KU-371-122

JULIUS CAESAR

A LIFE

PATRICIA SOUTHERN

AMBERLEY

LONDON BOROUGH OF SUTTON LIBRARY SERVICE	
30119 028 622 90 2	
Askews & Holts	Nov-2019
937.05	

This edition published 2019

Amberley Publishing
The Hill, Stroud
Gloucestershire, GL5 4EP

www.amberley-books.com

Copyright © Patricia Southern, 2019

The right of Patricia Southern to be identified as the Author of this work has been asserted in accordance with the Copyrights, Designs and Patents Act 1988.

All rights reserved. No part of this book may be reprinted or reproduced or utilised in any form or by any electronic, mechanical or other means, now known or hereafter invented, including photocopying and recording, or in any information storage or retrieval system, without the permission in writing from the Publishers.

British Library Cataloguing in Publication Data.
A catalogue record for this book is available from the British Library.

ISBN 978 1 4456 9619 5 (paperback)
ISBN 978 1 4456 5046 3 (ebook)

Typesetting and Origination by Amberley Publishing.
Printed in the UK.

30119 028 622 90 2

JULIUS CAESAR

About the Author

Patricia Southern is an acknowledged expert on the history of ancient Rome. She has an MPhil in Roman Frontier Studies from the University of Newcastle upon Tyne, where she was Librarian of the Archaeology Department for many years. She has written many books on Roman history and contributed numerous articles on Roman history to the BBC History website and the academic Roman studies journal *Britannia*.

Contents

Preface

Most authors who write about Caesar are immediately presented with a couple of dilemmas. The subject matter itself is awesome and overwhelming, because of the larger-than-life heroics that have become attached to Caesar, and then there is another problem: to include notes and references or just write the book? A full treatment of all the works that have been produced about Caesar would take a lifetime, so a choice must be made about which ones to include and which sections of the works to acknowledge as sources of ideas and interpretations of events in Caesar's life. The source material is uneven. Hardly anything in the ancient sources can be used to construct Caesar's early life, and then as he enters politics and begins to be noticed the amount of information increases exponentially, not least from his own literary works on the wars that he waged. We tend to lump together all ancient sources as primary evidence, but of course they are not exactly that, since some authors wrote at a considerable distance in time after Caesar's death and are almost as secondary as are modern works, so the primary evidence is derived from contemporary writers, like Cicero, who knew the man, his friends and his enemies, and lived through some of the most turbulent times in Rome's history. So having separated ancient works into contemporary and therefore primary sources and the work of later ancient authors into almost secondary sources, there is still the problem of evaluation of the worth of the information presented: did the ancient authors present a balanced or a biased view, did they tell the truth as they saw it, or did they never let the truth get in the way of a good story? This would fill a separate book, so the best plan for a librarian-cum-author, trained in finding sources and indoctrinated into acknowledging them, is to launch into the life of Caesar, present the reader with who said what and perhaps why, attributing all this various information to the endnotes, which, after all, nobody needs to read if he or she doesn't want to.

Patricia Southern
Northumberland, 2018

1

Caesar: An Extraordinary Life

Gaius Julius Caesar is without doubt a legendary figure, on a par with Alexander the Great, as Plutarch recognised when he equated the two men in his *Parallel Lives* comparing Greek heroes and villains with their Roman equivalents. Like Alexander, the name of Caesar resounded through the ages, eventually becoming a title used by Roman Emperors for their designated heirs and successors, and eventually re-emerging in more recent times as Kaiser in Germany and Tsar in Russia. The epithet 'legendary' should not imply relegation to the mythical realm, where there is more fantasy than fact, but such a description carries with it connotations of a personage larger than life, supremely clever, always victorious, head and shoulders above his or her puny contemporaries, to the extent that any embellishments or exaggerations that accrue meld seamlessly into the story and become an inextricable part of it, because nothing is too fantastic to be credible. To a degree the same process of accretion can be observed with very much more recent and equally legendary figures such as George Washington, Napoleon Bonaparte and Winston Churchill. In contrast to ancient personalities, so much more is known and verifiable about these modern counterparts, but nonetheless perception of their life stories undergoes significant changes, subtle or otherwise, with each succeeding era. The same is true of Caesar, because every generation cannot help but view him in the light of their own times, so in the end it is questionable whether there can ever be a real Caesar. Even his friends and enemies might have been at a loss to answer that question, and at a distance of 2,000 years, we are at even more of a disadvantage. We know much of what he did, and sometimes we know what he was trying to achieve and why. Occasionally we know what he was supposed to have said, the words preserved for us by the ancient authors, subject to misunderstandings and alterations to which reported speeches are susceptible. Less frequently, he is depicted in a darker light – when he lost his patience and acted rashly, or even deliberately cruelly, reminding us that he was after all a human being, subject to all the complexities of mood and temperament that made him less than heroic.

The difficulty for historians who attempt to document the lives of such household names is in getting behind the legend, and in telling the story to discard or ignore retrospective knowledge about their chosen subjects, including the course of their lives, what the individuals achieved and, most importantly, what happened to them in the end. Writing a historical biography, and also reading one, is always influenced by foreknowledge of the outcome, for even if the reader knows very little about the subject, probably the broad general outline is clear. Does anybody start a biography of Caesar without knowing that he was assassinated in 44 BC, or that Napoleon really should not have invaded Russia and that he died in exile on St Helena? Unlike revealing the killer at the start of a crime novel, it is highly improbable that the above statements are going to spoil the ending for readers.

Ideally, in order to retain a certain freshness in telling a story that has been told many times, the writer ought to try as far as possible to do what actors and actresses do: no matter that actors are speaking the lines for the umpteenth stage performance, or starting the same film scene all over again for take ten, they must make it seem as though they are speaking the lines or carrying out the actions in the script for the very first time, and their fellow actors have to pretend that they are hearing the lines, observing the actions, and reacting to them for the very first time. During his life (c.100–44 BC), Caesar met with people, events and problems for the very first time armed only with his own experience and family background, and the social customs and laws of the milieu in which he lived. He will have been forced to consider all the circumstances and decide what to do, how to act or react, and take a chance that his chosen course of action would be successful. The results that he wished for or tried to engineer were not necessarily pre-ordained or guaranteed, and in each episode of his life he did not have the advantage that modern audiences enjoy, that of knowing the outcome. Even without that knowledge, in reading a history book or a historical novel, or watching a play or a film, it is quite clear from the number of pages still unread, or the remaining length of the performance still to go, that until the very end the main character is going to survive the problems he or she is currently facing. The only question is *how* they will survive. In a Western film, for instance, early in the story a rifle points out of the upstairs window at the hero walking in the street below, and even as the voluntary suspension of disbelief allows the tension to mount, it is fairly certain that the gunman is going to miss, or he is only going to inflict a flesh wound. Since Caesar survived until 44 BC, it is certain for writers and readers that he will surmount whatever difficulties he is going to encounter before then, which rather takes the edge off the suspense. The narrative instead has to focus on how he surmounted the difficulties.

In documenting Caesar's life it is impossible to divest the account of all foreknowledge, to present the story as Caesar and his contemporaries witnessed it, living though it day by day, aware of a number of possible outcomes but not certain which it would be. At each significant moment during Caesar's career, it is tempting to recognise the traits and characteristics that carried him through successive dilemmas, and whilst this can be useful, it can also make it seem that his rise to power was inevitable, progressing smoothly from planned objective to planned objective, overriding obstacles and opposition until the final goal was reached. This approach does not take into account the recorded and unrecorded setbacks, the failures, the missed opportunities and the backtracking, the revision of plans and the sometimes ruthless manipulation of people and events that enabled Caesar to survive and move on with his ambitions intact. In the first line of his Foreword, Canfora quotes from Brecht's *Arbeitsjournal*: 'While writing my *Caesar*, I have realised that I must never for a moment let myself believe that things necessarily had to turn out the way they did.'[1]

Caesar most likely had a pronounced sense of his own worth and his abilities, and possibly he had clear notions about what he wanted to be, but even he could not predict how things would turn out. He was clever, certainly, but not omniscient, surviving sometimes by the skin of his teeth via a combination of determination, quick thinking, opportunism and, more often than not, a certain amount of luck. At any stage in his life he could have succumbed to disease or a fatal accident, or he could have been cut down in battle, or by an assassin, or he could have met with catastrophic military or political failure and been unable to overcome it, retreating into obscurity and being eclipsed by other astute generals and politicians. But already this last proposal sounds very uncharacteristic of Caesar, who did not give in and allow himself to be eclipsed. We know that he was not annihilated by total disasters until he was murdered, but neither Caesar nor his friends and enemies could have predicted the success or failure of any of his ventures before 44 BC. The legend obscures the possibility of failure; it infiltrates every aspect of Caesar's life and colours it with the rosy glow of heroism.

Foreknowledge of the course of someone's life and its end cannot fail to influence the interpretation of events that occurred, but with regard to Caesar not only the actual history but also the legend infiltrates and colours his own past. Where details are available about the childhood and youth of a legendary hero, or villain, it is easy to pick out those episodes which highlight the character traits that foreshadowed later eminence or infamy, and if details are lacking it is tempting to fabricate stories about what the child must have been like in order to achieve eminence in his chosen field. Since the focus of ancient audiences and modern readers alike are much more likely be on the success or failure of the adult personage, the predisposition or otherwise of the child to pursue his or her destiny is probably immaterial, but it does lend a sort of credibility to the concept that this destiny was somehow pre-ordained from birth. For one or two heroes or villains this may be correct, but in most cases, and in Caesar's case in particular, there was no such certainty, as just outlined above. Several modern authors have commented on the fact that Caesar's life and achievements were definitely not pre-ordained.

Nothing underlines this better than the game of 'what if', a purely academic exercise that serves no purpose in the light of hard facts but which can help to illustrate the uncertainty of life as it progresses in a forward direction, rather than being viewed in retrospect. What if Caesar had been killed, for instance, to choose an episode at random, when he had reached the praetorship in Rome and had been appointed governor of Further Spain?

Caesar's history until this point was varied, but quite decidedly it was nothing out of the ordinary. Caesar belonged to the senatorial nobility, but his family was not supremely important, despite the claim that the Julian clan was descended from the goddess Venus. Descent from deities was not peculiar to the Julian family. Several noble families claimed a god or two in their ancestry. But Caesar faced a disadvantage in his lack of illustrious human ancestors, and when he was only in his sixteenth year, according to Suetonius, his father died.[2] His only other male relative of importance was his uncle Gaius Marius, married to his aunt Julia, the sister of the senior Gaius Julius Caesar. But Marius' otherwise splendid career had ended badly, and was not an ancestral asset to the young Caesar. During his life Marius had been the sworn enemy of the Dictator Lucius Cornelius Sulla, so Caesar as Marius' nephew was potentially in grave danger after Sulla took over Rome. He defied Sulla's order to divorce his wife Cornelia, and survived, perhaps because of his youth, and in spite of the fact that Sulla allegedly recognised several Mariuses in him. After a brief spell as a fugitive, his life was spared, and he eventually left Rome. He saw some military action with the governor of the province of Asia, in modern terms western Turkey, where he had won a decoration for bravery, and in Cilicia. He returned to Rome after Sulla's death, and then went to Rhodes to further his education, as many young Romans did. On the way he was captured by pirates and eventually ransomed, then raised troops to go back and execute his captors, as he had promised to do.[3] Apart from this fantastic escapade, he followed the usual career pattern, serving in a legion as military tribune, then as quaestor or financial official of the governor in Further Spain. Between 67 and 62 BC he was appointed to civil and legal posts. The Romans combined military, civilian, political and religious appointments during their careers, so although it has been possible to write biographies of Caesar the politician or Caesar the general, in reality he combined both aspects as many other Romans did. Before the second century AD it is not really feasible to separate military and political careers into two distinct categories.

Until 62 BC Caesar's career had not been spectacular. In that year, in his late thirties, he was elected praetor. The official functions of the praetors, of which there were eight after Sulla's legislation in 81 BC, were primarily legal, but praetors could also command armies and, notably, the praetorship was the final rung on the ladder to the highest office, the consulship, which Caesar clearly aimed for and finally obtained in 59 BC. After a year of office in Rome, a praetor could go on to govern a province as proconsul, and after his praetorship Caesar was made proconsular governor of Further Spain. He embarked on a military campaign against the tribe of Lusitani, who may or may not have been causing trouble. In traditional Roman fashion and condoned by the Senate, such a venture would bring fame or at least notoriety, experience of government and of commanding troops, and the acquisition of loot. More importantly, it could bring election – one of the two consuls was within sight.

This diversion into a potted history of Caesar's life so far shows that he had already followed a protracted but normal military and civil career path to reach the praetorship, and perhaps his ambitions had become clear to his contemporaries, sufficient to engender mistrust or even fear of him. Though his career had not been extraordinary, it is possible that he was himself extraordinary; but it is careers and achievements that historians record, and not so much personal attributes and characteristics. If Caesar had been, say, thrown from his horse or killed by a tribesman in Further Spain in 61 BC, would he have been remembered as anything other than a footnote in history, if even that? Would ancient historians have remembered that Sulla was probably going to execute him but then changed his mind, exhorting his friends to watch the young man because, he said, Caesar had many Mariuses in him?[4] Or would anecdotes about his capture by Mediterranean pirates and his subsequent revenge have been preserved somewhere as an illustration of his ruthless determination? If Caesar's career was cut short before 60 BC, would any ancient historian have recognised in him a potential consul with a programme of reforms to put into effect in the teeth of senatorial opposition? Would they have been able to envisage him as the conqueror of Gaul? As first the friend and then the enemy of Pompey the Great, and finally Dictator for life?

If Caesar had died in 61 BC, not having reached the consulship, and not being descended from a currently important family with a long ancestral line of consuls who had performed various exploits in defence of Rome, he would have made scarcely any impression on Roman history. His great-nephew Gaius Octavius was his heir and became officially Gaius Julius Caesar Octavianus, but he never used this name. He called himself Gaius Julius Caesar, and insisted that others did so, until he was given the name Augustus. Octavius was coming up to two years of age when Caesar governed Further Spain, and it is unlikely that this infant would have been adopted and become Caesar's successor. If Caesar himself had not survived there would have been little except property to inherit, and certainly no political power or reputation. So without Caesar after 61 BC there would have been no Augustus, and the story of the Roman Empire would have been quite different. Conversely, without Augustus, the legend of Caesar would not have been promoted, fostered, manipulated and remodelled, to form the story that is well known today. The legend was potentially in danger of annihilation as Octavian-Augustus could have obliterated it, but he needed the more comfortable aspects of Caesar's achievements to shore up his power and influence, and his successors from Tiberius onwards likewise kept the Caesar legend alive, adopting the name, which became an Imperial title. By the third century the name Augustus denoted the senior Emperors, and the name Caesar denoted their junior partners and designated successors.

Caesar's true greatness and thus his reputation were formed only in the latter years of his life, between 60 BC, when he first stood for election to the consulship, and 44 BC, when he was assassinated. Only in retrospect does his earlier career assume any importance. In the face of his enormous reputation, it is sometimes startling to realise that his rise to prominence and his use of supreme power endured for a period of less than two decades. Before 60 BC it is possible that his friends and enemies had already recognised in him a burning ambition to rule the whole state and put its many wrongs to rights. Suetonius reports that there were allegations that early in his career Caesar was involved with Crassus in a plot to overthrow the government, and the author goes on to describe how the orator Cicero, in a letter to a friend, claimed to have recognised a tendency to despotism while Caesar was only an aedile, before he had been elected praetor and then consul.[5] Plutarch credits Cicero with being the first to detect a different Caesar behind his affable façade, implying that Caesar successfully masked how dangerous he was.[6]

Caesar was not alone in wanting to reform the state. It was not difficult to identify what was wrong with the government and the way it was run, nor was it difficult to discern the solutions, but only piecemeal efforts had been made to find a remedy for some of the problems, tackled a few at a time. No one after the two tribunes of the plebs, Tiberius and Gaius Gracchus, had yet taken on the entire task, and if anyone had tried to reform everything at once then the full weight of state machinery would have been set in motion to stop him, such was the abhorrence among the Roman ruling classes of one man assuming supreme power. Caesar may have discussed his ideas with friends, and outlined what he wanted to do. He had aired some of his views in the Senate and progressed far enough to alert a group of senators who united in opposition to him, with Cato at their head, but even this group perhaps could not foresee what he would become.

The formation of the legend and its survival grew steadily from Caesar's conquest of Gaul and his victories in the civil wars. He became something more than human. It was an uncomfortable fact that in his last years Caesar had been given unprecedented honours and had acquired more power than any previous or contemporary politician or general.[7] He had been creating his own legend for some time, presenting himself as he wished to be seen, most especially since his consulship and his ten-year conquest of Gaul. His *Commentaries* on his exploits in Gaul were not written primarily as historical records, but they were the news bulletins of their day, designed to impress the contemporary Roman public and enhance his own image. While the civil wars were fought against the opposing senators led by Pompey the Great, Caesar adopted a deliberate policy of *clementia*, being studiously merciful to his defeated enemies, an unusual measure which did not please everyone, because it meant that those whom he had forgiven were in his debt and everyone was literally at his mercy. Dissension did not matter all that much, because he had the state in his pocket. In summer 46 BC the Senate voted him all the trappings of supreme distinction, such as official thanksgiving for his victories for forty days, and seventy-two lictors to precede his triumphal chariot. Lictors were attendants who walked in single file before a magistrate who held *imperium*, the power to command armies. The lictors carried the *fasces*, or bundles of rods containing an axe, signifying the magistrates' powers of arrest, punishment and even execution. In modern times, this is the origin and symbol of fascism. Consuls, the most powerful magistrates of the state, were entitled to twelve lictors. Caesar was voted six times that number. Apart from the honours that set him apart from ordinary people, real powers were voted to him as well: the Dictatorship for ten years, overriding the law that it was to be held for only six months, and new powers as supervisor of morals, *praefectus morum*. He also had the right to nominate magistrates as electoral candidates, to sit between the consuls at meetings of the Senate, and to speak first on all questions arising. These honours and powers were ratified in laws passed by the people in public assembly. Finally, he was awarded the Dictatorship for life.[8]

In 44 BC, when Octavian first took up his inheritance from Caesar, he was not in the strongest of positions because of his youth. His inheritance was outlined in Caesar's will. He had added to the main document a codicil in which he adopted Gaius Octavius as his son and principal heir. Adoption by testamentary means may not have been entirely legal, but since the contents of Caesar's will had been made public by Caesar's consular colleague Mark Antony, Octavian had a foundation for his claim in the eyes of the people. However, he was careful to have his adoption ratified by law, being thwarted at the first attempt but succeeding later when he was made consul. After Caesar's assassination, thanks to Antony, backed by Marcus Aemilius Lepidus and his troops, a fragile peace had been restored with the assassins, who styled themselves the Liberators. Having rid themselves of the tyrant Caesar, they had made no plans for the government of Rome and the provinces, apparently thinking that the Republic would magically spring back to life. If Brutus and Cassius had opted for the death of Antony as well as Caesar and then taken over the state themselves, Octavian would have been deprived of any foundation on which to build his power base, because it would not have been practicable or wise to emphasize his connection with Caesar. As it was, Antony had persuaded the Senate to ratify all Caesar's acts, and had abolished the office of Dictator, in effect clearing the way for Octavian to play to the gallery about Caesar's victories and the popular appeal of some of his measures, without laying too much emphasis on the Dictatorship. He made no secret of his intention to wreak vengeance on the Liberators, upsetting some of what Antony had achieved in pacifying Rome. Later, Octavian played down Caesar in the earthly realm and concentrated on Caesar the god.[9]

Caesar had already experienced or possibly organised the first steps towards divinity. A statue of him was placed in the temple of the supreme god Jupiter on the Capitol Hill, with an inscription which probably proclaimed him as a demi-god, but the wording is not known for certain. Despite his family claim of descent from Venus, Caesar had the inscription removed.[10] It is not certain that Caesar was declared semi-divine during his lifetime, but if it was not official, it seems that the people were ready to accept him as such, and were even more enthusiastic after his death. Very soon after the Ides of March and the assassination, a certain Amatius, who claimed to be a relative of Caesar's uncle Gaius Marius, set up an altar to Caesar on the site of his funeral pyre.[11] Amatius had vowed to avenge Caesar, and gathered around him a gang of toughs. In order to calm the situation Antony executed him without trial, acting peremptorily and illegally. The people protested and demanded the official dedication of the altar so that they could make sacrifices on it. This ready acceptance was highly useful to Octavian, because divine Caesar was infinitely more respectable and squeaky clean than Caesar the Dictator. The altar was retained and eventually the cult of the divine Caesar was established in 42 BC, during the triumvirate of Antony, Octavian and Lepidus. Antony had been designated as *flamen* or priest of the cult.[12] Although the cult was established, the Temple of *divus Julius* on the site of Caesar's funeral pyre was not dedicated until 29 BC. Nowadays there are only shapeless remains of it in the Forum Romanum in Rome, consisting of the square block of its podium, from which all the facing stones have been removed. In the side facing the Senate House there is a semi-circular recess, containing the remains of a round structure, which may have been built on the site of the altar set up immediately after Caesar's funeral. Modern visitors still place offerings of flowers and candles on this truncated round ruin.

The debate about Caesar as a living god, or merely a god-in-waiting until after his death, can be left until the relevant chapter at the end of this book; the important point is that Octavian made mileage out of the willing consent of the people to endorse the cult, and presented himself as *divi filius*, the son of the god, which served the dual purpose of sanitising the memory of Caesar and supporting Octavian's claim to power. The first recorded use of this title is in 40 BC, but Octavian may possibly have used the concept from 44 BC onwards, an innocent phrase that evokes much debate. Whether or not he was overtly using a title associating himself with the divine Caesar so soon after the assassination, Octavian quickly exploited a timely astrological phenomenon, the comet that appeared during the celebration of games that he had arranged in honour of Caesar, in the summer of 44 BC. The comet was visible for seven successive days while the games were celebrated, and was immediately labelled the *sidus Iulium*, the star of Caesar.[13] A comet would usually have been interpreted as a bad omen, but Octavian successfully converted it into a sign of Caesar's apotheosis, and the people did not raise objections to his acceptance in the heavens as a god. Octavian placed a star on the head of Caesar's statues, and on his posthumous coin portraits. Underlining Caesar's divinity and thereby enhancing his own favoured position, Octavian courted and won over Caesar's adherents and supporters. The *sidus Iulium* was remembered and exploited long after Octavian's first use of it. When he was firmly in command of the Empire as Augustus, the comet or star featured in the works of the poets and writers of his literary circle. When the later biographers and historians wrote accounts of Caesar and Augustus, the star had receded in importance and they did not take as much notice of it.

The legend created and maintained by Octavian-Augustus would crystallize the ideology that Caesar must have been destined to rule the state, because that is what he did. But the legend did not crystallize completely. It changed during the long reign of Augustus. Octavian-Augustus utilised the story of Caesar in different ways as time went on, never renouncing his relationship with him, and always accentuating the positive, but selecting the aspects that suited him best in the circumstances in which he found himself. His long reign furnished him with sufficient time to manipulate the legend for posterity without entirely suppressing the record.

The memory of Caesar the Dictator was allowed to fade away because the Dictatorship was not quite such a solid foundation for Augustus to build on, whereas the divine Caesar was infinitely more acceptable. Augustus apparently obliterated some of Caesar's very early literary efforts, such as a tragedy about Oedipus, and a work on Hercules. According to Suetonius, Augustus wrote to his librarian Pompeius Macer to forbid publication of Caesar's minor works.[14] The Dictator's youthful literary works may have detracted from Augustus' carefully groomed image of himself and the presentation of his adoptive father Julius Caesar. Such works would probably not have helped ancient or modern historians to construct a personal portrait or a history of his life.

There may have been other works by different authors to which Augustus took an exception, particularly if they were hostile in intent or derogatory towards Caesar, but the fact that ancient historians and biographers from Augustan times onwards had access to information and official records implies that there was no wholesale destruction of documentation concerning Caesar. The materials that were available to the ancient writers were clearly more abundant than those that have survived to the present day, for instance Suetonius refers to some of Caesar's private correspondence to Cicero, and to others in his circle, which have since been lost, probably at some time in later antiquity. It cannot be discerned whether the losses of ancient works were accidental, or occurred as a result of deliberate policy on the part of later Emperors. In some cases, the ancient biographers acknowledge their sources, and therefore provide modern scholars with information about works that are no longer extant. Fragments of lost works sometimes appear in the accounts of later writers, and can be useful in constructing Caesar's life story, although, as with all ancient works, questions should be asked about reliability. Consideration should be taken of the context in which writers worked, their prejudices and biases, and whether they had an axe to grind, though it has to be admitted that information to elucidate these questions is not always forthcoming. Just as modern history books can be subject to an author's biased approach, ancient historians could be influenced by their social environment and their personal experience. Each age writes its own version of Caesar, compatible with the mindset of the time. In an imperialist age, Caesar can be a hero. In the modern age, it would not be interpreted as heroism when Caesar wiped out the Gallic tribe of the Eburones, nor would it be considered merciful to spare the lives of Gallic prisoners but to cut off their hands and send them on their way. People of the modern era have got as far as deploring such acts, but not as far as stopping them.

Nonetheless the legend of Caesar survives, based on the evidence that has been passed down to us. Foremost among the literary works is Caesar's *Commentaries*, describing in his own words the conquest of Gaul, and his accounts of the civil wars that brought him to supreme power. Caesar never finished his books on the civil wars, but they were completed by his officers, most probably using notes that he left behind. These works formed a large part of the Caesar legend throughout the ancient and medieval eras. Many a king or military leader read about and analysed Caesar's campaigns. The events that are described cannot have been entirely fabricated or mendacious, though they were possibly amplified a little for greater effect. Disarmingly, Caesar acknowledges his mistakes and failures, but then he could hardly pretend that mistakes did not happen, or simply tell lies by omission, because too many people witnessed the events. On the other hand, admitting that he got himself into dilemmas merely served to emphasize his success in overcoming them.

The last five years of Caesar's supremacy are the best documented of his life and times. As with the Gallic wars, there are accounts of the stages of the civil wars purportedly written by Caesar himself, though authorship of *The Civil Wars* and *The Alexandrian, African and Spanish Wars* is not certain. *The Alexandrian War* was probably written by Caesar's officer, Aulus Hirtius, who is also credited with finishing off *The Gallic War*. The authorship of those on the wars in Africa and Spain is not known, and these accounts differ in style and in their approach. Caesar may have made rough notes with which the author or authors worked. For the sake of simplicity and convenience, the books are attributed to Caesar and quoted as such. Much detail is included in these works, and additional details are found in the letters of Cicero to his friends, especially Atticus. The later historians Plutarch, Suetonius, Appian and Dio used Caesar's accounts, but sometimes give different versions of events. It is impossible to reproduce the whole story of the wars in a couple of chapters, because they would turn out to be longer than the entire book, so a choice has to be made as to which details to include – a problem that faced the ancient authors as much as it affects modern works.

The usefulness of Caesar's works to modern historians can be debated. There is little else which provides so much detail about the Gallic wars and the civil wars towards the end of Caesar's dominance, but it must be remembered that they were written with self-advertisement and promotion in mind, not necessarily for historical purposes, and the works do not necessarily illustrate the politics of the time, or anyone else's point of view. For that, it is Cicero's letters that provide an immediate contemporary view of what was happening, and what some people thought of Caesar's actions at the time.

It was once thought that Cicero's correspondence was not published until the reign of Nero, but it now seems certain that it was Cicero's friend Titus Pomponius Atticus who was responsible for preserving and assembling the letters exchanged between them, and some of the correspondence between Cicero and his other friends has also survived. It is not known whether some of the correspondence was perhaps deliberately edited out, either by Augustus, as Carcopino suspected, or by another hand.[15] Goldsworthy suggests that before publishing the letters Atticus omitted certain items that could have compromised him. Whether or not there was some tampering with the extant correspondence, it is clear that although in ancient times there were extant volumes of letters between Cicero and Caesar, and Cicero and Pompey, these and probably much else besides have been lost. When Augustus was firmly established in his all-powerful position, he could afford to be magnanimous to his erstwhile enemies, among whom was Cicero, an opponent of Caesar with a persuasive tongue and pen. Although Mark Antony shoulders all the blame for the murder of Cicero, it should not be forgotten that Octavian played his part in the proscriptions of potential enemies of the new regime of the Triumvirate. Cicero had helped the young Octavian to initial power, while at the same time thinking that he could use him and discard him just as easily, and he had said so, using a witty pun in Latin that indicated that Octavian should be praised to the skies, but the word that he used, *tollere*, had another meaning, implying that the young man should be annihilated. Octavian had no reason to love Cicero, but as Augustus, after he was as secure as possible in control of the state and the deceased orator was no longer a threat, he could tolerate him.

Augustus could also tolerate Marcus Porcius Cato the Younger, who had consistently and sometimes virulently opposed Caesar. When it was clear that the Republican cause was lost, Cato committed suicide rather than succumb to Caesar's policy of *clementia*. Far from becoming *persona non grata*, Cato became a hero in Augustan literature. One of the first writers to depict him as such was the historian Sallust, who retired from public life shortly before Caesar's death. Sallust had started out as a partisan of Caesar, but his later opinion was more equivocal, and his earlier opinion of Cato had been hostile, but when he came to write about Lucius Sergius Catilina and his alleged conspiracy, Sallust presented the two most virtuous men of his own times as Caesar and Cato, who had first clashed during this upheaval. What is remarkable is that this portrait of Cato appeared before Octavian had fully established his power, when he had not yet eliminated Antony and Cleopatra. In the Augustan age, both Virgil and Horace extol Cato as a Republican hero, but for Caesar, the emphasis is not usually on his exploits in the mortal realm but on his apotheosis and the *sidus Iulium*, the comet that appeared after his death, and which Octavian-Augustus interpreted as a sign that Caesar had entered the realm of the gods, or, as Suetonius says, *in caelum recepti*.[16]

Another historian who retired from public life, like Sallust, was Asinius Pollio, who began his career with Caesar and joined Antony, but survived under Augustus until AD 4. His history, now lost, covered the years from 60 to 42 BC, from the period of Caesar's first consulship to the Battle of Philippi, in which Antony and Octavian defeated the Liberators Brutus and Cassius. The loss of his work is to be regretted, but it was used by the second-century historians Plutarch and Appian, who probably found it more accurate and analytical than Caesar's own accounts of the Gallic and the civil wars, and a counterweight to the Augustan versions of late Republican and early Imperial history.[17] These later historians also used the work of Titus Livius, or Livy as he is better known, who was born *c.* 59 BC and died probably in AD 17, though his dates have been disputed. His great history of Rome was written during Augustus' reign. It is fortunate that later historians utilised Livy's work and sometimes quoted him, because the last thirty-one books of his history, covering the four eventful decades between 48 and 9 BC, are lost, preserved only in brief summaries (*Periochae*) which were probably drawn up in the fourth century AD. Judging by the number of books that Livy required to describe the events of this period, there must be a great mass of detailed information that is denied to modern historians. Livy's view of Caesar was not adulatory. One of the more interesting references is found in the work of Seneca, who says that Livy wondered whether the birth of Caesar was necessarily a good thing for the Roman state.[18] Augustus was established in power by this time, and could afford to be indulgent, recognising Livy's confirmed Republicanism, and calling him, affectionately, a Pompeian.

Livy's history was also used by Velleius Paterculus, writing in the reign of Tiberius, by which time the Augustan Caesar-cult was entrenched. The passages that Velleius takes from Livy are not mentioned by other authors, so he partially fills the gap in knowledge. He provides a succinct summary of the prelude to Caesar's rise to power, devoting twenty chapters of his second book to the period from Caesar's consulship in 59 BC to the advent of Octavian. He says that Caesar 'lays hold of my pen and compels me to linger a while upon him'.[19]

When the two main surviving biographies of Caesar were composed by Plutarch and Suetonius in the second century AD, the Caesarian legend was already crystallized. Emperors used the title Imperator Caesar in decrees and on inscriptions, which up to the reign of Nero, the last of the Julio-Claudians, denoted a slightly tenuous family connection as well as the trappings of power inherent in Caesar's name, but from Vespasian onwards Emperors could not legitimately claim descent from Caesar's extended family, and the name became an Imperial title. This ensured that Caesar was remembered, even into modern times when his name was transformed into Kaiser and Tsar. In ancient times as in the modern era, it is disputed whether Caesar or his great-nephew Augustus was the true founder of the Empire. Given that Caesar was firmly embedded in the Imperial power structure, anyone attempting to write about him would have to acknowledge his greatness and achievements, since denying them would be construed as derogatory to the reigning Emperor. Even so, it seems that authors could also document Caesar's faults without retribution, provided there was some basis of truth to them. As already mentioned, Livy could suggest that the advent of Caesar was not necessarily the best thing for Rome without incurring the wrath of Augustus and swift punishment, which, if it had occurred, would only have served to prove Livy's point.

Plutarch was born perhaps in the mid-40s AD, though the date is not certain. He hailed from Chaeronea, in Greece, and used his native language for his work, commonly called *Parallel Lives*, in which he twinned a historical Greek personality with a Roman one, equating Caesar with Alexander the Great. In choosing his paired subjects, Plutarch did not limit himself to strict contemporaries, but described men from different ages whose careers seemed to him comparable. His stated aim was to produce biographies not histories, documenting personalities rather than events, so he did not provide detailed descriptions of battles or even political problems because such descriptions do not reveal much about a person and his mindset. Plutarch and other authors used the now lost work of Asinius Pollio, who was generally considered to have carefully analysed events and personalities, and to have provided a balanced view of the works of Cicero and Sallust, and of Caesar himself. It is known that when Plutarch was writing, more of Cicero's work survived than is available in the modern collections.

Like Plutarch, Suetonius also had access to sources denied to modern historians, possibly including material in the Imperial archives, at least for the first of his biographies, when his relations with the Emperor Hadrian were still cordial. It has been suggested that there was a serious falling out between the Emperor and Suetonius, and perhaps from the biography of Domitian onwards there is less use of archival material and more use of anecdote and hearsay. But for Caesar, Suetonius could utilise information that had been preserved among contemporaries of the great man, thus providing a unique freshness in his work that does not appear anywhere else.[20]

Plutarch and Suetonius were not concerned very deeply with the social, political or military backgrounds of their subjects' lives. Even though Suetonius and Plutarch were writing at a remove of two centuries after Caesar, it could be argued that the pace of change was slow in the last century before the Christian era and the first couple of centuries thereafter, so the readers of the biographies would be familiar with the lifestyle and customs of the period in which each subject lived. Authors such as Appian and Dio dealt with Julius Caesar as part of their wider history of Rome, so although they did not set out specifically to document the changes that occurred in social and political life, it would be apparent from their narratives that precedents were set which brought about long-term consequences. These authors would not need to comment on changes, except where it served some purpose, as when Dio described the era before the death of Marcus Aurelius as a golden age, which thereafter disintegrated into iron and rust. There could be no better or more bitter way of expressing his opinion of the reign of Commodus and his successors, based on personal experience.[21]

In a modern work dealing with a historical figure, most especially one who lived over two millennia ago, some account of the background against which the person lived and worked is more or less mandatory, if only to avoid the necessity of explaining laws, customs, precedents and procedures each time they are met with in the life of the chosen subject. Ideally Caesar should be judged in his own historical context before condemning him as a haloed hero or a murderous monster. Accordingly, the next chapter describes the milieu into which Julius Caesar was born and in which he grew up.

2

The Last Years of the Roman Republic

An overview of the background to Caesar's career and rise to power is advisable if only to set the scene and avoid having to explain complex issues in the main text, but it involves simplification, which always borders on half-truths and being economical with details. As the saying goes, the devil is in the detail, and with all of them included, this subject could well occupy several volumes. With those caveats in mind, this chapter outlines some of the problems and trends of the later Republic, before Caesar and then Octavian-Augustus began to transform it into the Empire.

The Roman world of Caesar's early life was violent, corrupt and rent by struggles among the factions gathered around the political power seekers, sometimes leading to armed conflict and even civil war. These events tend to be in the spotlight in history, leading to the assumption that Roman political life was in perennial turmoil, but in the spaces in between the violence life went on peacefully enough. Power-seeking individuals could sometimes realise their aims within the bounds of the legal system, but if thwarted they tended to try to bend the rules, or even break them. Power was necessary to make changes to the way in which the state was run, but although self-interest ruled among late Republican politicians, power was not always sought by evil megalomaniacs who simply wanted it for the sake of elevating themselves. The men who reached the pinnacle usually had an agenda for reform, in itself no bad thing, but the way in which they went about it was usually at best forceful and at worst bloody.

The form of government of Rome, Italy and the provinces evolved from the late sixth century BC after the kings were expelled and the Republic was founded, traditionally in 509. The chief governing body was the Senate, composed of the most important men of the state, but there was also a wealth qualification, below which men could not become senators, nor remain as such if their census rating dropped. Assisting the Senate were the people in their various assemblies, with restrictions on their executive capacities, but still technically justifying the famous title Senate and People of Rome, represented by the initials SPQR. The Senate could not convene without being summoned by one of the senior magistrates, and could not direct policy. Senators could debate matters put to them by the magistrates and give their opinions, after which voting would take place and the majority decision would win the day. There was a prescribed order of speaking, the most senior members being approached first. The term magistrate as applied to Roman officials has much broader connotations than it does in modern English, for instance as used in magistrates' courts, denoting legal responsibilities. Roman magistrates were responsible not just for legal affairs, but also civil administration, military commands and religious matters.

The chief magistrates of Caesar's day were the two consuls, elected annually, holding office for one year, each endowed with equal civil and military powers. Collegiate rule replaced that of the kings, so determined were the Romans never again to endure the rule of one man. The consuls held civil, legal and military powers, the latter officially bestowed on them by the Senate with the grant of *imperium*. Hereditary rule was abolished in favour of elected magistrates, but although political power could not be bequeathed to senators' sons, there was a hereditary aspect in that powerful families expected their heirs to follow them into political life and military commands, where they would make their own way, hoping for success but risking failure.

Only in times of dire emergency could a single individual have power bestowed upon him, with the title Dictator. His powers exceeded that of all other magistrates including the consuls, who remained in office but in a subordinate capacity. The Dictator held office for only six months, and the consuls resumed office when his term came to an end. If the emergency was resolved before his term expired, the Dictator was expected to stand down, or if the problem extended beyond his term, another Dictator was to be appointed. At least this was the theory, belied by events of the late Republic when individuals clung on to power by fair means or foul, the most notorious example being Lucius Cornelius Sulla, who used the powers of Dictator not to resolve an emergency but to push through his reforms. His saving grace was that he stood down and retired into private life when his reforms were complete. The last example was Caesar himself, who was legally appointed Dictator more than once, for longer than the usual term, and eventually for life, apparently remarking that Sulla did not know what he was doing to lay down his powers voluntarily.[1]

Subordinate to the consuls were the praetors. In the earliest days of the Republic the praetors may have been the chief officials of state, but the consuls soon overtook them. The main responsibility of the praetors was to conduct legal business, but like the consuls they could be invested with *imperium*, which entitled them to command armies as well as carrying out civil administration.

Although the state in Caesar's day was nominally a Republic it was already worthy of the title Empire by dint of its territorial acquisitions. The Romans had first absorbed the Italian tribes and states and then acquired territories outside Italy. The lands were called provinces, a term which at first had no connotations of territory, but referred to the tasks undertaken by consuls and praetors after holding office, such as road repairs or control of woodlands and forests, or dealing with bandits in Italy. In times of war the consuls of the early Republic commanded the armies, but as the territories under Roman control expanded, it became the norm for consuls and praetors whose term of office ended to go out to govern the new territories, so the name 'province', describing their task, was also applied to the land. The first provinces were acquired almost by accident, and the process of accretion has been labelled by modern historians as a perpetual quest to find safe boundaries. Most imperialistic states could make that excuse, but in fairness expansionism for its own sake did not take hold in Rome until the mid-second century BC, when it dawned on the Romans that extra territories could be profitable in the form of taxation, trade, mineral wealth and exploitable provincials, who as non-Romans were regarded as somehow inferior, not part of the whole. Integration into the Roman world took a long time, but eventually Roman citizenship with its legal and civil privileges was bestowed on the

Italian allies, then on individuals or groups of people within a province, then to all inhabitants of a selected province, and finally to all the free-born provincials, but this did not happen until the early third century AD. Roman citizenship was a prized asset. It gave the possessors voting rights, but only if they were prepared to travel to the city of Rome. It also bestowed rights and privileges besides the franchise. A citizen could not be flogged or crucified, received better treatment at law, and held higher status than non-citizens. In the early first century BC, in Caesar's lifetime, the Italian allies of Rome went to war to claim a share in the government that they supported by contributing troops and paying taxes. They had been promised citizenship more than once, only to be disappointed at the last moment each time, and so they lost patience. The Latin term for allies is *socii*, and the war that broke out in the late 90s and early 80s BC is called the Social War. After some bloody fighting, in which the Italians were a match for the Romans because they had fought for them in several wars and had been trained in Roman methods, citizenship was offered somewhat grudgingly, but it set the precedent at last for integration into the Roman Empire. Caesar was one of the first to envisage the Roman world as a unified entity, not just a collection of territories and tribes to be exploited for the benefit of Rome. In 49 BC he enfranchised the Transpadane Gauls, the tribes across the River Po who had been given only Latin rights, not full citizenship, when Pompeius Strabo granted such rights to the Cisalpine communities. The rest of Gaul had to wait for the Emperor Claudius to grant the same privileges nearly a century later.

In order to govern the provinces, the Romans adapted and expanded their systems designed for the governance of a single state. They did not create a whole host of new magistrates but instead they employed the existing officials in new ways. The first recorded evidence for the beginning of this procedure dates from 326 BC when one of the consuls currently in office, Quintus Publilius Philo, was besieging the largely Greek city of Naples, and it was about to fall. Philo's consulship was nearing its end, but rather than appoint a new consul to take over the army the Senate voted him an extension of his command, so he ceased to be consul in Rome but retained the powers of a consul so that he could continue his military operations. The process was called *prorogatio imperii* and Philo's title became proconsul, or *pro consule* in Latin, indicating that he was acting on behalf of one of the official consuls. Thus the powers of the consuls were separated from the office. Occasionally proconsular powers could be bestowed on men who had not yet held the consulship, and the title of proconsul was given to some provincial governors of praetorian rank. In the same way that consuls could be made proconsuls, praetors could become propraetors to govern the smaller or less important provinces, though in the case of the praetors, while the number of consuls remained at two throughout the Republic, the number of praetors was increased because the legal and administrative business conducted in Rome itself had grown to much larger proportions. Via the institution of the pro-magistracy, a useful tool was thus created to facilitate the government of the provinces without appointing new officials with completely new titles and functions. It kept everything close to home and Rome.

In the evolved system of government and administration, there were lesser officials ranking below the praetors. These were the aediles, originally two, later raised to four, who were responsible for a variety of tasks, which increased and changed over time, including upkeep of the plebeian temples, control of markets, maintenance of the streets, and some policing functions. Latterly they were also responsible for putting on games and shows to entertain the populace, and the more magnificent the games, the greater was their popularity, so it was worth the expense to create a good foundation for a future career. Ranking slightly lower than the aediles were the quaestors, originally two of them, one appointed by each consul. By the fifth century BC they were elected by the people. Their numbers increased in accordance with growing administrative needs, and in the first century BC there were twenty under Sulla, who made this most junior of the magistracies an automatic entry to the Senate for young men who had served in various administrative posts, usually in their mid-twenties. Their duties combined financial, judicial and legal matters.

The government of the provinces was kept well within the senatorial realm, and therefore facilitated extortion and maltreatment of the provincials, because legal cases brought against venal governors were judged by senators who were mostly reluctant to condemn their peers. Provincial government therefore had an impact on legal proceedings and occasioned various attempts to reform the jury courts. Special *quaestiones* were set up to deal with extortion, or *repetundae*, so that at least in theory the provincials could seek redress for the actions of unscrupulous governors who extracted wealth from them. It would not have been easy for provincials to travel to Rome and find an advocate to state their case, so several crimes probably went uncontested in the courts. Another problem was the fact that, for those provincials who did take their cases to Rome, the juries did not always convict the accused. The juries were composed of senators, who were just as eager to get rich quick in a territorial province, so if they condemned another senator they risked making enemies of those who might be asked to sit on juries if they themselves were accused.

The courts were reformed more than once, first being wrested from total senatorial control and bestowed on the equestrians, or non-senatorial middle classes, but this did not completely eradicate the troubles of the provincials. Although senators bent on extortionate practices may have been curbed, this did not necessarily work in the interests of the provincials. The taxation of the provinces was firmly in the hands of the equestrians, under the heading of *publicani* (nothing to do with running a tavern). The *publicani* were usually businessmen who bid for the tax farm of an area of the province, then if their bid was accepted went out to collect the legitimate taxes, plus as much in excess of their bid as they possibly could. Extortion was therefore not limited to the senatorial governors, and any governor who tried to stop the tax collectors from cheating the provincials was sure to be prosecuted by an equestrian, and convicted. This situation ensured that governors turned a blind eye to the activities of the tax collectors, and the equestrians likewise ignored the activities of the senators.

In 106 BC the jury courts for cases of *repetundae* were reformed once again, this time being composed of senators and equestrians. Then they were given back to equestrians alone, then to senators alone, this last measure put into effect by Sulla.[2] Control of the courts has rightly been termed a political football, a problem that was not resolved in Caesar's day. Despite the difficulties in obtaining a conviction of a senatorial governor if the jury courts were in the hands of senators, there was no lack of prosecutors. There was no central administration that brought about prosecutions, which were left to private initiative. A successful prosecution could bring fame and fortune to aspiring politicians, for example Marcus Tullius Cicero, who famously prosecuted Verres for his thorough pillaging of Sicily. Cicero travelled to Sicily to collect evidence, an unusual proceeding at the time, and Verres was convicted after only the first of Cicero's prepared speeches. Since he was deprived of the kudos of delivering them to an admiring public, Cicero published the rest of them, unwittingly providing texts for schoolboys and girls to labour over in Latin lessons.

Several conflicts arose in the later Republic as groups formed in opposition to other groups and factional strife took hold. One of the earliest, of long duration, was the so-called struggle of the orders between aristocrats, or patricians, and the ordinary people, or plebeians. This is to over-simplify who exactly were the patricians and plebs, but the struggle was long since resolved by Caesar's day. The plebs had achieved an equal share in the government and although patrician or plebeian origins were still recognised, a plebeian nobility had grown up, so that some plebeian families were wealthier than the patrician aristocratic families. Gnaeus Pompeius Magnus, more familiarly known as Pompey the Great, came from a plebeian background but even in his youth he could raise three armies from his estates, and eventually grew wealthy enough to rival or even overtake Marcus Licinius Crassus, who declared that no one could call himself wealthy unless he could raise and support an army. On the other hand, Lucius Cornelius Sulla, although a thoroughbred aristocrat, started out as an impoverished youth who rose via the army to become Dictator.

One of the measures that helped to resolve the differences between patricians and plebeians was the appointment of tribunes of the plebs, possibly only two at first, but eventually there were ten, taking up office in early December each year, before the new consuls came into power in January. The tribunes of the plebs were not the same as military tribunes who ranked just below the commanders of armies. The people's tribunes had to be of plebeian origin, and were not magistrates like the consuls and praetors, but while in office they were sacrosanct and could not be harmed without retribution. They were granted powers to intervene in cases where patricians oppressed plebeians, possessing the power of *intercessio*, more commonly described as the power of veto. With the exception of the Dictator, tribunes could block the proposals of any officials if those proposals could be considered harmful to the plebeians. In Caesar's day the tribunes could be used by unscrupulous politicians to manipulate proceedings of the Senate, either by proposing laws as they were legally entitled to do, or by blocking proposals from other magistrates. The office survived into the Empire, the powers of the tribunes (*tribunicia potestas*), but not the actual post, being adopted by Augustus and succeeding Emperors. It was renewed annually for each Emperor. The abbreviation *trib. pot.* appears on many Imperial inscriptions, followed by a figure in Roman numerals, representing the number of years that tribunician power had been held.

The political and social divisions in the first century BC were not between patricians and plebeians, but between senators and *equites* or equestrians, often translated as knights, but more accurately denoting the middle classes of non-senatorial status. Though the two classes were sometimes in opposition to each other, as for example in control of the jury courts, as outlined above, this class division did not always involve internecine strife and disruption to state proceedings. Senators and equestrians sometimes worked together, depending on their shared interests. There was a wealth qualification for each class, and senators' sons who had not yet entered public office ranked as equestrians, until they entered the Senate and took up one of the junior magistracies, the most important being that of quaestor. Many of the equestrians became businessmen, or the partners of senators, who were restricted to landownership and agriculture as a source of wealth, and were forbidden by law to run businesses or engage in trade directly. It was possible but not easy for equestrians to aspire to a political career and play a part in government, to become senators and take up office, but it was rare for them to reach the consulship.

There was great snobbery among the senatorial class about these *novi homines*, or new men, entering the Senate with no long-standing consular backgrounds. In the last century and a half of the Republic, there were only ten *novi homines* who were successful in gaining senatorial status. Gaius Marius, an equestrian from Arpinum, was one of them, being elected consul for 107 and earning military fame thereafter and six more consulships, the last one obtained not entirely legally. In the years after Marius, between 93 and 48 BC, only Marcus Tullius Cicero reached the consulship as a *novus homo*, rising to prominence via his legal work and appearances in the courts, acting either for the defence or the prosecution.[3]

While not every Roman male of senatorial or equestrian background aspired to the highest public offices and provincial commands, the men who were ambitious had to follow the stages in the career structure, aiming ultimately for the consulship. Many were bound to be disappointed simply because there were only two consuls each year. Their success or otherwise depended not only on wealth and status, or their declared policies, but also on their popularity, active canvassing, and ultimately on the elections. A new division among the politicians arose in the later Republic, between on the one hand the *boni*, or *optimates*, the self-styled 'best men' who upheld traditional values sometimes to the point of seeming hide-bound and unimaginative, and on the other hand the *populares* or demagogues, who played to the people and seemed far too liberal and imaginative for their own good.

These two terms describe only senators, not the ordinary people who gathered around their chosen senator as his clients, or *clientes* in Latin, and supported him in the social and political milieu in return for certain favours, financial or otherwise. Clients were not always from Rome, but could be drawn from a much wider circle outside the city, and as Rome expanded a senator could recruit clients in the provinces as well. It is not known if clients regularly swore an oath of loyalty to their patrons, but since an individual could attach himself to more than one patron, perhaps an oath was not generally called for. The number of clients accompanying a senator to the Forum or the Senate was testament to his relative importance. With his clients, his extended family swelled by marriage alliances with other families, his slaves and his freedmen, a senator was the head of a large organisation, forming a party of his own, and his personal interests took priority over any faction to which he belonged. Such alliances were fluid, and neither the *optimates* nor the *populares* should be considered as two opposing political parties, each with a central organisation, a party headquarters, and co-ordinated policies. Such an arrangement did not exist. There was no representative government with a senator acting on behalf of a group of people belonging to a defined geographical division, and no civil service or central political administration. Everything depended on the personal inclinations of the senators. There were politicians from both the *optimates* and *populares* with a genuine interest in the state and the people, and sometimes men from both groups could work together instead of opposing each other, but within each group there were also individuals following their own agenda. Romans did not have to toe the party line because there was no party line to follow, so factions could be formed or dismantled according to the needs of the moment. Such factions were not unusual, but the term 'faction' referred originally to a group of people with similar interests, and only later did it take on its derogatory connotations when violence entered into Roman politics. In the account of his achievements, known as the *Res Gestae*, Augustus began with his success on freeing the state from the domination of a faction (*a dominatione factionis*).[4]

The voting systems of the Republic show that it was not a democracy as we understand the term. Women had no voice in politics, and even for men the votes were not counted individually and then totted up. Voting on legislative matters or in elections was carried out in voting groups, where each man cast a vote, but the majority vote in each group decided the issue for that group, and the final outcome depended on the overall majority of all the groups. The main assemblies of the people in the early Republic were the *comitia curiata*, the *comitia centuriata*, the *comitia tributa* and the *concilium plebis*. The last named of these was for plebeians alone, but its decisions, called *plebiscita*, applied to all citizens including patricians. The *comitium*, from which the plural noun *comitia* derives, signified the meeting place of the assemblies. The *comitium* was not a building, but a designated area where the people could assemble, but the people could not decide to hold meetings unless they were summoned by a magistrate. The functions of the assemblies were limited to voting for candidates for the various magistracies, or voting yes or no to proposals laid before them. No discussion was allowed in any of the assemblies on the legislative or administrative matters devised by the magistrates, which were presented to the Senate first. At least that was the proper method, but increasingly often from the time of the tribunes Tiberius and Gaius Gracchus in the mid second century BC, magistrates presented bills directly to the people, and made laws without having them discussed in the Senate. The *comitia curiata* was the earliest assembly, made up of thirty groups called *curiae*, ten from each of the three original tribes. By the late Republic this assembly met only to bestow *imperium* on the consuls and praetors.

The *comitia centuriata* grew out of the *comitia curiata*. In the early Republic the divisions of the *comitia centuriata*, the centuries, were based on property and wealth, and the title century does not indicate that each one comprised 100 men. The wealthiest class of all formed the cavalry of the early Republic. These men had to provide horses and their feed and harness, and their own equipment as well, so only the wealthiest could belong in this category. There were subordinate classes based on the type of military equipment that each member of the class could afford, with the largest number of men crammed into the lowest class, the *capite censi*, who had no property and were not eligible for service in the armies, and were therefore counted by heads, not wealth. In Caesar's day, the *comitia centuriata* contained 373 centuries according to age and property values, supplemented by eighteen centuries of wealthy men who originally formed the cavalry, but each of their centuries contained the smallest number of individuals. Each man cast a vote within his century, and since the issue for each century was decided by the majority vote, this gave a preponderant influence to the centuries containing the wealthiest men. As Goldsworthy points out, since the wealthiest classes voted first, they could carry the elections without even calling upon the poorer men to cast a vote at all.[5] The *comitia centuriata* could be summoned only by magistrates who held *imperium*, usually the consuls and praetors. The bestowal of *imperium* gave the holder military and administrative powers, and in turn the *comitia centuriata* was responsible for electing these higher magistrates. It was also responsible for voting yes or no to proposed wars, and on occasion the people voted no, thus belying the reputation of the Roman people as bloodthirsty and eager for war at all times.

The *comitia tributa* was divided into thirty-five voting tribes, and this assembly was responsible for the election of the lesser magistrates ranking below the consuls and praetors. The *comitia tributa* could be summoned by consuls, praetors and also the tribunes of the plebs, and it voted on bills laid before it by the magistrates. When politicians went straight to the people with their bills this is the *comitia* that they summoned to vote on their measures, unless it was for going to war, which as outlined above was the responsibility of the *comitia centuriata*. After the Social War with the Italian allies, when Roman citizenship was finally offered to the allies, many new citizens were created, but their influence was curtailed by distributing them among only a few voting tribes, and for a long time thereafter various tribunes and magistrates tried to pass laws to redistribute them more fairly among all the thirty-five tribes.

The part played by wealth not only influenced the voting systems, but could also disrupt the elections, in that bribery was occasionally used, not to mention browbeating the electorate now and then. This became more common in the later Republic, though Gruen examined the evidence and concluded that disruption was not as frequent or as serious as has been claimed by ancient and modern authors.[6] Whether or not expenditure on canvassing for elections crossed the boundary between acceptable limits and outright corruption, most candidates usually looked forward not only to election, but after holding office as praetors or consuls they each hoped for an appointment as a provincial governor. Once comfortably installed in a province, most governors could rely on being able to recoup their financial losses, and much more besides. This was the key to continuing their political careers, especially for those men who did not hold vast profitable estates or inherited wealth. Enlightened Romans were forever framing preventative laws to try to keep up with the transgressions of their colleagues, and in the second century BC the tribune of the plebs Gaius Sempronius Gracchus passed laws to ensure that the provinces to be assigned to retiring consuls and praetors were decided before the elections, to discourage candidates from angling to obtain the most profitable territories just as they embarked on their canvassing for election. Tribunician veto on this procedure was forbidden, but this may not have been embedded in Gracchus' legislation and may have required a separate law.[7] Using the *lex Sempronia* passed by Gaius Gracchus, the Senate tried to muzzle Caesar when he stood for the consulship of 59 BC, by assigning the successful consuls for that year to the proconsular tasks of caring for woodlands and roads.[8] But Caesar circumvented them, and obtained Transalpine and Cisalpine Gaul and Illyricum as his provinces, which he retained for a decade.

Retention of power once a politician had gained high office always represented a potential threat. During the early history of the Republic, in the mid-fifth century, the normal government had been suspended, and ten men or *Decemviri* had been appointed to frame and codify the laws for the first time, resulting in the production of the famous law codes known as the Twelve Tables, which Roman schoolboys thereafter had to learn by heart. At the end of their task, the men refused to lay down their powers, the traditional villain of the piece being Appius Claudius, who apparently turned into a megalomaniac monster. Despite the accretion of probably fabulous legends about him, Appius represented exactly the vice that the Roman governmental system sought to avoid, domination by one individual with too much power.

Occasionally there were exceptional circumstances where the retention of power by means of legalised re-election was condoned. One such threat was the emergence of the tribes of the Cimbri and Teutones sweeping across northern Italy, probably intent on invasion. In this instance, the people insisted on electing the ex-consul and successful general Gaius Marius to his second consulship in 104 BC, and they did this each year until 101 BC, when he defeated the tribes at Aix-la-Chapelle. The repeated elections broke with tradition, but allowed Marius to retain his command in the north of Italy, at the cost of setting a precedent, because candidates were supposed to be present in Rome for the electoral process, and Marius did not leave his command.

In 60 BC, returning from his term of office as governor of Further Spain, Caesar sought to register his candidacy for the consulate; elections were to take place the following year. However, he had also been awarded a triumph in Rome for his military exploits, and this presented a dilemma. He could not register his candidacy without entering the city, and yet no commander was legally allowed to cross the *pomerium*, or city boundary, while still at the head of an army. If he wanted to celebrate his triumph, though, he had to retain his command. Caesar therefore asked permission of the Senate to canvass for the elections *in absentia*. The Senate, led by Cato, blocked him. Caesar was offered a choice. He could hold the triumph but forego any chance of election as consul, or he could come to Rome and canvass legally for the elections and forego the triumph. He chose Rome and the elections, and duly became consul in legal fashion.[9]

Politicians of the later Republic were adept at bending or ignoring the rules, achieving their ends by means which were dubious but not always totally illegal. In 133 BC, not too long before Caesar's birth, the tribune of the plebs Tiberius Sempronius Gracchus embarked on a programme of reforms which were sensible and necessary, but he overstepped the mark by his methods. Normally a tribune presented his ideas to the Senate for debate, and in the usual way the necessary laws would be framed and presented to the people's assemblies for approval. According to the *lex Hortensia*, a law passed in 287 BC, this became the preferred method but not actually a legal requirement, so Tiberius went straight to the people to have his laws passed, setting a precedent for by-passing the Senate, a method which unscrupulous politicians utilised thereafter. When his opponents persuaded another tribune to block him, Tiberius had the unfortunate fellow tribune forcibly removed, scandalously ignoring the sacrosanctity that tribunes were supposed to possess.

If Tiberius' opponents hoped that he would no longer be a problem after the expiry of his term of office, they were disappointed when Tiberius stood for re-election for a second term. One year of office was not enough to put into effect his agenda, and by standing for re-election he could avoid prosecution for offences against the state, which his enemies were sure to bring against him when he returned to private life. He came to a gory end because the Senate overreacted, fearful of his power. The consul was asked to use force to stop him, but refused. In desperation the Pontifex Maximus, head of the priestly college, stepped in, and gathered a mob of senators and their associates, who slaughtered Gracchus and his adherents. Their actions were a stain on the Republic, but the violence was repeated a decade later when Tiberius' brother Gaius Gracchus was elected tribune for two terms, and stood for a third. This time, the Senate passed the *senatus consultum ultimum*, or the last decree, which was used only in emergencies, and Gaius and 3,000 of his supporters were killed.

Factional strife and political murder now routinely entered Roman politics, but there was worse to come. During the struggle with Lucius Cornelius Sulla, Gaius Marius and his colleague Lucius Cornelius Cinna simply took over the state. They established yet another precedent by declaring themselves consuls for 86 BC without the benefit of regular election, and for 85 BC, after Marius' death, Cinna appointed his colleagues as consuls. It shocked Roman sensibilities, and yet only a generation later, beginning with Augustus, the elections faded away and appointment of consuls and other magistrates by the Emperors became the norm, without ruffling anyone's feathers.

The problem for politicians of Caesar's day, and for Caesar himself, was not only gaining power but retaining it, in order to put into effect their programmes, which were continually hampered by having only one year in which to achieve anything. Retention of office was not normally possible, and re-election immediately after holding office was discouraged, and eventually forbidden by laws outlining the number of years that should intervene between various posts.

Quaestors, for instance, were usually in their late twenties and early thirties before taking up office, and nine years were supposed to elapse between this post and that of praetor. In the intervening period there were a few options. An ex-quaestor would usually stand for election as one of the aediles, or if the individual belonged to the plebeian class he could become a tribune of the plebs. Some men would accompany a magistrate, either in Italy or a province, nominally with financial and secretarial duties, but sometimes gaining experience of war. All the time they would be building up connections with influential people, or networking as the modern term describes it.

After reaching the praetorship, the aspiring politician had to wait for three years before aiming for the consulship. Not all retiring praetors would become governors of the less important provinces, though they might accompany one of the consuls who had been allotted a provincial command, again forming contacts with people who might help the individual in his career, especially if he had the consulship within his sights. Though this career pattern was often flouted, it generally ensured that no one should become consul until he was around forty-two years of age and therefore he could be reasonably expected to be mature and experienced. Then another ten years were supposed to elapse between the first and second consulship. It was all good in theory.

Given that power on a prolonged basis was necessary to complete some of the desired reforms, where was the dividing line between the interests of the state and the growth of personal dominance? The Senate as a body was on perpetual alert for men bent on the accretion of personal power, and would block all proposals that seemed to be leading to dominance. The people would vote, not necessarily for a personality, but for their promises and avowed policies, but even when policies were necessary, sensible and thoroughly thought through, if they were also considered detrimental to senatorial interests they would be fought tooth and nail and squashed if possible. A politician could try to use strictly legal means to expedite sound polices that promised to remedy various ills of the state, but the author or authors of such policies would usually be suspected of harbouring ulterior motives, namely the attainment of personal power.

Were ambitious politicians altruistically concerned with providing solutions to problems of the state, or were they unscrupulous opportunists who identified problems and latched on to them to promise reforms, merely as a vehicle for gaining popular support? Sallust recognised this preponderance of self-interest when he described the activities of Lucius Sergius Catilina.[10] The fear of dominance by one man who had become too powerful ensured that the Romans more or less painted themselves into a corner, where any activity aimed at reforming the functions and administrative procedures of the state, no matter how necessary they had become, could be considered as a bid for supremacy. Conversely, a situation was created where dominance was necessary to achieve anything at all.

In the later Republic dominant figures emerged not only via the political scene but via the army, until the two became intertwined. The army could never be divorced from political affairs, but it had become significantly more important during the last two centuries of the Republic. Marius gained fame as a military commander, but in the end he used his military power to control Rome. Sulla used the army, with the exception of some of his officers, to violate all the regulations when he marched on Rome to gain what he wanted. In immediate terms, this was the military command against Mithridates of Pontus, which had been voted to him as consul and then given to his rival Gaius Marius, and ultimately he was determined to shore up the oligarchy and reinstate senatorial eminence.

Political and military careers were inseparable for Romans of the Republic. Consuls were responsible for administration of the state, but they also commanded armies, and at the bottom of the scale young men would take up political and military appointments on the career path to higher offices. The citizen army of the Republic was assembled for specific campaigns, recruited from Romans and their non-Roman allies, commanded by the consuls or the praetors and then disbanded when the campaigns ended. All eligible able-bodied men had a duty to serve when called upon, for a specified number of years or campaigns, but during the later Republic campaigns tended to last longer than one season, and on occasions there were wars to be fought in several different territories. This meant that there was usually an active army somewhere in the Roman world at all times during the first century BC, and ordinary soldiers could follow a military career by re-enlisting for successive campaigns under different commanders. A semi-professional coterie of soldiers developed, despite the disadvantage that a man who had been promoted and had possibly served as a centurion in one campaign usually had to start all over again in the ranks in the next campaign, unless the commanders knew him personally and appointed him directly.

Longer campaigns strengthened the bonds between commanders and soldiers, who swore an oath to obey their generals, which was taken very seriously. The commander was technically restrained by his obedience to the Senate, but in civil wars a private individual could raise an army, as when Pompey raised a total of three armies on behalf of Sulla, from his landed estates in Picenum, and Licinius Crassus too brought troops to fight for Sulla. In these circumstances the authority of the Senate could be by-passed. Neither Pompey nor Crassus held any political office, but they did not wait for permission of the Senate to recruit soldiers. Sulla held on to the power he gained via the army, and he used it to shore up the oligarchic Senate, and he did a very fine job that took some effort from succeeding politicians to unravel. Unfortunately, not all ambitious commanders had their sights set on bolstering the Senate, and they could use the army too. Marius gained fame as a military commander, defeating the rebel Jugurtha in Africa and saving Rome from the Celtic tribes. He was also famous (or notorious) for changing the rules by recruiting the poorest of the men in Rome, the *capite censi*, who were counted not by wealth but by heads, as their title suggests. They were not normally eligible to serve in the army because they had no means of equipping themselves.[11] It was not unreasonable to utilise the available manpower, but it meant that the state eventually had to provide arms and armour for the army. In the end, though, Marius could not resist utilizing his military power to control Rome, and Dio invents a speech for the senator Lutatius Catulus, to the effect that it was the wars in quick succession and the six consulships in a short period that made Marius the man he eventually became.[12]

Despite these examples, it was still necessary to grant unprecedented powers to a general when danger threatened, especially if the danger was widespread and embraced more than one province. The growing Empire had overreached itself. It was divided up between provinces and non-Roman territories bordering on them, and worked well if internal disruption or external threat could be dealt with by the governor on the spot, or, in extreme circumstances, the governor could request help from Rome or call upon Rome's allies within reach of his province to provide troops. Theoretically, a governor was not authorised to recruit new troops without permission from the Senate, but in emergencies it could be condoned. Where the threat extended across provincial boundaries or across the borders with non-Roman states, a commander could be appointed with more wide-ranging territorial powers, including authorisation to make peace or war and to raise troops.

Just such a problem was represented by pirates, who threatened coastal areas all around the Mediterranean, endangered merchants and travellers alike, and disrupted Rome's food supply. When Caesar was just embarking on his career, Pompey the Great was one of the most important men in Rome, with extensive military experience and less political expertise, but he had great influence by working in the background through his supporters. He was the only man in Rome with enough prestige to take on the task of eradicating the pirates after other commanders had failed, largely because they were awarded insufficient powers and resources to combat the problem.

According to his normal practice, Pompey left it to his supporters to work on his behalf while pretending that he was not seeking any appointment to deal with the pirates. The bill did not name any specific commander but outlined his powers. When the law was passed, the unnamed commander was empowered to control a large navy, and about two dozen subordinate commanders in charge of parts of the fleet and troops on land. For the first time one man had been given command not only of the whole Mediterranean, but also of all territories surrounding it up to 50 miles inland, taking precedence over existing governors of those territories.[13] He also had control over his subordinate officers, most of whom were of high rank and would normally have reported individually to the Senate but now reported to the commander himself. It made perfect sense to appoint a single high-ranking officer who operated within the war zone and could co-ordinate the activities of all his subordinate officers, thus avoiding unnecessary delays, not to mention confusion caused by each officer having to report to the Senate and await replies. Pompey was finally named as this extra special commander, which surprised nobody. This sort of extraordinary command became more common during the late Republic, and rules were bent or even flouted to accommodate them.

These extraordinary campaigns, of longer duration and wider extent than had been the norm, only served to strengthen the bonds between commander and soldiers, and a concomitant factor was the fact that pay, promotion and ultimately provision for retirement was in the hands of the commander. The dependence on the commander was exacerbated by the reluctance of the Senate to find lands or state funds to provide for any form of welfare for retiring soldiers. The land problem in all its aspects became a constant problem and a vehicle for rising politicians in the later Republic, and in certain respects was bound up with the army. The soldiers were mostly derived from the farmers of smallholdings, who went back to their lands when wars ended. As a rule, the army perhaps did not take all the men of eligible age from all the farms, leaving some behind to grow the crops, but as campaigns lengthened and men were absent for longer periods, or were killed, a decline set in and farms were abandoned. At least this is how it was perceived in Rome, to account for the numbers of people migrating to the city and swelling the ranks of the urban poor. Other factors were also perceived as contributing to the impoverishment and disappearance of small farms, such as the growth of wealthy estates that swallowed them up and were then farmed by slave labour, thus pricing the small farmers out of the market. The land problems were real enough, but from the time of the two Gracchi, the Romans perceived the disappearance of the small farmers as a threat to recruitment for the army, a factor which has been reviewed and revised by modern historians.[14]

When soldiers were dismissed without farms to go to or any other means of support, they turned to their commander if the Senate proved intransigent and refused to help them. Commanders were therefore under pressure to remain active on the political scene in order to have the necessary legislation forced through, and after a long period of failure to get his veterans settled after his defeat of the pirates and then of Mithridates of Pontus, this is what threw Pompey the Great into the arms of the new consul for 59 BC, Gaius Julius Caesar.

3

Caesar's Family and Early Life, 100–83 BC

The most important factors in Roman political life were the possession of wealth and illustrious ancestors who had been consul at least once, or better still had saved Rome from danger or enjoyed success in war. The Julian clan was one of the most ancient in Rome, but the particular branch of the Julii to which Gaius Julius Caesar belonged was not politically eminent, being quite undistinguished for the last three centuries, although other branches had consular ancestors. Julius was the family name, or *nomen*, signifying membership of the clan of the Julii. Gaius was the *praenomen*, or personal name, like Marcus, Publius or Lucius, and in Caesar's case Gaius was the name given to all first-born sons of the family. Following the *nomen* Julius was the *cognomen* Caesar, indicating the section of the Julii to which the family belonged. Neither Julius nor Caesar was a surname as we understand the term, and there was more than one branch of the Julii Caesares. It cannot be assumed that any Roman with the name Julius was a relative of Caesar, even if the individual was also a Julius Caesar. One of the consuls for 157 BC was Lucius Julius Caesar, as were the consuls for 90 BC and 64 BC, but these men belonged to a different branch of the Caesares, and were not close relatives of Caesar.[1]

Although the Julians were acknowledged as among Rome's original families and held patrician status, there is insufficient information to trace Caesar's ancestry back beyond his grandparents. In the mythical realm, the Julii Caesares were said to have descended from Iulus, the son of Aeneas, who brought his family to Italy from Troy after the city had fallen. Aeneas' parents were the mortal Anchises and the goddess Venus. This would be considered preposterous were it not for the fact that several other Roman families claimed descent from various gods, and were usually responsible for setting up and maintaining temples to these deities. In the earthly realm, Caesar's grandfather was Gaius Julius Caesar, married to Marcia, the daughter of Quintus Marcius Rex, whose family was allegedly descended from one of Rome's kings, Ancus Marcius. Beyond this, not even speculation is enough to elucidate Caesar's ancestry, though Caesar himself would have had access to family records. There were also official census records, and births had to be registered officially, but little has survived of these sources, except lists of population figures.

The elder Gaius Julius Caesar may have had a brother, Sextus Julius Caesar, who was consul in 91 BC, and may therefore have been Caesar's uncle, but although the existence of this man is proven beyond doubt, his exact relationship to Gaius is not, so he could have been a cousin of Caesar's father. The elder Gaius definitely had a sister, Julia, who married Gaius Marius, probably in 113 or 112 BC. Marius was not yet famous, just an aspiring equestrian politician who had been elected praetor for 115 BC, and after his office expired he had served as governor of Further Spain in 114 BC. He was destined to become much more famous and is considered to have been influential in the young Caesar's life.

Caesar's mother was Aurelia, from a plebeian noble family. She had consular ancestry, her grandfather having been consul in 144 BC and her father in 119 BC, but this would not necessarily help Caesar in his career since his paternal ancestry was what counted most. Aurelia did have influential relatives in the three brothers Gaius, Marcus and Lucius Aurelius Cotta, who were probably her cousins. Aurelia and Gaius Julius Caesar had three children: Caesar and two girls named Julia. Girls were named according to their paternal family. The two Julias would be distinguished officially as Julia Prima and Julia Secunda, but more than likely had special distinguishing nicknames as well.

The relative obscurity of Caesar's family background is illustrated by the lack of a precise record of the year of his birth, though this lacuna in our knowledge would probably be remedied instantly if the lost first sections of Suetonius' and Plutarch's biographies were ever to be discovered. Caesar's birthday is known to be the third day before the Ides of Quinctilis, which translates into modern terms as 13 July. The month was later named after him, just as August was named after Augustus. In Roman terms, the year began in March, and before the month of July was renamed in Caesar's honour it was called Quinctilis, the fifth month after the beginning of the year. But although the day and month are known, the year of Caesar's birth is not established. Traditionally he was born in 100 BC, but it has also been argued that the birth occurred in 101 or 102 BC. The point is academic, and ascertaining the exact year hardly makes any difference to Caesar's personality, ambition or success.

The career of Caesar's father is known only in broad outline, without the benefit of precise dates. It has been suggested that Gaius was appointed to a board of ten men charged with providing lands and setting up colonies for the discharged veteran soldiers of Marius' army after the defeat of the tribes of the Cimbri and Teutones who had threatened to invade Italy for the past four years or so. Given that the elder Gaius Julius Caesar was Marius' brother-in-law from about 113 BC onwards, it is highly likely that some appointment would have been awarded to him, and the settlement of the veterans was a likely option, perhaps in 103 BC, or more likely 100 BC when Marius was consul for the sixth time.[2] This task was probably followed by the quaestorship, perhaps around the time of Caesar's birth.

The ensuing years between Gaius' service as quaestor and then praetor are obscure. The exact dates are not proven, but he may have been praetor in 92 or 91 BC, and then proconsul of Asia in 91 or 90 BC. His title as proconsul does not indicate that he had been consul, since it was the customary designation for provincial governors of praetorian rank who had not yet reached the consulship. The province of Asia was wealthy, with flourishing agriculture and industries, especially in woollen products. Trade routes through the province brought goods to the ports of the Aegean Sea. The land had been bequeathed to Rome by its last king, Attalus III of Pergamum. In 133 BC his kingdom became the Roman province of Asia, not to be confused with the much wider area of the same name in modern English. The province covered most of western Turkey, together with some of the islands off the coast, though there was an accretion of territories and adjustment of boundaries after it came under Roman control. Most Roman governors saw the provinces as a quick way of getting rich, especially Asia, so it was hardly surprising that Mithridates VI, King of Pontus, who had been thwarted by Rome in his bids for territorial expansion, was easily able to foment revolt among the population of Asia in the early 80s BC. Virtually no information about the behaviour of the governor Gaius Julius Caesar has come to light, so it is possible that he made a fortune during his term of office, like the governors before and after him, but a brief inscription in his honour was found on the island of Delos, near one of the granaries set up by the *olearii* or olive oil merchants, which may mean that he had treated them fairly if not magnanimously.[3] Perhaps Caesar's father was as scrupulously honest as we would wish him to have been.

At the time of Caesar's birth, his father was just embarking on his political career as quaestor, the first post that really mattered in the senatorial path to the consulship, while Caesar's uncle Marius had reached the peak with his sixth consulship in 100 BC. Unfortunately, his consulship did not work out as he had hoped and planned. He made a mistake in trusting the men he chose to push through his legislation for the settlement of his veteran soldiers. These men proved unreliable and violent, and escaped from his control, so he was obliged to suppress them with force. Thereafter his career was in abeyance, until his final years, when his brief resurgence brought both his career and his life to an ignominious end.

It is worthwhile to examine Marius' career, in that it shaped Caesar's early background if not his character. Caesar was about thirteen years old when Marius died. He was an extraordinary general, but not a successful politician. It cannot be proven how much contact Caesar had with his uncle during his childhood and early youth, nor is it certain how much influence Marius had on Caesar's development, opinions and ambitions. Plutarch was certain that the relationship provided a role model for Caesar.[4] Even without direct contact, it is likely that Caesar derived valuable lessons from his uncle's career, even if only in retrospect when he had grown up and achieved better understanding. Marius had shown that relatively humble origins could be overcome, and much could be achieved with a combination of luck, a determined mindset and the right choice of patrons.

Anyone who wanted to rise in the Roman political world needed an influential group of friends who could provide the necessary funds and political backing, who could pull strings to help their protégés to obtain appointments with their relatives or friends, and could persuade the Roman electorate to cast favourable votes. Marius was backed by the Caecilii Metelli, an influential family with consular ancestry dating back to the third century BC. According to Plutarch, the Metelli had always been patrons of Marius' equestrian family, and with their support he was elected tribune of the plebs. The relationship was not always smooth. Plutarch reports that as tribune, Marius proposed a change to the voting system, which would have threatened the dominance of the most powerful men in legal cases. He was challenged by the consul Lucius Aurelius Cotta, who asked Metellus for his opinion. There were several politically active Caecilii Metelli, and though Plutarch does not specify which Metellus was asked for his opinion, it was probably Cotta's colleague, Lucius Caecilius Metellus Delmaticus. When Metellus said that he thought the consul was correct to oppose the proposal for changing the voting system, Marius ordered one of the lictors outside to take Metellus to prison. According to Plutarch, Marius asked the other tribunes to support his bill, but they refused, so he left the Senate, presented the bill to the people and got it passed.[5] After his year as tribune, Marius stood for election as curule aedile, the more important of the two types of aedile, the lesser version being plebeian aedile. Voting took place first for the curule post, and Marius was not successful, so he presented himself as candidate for the second type, and failed there as well.[6] These stories demonstrate Marius' determination, fearlessness, and potential ruthlessness. His failure to impress the voters for the aedileship did not prevent his election as praetor, and after his term of office, he was appointed governor of Further Spain.

The Metelli may not have realised the extent of Marius' determination to rise in politics. He was, after all, of humble background, and a *novus homo*, or new man, with no money and not skilled in the rhetoric that upper-class Romans so valued. Perhaps it was unthinkable that he could ever become consul. The first step towards this goal came in 109 BC, when Marius was appointed one of the legates, or deputies of Quintus Caecilius Metellus, the brother of Metellus Delmaticus, who was consul for that year. Metellus was appointed to conduct the war against Jugurtha, King of Numidia, after which he earned the name Numidicus. Jugurtha had fought on the Roman side in Spain, in the army of the illustrious Scipio Aemilianus, in which campaign Marius had also served. In fighting for his claim to the Numidian throne, Jugurtha had eliminated his rivals, but he had also massacred some Italian businessmen. The Romans declared war on him, but the initial campaigns under different commanders had not gone well. The historian Sallust wrote an account of the Jugurthine war.

There was greater success when Caecilius Metellus was sent to take command, but he was not able to conclude the war. After fighting under Metellus for a short time, Marius asked for leave to return to Rome in 108 BC to stand for the consular elections for 107 BC. Metellus was from a noble house of long-standing fame, while Marius was regarded as an upstart nonentity, and Metellus advised him to wait, perhaps with the trace of a sneer. Marius went home anyway, leaving only a few days for canvassing. The fact that he was elected indicates that Marius already had a circle of friends and adherents in Rome to do his canvassing for him, and, more importantly, it shows that this was not a decision made on the spur of the moment, but that he had planned his campaign in advance.

As consul, Marius manoeuvred for the recall of Metellus, and successfully proposed that he himself should be appointed as the new commander in Numidia. When he returned to Africa, Marius went on to win the war against Jugurtha, with significant assistance from one of his deputies, Lucius Cornelius Sulla, an impoverished but blue-blooded aristocrat, who, according to Sallust, soon became the best soldier in Marius' army.[7] Just as Marius had turned against Caecilius Metellus, Sulla was to become Marius' nemesis.

While he was in Rome, Marius had recruited more troops to augment the army in Africa. He did not raise the new soldiers via the usual levy from among the classes who could afford to equip themselves, but from the men who had no property and were grouped together under the heading *capite censi* and were technically ineligible for service in the army.[8] This meant that the state would have to provide their equipment, but this was not a new idea – the tribune of the plebs Gaius Gracchus had already made a move in this direction, and the state was already providing equipment for some of its soldiers. It made sense to utilise all the available manpower, regardless of their property status, but Marius has been blamed for starting off the mutual dependence of the generals and their soldiers, in effect creating armies whose loyalty was not primarily to the state but to their commanders. The accusation is not entirely fair, because this new element had already entered Roman politics. Plutarch blames Lucius Cornelius Sulla, not Marius, for starting the trend. In a succinct analysis of the ills of the later Republic he points out that the consuls of earlier times did not pander to their troops, but the generals of later times won political fame not by merit but by force, backed by their soldiers, and spent more time fighting other Romans instead of external enemies. To keep the loyalty of their troops the commanders had to gratify them and in effect buy them, and had to become political leaders as well as commanders, and Plutarch emphasises that it was Sulla more than any other commander who began this process.[9]

Between 104 and 101 BC Marius was the saviour of Rome, having finally defeated the Cimbri and Teutones and prevented an invasion of Italy. His track record was glorious so far, until his consulship of 100 BC. The end of his life was even worse. During Sulla's absence in the East, Marius and his consular colleague Lucius Cornelius Cinna eliminated their political rivals in a notorious bloodbath, but only a few days into his consulship Marius died. His sudden and rapid fall into disfavour was probably not lost on the young Caesar.

The scant details of the career of the elder Gaius Julius Caesar, and the better-documented life of Marius, can provide only a glimpse of Caesar's early life. There is little if any knowledge of the friends and enemies Caesar inherited from his father. Next to nothing is known of the family's source of wealth, which would have been derived from the landed estates that the Julii Caesares surely possessed. The property or properties belonging to Caesar's father may not have been extensive. The location of the estate, or more likely estates, is not known, nor is there any evidence as to how extensive they may have been. In any case, Caesar may have lost them when Sulla returned from the East and deprived Caesar of his inheritance. According to Suetonius, Caesar lost everything at this time. It is known that as an adult Caesar possessed estates near Nemi, and at Labici, where he wrote his will towards the end of his life, adding a codicil naming Gaius Octavius as his heir. These may have been estates that he acquired much later.[10]

His childhood home was in the Subura, in a modest house, says Suetonius.[11] The area covered the slopes of the Viminal, Esquiline and Quirinal hills. Its territorial limit next to the Imperial Forums is today marked by the high and imposing fire-wall that Augustus built behind his Forum and Temple of Mars Ultor. The Subura was not a desirable address, nor was it a wealthy area. Nothing is known about Caesar's childhood, and perhaps mercifully there are no prodigy stories comparable to the infant Hercules strangling snakes whilst in his cradle. Historians can only assume that Caesar was a normal Roman boy, brought up and educated in the normal fashion. The persistent legend that Caesar was delivered by Caesarian section is now dismissed, because although the doctors of the ancient world knew how to deliver babies in this way, the procedure was usually fatal for the mother, and Caesar's mother obviously survived, until he was in his forties. It is possible that an ancestor of Caesar was born in this way as a later source suggests, with unrecorded detrimental consequences for the mother.[12] When he was born, Caesar's father would have had the power of life and death over him, refusing to accept him into the family if he had any serious physical defects or deformities. Having lifted the newborn Caesar from the floor, thereby acknowledging him as his son, the elder Gaius would preside over the religious ceremonial to celebrate the birth, and would have to register his son's name for the census records. This would take place nine days after the birth, perhaps to allow for any mishap which would render registration unnecessary, since infant mortality was high in ancient Rome.

In the early years, the mother took most of the responsibility for bringing up the child. The most common description of Aurelia in modern works is 'formidable', a description probably derived largely from the way in which she dealt with the intrusion of Publius Clodius, dressed as a woman, at the festival of the Bona Dea, the Good Goddess, which was held in Caesar's house. Men were strictly excluded from this festival. Plutarch describes how Aurelia possessed strict moral values.[13] Despite the lack of detailed biographical information about her, Aurelia has acquired legendary status, along with Cornelia, the mother of Tiberius and Gaius Gracchus. The sanctity of motherhood and family values were promoted by Augustus. One of the sculpted panels of the Ara Pacis, the altar to Peace, shows the figure of a woman holding two robust babies, first interpreted as Mother Earth and now thought to represent Peace, but it is still an idyllic scene of motherhood. Aurelia's reputation may have been enhanced by Augustan propaganda, and though there is little about her that survives in the extant literature, what is known is reminiscent of Augustus' own mother Atia, renowned for her exemplary upbringing of her son.

As a child, Caesar's early development would have been in his mother's hands, but there would also have been slaves to take care of his daily needs, and eventually a tutor, or tutors, may have been appointed. One of his teachers when he was older was Marcus Antonius Gnypho or Gnipho, recorded by Suetonius in his biographies of grammarians.[14] Gnipho was born in Gaul and, abandoned by his parents, he was rescued by an unknown family and brought to Alexandria for his education. Suetonius says he first taught rhetoric in the house of Julius Caesar, while Caesar was still a boy. He was said to be highly talented, fluent in Greek and Latin, and of a kindly nature. Perhaps something of his disposition influenced Caesar.

Roman boys of Caesar's social class would be expected to have a high standard of literacy, reading and writing Greek as well as Latin, and the main aim of their education was to produce articulate young men to whom public speaking should come easily. Teachers of rhetoric were engaged to help these pupils at home, and schools were established in Rome for young boys, but when they were older some Roman youths went to Greece, to the schools in Athens and Rhodes. Their teachers would instruct the young men not only in composition of speeches, but also in using appropriate gestures and stance, because public speaking, in front of crowds in the open air, was like acting in a play but with natural acoustics and without the aid of microphones; voice projection, good delivery and gesturing with hands and arms were essential parts of the repertoire, which perhaps summon images of Douglas Fairbanks in silent films.

Cicero had a high opinion of Caesar's rhetorical skills. Suetonius says that Caesar spoke in a high-pitched voice, and made impassioned gestures, which were not ungraceful.[15] Since he wrote long after Caesar's death, it could be asked what source was available to

Suetonius, recording these details for posterity. Plutarch may have had access to sources describing Caesar's rhetorical skills, but if so he did not quote them, falling back on the nonspecific formula that 'it was said that' the adult Caesar possessed a gift for political oratory, but Plutarch also considered that Caesar was too engrossed in honing his military talents as his path to fame, and did not give his whole attention to public speaking. On one occasion Caesar urged his audience not to compare him, a man of war, with an orator whose gifts came naturally, improved with long practice. False modesty, of course: Caesar well knew how to control an audience.[16]

From an early age Roman boys were included in adult affairs, absorbing how the household was run and how their landed estates functioned. Suetonius says that Caesar was strict in managing his household, though Suetonius' main point concerns the disciplining of his slaves.[17] It would have been essential to learn how the family businesses were organised. Businesses and trading activities were run on behalf of senators by equestrians, because senators were forbidden by law to engage in work of any kind, though it was acknowledged that senators owned ships and laws were passed to try to limit the number of vessels that they could operate. Whilst there was perhaps no strict sense of budgeting in the household accounts, in balancing income against expenditure a boy would soon learn which enterprises were most profitable, and would understand the vagaries of agriculture, as documented by their stewards or bailiffs, who would be slaves or perhaps freedmen.

As an introduction to political life, boys would be taken to the Forum by their fathers or guardians to hear speeches, or to listen and observe at the courts when the advocates were speaking. Instead of being shut away in a nursery, boys would be allowed to join dinner parties and social gatherings, as well as being seen with their fathers and clients in the public spaces. This enabled the offspring of the political figures to see and be seen by friends and enemies of their families, which they inherited along with their fathers' clients. This was the Roman version of networking, while the boys and young men discovered how public life worked. Another form of networking was the physical exercise regime in the Campus Martius, where boys performed on horseback or on foot, and swam in the Tiber – no mean feat since the river can flow very rapidly. Swimming as a boy no doubt helped Caesar much later when he had to flee for his life by swimming, allegedly carrying documents above his head, when he was under siege at Alexandria.[18]

There is little information as to how proficient Caesar was as a boy, just glimpses of him as an adult. He was said to have been a good rider, riding bareback without a saddle, according to the writer and polymath Varro, who grew up in the same era as Caesar.[19] This brings up the question as to whether the Romans used saddles – long denied, but now accepted. The slightly raised rear sections of the saddle have always been visible on sculptures, especially on the tombstones of cavalry soldiers, but they were not necessarily recognised for what they represented. The Romans did not have stirrups, however. Plutarch reports that Caesar rode very fast and made a habit of putting his hands behind his back, which means he was not controlling the horse via the reins and the bit, but with his knees. This was good practice if a boy was to learn how to use his weapons while controlling his horse, but also comes under the heading of showing off.[20]

There were no actual military schools in Rome like the colleges of today, but there were private tutors, military manuals and the personal assistance of family members who had military experience, which all served to prepare young men for military command. Political, military and religious life was intertwined, so the boys and youths doing their exercises in the Campus Martius would expect to be involved in all these spheres. The first important military post was as a military tribune, of which there were six in each legion, and in the early days there were usually up to four legions, raised for specific campaigns and disbanded when the wars ended. Hence there were normally twenty-four military tribunes. The most senior in each legion was the *laticlavius*, or the broad stripe tribune, from a senatorial family but not yet a senator. These were second in command after the consuls, who commanded the armies. The other five tribunes were *angusticlavii*, or narrow stripe tribunes, from equestrian backgrounds, usually with some military experience. The broad stripe tribune would have little military experience and no real qualifications except his family background, where he would have become accustomed to dealing with slaves and clients. Roman boys were not usually shy, retiring wallflowers, so making themselves understood and being obeyed would have been natural to them by the time they met grizzled soldiers much older than they were themselves. To gain an appointment, the young man himself, or his family, would probably have some acquaintance with the commander. In the Roman world the old adage was true: it was not what you knew that counted, but who you knew, and recommendations from relatives and friends for posts was not frowned upon.

It can only be assumed that Caesar experienced the same sort of education briefly outlined above. The events in politics and military history from 100 to 84 BC would also have served as part of his education as soon as he was old enough to understand them. He may have discussed such matters with his parents, or his father may have taken the time to explain things. Uncle Marius may have had a hand in the young Caesar's development while he grew up in a world where not only foreign wars were fought, but also wars between Romans. Half a century before Caesar was born Roman politics had become dangerous and potentially bloody, and it was not destined to improve. Perhaps he watched, listened and learned.

Caesar was about nine years old when the preliminaries to the Social War began, in which the Italian communities allied to Rome decided to fight for Roman citizenship and more privileges. The term Social War refers to the allies, or *socii* in Latin. By the terms of their individual alliances with Rome, the Italian allies had faithfully sent their young men to fight alongside the Romans in wars that did not directly concern them, and now they wanted equality with the Romans. Citizenship had been promised to the allied states and tribes of Italy on a few occasions, and then, each time, all hopes had been dashed. The Senate objected and squashed the proposals. In 91 BC, it seemed that the programme of Marcus Livius Drusus, tribune of the plebs, might succeed. He attended to various problems, proposing among other things to redistribute land to benefit the poorer citizens, and to found colonies where the swelling population of Rome could settle, thus relieving the difficulties with food supply to the city. More importantly for Rome's Italian allies, he proposed to bestow Roman citizenship on them all. Then he stepped out one morning through the crowd of people gathering to meet him, and he was killed.

The response of most of the Italians was to secede from their alliances, each of which was made separately with Rome and contained a clause forbidding the state or tribe to join with any other. The allies defied the rule, amalgamated and mobilized their troops, all well trained in Roman fighting methods. They set up their own state, issuing coinage, refusing to use the Latin language and substituting Oscan, the most widespread language in the Italian peninsula. The fighting began in 90 BC, provoked in part by an offer of citizenship to the Latin communities, which had always been physically and temperamentally closer to Rome, and to any of the Italian allies who had not joined the rebels. It was not enough. The allies fought well, and in 89 BC the Senate offered citizenship to all who applied within sixty days.

Two men emerged from the war with prestige: Gnaeus Pompeius Strabo, the father of Pompey the Great, who calmed everything down in the north by offering citizenship to the Cisalpine communities; and Lucius Cornelius Sulla, who rounded up the die-hards in the south, putting the recalcitrant city of Nola under siege. By 88 BC the war had fizzled out, but not entirely. Nola was besieged for some years to come, and the Samnites, arguably Rome's fiercest enemy from earliest times, continued to fight. Some resentment remained, because the Romans put all the new citizens into only a limited number of voting groups, and thereby much reduced their influence, so it was business as usual in the city for the senators who begrudged the citizenship granted to those whom they considered their inferiors. The question of a fair distribution of the newly enfranchised allies among all the thirty-five voting groups surfaced again and again in politics.

Late in 89 BC, Lucius Cornelius Sulla and Quintus Pompeius Rufus were elected consuls for 88 BC. Sulla had achieved modest fame, and was to find even more fame in a new war that had been threatening in the eastern provinces for some time. Mithridates VI of Pontus was expanding his territory at the expense of Rome's provinces. He exhorted the inhabitants of Asia, where Caesar's father had been governor a short time before, to rebel against the extortionate Romans, and the result was a massacre of Roman tax collectors and Italian businessmen in 88 BC. Then Athens joined with Mithridates because they did not like the way in which the Romans had imposed upon them a pro-Roman government. Mithridates showed no signs of stopping his aggressive expansion, so Rome declared war, and Sulla was appointed to lead the army in this war.

The rest of Sulla's consulship did not bring him much credit. The tribune of the plebs, Publius Sulpicius Rufus (the cognomen Rufus is disputed), agitated for the distribution of the new Italian citizens among all the voting tribes, and tried to recall the exiles who had been forced out of Rome during the recent troubles. This was a complete *volte face* for Sulpicius, who had previously argued against the recall of the exiles. In both cases, for the redistribution of the Italian allies among the voting tribes and the recall of the exiles, Sulla and Pompeius Rufus blocked him. They declared that the omens were unfavourable, and suspended all political activity. Sulpicius tried and failed to organise voting on his bills. The people expressed their own opinions by rioting. In the disturbance, Sulla had to take flight, and ended up in his rival Marius' house for safety. Sulla's version, relayed by Plutarch, is that he was surrounded by Sulpicius' men with swords drawn, and driven into Marius' house, where he talked over some issues, then left to go to the Forum, where he rescinded the decree suspending public business.[21]

Sulla withdrew to the army which was still besieging Nola, fortunately with his rank as consul intact. He was still there when he heard that Marius had engaged Publius Sulpicius Rufus to transfer the command against Mithridates to him, despite the legal award to Sulla.[22]

They could not have expected Sulla to accede meekly to the new situation, and the contest was unequal from the start. Sulla commanded six legions, which were loyal to him and quite keen to go to the East so that they would not have to be discharged, and also there was the prospect of plunder and booty in the East. Marius had no army, and was getting on in years. He would have to take over the troops under Sulla, but this would prove to be difficult because he was not as ruthless as Sulla – at least not yet.

Marius sent his officers to take command of Sulla's army. They were killed, and Sulla then marched on Rome with his troops. This was a major gesture given that generals were forbidden from crossing the *pomerium* at the head of an army. It says something for the integrity of Sulla's senior officers that they refused to accompany him; only his quaestor, probably Lucius Licinius Lucullus, went with him.[23] This lack of support was not enough to dissuade Sulla, because the soldiers were in favour of his march. He wanted the command against Mithridates more than he cared for propriety.

Sulla did the unthinkable, and Marius and his tribune Sulpicius Rufus were quite unprepared for it. They put up a doomed defence of the city, but were overpowered and had no alternative but to leave Rome, with the younger Marius in tow, and go into hiding. Sulla declared both Mariuses, Sulpicius and nine others as *hostes*, or enemies of the state, reinforcing his decision by means of a law. As *hostes* Marius and Sulpicius were to be refused help of any kind, and could be hunted down and killed without retribution. There would be men who were perfectly willing to do this, seeking Sulla's goodwill. Sulpicius was killed, and Marius and his son travelled separately to Africa. Caesar would have been eleven or twelve years old at the time, and this event was of direct concern to his family. It is improbable that he was left out of discussions, since by dint of the relationship to Marius the whole family was potentially in danger. Fortunately, Sulla was keen to depart for the coming war against Mithridates, and thereafter, for a short time, his opponents could take a breath.

The new consuls for 87 BC were Gnaeus Octavius and Lucius Cornelius Cinna. Sulla made them swear an oath that they would not interfere with his recent legislation, knowing that as soon as he left Italy they would set about doing exactly that; but swearing an oath was a sacred act, not to be broken lightly. To do so would incur the wrath of the gods and the distrust of the people. Cinna, apparently, was willing to risk this. One of Sulla's consistent main aims was to prevent tribunes of the plebs from wielding so much political power, so Cinna tried to overturn his legislation, and to revive the questions of distribution of the new Italian citizens and the recall of the exiles. His colleague Octavius persuaded most of the tribunes to veto the proposals, and once again there were riots, in which some of the newly enfranchised citizens were killed. Cinna was deprived of his consulship by a decree of the Senate, and left Rome to recruit men to help him regain it by armed force. Octavius was now sole consul, an anomaly in political terms, so he arranged the election of Lucius Cornelius Merula, who was *flamen dialis*, a priest of Jupiter, a religious post with so many taboos and restrictions attached to it that Octavius was effectively the only one of the two consuls who could act.

With Cinna at large and gathering troops, Octavius and Merula made an effort to fortify the city before he could march on it as Sulla had done. In the meantime, Marius had heard of the situation and arrived to join Cinna. Octavius and Merula turned to Metellus Pius, the general commanding in the ongoing war against the Samnites, asking him to make peace and come to their aid, but the Samnites imposed strong terms, demanding citizenship and the return of prisoners and all booty carried off by the Romans. At this point Marius and Cinna leapt in, offering to meet all the terms of the Samnites, hoping that the tribes would join them. Their plan was to blockade Rome and starve their opponents, and at one point they nearly managed to enter the city, but were driven back.

The Senate declared them enemies of the state, which was no change for either Marius or Cinna. In 87 BC they took Rome. No one could stop them now because they were backed by troops, some of them freed slaves (although eventually all the ex-slaves had to be eliminated because they had gone on a killing spree and would not obey the command to stop). The consul Octavius was advised to flee, but refused to do so and was killed, his head suspended before the Rostra where politicians addressed their speeches to the people. Other heads were displayed there shortly afterwards. Appian says that this horrendous act started a trend in other massacres.[24] Much later, Mark Antony nailed Cicero's head and hands to the Rostra, following a precedent set by Cinna and Marius. The other consul, Merula, committed suicide, first removing his priestly cap, called the *apex*, which he apparently wore at all times and not just when he resided over sacrifices.[25]

Marius and Cinna ruthlessly avenged themselves on their real or suspected enemies, and in the carnage there were several men who were ready to make false charges against their own enemies, or simply to murder them and disguise their deeds as part of the process set in motion by Marius and Cinna. Sulla's house and country villa were destroyed and his family fled to join him in Greece. The whole sorry business is described at length by Appian, giving the names of the more prominent victims, and commenting that Marius and Cinna displayed 'neither reverence for the gods, nor the indignation of men nor the fear of odium for their acts'.[26] Apparently without benefit of elections by the people, or the approval of the Senate, Cinna and Marius became consuls for 86 BC. It is suggested that elections were in fact held, but with only the two candidates in the running, which kept up the appearance of legality.[27] Marius thankfully died in January 86 BC, seventeen days (some say only thirteen days) into his consulship, his career and reputation in ruins after its glorious beginnings.[28]

What was it like to be the nephew of the man who had caused so much bloodshed in Rome? Did the young Caesar approve of the removal of suspected enemies, or was he appalled by it? Worse was to come under Sulla, who published lists of those he proscribed, but this does not excuse the actions of Cinna and Marius. Whatever suffering Caesar inflicted on the Lusitanians, the Gauls and the Pompeians in the civil wars, it is notable that he did not produce lists of proscribed individuals in Rome and the provinces, as his predecessors and his successors infamously did. Is this early experience one reason why he refrained from doing so? Did Caesar shed any tears over Marius when he died?

Caesar may have shed tears over a scheme hatched by his uncle and Cinna to appoint him *flamen dialis* in place of Merula. The priesthood was prestigious, but highly restricted by antique taboos lost in the mists of time. The *flamen* was not allowed to be absent from Rome for two (some say three) consecutive nights, could not ride a horse, was forbidden to look on a dead body, and could not witness an army on campaign. These and several other restrictions excluded the post-holder from a political, and especially a military, career.[29] Plutarch has a slightly different tale, placing Caesar's personal bid for a priesthood, which is not specified as *flamen dialis*, after Sulla's return to Rome, because he was disgruntled at Sulla's lack of attention to him.[30] This sounds suspicious because in the circumstances of Sulla's reappearance in Rome Caesar would more likely have wanted to avoid his attentions completely. Plutarch goes on to say that Sulla prevented Caesar from gaining the priesthood, possibly a slightly garbled reference to the fact that Sulla appropriated Caesar's inheritance and cancelled his priesthood, or even to the legislation of November 82 BC, when Sulla cancelled all the actions of his predecessors, and probably the designation as *flamen dialis* was included in this pronouncement of Sulla's.

It is impossible to say whether Caesar desired the appointment, for reasons unknown, or whether it was imposed upon him, possibly in a bid to keep him sacrosanct and safe, and possibly to fill the post before anyone else could be proposed for it. Meier suggests that Caesar probably did want the post, because to a family which had not been distinguished for such a long time, it would have helped his career, possibly leading to the consulship, since the priesthood had not deterred Merula.[31] But Merula was an anomaly and a special case. If Caesar had been appointed *flamen dialis* his career would have been obliterated before it had begun, but the point is merely academic, because he was too young to become a priest when it was first proposed. It is unlikely that he was ever officially inaugurated as *flamen dialis*, since Merula's post remained vacant until about 12 BC, or possibly two years later.[32] It is not known if Caesar had to observe all the taboos while he was proposed as *flamen dialis*. Matthias Gelzer was convinced that even if Caesar had been confirmed in the priesthood, he would have found a way around the restrictions.[33] Suetonius says that Caesar was never deterred from carrying out his plans on the grounds of religious scruples.[34]

After Marius' death Cinna appointed Lucius Valerius Flaccus as his consular colleague to preserve legality. It was clear that sooner or later Sulla would be back, so Cinna started to prepare for his arrival and the beginning of another civil war, collecting recruits, food supplies and money.[35] It has been suggested that the elder Caesar participated in these activities on Cinna's behalf, gathering food supplies and cash.[36] He may have been engaged on this task when he died at Pisae (modern Pisa), in 85 or 84 BC. Both dates have been suggested, the modern consensus being for 84 BC. Caesar's father may therefore have been one of Cinna's active supporters instead of hiding in the background. In any case, Sulla's vengeance would probably not be averted by inaction.

The relationship between the elder Caesar and Cinna is not elucidated, but there was a marriage alliance in 84 BC, when the young Caesar married Cornelia, Cinna's daughter. To do so he had first to break off an engagement which had been made when he was still a child, to Cossutia, the daughter of a very wealthy equestrian, who presumably would have brought a rich dowry. Perhaps it is not too cynical to interpret this early engagement as a means of launching Caesar on his political career when the time came; it was an expensive business, so a monetary rather than a prestigious political alliance was planned for him. Plutarch actually says that when Caesar married Pompeia she was his third wife, thus counting Cossutia as his first wife and Cornelia as his second.[37] Perhaps if Cossutia had been a patrician then Caesar would have gone through with the marriage, but the *flamen dialis* and his wife both had to be of patrician birth. Caesar's alliance with Cinna and the marriage to his daughter Cornelia may have been arranged by Caesar's father, or by Cinna, but since both these men died in 84 BC, it may have been Caesar himself who brought about his marriage to Cornelia. Perhaps he was in love with her, and perhaps it was not simply stubborn opposition to Sulla that made him refuse to divorce her at the Dictator's bidding. Cornelia was the mother of Caesar's only legitimate child, Julia, who married Pompey the Great and died trying to give him a son.

Sulla was in Greece, having rounded off the war before winning a complete victory. He spent some time shoring up his achievements to arrange at least a temporary peace so that he could return to Rome. Cinna, who was consul for the third time in 85 BC, planned to take the war to Greece instead of allowing Sulla to land in Italy. Cinna engineered the election of himself and Papirius Carbo as consuls for 84 BC, but in that year he was murdered by mutinous soldiers who did not want to fight another civil war and did not want to go to Greece to fight it. There was little profit to be made in civil wars. Cinna's removal from the scene left Carbo alone, and contrary to all precedent he did not appoint a colleague or ask the populace to vote for one. Whether he wanted to fight Sulla or not, Carbo was forced into war when Sulla landed in Italy with five legions in 83 BC.

Caesar's father had been dead for some time, and the young Caesar was now the head of his family, responsible for his mother and sisters, his wife Cornelia and his household. He was the nephew of Sulla's enemy Marius, and the son-in-law of Cornelius Cinna, who had determined to fight Sulla in Greece and raised an army to do so. Caesar was in entirely the wrong camp, and co-operation with Sulla was out of the question.

4

Early Career, 83–69 BC

What was he like, this young man who was so firmly in the camp of Marius and Cinna, now married and head of his household? Tall and fair, with black eyes, says Suetonius; slightly built, says Plutarch.[1] By the time Suetonius and Plutarch wrote their biographies, there was probably no extant literary or official record that gave an exact physical description of Caesar, and there was definitely no one around with living memory of Caesar. There would be surviving sculptured portraits and statues, but even though statues were routinely painted, these would not necessarily verify dark eyes and a pale complexion, and the authors give no hint of the source or sources they used. In the modern era, not all the portraits confidently labelled as Caesar are unequivocally accepted, except for the coinage where the name of Caesar is included. There is nothing to help modern historians to describe Caesar as a youth.

Assessing his character is a little easier, provided that the anecdotes relayed about him are treated with a pinch of salt. In appearance, he was said to be scrupulous about shaving and removing body hair, and in dress he may have been a trend-setter rather than a dedicated follower of fashion. He wore tunics with fringed sleeves extending to his wrists, not very practical, one would have thought, and he wore a loose belt around the tunic, contrary to the accepted norm. The belt came to the notice of Sulla, who warned his aristocratic contemporaries to beware of the ill-girt boy (*ut male praecinctum puerum caverent*).[2] This description may belong to Caesar's youth, when he wanted to stand out from the crowd. Later, he would be more worried about hair loss.

The two years before Caesar reached the age of twenty were probably the worst of his entire life, but also probably helped to mould characteristics that were already forming, to stand up to enemies and to take risks in pursuit of his aims. In 83 BC one major aim would be to stay alive. Sulla had concluded the war against Mithridates, knowing that he had not won a decisive victory, but he needed to return to Italy before his opponents gained the upper hand. Some senators and Sulla's wife Metella had fled to him to ask him to help his adherents still left in Italy, where they were being oppressed and even murdered by Cinna and Carbo.[3] He made the best possible arrangements to contain Mithridates, taking several months to do so, then gathered his army and landed at Brundisium in the spring of 83 BC. The inhabitants of the town wisely and pragmatically decided not to oppose him, and were rewarded by a grant of exemption from customs dues, which they still enjoyed in Appian's day.[4]

Sulla brought with him five legions. The soldiers were battle hardened and loyal, if only because they knew that they could not expect lenient treatment at the hands of Sulla's enemies in the war that was about to start in Italy, much less earn any rewards. Only Sulla could arrange rewards for them.

As Sulla fought his way towards Rome, three men leading extra troops joined him. Probably the first to reach him was Marcus Licinius Crassus, with troops that he had raised in Spain and brought by way of Africa, where he had initially teamed up with Quintus Caecilius Metellus Pius. The two men had fallen out, although both were still loyal to Sulla. Gnaeus Pompeius, more familiar as Pompey, was only in his early twenties but confident beyond his years, and had raised a legion in Picenum where his deceased father Pompeius Strabo enjoyed a better reputation than he had in the rest of Italy. Pompey later raised two more legions, and was to become one of Sulla's most successful generals.[5] He was also destined to play a large part in Caesar's life, but not for a few years yet.

The war did not begin in earnest until 82 BC. Both sides concentrated on recruiting and preparing, though there were a few skirmishes and some changing of sides. Papirius Carbo went to Rome to organise the consular elections for 82 BC, succeeding in gaining his third consulship with the younger Marius, the nephew of Gaius Marius, as colleague. Marius was underage, but the rules were ignored. In contesting Sulla's advance, Marius was driven into Praeneste and besieged there, but managed to send a message to the praetor, Brutus Damasippus, to eliminate supporters of Sulla in Rome.[6] Damasippus accordingly summoned the Senate, and unsuspecting Sullans were killed, some in the meeting house and others while trying to escape. This incident probably paled into insignificance next to the carnage that followed when Sulla finally won, but it was a sign of the times. Ruthless violence was not restricted to Sulla and his adherents. The murders did Sulla a good turn. After this example on the part of Carbo and the young Marius, it was generally decided that declaring for them would be no better than declaring for Sulla, so the city was opened to him.

A bitterly contested battle for Rome took place after Pompey defeated the relief force sent to extricate Marius from Praeneste. Sulla reaped what he had sown when he captured and killed all the Samnites who had fought against him at Praeneste – understandably resentful, the surviving tribesmen joined with the Lucanian tribes and the troops under Damasippus and marched on Rome to draw Sulla there. In this battle outside the city, Licinius Crassus on Sulla's right wing won a victory and chased all his opponents to Antemnae, but Sulla's left wing collapsed.[7] Soldiers fleeing to the city gates found themselves locked out, so had to turn and make a stand, and achieved a hard-fought standstill. Only later did Sulla learn that it was not a total defeat, and that Crassus had turned the tables. Crassus was at Antemnae, where Sulla joined him. Infamously, once he arrived there, he accepted the surrender of his enemies, promising them their lives. But there was one condition: they would only be spared if they killed the members of the anti-Sullan faction in the town. After complying, they went with Sulla to Rome, where they were herded together and killed while Sulla himself addressed the Senate in the Temple of Bellona to a chorus of screams and yells from the dying men. It was only the execution of some criminals, he said dismissively; 6,000 of them, according to Plutarch.[8]

The civil war was not limited to Rome and Italy. One of Cinna's adherents, Quintus Sertorius, made his way independently to Spain, where he was only defeated with difficulty some years later. There was fighting in Sicily and then in Africa as Pompey and his army won victories for Sulla. He eliminated Carbo in Sicily, for which act he later and retrospectively earned the nickname young butcher, *adulescentulus carnifex*. Next he was sent to Africa to fight against Domitius Ahenobarbus, and won.[9] This left only Sertorius in Spain.

When Pompey returned to Rome in 81 BC, he asked permission to celebrate a triumph, where he would parade through the streets with his spoils of victory. Sulla refused. Pompey was too young, and besides it was in bad taste to celebrate a triumph over Romans; these events were more appropriately reserved for victories over foreign enemies. Pompey sulked, and said that more people worshipped the rising sun than the setting sun, making it perfectly obvious that he was describing himself and Sulla in that order. Anyone else would probably have been executed, but Pompey was allowed his triumph.[10]

Rome was firmly under Sulla's thumb, and he began to eliminate his enemies. After some random killings, Plutarch says that Gaius Metellus, whose precise identity among so many Metelli has not been established, was brave enough to ask Sulla when the killings would end, and who was to be spared. When Sulla answered that he had not yet decided who was to be spared, Metellus asked him at least to produce a list of those he intended to punish, so that the people who were not on it could relax.[11] Thus the first dreadful proscriptions began. A list of perhaps eighty men was issued to begin with, though the numbers vary in the ancient sources, then another list was drawn up of 220 men. These men could be killed with impunity. Senators and equestrians were killed, because in removing a senator it was necessary to remove his entire circle, and some senators were closely bound to equestrians as their clients, and as agents in their business activities as well as in political endeavours. There were rewards for murderers of the proscribed, and for informers who denounced individuals and had them added to the list. Naturally there were punishments for any who sheltered the named victims, a system which anticipated a similar and even more widespread system in Europe in the 1940s. The murders did not end with Sulla's named victims. Arbitrary killing took place, against which no one seemed interested enough or brave enough to protest. Names were added to the list, because anyone who killed one of the proscribed individuals would not only be rewarded but could inherit the property of the deceased.

As the nephew of Marius and the son-in-law of Cinna, it was likely that Caesar should be included in the lists of proscribed individuals. Suetonius describes Caesar refusing Sulla's demand that he divorce Cornelia, which led to the confiscation of Cornelia's dowry, the cancellation of his priesthood and the loss of his family inheritances, and then Caesar's flight from Rome.[12] Plutarch orders events somewhat differently, in that Sulla thought about killing Caesar, and when some men protested on account of his youth Sulla said that they were fools not to realise that there were many Mariuses in the boy. Plutarch relates that it was only after Caesar heard of this remark that he fled from Rome.[13]

If the exact order of events is not clear, it is certain that Caesar refused to divorce his wife, unlike Pompey who complied with Sulla's demands, divorcing his first wife Antistia and then marrying a lady of Sulla's choice, his stepdaughter Aemilia, even though she was already married and pregnant.[14] Did Sulla have some other hapless girl in mind to try to bind Caesar to him in a marriage alliance, as he had done with Pompey? The sources are silent, but any plans that Sulla may have had would have been purely academic when Caesar dug his heels in and refused to divorce Cornelia. Did Caesar have an unpleasant interview with Sulla, or did the great man send a couple of soldiers to his house with a note? Having defied Sulla, either directly to his face or indirectly through agents, Caesar spent some time away from Rome, fleeing into Sabine territory, staying continually on the move to evade Sulla's agents. He contracted malaria, and had to bribe an officer to spare his life. He probably never forgot this episode. It came to an end when several people interceded on his behalf, including the Vestal Virgins, who were perhaps alerted by Aurelia. Mamercus Aemilius, a relative of Caesar's, and Aurelia's relatives the Cottae brothers, also appealed to Sulla. Suetonius claims this as the occasion when Sulla pointed out that there were many Mariuses in the young Caesar, prophesying that he would one day obliterate the aristocracy, which may owe more to the author's retrospective knowledge than to Sulla's perspicacity.[15]

If Sulla had confiscated Cornelia's dowry and Caesar's family inheritance, what happened to Caesar's finances? Was he destitute, forced to rely on help from friends, or could he borrow money in the expectation of regaining some of it once he had begun his career? Since nothing is known of the family affairs in the first place, it is unlikely that an answer to this question can be found. Caesar and his family obviously did not starve to death, but his income and expenditure is unknown. There is no hint in the sources that when Sulla decided not to have Caesar eliminated he also gave him back his inheritance. If it was an official pardon, Caesar's property may have been restored, but there is no evidence. Cornelia's dowry was probably lost forever. The money was paid into the public treasury according to Plutarch, and since Cornelia was the daughter of Cinna it would seem highly unlikely that Sulla would reverse his decision.[16] For Caesar, there was money enough to send him to Rhodes to further his education and to support him while he was there, and when he was captured by pirates before he arrived in Rhodes his friends were able to raise a substantial ransom for him, presumably on some solid security rather than Caesar's promise that he would capture and execute the pirates, thus regaining the ransom money. The most that can be said is that Caesar probably emerged from his encounter with Sulla with a keen appreciation of the value of money and what it could do for him.

The need to re-establish his finances may have been one of the reasons why Caesar looked for a post in the provinces, another reason being the need to remove himself from Rome once again, this time going somewhere much further away. Sulla's reach was probably limitless but in a province it was better than being anywhere in the immediate vicinity of Rome. One of the praetors in 81 BC was Marcus Minucius Thermus, a confirmed Sullan, who was to be governor of Asia. It was the province that Caesar's father had governed, which may or may not have influenced Caesar's next move. Somehow, he recommended himself, or persuaded someone else to recommend him to Thermus. As Goldsworthy points out, there is no immediately obvious connection between Thermus and Caesar.[17] When Thermus left for Asia, Caesar was included on the governor's personal staff. Thermus could hardly have accepted Caesar as part of his entourage if he was under threat from Sulla. No further names were added to the proscription lists after 1 June 81, the deadline set by Sulla, so it may have been after this date that Caesar looked around for a suitable patron who would take him on. It was probably congenial to Sulla to see the back of Caesar at least for a time, and for Caesar himself, it was the beginning of his career, starting on one of the lowest rungs, in the normal way. No experience was required for young men on the staffs of governors, where they would perform whatever task was allotted to them and gain experience of government and probably of military action along the way. Caesar would not be all alone in any expedition in the company of a provincial governor, but like other young officers in any entourage he would have slaves, probably some friends, several horses, baggage and baggage animals to carry it.

The governor of Asia had to be a dependable man, like other Roman governors of the eastern provinces, because Mithridates VI had not been decisively defeated and had not renounced his expansionist tendencies. Expansionism was fine when Romans were doing it, but not when any of their neighbours tried it, most especially if the neighbour had incited the provincials to rebel, as Mithridates had done in Asia. Those states which had sided with Mithridates were to be taught the error of their ways. Some communities in the province of Asia were still not reconciled with Rome, one of the recalcitrant cities being Mytilene, in the south-east of the island of Lesbos, off the western coast of modern Turkey. Mytilene consistently backed the wrong side in any trouble with Rome and as a result Thermus prepared to besiege the city.

A siege of an island fortress necessitates combined operations between the fleet and the army, and the Romans requested extra vessels from King Nicomedes IV of Bithynia, one of their allies who had not succumbed to Mithridates. Friendship had to be fostered and maintained with those which had not supported the king, if only to dissuade them from leaning towards Mithridates when, not if, he started to mobilise again. Friendship with Rome was a mutually supportive agreement, with each party obliged to help the other in times of need. The arrangement was usually formalised, each king or ruler being bound to Rome under the terms of friendship with the Roman people, and their obligations would probably be specified, tailored to the circumstances of each allied state. In modern terms the chosen rulers are called client kings, since the relationship was similar to the client system that bound a senator and his supporters, but in Latin the formula was *rex sociusque et amicus*, king and ally and friend. This title was officially awarded after the king had been recognised as such by the Senate in a process called *appellatio*.

Caesar's first recorded major task under Thermus was to journey to the court of Nicomedes to collect the ships that the Romans had asked for. Allegedly he stayed for a suspiciously long time at the court, and was accused then, and for the rest of his life, of having a homosexual relationship with the king. Such accusations were often levelled at Roman youths, especially if it was suspected that the young man in question was the passive partner in the relationship, or had even solicited it, both of which implied that he was effeminate. Mark Antony, for instance, was accused of homosexual acts with Curio, one of his best friends, when they were both young, and even before this, said Cicero, Antony was nothing but a common prostitute offering himself for a substantial fee to other men.[18] The accusations made entertaining speeches and good copy when the speeches were published, but probably became somewhat worn out in the retelling. Besides, any hint of effeminacy levelled at either Antony or Caesar was patently not true. Both men had such consistent records of seducing queues of women that charges of effeminacy and homosexuality seem far-fetched, but lurid stories circulated about Caesar, exacerbated when he returned to Bithynia a short time later. He said that he was to collect a debt for one of his freedmen, but it looked like an excuse to resume relations with Nicomedes. Well, did he, or didn't he? Does it really matter? Caesar tried to deny the accusations, but on the whole he was not too ruffled until much later. He lost his temper towards the end of his life, when at one of his four triumphs after the end of the civil wars the soldiers sang or shouted verses about Caesar's amatory conquests, and how he was 'vanquished by Nicomedes'.[19] Perhaps Caesar was tired and irritable when he had his triumphal tantrum.

At the Siege of Mytilene, Caesar took an active part in his first military action. No details of his exploits have been preserved so it is not known what he did to earn his award of a civic crown (*corona civica*) from Thermus. It was usually awarded for saving the life of a fellow citizen, or possibly the lives of several citizens.[20] It was made of oak leaves, and the award carried with it certain privileges, releasing the wearer from civic obligations and bringing him distinction in civil life. When Caesar attended the public games everyone was obliged to rise in his honour, and even senators were not excluded from the obligation.

From Thermus' command, Caesar moved on to Cilicia, to join Publius Servilius Vatia Isauricus, perhaps joining him in 79 BC. Caesar would know him simply as Servilius Vatia, since he earned the name Isauricus when he took the town of Isauria Vetus during fighting against the pirates who infested the Cilician coast. One of the officers serving under Isauricus was Titus Labienus, who hailed from Picenum, Pompey's homeland. He and Caesar may have become acquaintances if not friends in Cilicia, since Labienus later became one of Caesar's trusted lieutenants in Gaul. Suetonius provides no details of what Caesar achieved under the command of Isauricus, except to say that he held the post for a short time.[21] This was probably because news came in 78 BC that changed Caesar's whole situation. Sulla was dead.

Caesar returned to a version of Rome that had been moulded by Sulla in accordance with his view of the proper order of things. He had put the Senate and the oligarchy firmly at the head of state, and passed laws to maintain his vision. Soon after he had taken over the city and removed his enemies, he played the game to the letter of the law to gain unrivalled power. The consuls were dead, so officially the state was rudderless. In the days of the kings, far back in Roman history, when a king died he was replaced temporarily by an *interrex*, who held power for five days to oversee the appointment of a new king. If this had not occurred before his five-day term ended, he stepped down and another *interrex* was appointed for the next five days. Sulla revived this custom, and the Senate duly elected the *princeps senatus*, the leading senator, Lucius Flaccus, as *interrex*.

Sulla required supreme power if he was to put into operation his ideas for reform. He could not have achieved such unlimited power as consul, because he would be subject to the approval of the Senate and of his colleague, and in any case he required power for a longer period than one year. He may have been able to engineer his election time and time again for each successive year, but this would have seemed inappropriate, and besides, one of the laws that he passed was designed to prevent anyone from re-election as consul before a period of ten years had passed, so it would have been hypocritical to act contrary to his own legislation. He suggested to Flaccus that what was called for in the circumstances was the appointment of a Dictator, an office which had lain dormant for over a century. There was no doubt as to whom he had in mind to fill the post. He set his ideas down in a letter to Flaccus, according to Appian.[22]

One slight problem with the scheme was that the Dictator was customarily appointed in dire emergencies, and his post was only for six months. After this term, he was then expected to resign the office. Sulla got around this by suggesting that the fixed term should be waived, and instead the Dictator should be appointed for an arbitrary term, namely until the government of Rome, Italy and the provinces was restored and there was peace and the return of law and order. This purpose was made clear by a law defining his task, as *Dictator legibus faciendis et rei publicae constituendae*, to make laws and reconstitute the Republic. The law did not limit his powers in any way, and only Sulla himself could decide precisely when the government had been restored.

By this means Sulla was able to take power more or less on constitutional lines. There was no written constitution as such, but he adapted accepted custom and existing law to his own purpose. He was not the first or last to do so. Appian says that the Romans did not like it, but acquiesced. They had experienced the rule of autocrats before, but there had always been temporal or legal limits on Dictators. Sulla was not subject to such limits, and therefore his rule qualified as tyranny.[23] Being aware of the possible hiccups even though his hold on power was absolute, Sulla had all his acts ratified in advance by the Senate, and he was not obliged to go to the people for approval of his laws, though he could do so if he wished. This meant that he allowed himself *carte blanche* to pass laws as he saw fit. He had had a long time to think about what was wrong with the state in his view, and what to do about it.

Keeping up the semblance of a normal Republican government, Marcus Tullius Decula and Gnaeus Cornelius Dolabella were elected consuls. Sulla as Dictator had supreme power over them. Since he had achieved power at the head of an army, he tried to ensure that no one else could do the same. He could execute anyone he chose without trial, and in this way he eliminated one of his own officers, Quintus Lucretius Afella, sometimes rendered as Ofella. This man had done good service for Sulla in the war that brought him to power, especially in the capture of Praeneste, but he now expected that he should receive some reward. He stood for the consulship, perhaps when Decula and Dolabella were elected, though it is also suggested that it was in the following year. Afella had not yet entered the Senate and consequently he had not served as quaestor or praetor, so he was quite out of order. The date when he became a consular candidate is not known, but if it was in the second year of Sulla's Dictatorship, when laws had been passed to establish a proper order of office-holding, requiring the candidate to have begun at the bottom rung as quaestor and worked his way up, then Afella's bid for the consulship was nothing less than insane. Sulla had Afella killed. Appian describes how he did the deed himself, in the Forum, declaring that Afella had disobeyed him and this was the punishment.[24] The murder served to encourage the others, as the French phrase has it.

For some time Sulla had resented the way in which the tribunes of the plebs were being used to manipulate political practice, so he set out to curb their power while not abolishing the office altogether. The main method of achieving this was to prevent any man who had been tribune from obtaining further offices. This would mean that only the most dedicated individuals would become candidates for a post as tribune of the plebs. If men still wanted the office, there were further restrictions, the nature of which is disputed. It is suggested that Sulla abolished the tribunician right of proposing laws, but it may be that he stipulated that tribunes were forbidden to take bills straight to the people's assemblies, and were obliged to submit their proposals to the Senate for approval. This is perhaps the most likely explanation, since one of the devices used by tribunes in the past was to go directly to the assemblies and have laws passed without consultation and debate in the Senate. The traditional right of *intercessio* or veto was retained, perhaps because it would have caused much discontent if Sulla had tried to abolish it.

The *lex annalis* was passed to establish the career structure on more rigid lines, and to stipulate the age qualification for the offices of quaestor, held at about the age of twenty-nine, praetor at thirty-nine and consul at forty-two, and as already mentioned, ten years had to elapse before anyone could try for re-election. Provincial governors were restricted to the confines of their provinces, and not to leave them or to lead an army across the boundaries. The penalty was a charge of *maiestas*, or treason. In theory this would prevent a governor with troops at his disposal from using his army to march on Rome, as Sulla himself had done. It was theoretically sound, but all that was required was a determined governor who had cultivated the loyalty of his troops and was willing to risk everything on this one manoeuvre. Caesar for instance.

The numbers of senators had been depleted in the civil wars, and the Senate required reinforcement. The tribune Marcus Livius Drusus had planned for the conversion of 300 equestrians into senators. There was usually a supply of wealthy equestrians with the necessary qualifications for entry to the Senate, but not all of them wished to do so – one example, much later, being the future Emperor

Vespasian, whose brother Sabinus became a senator before him and for some time tried unsuccessfully to persuade him to follow suit. Sulla put Livius Drusus' measure into effect, bringing the Senate back up to strength at about 600 senators. He also returned the juries for the *quaestiones* to senators. The number of praetors was increased to eight, and the number of quaestors to twenty. Sulla's legislation ensured that as quaestor a young man automatically became a senator and began his political and military career.

A perennial problem that plagued the Republic was the discharge of soldiers when campaigns were ended. Some of the soldiers of later Republican armies were usually able to re-enlist in another army, given that wars were nearly always being fought somewhere in the Roman world, or if there were no wars, troops were more frequently required for policing some of the less settled provinces. A few soldiers could return home to their farms, but increasingly in the late Republic lands were not readily available, and had to be found to convert ex-soldiers into farmers, and it was usually at someone else's expense. Sulla settled his own veterans in Campania, but in doing so there had to be evictions and appropriation of lands, causing widespread discontent among the displaced persons, who only needed a leader to unite them against the state.

In 81 BC Sulla and Metellus Pius were elected consuls. Sulla considered that his work was almost done, and he felt that in accordance with a prophecy he was approaching death. He resigned in 79 BC. Appian says that it is not true that Sulla was failing in health or bodily strength, but he was tired of war and had fallen in love with rural life.[25] In reality, it is said that Sulla was eaten away with disease, probably syphilis, though Plutarch says he had an intestinal ulcer.[26]

When the news of Sulla's death reached Caesar, he also heard that one of the consuls of 78 BC, Marcus Aemilius Lepidus, had started a rebellion. Pompey had backed Lepidus for the consulship, and Sulla had warned him of future trouble with him. Lepidus was intent on overturning most of Sulla's legislation and was presumably not prepared to bring this about in piecemeal fashion, patiently setting out proposals for senatorial debate and then battling for his ideas with only one year to gain assent for his legislation, during which his enemies could employ any number of delaying tactics as well as open opposition. Whatever his reasoning, Lepidus went straight for armed force. His colleague as consul was Quintus Lutatius Catulus, a confirmed Sullan, and he naturally upheld what Sulla had achieved. He defeated Lepidus, with the help of Pompey, but this still left a lot of discontented people, especially the displaced farmers who had lost lands to the veterans of Sulla's army. Suetonius says that Caesar was offered considerable incentive to join with Lepidus, but once back in Rome, either by good luck or more likely good management, he steered clear of Lepidus and his schemes, because as Suetonius says he had no confidence in Lepidus' capacities to lead a revolt.[27] Meier points out that Caesar probably assessed the number of soldiers that Lepidus had at his disposal as against the much greater number at the disposal of his opponents, and concluded that the chances that Lepidus would succeed were slender.[28] The defeat of Lepidus launched Pompey on his post-Sullan career. He had obtained a military command to assist Catulus, and kept his troops together while he angled for another command, to assist Metellus Pius against Sertorius in Spain. He succeeded, left Rome, and did not return until 71 BC.

Having experienced his first taste of military activity abroad, Caesar turned to the law courts to make a name for himself, as many other young men had done. In 77 BC, he prosecuted Gnaeus Cornelius Dolabella for extortion when he governed Macedonia.[29] This Dolabella is no relation to Publius Cornelius Dolabella, consul in 44 BC, who marred Cicero's daughter Tullia. As one of Sulla's generals, Gnaeus Dolabella used his favoured position to accumulate riches from the provincials. Since there was no state machinery and no public prosecution service in Rome to bring miscreants to court, prosecutions were instigated by a private individual acting on his own initiative, or on behalf of a grieved party. It may be that representatives of the Macedonian people approached Caesar for help, and he agreed to act as their advocate. Goldsworthy suggests that the Macedonians may have had a connection with Caesar's father.[30] On the other hand, young men could earn fame and possibly fortune in prosecuting someone in the courts.

Caesar's rhetoric was not sufficient to secure a condemnation in the extortion courts. Dolabella had influential friends, and he was defended by the famous orator Quintus Hortensius, and Gaius Aurelius Cotta, cousin of Caesar's mother, who with his two brothers had stood up for Caesar against Sulla. There were usually no hard feelings among families who found themselves temporarily in opposition in the courts. Prosecution and defence were tasks to be performed, not emotional actions, and even if the result was acquittal, the prosecutor lost nothing. Next, in 76 BC, Caesar was asked by other Greek cities to prosecute Gaius Antonius Hybrida for extortion. The result went against him once again. Presiding over the court was Marcus Terentius Varro Lucullus, *praetor peregrinus* in charge of affairs concerning non-Romans, who were termed *peregrini*. He pronounced Antonius guilty, which he clearly was, but Antonius appealed to the tribunes to veto the proceedings, and thus he escaped condemnation. As strenuously as Sulla had tried to reduce the power of the tribunes, they could still exercise strong influence on affairs.

Failure to secure a conviction for either Dolabella or Antonius did not harm Caesar's career. He had shown confidence and eloquence in his speeches, and according to Plutarch he was beginning to cultivate the loyalty of the populace by giving banquets and engaging people in friendly conversation.[31] Suetonius does not mention the prosecution of Antonius, and says that Caesar left Rome in 75 BC because of the unpopularity he had earned by his action against Dolabella.[32] There were bound to be some men who disapproved of Caesar, but Plutarch says that they did nothing to stop him because they thought that his popularity would disappear as soon as the money ran out.[33] If he was to rise to prominence and start a political career Caesar had to manufacture a positive image, like any other aspiring politician, and this meant continued expenditure on a lavish scale. It is not clear where the money was coming from, except in so far as it was most likely borrowed, perhaps from a number of lenders, principally Crassus, even at this early stage.

Having established a good reputation so far, in 75 BC Caesar decided to further his education. Learning to read and speak Greek and Latin as a child was not the final goal of his education. It was gradually becoming fashionable for young men to turn to Greece to study rhetoric and philosophy. Mark Antony, for instance, went to Athens, but Caesar chose to attend the schools in Rhodes, principally that of Apollonius Molo. On the sea voyage, he was captured by pirates, off the island of Pharmacussa, which lay 6 miles south of Miletus. Caesar may have had some experience of pirate activity while serving under Servilius Isauricus in Cilicia. Plutarch describes Caesar's capture by the pirates in some detail, but places it out of context, together with Caesar's visits to Nicomedes in Bithynia.[34] Suetonius recounts the episode in the correct chronological slot, adding that when Caesar set sail the winter season had already begun.[35] The pirates demanded a ransom, which Caesar scorned. Never in doubt as to his own merit, he told the pirates that he was worth much more than they asked, sending off some of his friends to gather the required sums from the coastal communities of the eastern Mediterranean, whose duties included keeping the sea lanes safe. For a month while the cash was raised, Caesar allegedly lorded it over his captors, ordering the pirates to be quiet if he wanted to sleep. The story will have gained in the retelling, but it seems that Caesar kept up a cool façade in circumstances that could have proved fatal. He promised to return and execute all the pirates, and Plutarch says that they thought he was joking. But he was in deadly earnest. When the money was paid and he was freed, he assembled some ships at Miletus, took the pirates by surprise at Pharmacussa, and hauled them off to prison at Pergamum. He claimed all the money the pirates had accumulated as booty.

As a private individual with no official appointment, he required the backing of someone in authority before he took any further action, so he approached Marcus Juncus, governor of Asia, who had gone to the neighbouring territory of Bithynia. King Nicomedes had died in 75 BC, bequeathing his kingdom to Rome, and Juncus was busy organising the territory as a Roman province. According to Plutarch, Juncus was more interested in the cash that Caesar had taken from the pirates than in helping Caesar to wreak vengeance on them.[36] Juncus said that he would deal with the pirates when he had time, and recommended that they should be sold as slaves. This would have brought in more cash, but Caesar wanted revenge, not profit. He returned to Pergamum and crucified the pirates. Suetonius says that he was merciful in having their throats cut first, and indeed it was merciful in the sense that it would be a quicker death than hanging on a cross for up to three days before finally dying of slow suffocation.[37] The dead bodies hauled up on to crosses were presumably intended to teach other pirates what to expect from Rome. Caesar organised the executions presumably without any authority at all, but then the inhabitants of the coastal cities would not have raised any objections at the deaths of some pirates.[38]

Caesar continued on his interrupted journey to Rhodes. He had not been there for long when some troops of Mithridates, King of Pontus, launched raids on the Roman province of Asia. Mithridates had not been decisively defeated by Sulla, and he was now angry because neighbouring Bithynia was to be ruled by Romans instead of one of his allies, or as he would have preferred, one of his own vassals. This raid is not securely dated, but it was probably in the summer of 74 BC. Determined to take action, Caesar left Rhodes to enter Asia, to gather troops and repel the raiders sent by Mithridates.

No source mentions that Caesar was invested with any kind of official powers, and in fact Velleius Paterculus specifically says that he was a *privatus* when he raised the militia or collections of auxiliaries.[39] It is probable that there was no overall commander in Asia at the time. The governor, Marcus Juncus, may have still been engaged in organising the new province of Bithynia, or he may have already started on his return journey to Rome. Marcus Aurelius Cotta, cousin of Caesar's mother, was to be the governor of the new province of Bithynia, but may not yet have arrived there. Perhaps there had been correspondence between Cotta and Caesar, but there is no proof for this. Just as Caesar had acted as a private individual against the pirates, he now did the same in Asia and successfully fought the raiders. Meier questions the effectiveness of Caesar's military action, and calls it an act of presumption.[40] So it was, and Caesar would have been the first to agree, but it was not his last act of presumption, indeed his whole career could be labelled as such. If not a resounding military success, Caesar's action helped to stabilise the loyalty of those states which were wavering in their choice between Rome and Mithridates.[41]

The following years saw the beginning of a troublesome time for the Romans. Appian lists the wars that were going on around this time. It was not only Mithridates who worried the Romans. The rebel Sertorius was still in command in Spain, where Metellus Pius and Pompey were not yet enjoying success against him. The perennial problem of the pirates affected the whole Mediterranean, and there was a war against the people of Crete. Then, in 73 BC, the gladiator Spartacus raised rebellion in Italy and gathered a large force of slaves and discontents.[42] At first the Romans were confident that they could crush Spartacus and the slaves fairly easily, but they soon found out that it was not as easy as they first thought. There was a scramble for military commands in 74 BC. The consuls of 75 BC, Lucius Octavius and Gaius Aurelius Cotta, were respectively assigned the provinces of Cilicia and Cisalpine Gaul for the following year, but the increasing threat from Mithridates influenced affairs in Rome. At some unknown time, Lucius Licinius Lucullus realised that here was a chance to earn glory and distinction in a command against Mithridates. Octavius died early in 74 BC, and Lucullus obtained Octavius' province of Cilicia, not without some sordid intrigue. He also obtained Asia, when Marcus Cotta was assigned to Bithynia. It was essential to protect these two Roman provinces, and even more essential to neutralise, if not defeat, Mithridates, especially since he made a pact in 74 BC for mutual assistance with Sertorius in Spain, which threatened war on two fronts at the same time.

After his success in repelling the raiders of Mithridates, it is suggested that Caesar may have been attached to the staff of Marcus Antonius (the father of Mark Antony), on whom the Senate had conferred a special three-year command against the Mediterranean pirates in 74 BC. If so, the post, whatever it was, did not last long. Gaius Aurelius Cotta had died, probably in 74 BC, and as he was also a priest, one of a college of fifteen members, there was a vacancy, which was awarded to Caesar. He returned to Rome in 73 BC to take up his new appointment. It was a considerable honour and a mark of prestige, signifying his arrival on the political scene. The duties were nowhere near as restrictive as those of the *flamen dialis*. The college of fifteen priests, or *pontifices*, with the chief priest or Pontifex Maximus at their head, was an exclusive elite of nobles. It was not possible to become a member without being asked, and often when a member died his replacement was chosen from among his relatives. It was not unknown for young priests to be co-opted before they entered the Senate, so in this respect, Caesar, as a non-senator, was not an unusual choice, and his relationship to Cotta, added to his recent success in Asia, presumably influenced his appointment.

In this same year Caesar prosecuted Marcus Juncus for extortion while he was governor of Bithynia. It was Juncus whom Caesar had approached for assistance in executing the pirates he had captured, and who had dismissed him with the instruction to sell the pirates as slaves. Is there a hint of revenge in Caesar's prosecution? The verdict is not known, but if Juncus was acquitted, like the other men whom Caesar had prosecuted, the action did not harm Caesar's career.[43]

Probably in 72 BC Caesar was elected by the people for a post as military tribune in a legion. As a patrician he would have been *tribunus laticlavius*, senior to the other five tribunes.[44] It was the first time he had been elected to any post and it served to demonstrate his standing among the people. Where and with whom he served as tribune is not known, and the extant sources give no clues. He may never have left Italy, possibly serving in one of the legions of Marcus Licinius Crassus in the struggle against Spartacus.[45] Crassus had served as praetor in 73 BC, and was appointed to the command against Spartacus in 72 BC after the defeat of the consuls by the slave army, which was still despised even after its success against the Romans. Since Spartacus and his slaves were not considered worthy opponents, Crassus did not earn much glory in his eventual success against them, certainly not enough to rival Pompey, who came home from Spain via northern Italy just as the remnants of the slave army was feeling its way northwards. Pompey made short work of the survivors of Spartacus' band, and claimed his action as a victory in 71 BC.

Despite their personal differences, Pompey and Crassus co-operated in 71 BC in an election campaign to secure the consulships for 70 BC. Their canvassing was not innocent of bribery. Crassus knew the value of money and spent all his life acquiring it. Having followed the career structure that Sulla had laid down, Crassus as an ex-praetor was perfectly eligible for his candidacy for the consulship. Pompey, however, was not. But he was a successful general, and he had always been an exception to the rules. He was underage, and had not even become a senator. The Senate obligingly waived Sulla's rules demanding a progression though the quaestorship and the praetorship before the candidacy for the consulship, normally only reached by men in their early forties. The senators may have been influenced by the presence of Pompey's army outside Rome. He had technically given up his command and become a mere private citizen, as was required for the candidacy for the consulship, and as a *privatus* he could have been prosecuted in the courts, but there is no doubt that although he was no longer the commander of the troops they would have supported him. This meant that they would have to be settled on the land or offered some rewards, and for once the legislation for the settlement of Pompey's troops and those of Metellus Pius went smoothly.

Crassus too had kept his army together, and since the rivalry between Crassus and Pompey was well known, the people were afraid that the two would come to blows and use their armies against each other. Appian relates how the people beseeched the two men to be reconciled. Crassus was the first to yield and offered his hand to Pompey, who accepted the reconciliation. Nevertheless, the people would not disperse until the order had been given to disband the armies.[46] Plutarch recounts the same episode but places it at the end of the consulship, when Crassus was first to yield and offered his hand to Pompey.[47]

Pompey, as a non-senator, had never been party to the workings of the Senate, and consequently had no experience of senatorial procedures or protocol. To remedy this defect, and no doubt to maintain credibility, he asked his friend Marcus Terentius Varro to write it all down for him in an instruction manual. At this stage in his career, the young Pompey was in touch with reality. He knew where his deficiencies lay, he was willing to remedy them, and he was courageous enough to enter on his consulship, aware, but blithely unconcerned, that he did not know everything.

During their joint consulship, Pompey and Crassus dismantled parts of the Sullan legislation, notably restoring the tribunate. There was little enough to do to eradicate the work of Sulla, since previous politicians had already started the process as soon as Sulla was dead. In 75 BC the consul Gaius Aurelius Cotta had reversed Sulla's ruling that had banned tribunes from seeking further offices. Suetonius says that while Caesar was military tribune he ardently supported the efforts of politicians to restore the authority of the tribunes of the plebs, without specifying who was making the efforts, or what the legislation entailed.[48]

There was one area besides the tribunate that had not been fully remedied; this was the composition of the jury courts. The Gracchi had placed them under the control of the *equites*, who had a sorry track record, but when the courts were handed back to the Senate, the members of that august body had proved no less partial or corrupt. At the beginning of 70 BC, the notorious Verres returned from his post as governor of Sicily, where he had outshone all previous governors in rapacity and personal greed. Marcus Tullius Cicero eagerly took up the case for the prosecution, even going so far as to visit the scene of the crimes and collect evidence. He wrote five stirring speeches, but after he had delivered the first one, the defence conducted by Quintus Hortensius – with whom he was to lock horns many times – had already crumbled. Thoroughly miffed because he was denied the chance to show off his oratorical talents in a long trial, Cicero published the speeches. The major point raised by the trial of Verres was that the deplorable level of exploitation of provincials could not continue unchecked. It never disappeared entirely, and it was highly unlikely that it ever would, but at least the Romans attempted to set up jury courts that would be a little less biased towards the profit seekers.

At the trial of Verres, the senators on the jury did show their usual bias towards their own kind, but the need for reform was still paramount. Caesar's kinsman, Lucius Aurelius Cotta, put through a bill to restructure the composition of the juries, which would henceforth be divided between three elements of society: senators, *equites Romani* and *tribuni aerarii*. There is no consensus among modern historians as to who the last two groups of jurors were. It is possible that *equites Romani* indicates those who were members of the early Republican cavalry and entitled to receive the public horse (an antiquated means of equipping the cavalry at public expense), but none of this is certain. The *tribuni aerarii* were originally officials of the treasury (*aerarium*), but the treasury post seems to have gone out of use before 70 BC, and the title may have been revived specifically for the jury courts. It may refer to *equites*, who were not included in the original eighteen voting centuries of their class. No one from any lower class was included in the composition of the juries.[49] Whatever was the distinction between the *equites* and *tribuni aerarii*, the law was passed in an attempt to make the courts less uniformly biased. Since the new *lex Aurelia* was the work of Caesar's relative, he may have had some private discussion about it; at any rate he removed the *tribuni aerarii* when he came to power himself. This was not to be for some years yet, but as a first step Caesar stood for election as quaestor for 69 BC.

5

Senator, 69–63 BC

Caesar was one of twenty new quaestors elected for the year 69 BC. The duties were varied, sometimes limited to the city of Rome as an assistant to a magistrate, and sometimes to be carried out in one of the provinces. Caesar was sent to Further Spain, to serve under the command of Antistius Vetus. This post as quaestor gave him immediate access to the Senate, one of Sulla's measures that had not been overturned. One of Caesar's first recorded actions in the Senate is his speech in favour of a proposal put forward by Plotius, or Plautius, to grant an amnesty to the followers of Lepidus and Sertorius who had taken refuge in Spain. Caesar's brother-in-law, Lucius Cinna, would be included in the amnesty.

Before Caesar was due to depart for Spain, his aunt Julia died, and he also lost his wife Cornelia. Plutarch describes how he earned even more popularity by giving the oration at his aunt's funeral.[1] Since Julia was the widow of Gaius Marius, whose last acts had been among the bloodiest that Rome had seen so far, Caesar risked the opprobrium of some of the senators and equestrians whose families had suffered at Marius' hands. Sulla had destroyed statues of Marius on the Capitol, and had forbidden the display of any images of him. Caesar ignored the ban, and had images of the family of Marius carried in Julia's funeral procession. Everyone knew his connection to Marius, so his best option was not to try to hide it, but to organise a splendid funeral, making it clear that he was not ashamed of his family origins.

The same applied when his wife Cornelia died. The exact date is not known. She was the daughter of Lucius Cornelius Cinna, and Caesar did not try to cover up her origins either. He gave her a public funeral, unprecedented because as Plutarch points out, relatively young Roman matrons did not receive this honour.[2] Apart from any love and respect that Caesar felt for his aunt and his wife, he was also making a political statement for himself.

The two provinces of Hither and Further Spain (*Hispania Citerior* and *Ulterior*) had been annexed by the Romans in 197 BC. There remained large areas of what is now modern Spain where neither Roman conquest nor colonisation had penetrated, but the areas marked out as provinces had attracted many Roman settlers and businessmen. This appointment offered Caesar opportunities to gain experience, and also some personal profit. As quaestor he was responsible for pronouncing judgements in the courts, and though he was still small fry on the greater Roman political scene, he was all-important to some provincials. He probably used the post to line his own pockets, perhaps in the form of gifts, loosely interpreted and freely given. Without resorting to bullying and extortion, he could make friends and allies in the province, all of whom might come in useful later in his career. Gelzer puts it more cynically, describing how Caesar would have many opportunities to put provincials under obligation to himself.[3]

A telling episode that occurred during Caesar's tour of duty in Spain is recorded by Suetonius. In the town of Gades (modern Cadiz) Caesar noticed a statue of Alexander in the Temple of Hercules and became upset, because he had reached the age when Alexander had already conquered the world, while he himself had achieved nothing worthy of note.[4] Plutarch relates this episode in a later context, when Caesar had served as praetor and was in Further Spain as governor. There is no mention of the statue, but Plutarch says that Caesar was reading a book about Alexander and told his friends that so far he had achieved very little, especially in comparison with Alexander.[5] Suetonius goes on to suggest that Caesar's dismay and self-deprecation at Gades led immediately to his decision to ask for discharge from his post before his tour of duty had officially ended.[6] There may be some confusion with his later appointment as governor of Further Spain, when he definitely did depart early, because he wanted to be back in Rome in time for the elections in 60 BC for the consulship of 59 BC.

Before he left Spain, Caesar had a disturbing dream in which he raped his mother, but was comforted by the interpretation of soothsayers, who told him that it was purely symbolic, his mother representing the earth, which he was destined to rule.[7] This dream is also reported in a different context, just before the civil war with Pompey. On his way home from Spain, Caesar visited the colonies of the Transpadane region, which had received only Latin rights after the Social War instead of full Roman citizenship. There was a detectable restlessness and a hint of rebellion among the communities, and Suetonius accuses Caesar of hoping that armed insurrection would break out. Fortunately, says Suetonius, this was prevented by the foresight of the consuls, who had temporarily stationed legions in the area before they were to depart for service in Cilicia.[8] Opinion is divided as to whether Caesar was guilty as charged. Gelzer thinks Caesar was hoping for rebellion, Meier says such action would have been irresponsible, and it was more likely that he preferred to foster enormous pressure on the government, so he could emerge as champion of the cause and win over many clients.[9] It is unlikely that Caesar would have staked his career, which was only just beginning, by embroiling himself in rebellion in an effort to enfranchise the Transpadane communities. This could be achieved much more peacefully by other means, though it was to take several more years.

The story of Caesar's disruptive tendencies serves as a link in Suetonius' narrative with his next remarks, leaping out of context to 65 BC, when Caesar was aedile. It was suspected that Crassus and Caesar were forming a conspiracy, together with Publius Sulla and Lucius Autronius, who had been elected consuls but then dismissed because they had been found guilty of corruption. Crassus was to be Dictator and Caesar his master of horse, so the story runs, but Suetonius acknowledges that his sources were Tanusius Geminus and Marcus Bibulus, both of them virulently anti-Caesarian, but Suetonius backs up their stories by quoting one of Cicero's letters, written much later than the alleged plot, in which he says that Caesar's despotism was evident when he was only an aedile.[10]

Grouping together all the alleged plots in which Caesar was allegedly involved, Suetonius goes on to outline the plans of Gnaeus Piso to raise revolt with the help of the peoples beyond the River Po, a scheme which fell through because Piso died. Once again, is it likely that Caesar would have risked everything on a coup d'état at this stage, even with the backing of Crassus? In each alleged plot, Caesar is cast in the subordinate role, which was not his style. A famous anecdote demonstrates that he was unwilling to act as a subordinate. Travelling to Spain as propraetorian governor, he and his friends passed through lowly villages, and one of his companions asked him if he thought that the inhabitants fought for position and prestige in a village, just as men did in Rome. Caesar replied that he would rather be the first citizen in one of these villages than second in Rome.[11]

On his return to Rome, Caesar married again, this time to Pompeia (no relative of Pompey). Her mother was Cornelia, Sulla's daughter, and her father was Pompeius Rufus, the son of Sulla's colleague Quintus Pompeius Rufus. Caesar's new wife was therefore rooted in the Sullan regime, being the granddaughter of both Quintus Pompeius Rufus and of Sulla himself. Caesar had made an unequivocal statement before he left Rome that he maintained his connections with Marius and Cinna, and he now made another that he was not automatically the foe of any relatives of Sulla. His household was now complete again; he had a wife with solid connections, and a young daughter, Julia, who would now be about eight years old, though her date of birth is not attested. It is likely that his mother Aurelia lived in his household. In 63 BC, when Caesar left home on the day of the elections as Pontifex Maximus, she was said to have kissed him before he left, so she was present in his house, and she was there when Clodius dressed as a woman and profaned the ceremonial devoted to the Bona Dea.

Caesar's rise was hardly meteoric. His path to the consulship was progressing at the usual pace, but it was hardly in doubt that the consulship was his aim. His family connections, though noble, were not outstanding, and he had no immense private fortune, so Caesar had to start at the bottom. He presumably borrowed money to finance his career, and was perhaps already embroiled with Crassus as one of his creditors. Crassus lent money to several other young men, so Caesar was not necessarily one of his favourite protégés. After his quaestorship Caesar required further posts, which would enable him eventually to become praetor and then a provincial governor. In order to repay his creditors, Caesar relied, like many another politician, on being able to make a profit from whichever province he was to govern. But the praetorship was some way off, so Caesar accepted whatever post he was offered, not without string-pulling, of course. Probably in 67 BC he was made *curator* of the Via Appia, though the date is not certain and this task may belong to Caesar's term as aedile, two years later. The Via Appia was one of the earliest roads out of Rome, dating from the fourth century BC. It ran from Rome to Brundisium, the ancient equivalent of a modern motorway linking Rome with the southern coast of Italy and the Mediterranean. There was no permanent centrally controlled system for the upkeep of roads, so *curatores* were not assigned to the roads on a regular annual basis. The roads had usually degenerated badly by the time an official was appointed to improve them. The paved roads that are now taken as the hallmark of the Roman Empire were not yet common. Some road surfaces were impermanent, more vulnerable to wear and tear than paved roads, and maintenance was essential. It was a post in which Caesar could earn respect and gratitude as well as notice from his superiors if he carried out his duties assiduously. Travellers expected the *curator* to repair routes where necessary and attend to their proper functioning, such as drainage and the removal of obstacles; without doubt if improvements were made under Caesar as *curator*, he would advertise the fact by means of inscriptions on milestones, which had been in common usage for about a century, or whatever other facilities were offered. Funds were allocated by the Senate for the curator appointed to the task of road repair, but Plutarch says that Caesar also spent a lot of his own money.[12] He had no doubt borrowed money for the purpose, not simply to facilitate transport but to cultivate public approval and therefore votes for whatever post he decided to stand for next.

When Caesar was busy organising road repairs, the Roman political scene still revolved around Pompey. In 67 BC the tribune Aulus Gabinius put forward a bill to create a special command with the aim of eradicating the menace of the pirates in the Mediterranean. Unprecedented military and naval authority was to be bestowed on an unnamed individual over the whole Mediterranean and up to 400 *stades* inland according to Plutarch, approximating to 50 miles inland in all the coastal areas around the Mediterranean.[13] Everyone knew that Pompey was behind the proposal. His method was to feign indifference while a problem grew worse and worse, not offering his services or any opinion on the matter, and then reluctantly accepting the command or office when it was finally bestowed on him, usually after his agents had done the background work that was necessary to convince people that he knew how to deal with the situation.

Opposition to the bill arose from the right-wing senatorial party led by Quintus Lutatius Catulus. Many other senators may have been opposed to the special command because of the extent of the power over land and sea that the commander would be given. The people, who saw it as an end to food shortages caused by piratical disruption of supplies, were firm in their support of it. When Catulus addressed the people outlining objections to the bill, he asked what would happen if Pompey failed? Who else would they find to take his place for more urgent tasks? And the people shouted in unison, as if by previous agreement, 'You Catulus'.[14]

The story arose that Caesar was the only senator who spoke in favour of Gabinius' bill. This is Plutarch's version, but the motives that he attributes to Caesar do not concern common sense or support of Pompey, but Caesar's desire to cultivate popular support for himself.[15] Matthias Gelzer accepted that only Caesar 'had the impudence' to speak in favour of the bill, as does Meier, who suggests that there may have been a session for debate without Gabinius being present, but Caesar's lone voice was an act of great courage.[16] But as Goldsworthy points out, it surely cannot be the case that Caesar was a lone voice in favour of Gabinius' bill, especially since Pompey had no difficulty in finding men to fill the fifteen posts as *legati*, each with praetorian powers, and two quaestors, to operate on land and sea.[17] A short time later the number of subordinates was raised to about two dozen. Some of the officers serving under Pompey were actually higher ranking than he was at the time, but they did not quibble about precedence. Integral to the proposal there was a departure from normal practice, in that the commander was to be in sole charge, with all his subordinate officers reporting directly to him instead of to the Senate, so that he could receive situation reports at his headquarters and then rapidly coordinate all the necessary actions, without waiting for the authorisation of the Senate to be sent to each individual subordinate officer under his command.

Caesar was most likely in favour of the bill because he had experienced at first hand something of the problems involved in any official operations against the pirates. Not only had he been imprisoned by a group of pirates to whom he paid ransom, then captured and killed, but also he had probably served briefly under the command of Marcus Antonius, Mark Antony's father, whose task was to combat the pirates. Thus Caesar had viewed the problem from both sides, as victim and opponent. Antonius' command was imbued with wide-ranging powers but not nearly wide-ranging enough, and the result was failure when Antonius was killed or died in post. Antonius had earned the posthumous name Creticus, which would normally have been in celebration of a victory, but in this case the name denoted abject failure. The necessity for a wide-ranging command with vast resources at the disposal of the commander and his officers was quite clear. Penny-pinching ways of dealing with serious situations irked Caesar, who probably voted openly for the grand plan, and tacitly for Pompey as the best man to put it into operation. Caesar's fingers may have itched for the opportunity to conduct the campaign himself. Gelzer asserts that Caesar would have been just as capable of dealing with the pirates as Pompey was.[18] But Caesar could not possibly hope to be a political rival to Pompey the Great, who for the next few years was at the zenith of his career.

The Gabinian law was passed despite the opposition, some of it from the tribune Trebellius who tried to veto the proposal. Gabinius had him deposed. This attempt to veto the bill reveals that the restoration of the tribunate had not benefited the populace at all; it had achieved nothing except to perpetuate the use of the office as a mouthpiece for the strongest men in Rome, whoever they were. There was no further opposition to the bill, and all that was required now was to name the person to whom this extraordinary command with extraordinary powers was to be allotted. Pompey leapt into action as soon as he was named as commander against the pirates. His prompt action suggests that he had been thinking about how to deal with the Mediterranean and the coastal areas, how to sweep the seas clear of the menace, and what to do with the pirates afterwards. He divided the Mediterranean and the coasts into thirteen regions and placed a squadron of ships in each. When he embarked for the first assault he was told that it was not propitious to set sail at that moment, but he swept aside all opposition with the bold observation 'It is necessary to sail; it is not necessary to live'. If his ship had foundered, of course, the adjective 'bold' would have been replaced with 'reckless' or 'misguided'. But Pompey was sure of himself and determined. In less than two months, the seas were clear of pirates, who had been resolutely netted up and herded to the coasts of Cilicia. Instead of executing them all, Pompey settled his defeated captives in the coastal cities they had ruined, in the hope that they would learn the arts of peace and make their own living from the lands allotted to them. Now he needed another command.

Lucius Licinius Lucullus had been awarded the command against Mithridates of Pontus, and had begun well, forcing Mithridates to leave all the territories he had occupied, and to take refuge in Armenia. Lucullus had also ironed out many abuses against the provincials in an attempt to clean up the dreadful exploitation that had been normal since Sulla's campaigns. Lucullus was one of the very few governors to whom the provincials expressed gratitude. He had marched into Mithridates' kingdom of Pontus and captured the cities, and was on the point of annexing the territory. From the point of view of Rome, Lucullus had done well, but from the soldiers' viewpoint he had cheated them of legitimate booty, because in taking the cities, he had prevented them from sacking them and helping themselves to loot. The promise of booty was what encouraged soldiers to enlist in the first place, so fighting for Lucullus without profit soon palled. They obediently helped him to win a great battle against Tigranes, the King of Armenia, who had allied, or been coerced into an alliance, with his refugee-guest Mithridates. As a belated reward to keep his soldiers happy, Lucullus allowed them free rein to gather portable wealth after they had captured the Armenian capital city of Tigranocerta. But Lucullus is generally agreed to have lacked the brilliant touch that Pompey or Caesar had with their armies. In the inhospitable highlands of Armenia, where perhaps the soldiers could no longer see the point of what they were fighting for, they mutinied. According to Dio it was Publius Clodius, who was destined to fulfil a notorious political role in Rome, who encouraged the troops of Lucullus to mutiny.[19] By political means at Rome Lucullus was gradually deprived of parts of his command. A new commander, Manius Acilius Glabrio, was sent out to take command because it was thought that Lucullus was prolonging the war, but Glabrio found that it was not as easy as it seemed, and halted in Bithynia. Marcius Rex commanded in Cilicia. The campaigns in the East were not going well.

What was required was a new overall commander, and there just happened to be one in the vicinity who was rounding off a successful campaign against the pirates and would soon be free to assume command almost at once. The tribune Gaius Manilius had little trouble in passing his law to bestow the command on Pompey in 66. The commander was to have control of all the provinces in Asia Minor, essential if he was to conduct the war properly. He would need supplies from a large area, since he may be forced to chase Mithridates and Tigranes from kingdom to kingdom, through several different provinces, allied kingdoms, and foreign states. The protocol of crossing boundaries between provinces would have to be waived. Pompey would have the power to make war on other enemies if necessary, and to conclude peace treaties as he saw fit. The Senate was therefore by-passed while Pompey was in command, just as it had been in the war against the pirates. All well and good for the moment, but Pompey's problems would begin when he returned to Rome, when he could not persuade the Senate to ratify the measures he had taken in concluding peace and making treaties with the states and people of the East.

Cicero, who was praetor in 66, made a speech in support of Manilius. Caesar voted in favour of this bill, 'out of bitter necessity', says Gelzer, and Meier interpreted Caesar's vote in the same light, because by voting for the bill, Caesar placed himself in a favourable light with Pompey and also with the people, because Pompey was the man of the moment who had ensured the safety of the food supply by defeating the pirates.[20] Gelzer traced Caesar's *popularis* tendencies to his connection with Cinna, tendencies which became so distinct at a later time.[21] That time may have been now, when Manilius' bill was being debated. Meier identifies this moment as a turning point when Caesar turned away from Crassus and the *optimates*, and instead made a decisive move towards the people and Pompey.[22] A recurring theme of Gruen's work is that Caesar was concerned to ally himself with Pompey throughout his early career.[23]

Writing two centuries later and with the benefit of hindsight, Dio says that Caesar voted for the Manilian law because he foresaw that he might need something similar for himself one day.[24] This may be true, not just derived from Dio's judgement based on his historical knowledge. The problems of the late Republic could never be solved by two consuls who held power for only a year, with the distinct possibility that their legislation could be overturned as soon as they stepped down. Greater powers, together with more time to execute any long-term schemes, were necessary if the problems were to be tackled effectively. No doubt many politicians realised this, but no one except Sulla had been willing to risk accumulating so much power, and with it the condemnation of his fellows. The difference between other politicians and Caesar was that Caesar was willing to go one step further and aim for more extensive powers, regardless of the opprobrium of his contemporaries.

While Pompey was absent Caesar concentrated on building up his own influence in Rome. When Pompey came back, he would be more than ever the man of the moment, eclipsing everyone else; he might be cultivated as a patron for Caesar, but it would be much better to be in a position of relative independence, but also clearly in favour with the great man. Caesar decided to stand for election as curule aedile for 65 BC, the most senior of the two sets of aediles. Having obtained the post, Caesar planned his lavish entertainments for the people. His colleague was Marcus Calpurnius Bibulus. These two men were fated to run parallel in more than one post, with Bibulus the loser every time. He spent money on entertaining the people, just as Caesar did, but all the credit went to the man who knew best how to advertise and promote himself. Bibulus compared himself to the god Pollux, twin of Castor, but people only ever remembered Castor and never his twin.[25] Bibulus never developed the charm, charisma, and ability to sell himself to the public that Caesar had already mastered. The aediles were responsible for policing of the streets and markets in Rome, and for the upkeep of temples and public buildings. There would probably be a kernel of experienced subordinate staff or slaves already in place to carry out some of the work, and the Senate voted an allocation of money from public funds to help with expenses, but holders of these posts were expected to contribute from their own pockets, especially to finance the games and shows that they were under obligation to put on. Customarily there were seven days devoted to games and shows in April, in honour of the Mother Goddess Cybele, a cult that had been imported to Rome in 204, according to a prophecy in the Sibylline Books and advice from the oracle at Delphi. In September fifteen days of games were voted in honour of Jupiter Capitolinus. Caesar determined that his games, shows, theatre performances and banquets were to outshine anything that had gone before.

He arranged gladiatorial combats in honour of his late father, putting on 320 pairs of combatants, so many that the Senate had to pass a law to limit the number of gladiators that could be kept in Rome.[26] The memory of Spartacus was still too raw. In addition to his gladiatorial games, Caesar also decorated the Forum and the adjacent public buildings, and the Capitol, and Plutarch says that Caesar topped off the lavish expenditure of his term as aedile by restoring Marius' trophies from his wars, which had been displayed on the Capitol Hill, but destroyed by Sulla. Caesar had secretly commissioned the production of statues of Marius and of Victory and installed them on the Capitol, presumably overnight, because Plutarch describes the amazement of people who saw them the next day, statues glittering with gold, with inscriptions recording Marius' victories over the Cimbri.[27] It was a notable achievement, anonymous in intention, but it can scarcely have been difficult to recognise who was responsible. According to Plutarch, the action provoked Quintus Lutatius Catulus to make a speech in the Senate, in which he remarked that Caesar was not content with undermining the constitution but he was now figuratively battering the walls with siege engines. Plutarch adds that Caesar managed to convince the Senate of his innocence, presumably regarding the charges that he was intent on overthrowing the constitution, not the charge of putting up statues. This no doubt involved much smooth talking by Caesar. The morale of his friends was considerably enhanced, and apparently they told Caesar that the populace would be glad to see him overcome the opposition and achieve supremacy in Rome. This is most likely Plutarch's retrospective opinion, and not derived from a contemporary archival source.[28] It is not recorded that Caesar was ordered to remove the trophies.

It was an accepted procedure for most young men who aspired to a political career to gain a reputation for generosity and extravagant display while serving as aedile. It was a means to an end, namely votes. Cynically but accurately, Appian describes how Caesar borrowed vast amounts of money to make himself popular among the masses, who always sing the praises of those who are lavish in expenditure.[29] Meier says that Caesar's extravagance reflected the insecurity of the young outsider, craving notoriety and wanting to build up electoral power rapidly and on the grand scale instead of by slow degrees. For Meier, Caesar was always an outsider, which may be how Caesar viewed himself and how his contemporaries viewed him.[30] But the question could be asked, did Caesar ever feel insecure, even at the comparatively young age as aedile?

Caesar needed popular favour, especially in 65 BC as dark rumours started to circulate about his possible involvement in the so-called first conspiracy of Lucius Sergius Catilina, better known as Catiline. This individual had a bad reputation while living and an even worse posthumous press, having been accused of various crimes, including extortion while he was governor of Africa. So far no one had been successful in condemning him. Prosecutions were arranged but he emerged almost unscathed each time, not that anyone truly believed in his innocence, but happily for him, firm evidence of what he was supposed to have done was simply not available. No one will ever know to what extent Caesar was implicated in this alleged plot, nor in the next one that was ended by Cicero in his first and only consulship in 63 BC. In recent times, the Catilinarian plots have been played down, attributed mostly to Cicero's over-reaction and his determination to be the saviour of the state. The plotting that was supposedly detected in 65 BC was attributed to the initial machinations of Publius Autronius and Publius Sulla, the two men who had been elected consuls for that year, but they were both found guilty of corruption in their election campaigns, and were deposed. In their places Lucius Manlius Torquatus and Lucius Aurelius Cotta were elected. It was said that the new consuls were to be assassinated in January, but the plans failed and the assassinations were re-planned for February. This plan also failed, and left the culprits even more discontented. Caesar's name was mentioned in association with this plot, but as Gelzer points out, the so-called evidence for Caesar's involvement was compiled retrospectively in 59 BC, not in the relevant context, so it is doubtful that Caesar was involved in any scheme, especially if it involved killing his mother's cousin, Lucius Aurelius Cotta.[31]

It was alleged that Autronius and Sulla had contacted Catiline. In 65 BC, it was thought that the main aim of the disappointed consuls, and possibly Catiline as well, was to take over the state, but the story is smoke without fire, rumour made pseudo-fact. No one can even be sure that there was ever a plot in 65 BC, and if there was, it is still doubtful whether Catiline was involved in it. Cicero, who wrote about these events in a contemporary pamphlet called *de Consiliis Suis*, which was not published until after his death, was certain of the existence of some shady dealings, but he did not mention any involvement of Caesar in this first conspiracy. He did think that Crassus was implicated, however, and if Crassus was involved then it might follow that Caesar, who was associated with Crassus by dint of borrowing money from him, at least knew of the plot. Rumours circulated that Crassus was going to make himself Dictator in the ensuing mayhem after Catiline's plot, and Caesar was to be his master of horse (*magister equitum*). In that case, it might seem that Catiline was to be used to stir up trouble that Crassus and Caesar could then heroically stamp out. The situation is even more nebulous now than it was at the time, but it does demonstrate that the association of Crassus and Caesar was considered to be strong and their joint ambition unbounded. This perception may have been retrospective, and even if it were contemporary it does not necessarily have any basis in fact.

Other stories were told of the mutual scheming of Crassus and Caesar in 65 BC. Crassus was censor in that year with Quintus Lutatius Catulus as his colleague. The duties of the censors were to conduct the census which was held every five years. Their appointment lasted for eighteen months, unlike the other magistracies which were annual. As well as compiling the lists of Roman citizens, the censors were responsible for reviewing the membership of the Senate, with powers to demote and remove any senators who were considered unsuitable. They could also adlect to the Senate anyone whom they considered worthy, so they had tremendous influence on the conduct of the senators, but they seem to have spent most of their terms of office in squabbling with each other. Catulus had spoken against Gabinius' and Manilius' bills to bestow the special commands on Pompey. He was a devout follower of Sulla, and had given him a state funeral, and he had done most to put down Lepidus' ill-judged rebellion after Sulla's death. He stood for everything that was conservative, and was the antithesis of men like Caesar. Crassus tried to put into practice Caesar's wish to bestow full citizenship to the Transpadane communities, which Caesar had visited on his way home from Spain after his quaestorship. Catulus blocked the proposals.

He also blocked the proposal to annexe Egypt as a Roman province, a real possibility since the ruler set up by Sulla in 80, Ptolemy XI

Alexander, had been murdered after a very short reign, but he had apparently left a will that would have bequeathed the kingdom to Rome, just as Attalus of Pergamum had done in 133.[32] It could be said that Ptolemy Alexander's successor, Ptolemy XII, nicknamed Auletes 'the fluteplayer', had no legal claim to the throne of Egypt. Roman interest in Egypt was of long ancestry, and sprang from only one major cause: it was the wealthiest land in the world. It was also the bridge between the African and eastern provinces, and via the Red Sea there was access to the trade routes to and from places as far away as India and China. Given that Caesar did not actually annexe Egypt when he had the opportunity after the Battle of Pharsalus, but instead set up Cleopatra as its Queen, there may be some soupcon of doubt about the story that he hoped to be given the command of Egypt in accordance with the terms of Ptolemy XI Alexander's will. At the time when the proposal was made he had not reached any of the higher magistracies, so as aedile, was he aiming too high? It is hardly to be wondered at that people saw Crassus as the mastermind behind the proposal and Caesar as his tool.

All Crassus' proposals during his term as censor were defeated by Catulus, so the Egyptian adventure came to nothing. Perhaps because of the implacable discord between the two men, giving rise to a period of non-achievement, the censors resigned before they had conducted the census.

The following two years were even more fraught. Catiline refused to be discouraged at his lack of political success. He had been defeated in the consular elections in 66, and had been unable to stand as a candidate in 65 BC because he had been undergoing prosecutions at the time, and anyone brought before the courts was not allowed to stand as a candidate for any office. Catiline had not been condemned, but the case had ruined his chances of election for that year. He had friends in high places; several aristocrats, including ex-consulars, spoke favourably of him, not that this is any recommendation of good character, only of solidarity with his peers. At one point, even Cicero had considered defending him in court. Catiline could be affable and charming, and it is likely that his reputation has been blackened retrospectively after he had been accused of raising revolt and then been defeated. He made it known that he desired the consulship for 63 BC, so he started to agitate in the run up to the elections in 64 BC. There were only three candidates, and still Catiline failed to be elected. The new consuls for 63 BC were to be Gaius Antonius Hybrida, the uncle of Mark Antony, and the man who had appealed to the tribunes to veto his trial by Caesar some years before, and Marcus Tullius Cicero, the *novus homo* who had made his name as a prodigious orator in the law courts. Catiline bided his time; it was supposed that he would try again next year.

Between his term as aedile in 65 BC and his election as praetor in 63 BC, Caesar served as president of the *quaestio de sicariis*, a court dealing with murder charges. In this capacity he brought about prosecutions for those men who had murdered Sulla's proscribed victims. They had usually brought in the heads of the outlawed men, and received payment for their actions from the state treasury. Laws had been passed exempting the murderers from punishment, because in legal terms, as enacted by Sulla, anyone could kill proscribed men without facing punishment, so in view of the laws still standing it was doubtful if prosecutions were legally acceptable. Caesar decided that they were. As president of the court he had no say in the final judgement, but at least two men were condemned. Caesar challenged the law, but at a time when not too many people would have been upset to see men prosecuted and condemned for murders that they had committed from the worst of motives in the worst of times.[33]

Appian provides a retrospective portrait of Caesar around this time, describing him as still a young man, powerful in speech and action, audacious in all things, calm and collected in everything, and profuse beyond his means.[34] This is a portrait that is accepted with historical hindsight, but was probably becoming common knowledge in the late 60s BC, in that people judged Caesar by what they had witnessed so far. Caesar would need all these attributes during the year 63, a tempestuous year in politics, and a successful one for Caesar himself, as he aimed for higher offices with his usual vast expenditure and confidence in himself.

On 10 December 64 BC, the ten tribunes for 63 BC entered office. A small group of them had formulated plans for reforms, and they worked together and held meetings to outline and plan their legislation.[35] One of them, Publius Servilius Rullus, introduced a land bill at the beginning of the year. Rullus had not been heard of in Roman politics before this time, and faded into obscurity afterwards. He was said to adopt a dishevelled appearance and sported a beard, harking back to the original tribunes of the plebs of the fifth century BC. Rullus' bill has been repeatedly discussed and disputed by modern scholars. The only source for this bill and its clauses derives from three speeches on the land bill by Cicero, called *De Lege Agraria*. Since Cicero was not in favour of the proposal, these speeches are not unbiased. The bill was never converted into law, so discussion is perhaps somewhat academic, but its failure may have inflamed those who had hoped to gain from it, and thereby served to provide Lucius Sergius Catilina with a band of thwarted discontents in Rome and Italy. Rullus' bill would not have solved all the problems of the later Republic, but it would have alleviated several of them all at once, and a lot of thought had gone into the preparation of its clauses. Gruen considers that it was 'intelligent in design and farsighted in conception'.[36] Rullus attempted to satisfy many needs while also treading carefully between forced sales or seizures of lands, both public and private, and he wanted to avoid making insufficient allocations for the needy. The urban poor were to be given lands, which would dramatically reduce their numbers in the city of Rome and therefore also reduce the potential riots because of food shortages. The soldiers settled by Sulla on confiscated land were to be left unmolested, unless they expressed a wish to sell, in which case the law provided for them. Some public lands in the provinces, owned by the Roman state, were to be included in the allotments, and since public lands in Italy and the provinces would not be sufficient, it was proposed that lands would be purchased as well. The finance for this would soon be provided from the wealth that Pompey would bring to Rome, in the form of taxation and tributes when he had settled the eastern territories, some parts of which were to be annexed and others were to be allied to Rome. Generous offers were to be made to owners of land to encourage them to sell, partly aimed at men who had got into debt but with falling land values could not discharge their debts by selling in the ordinary market.[37]

To put all this into practice there was to be a commission of ten men, each with praetorian powers for five years, with a staff of land surveyors, administrators, secretaries and clerical staff. The commissioners were not to be responsible to anyone, so they could not be harassed by rising or established politicians, and there could be no question of any predominant personal interest. Pompey would not be allowed to join the commission of ten, but besides settling the urban poor, the bill would have ensured that there was a ready-made solution for the settlement of his veterans when he returned to Rome and disbanded his armies. Cicero as consul bludgeoned the bill to an early death. He sold it to the populace as a scam, protesting that the allocations of lands would be worthless, consisting of marshes or swamps, and that selling public lands would entail loss of revenues to the state. On this last point he was at least consistent, since he made the same objection about Caesar's land bill of 59 BC. Chiefly Cicero was protesting on behalf of Pompey. His argument ran that the commission of ten excluded Pompey or any of his representatives, but this is not entirely true because originally all ten tribunes of the plebs supported the bill, and it is suggested that two of them, Titus Labienus and Ampius Balbus, were Pompey's men. It was thought by some men at the time, and ever since, that Rullus, an otherwise obscure character, must have been a front man for some other politicians. After all, this is how tribunes were used by politicians in the later Republic. It is usually said that Cicero believed Crassus and Caesar to have been behind the bill, and that he thought that these two were trying to build up a power base against Pompey before he came home. This has been challenged by Gruen, who points out that the suspicion falling on Crassus and Caesar is a modern interpretation, deduced from Cicero's hints that some prominent men were behind the bill, but Cicero uses careful language and does not go so far as to name anyone.[38] It has been pointed out that no one dared to attack Crassus directly.[39]

Nonetheless, some modern historians follow Cicero's line of reasoning that the plan was to embarrass Pompey, and could therefore have been a ploy on the part of Crassus and Caesar to hold him to ransom when he returned, needing above all else land for his soldiers. Gruen argues that, contrary to Cicero's claim that the bill was inimical to Pompey, the great general was honoured by a clause that exempted him from turning over all the spoils of the Mithridatic war to the state.[40] The evidence is not detailed enough to refute or strongly support the arguments that Rullus' bill was promoted by Crassus and Caesar for their own ends, and that it was aimed at damaging Pompey, and so any resolution depends, like much else about this period, on opinion.

Whatever his stance on Rullus' bill, Caesar was beginning to make a name for himself in 63 BC. He prosecuted Gaius Calpurnius Piso for extortion when he was governor of Cisalpine Gaul, but there was also the fact that Piso had executed a Transpadane Gaul. Caesar had taken the Transpadanes under his wing, and though they had not received the citizenship that he had promised them, thanks to the opposition of Catulus, Caesar must now keep faith with them to preserve his credibility, otherwise it would seem that he was simply toying with any device that might bring him fame. Piso was acquitted, but Caesar had made his statement; he would not be blamed for his failure when it was clear that the nobility of Rome closed ranks against outsiders. Caesar also defended a Numidian chief called Masintha, in a case against king Hiempsal, who was attempting to reduce the chief and his people to the status of vassals. Hiempsal's son Juba came to Rome to appear at the trial, during which Caesar lost his temper and seized Juba's beard. If it was done for effect it made the wrong impression, and earned the enmity of Juba, who fought against Caesar in the civil wars. The judgement went against Masintha, who was declared along with his people to be a vassal of Hiempsal, owing tribute. Suetonius describes how Caesar rescued Masintha from the court, and concealed him in his house, until he was due to depart for Spain as governor. Then he hid Masintha in his litter and smuggled him out of Rome.[41]

Not entirely to his credit, Caesar acted in collusion with Titus Labienus, one of the tribunes in 63 BC, who brought about the prosecution of the aged Gaius Rabirius, who was accused of killing the tribune Saturninus nearly forty years earlier.[42] Saturninus had been associated with Marius, and in 100 he had put forward a land bill, one of the aims of which was to provide allotments for Marius' veterans. Another land bill concerning Cisalpine Gaul met with opposition not only from Saturninus' opponents but also from the urban mob. Saturninus managed to have the bill passed into law only amid considerable violence. Thereafter Saturninus became increasingly violent, being elected tribune for a second term, and associating himself with Glaucia, who wanted to stand for the consulship immediately after his praetorship. Marius had been content to use Saturninus to provide for his veterans, but the tribune had got completely out of hand, eventually gathering supporters and seizing the Capitol Hill. Plainly he had to be stopped, and the Senate passed the *senatus consultum ultimum*, or last decree, empowering the consuls to defend the state. Marius took charge of troops, besieged Saturninus on the Capitol, forced him to surrender and imprisoned him and his followers in the Senate House, promising them protection from summary execution. The mob thought otherwise, broke through the roof of the Senate House and killed most of the prisoners. Saturninus was one of the casualties. One of the men who had participated in the affair was Gaius Rabirius.

Tribunes were theoretically sacrosanct, no matter how unscrupulous they had been, so the murder of Saturninus was a terrible crime; it was not the last time that Caesar would place great emphasis on the sacrosanctity of tribunes. The combined action of Labienus and Caesar was not directed solely at Rabirius, but at the senators who had passed the *senatus consultum ultimum* when the crisis caused by the actions of Saturninus and Glaucia came to a head. The last decree of the Senate had been used to justify putting men to death without trial, and this was the major point. There was no standing jury court to deal with the charge that was brought against Rabirius, that of *perduellio*, or treason.[43] This was an antiquated charge which had lapsed and it was more usual to bring a charge of *maiestas*. In accordance with the antiquated charge, Caesar and Labienus chose an antiquated court. Caesar was selected by lot as judge, along with a distant relative, Lucius Caesar. They gave the death sentence, but Caesar had displayed such rampant hostility that this worked against him and in Rabirius' favour.[44] Rabirius appealed to the people and was defended by both Cicero and Hortensius. Conveniently, it was discovered that the man responsible for the murder of Saturninus was a slave, and Rabirius was not put to death. If he had been found guilty, the punishment would have been barbaric, even for the Romans. The old man would have been tied to a stake in the Campus Martius and flogged to death. The whole procedure was brought to an end by lowering the flag on the Janiculum hill. In Rome's past, this meant that the city was about to be attacked, and any public business had to be terminated. According to Dio, it was the augur and praetor Quintus Caecilius Metellus Celer who ordered the flag to be lowered, and modern historians have suggested that this was prearranged between Caesar and Metellus, especially since the trial was not resumed. Dio points out that Labienus would have been entitled to prosecute again, but he chose not to.[45] Perhaps Caesar never intended the case to be anything but a show of strength, aimed at the Senate and its propensity to allow executions without trial. This would become a serious issue towards the end of the year, and Caesar was consistent in his opposition to summary executions of this nature.

The most important steps that Caesar took at this time were to stand for election as praetor, and also for election as Pontifex Maximus, high priest and head of the college of pontiffs. The elections for the praetors went well, and Caesar became praetor elect for 62 BC. There was nothing abnormal about his candidacy and his election, since he had served as quaestor and aedile and was about the right age for the post. It was his candidacy for Pontifex Maximus that was completely unexpected.

The office of Pontifex Maximus was bestowed for life, and the post holder was usually co-opted by the Senate, one of the measures that Sulla had instituted. Two things happened concerning the Pontifex Maximus, but the chronological order in which they occurred is not established. The post-holder Metellus Pius died, creating a vacancy, and the tribune Titus Labienus passed a law to restore the election of the priests to the people. This included the augurs, the pontifices, and the *quindecemviri sacris faciundis*, as well as the head of the college, the Pontifex Maximus.[46] There was no recorded opposition to this law. Dio links the new law directly to the election of Caesar as Pontifex, but Gruen says that this is erroneous.[47] It was an excusable assumption that Labienus and Caesar had collaborated to pass a law that facilitated Caesar's appointment as Pontifex Maximus, but there are too many unknown factors to make this connection. The exact date when Metellus died is not established, nor is the date when Labienus presented his bill. It could have been presented at any time during his tribunate, which ran from 10 December 62 to 9 December 63, but obviously the law had to be proposed before the elections were held. It may be the case that at some point in 63 BC Metellus Pius was ill and likely to die, and Caesar saw his chance to obtain the highest priesthood, relying on Labienus to transfer the selection of priests from the Senate to the people. Alternatively the bill may have been formulated and passed as soon as possible after Metellus' death.[48] If either of these scenarios is correct, it reveals

Caesar as the opportunist that he was, with a finger on the pulse of political developments, quickly forming plans to promote himself whenever the opportunity arose. Whatever the chronology, it was a fortuitous development for Caesar. He would have had scant hope of being co-opted to the post of Pontifex Maximus by the Senate, but he had a much better chance of success by standing for election by the people, to whom he could distribute lots of cash or promises of favours as he presented himself as a candidate. According to Dio, Caesar flattered everyone and did not mind grovelling now and then to his superiors, the very men whom he was intent on dominating.[49]

Caesar announced his candidacy, competing against Quintus Lutatius Catulus and Publius Servilius Vatia Isauricus. These men were of the usual calibre expected of candidates for the post of Pontifex, influential senators of consular rank, older and more experienced than Caesar, who had served as aedile, and was probably praetor elect by the time of the elections, but he had not yet attained anything more prestigious. Gelzer underlines Caesar's audacity in his bid to become Pontifex Maximus.[50] In ordinary circumstances Catulus was the prime candidate, but he knew that Caesar's money would speak more loudly and find the right targets. Catulus clearly thought that Caesar had a very good chance of election and tried to buy him off.[51] But Caesar was not interested in money, not even to pay his debts. He wanted the supreme priestly office for its political influence. He was elected, by a vast majority according to Suetonius, including more votes from the tribes of Catulus and Isauricus than these candidates received themselves. Plutarch tells it differently, that Caesar was elected only by a close margin.[52] The numbers of votes do not really matter. Caesar was elected. The world may have heard no more of him had he been unsuccessful, since he told his mother that he would return home as Pontifex Maximus or not at all. It might seem uncharacteristically melodramatic to go off into exile somewhere or even commit suicide in the event of failure. Presumably he meant that he was sure of victory, having bribed enough men to ensure that the elections would go in his favour. Perhaps it was not simply cash that helped Caesar to gain votes. Gruen suggests that Pompey and his men supported Caesar, and canvassed for votes for him so that Pompey's enemy Catulus would be defeated.[53] If by some quirk of fate Caesar had been foiled, he would have thought of something else.

In the autumn of 63 BC, when Caesar was praetor elect, there was a birth in Caesar's extended family. His sister Julia had married Gaius Atius, and they had produced a daughter, Atia, who had married Gaius Octavius, and on 23 September Atia and Gaius had a son, named Gaius Octavius, after his father. It may not have been considered a significant event, especially since infant mortality was so high, but nineteen years later, Gaius Octavius junior was destined to become the foremost politician in Rome, the heir of Caesar, and as Augustus, the man who presided over the transition of the Republic into the Empire.

Towards the end of 63 BC the infamous Catilinarian conspiracy was brought to light by the consul Cicero's vigilant investigations. The episode has been discussed many times, using the only contemporary evidence that is available, namely Cicero's speeches made at the time but not published until he had polished them for public consumption. The next most important evidence is Sallust's retrospective work, called variously *Bellum Catilinae*, or *de Catilinae Coniuratione*, referring to the conspiracy and the war that broke out after the conspiracy was discovered. These surviving accounts of the so-called rebellion are hostile. Cicero had a vested interest in portraying Catiline as a thoroughly unprincipled villain, so that his brave stance against him would seem all the more worthy. Sallust wrote his book nearly two decades later, when he was firmly in Caesar's camp, so although he accepts Cicero's portrayal, he plays down the consul's achievements and writes at length about the contributions of Caesar and Cato, contrasting their completely opposite opinions.[54] Modern opinion is polarised. Catiline has been seen as a revolutionary whose aim was to bring down the state, and at the opposite pole he has been portrayed as a man dedicated to reforms to improve the situation of the poor and the ultimate benefit of the state.[55] He may have been the tool of equally irresponsible politicians, or a mad man bent on personal power. Initially Crassus and Caesar may have supported him, not necessarily aiming at revolution, but they would probably have continued to back him if they thought that he would have been successful.[56] There is no voice, contemporary or later, from Catiline's side of the affair that might explain what he was trying to achieve, and the multiplicity of modern opinions indicates that modern historians cannot decipher what Catiline intended to do if he had gained power.

According to Dio a law had been passed in 63 BC, strongly supported by Cicero, stating that for those found guilty of bribery at elections, banishment for ten years should be added to the penalties. Catiline thought that this was aimed directly at him.[57] For the third time he was defeated in the elections, this time for the consulship for 62 BC. It may have been only at this moment that he hatched a plot in a monumental fit of pique, frustrated that power and influence, and the means to repay his debts, were denied him yet again. It was unlikely that he would be any more successful in subsequent elections, and he did not wish to wait for another year. There were plenty of men in Rome who bore any number of grudges or who shared similar frustrations. The promise of land had been dangled before the urban poor and then obliterated when Rullus' bill came to nothing. There were some senators whose careers had been blighted, and who found association with Catiline an attractive proposition.

Catiline's following was not overwhelmingly numerous, but it comprised a cross-section of Roman society, rich and poor alike, of those who could be persuaded to follow an aristocrat who promised reforms, cancellation of debts, redistribution of wealth, and, in short, a better world. He refused at first to recruit slaves, a point which Lentulus Sura contested. Sura made the mistake of committing his thoughts to writing, and the letter that he wrote incriminated him. At the end of October it seems that Catiline planned to begin an armed rebellion outside Rome, and to assassinate the consuls and other senators, but the assassinations failed, or were foiled. As yet Cicero had not enough incontrovertible evidence to persuade the whole Senate to act, but by mid-November Catiline joined his army in Etruria, and was declared *hostis*, or a public enemy. In December the Catilinarians made another fatal mistake; Lentulus Sura and other senators tried to convert to the Catilinarian cause some Gallic envoys from the tribe of the Allobroges, who were leaving Rome after presenting an unsuccessful petition. It was thought that the Gauls may have been sufficiently discontented to turn against the Roman government and join in the plot, but rather than embroil themselves in what could turn out to be a Roman civil war, they reported to their patron in Rome, Fabius Sanga.[58] The matter was referred to Cicero. Another conspirator, Gaius Cornelius Cethegus, had hidden a collection of arms in his house, enough to convict him, despite his claim that the weapons were just his private museum pieces. Cicero arrested Cethegus and three other conspirators. Four more arrests were made shortly afterwards. Also arrested was Publius Cornelius Lentulus Sura, who had unwittingly given Cicero evidence of the plot. He had been consul in 71 BC, but had fallen foul of Pompey and his party, and had been removed from the Senate by the censors during the consulship of Pompey and Crassus in 70 BC. Lentulus had to embark on a second career from the beginning, and had become praetor by the time of Catiline's conspiracy.[59] He had the further distinction of having married Julia, the widow of Marcus Antonius Creticus and the mother of three boys, the eldest of whom was Mark Antony, who never forgave Cicero for his treatment of his stepfather Lentulus.

It was a tense moment for Caesar and Crassus. They were not accused outright but there was suspicion that they had aided and abetted Catiline, if not instigated the whole plot. They had enemies who wished to see them brought down. Catulus was still bitter after his failure to be elected Pontifex Maximus, and Calpurnius Piso was embittered after his trial instigated by Caesar. Both these men tried to browbeat Cicero into accusing Caesar, but Cicero refused to do so.[60] Appian says that Cicero did not wish to bring Caesar into the controversy because he was so popular with the people.[61] It is also possible that, at the time, Cicero did not believe that Caesar was deeply involved with Catiline.[62] In his published speech about the Catilinarian conspiracy, Cicero treated Caesar quite deferentially, but this may be a revision of what he actually said in the Senate, since the published version was worked up later, in 60 BC. By this time, Caesar was due to return to Rome and it was clear that he intended to become consul in 59 BC. Cicero was perhaps hoping to conciliate Caesar and work with him. In a letter to Atticus, Cicero said that he hoped to be able to influence and perhaps modify Caesar's policies.[63] But Cicero's real opinion emerged much later in a work called *de Consiliis Suis*, which he did not intend to publish during his lifetime. The work was made public some years after his death, and long after Crassus and Caesar were dead, so then it did not matter that Cicero set down in writing his conviction that both of these men were behind the Catilinarian plot.

There was a debate in the Senate on 5 December to decide the course of action concerning the first five men who had been arrested. Crassus did not attend. As consul, Cicero opened proceedings with the statement that he preferred an immediate death penalty, but left it to the Senate to make the final decision. The debate in the Senate is summarised in a letter from Cicero to Atticus.[64] Senior members of the Senate suggested that the death penalty should be adopted. There was no suggestion of a trial. Caesar was praetor elect, so he was entitled to speak after the consulars and the praetors for the year. The gist of what he said is preserved by Sallust in his account of the conspiracy of Catiline.[65] By the time Sallust wrote this work, he was in Caesar's camp, but this does not mean that he deliberately created a speech that would present Caesar in a better light than had been the case at the time. According to Suetonius, Caesar was the only senator who proposed leniency.[66] Caesar pleaded for the lives of the Catilinarians by advising that the arrested men should be separated and held in different Italian towns, never to return to Rome. Dio adds that there was to be no discussion of a pardon for them, and if the men escaped from the cities where they were held, the communities should be fined.[67] Appian says that Caesar advised that the men should be imprisoned until Catiline was defeated, and then trials should be held. This suggestion swayed some of the senators.[68] Sallust's version is different. He reproduces a long speech by Caesar, mostly reminding his audience of Rome's history and objecting to Decimus Silanus' recommendation for the death penalty. Sallust then gives Caesar's own recommendations, that the conspirators should be imprisoned in free cities, and anyone trying to bring their case to court should be considered to be working against the state.[69] Apparently Caesar rounded off his speech with the warning that there would be repercussions later if the death penalty were passed without giving the accused the benefit of a trial, but this may be a retrospective insertion, made in the knowledge that Cicero suffered exile after Clodius passed his law condemning anyone who had executed men without trial. On the other hand Caesar had strong reason to warn Cicero not to act too hastily. He had been instrumental in prosecuting Rabirius four decades after the murder of Saturninus, in which the major point was not Rabirius' guilt, but the irresponsibility of the Senate in passing the last decree which enabled men to be killed without trial. Caesar may have been impertinent enough to issue a warning to his audience, and it is said that some of the senators were influenced by it, and were now unwilling to risk the enduring hatred of the people if the so-called conspirators were executed after being refused a trial. Suetonius says that some men had already begun to side with Caesar, including Cicero's brother Quintus, and he would have prevailed in bringing the whole Senate round to his point of view, but met his match in Marcus Porcius Cato, whose speech brought the Senate back into line.[70] According to Plutarch and Appian, Cato also managed to cast suspicion on Caesar while making his speech.[71] Even after this, Caesar kept up his argument, only ceasing when the armed guards around the Senate threatened him with weapons drawn. Some of Caesar's friends moved away, while the few that were left shielded him and somehow got him out of the way. For the short time until the end of the year, Caesar did not attend any further meetings of the Senate.[72] He had made his point, and he had succeeded in winning election as praetor for 62 BC, so he did not need to risk the rest of his career on trying to enforce his viewpoint in the face of such opposition. When payback time came around, as it surely would, Caesar's hands were squeaky clean.

Since Cicero as a lawyer knew very well how a proper trial could be dragged out, and how defence lawyers could work up a good case, he also realised that obtaining a conviction would not be guaranteed. He required a rapid result because his consulship was nearing its end, and it would be an anti-climax to exit from his term of office having revealed the plot but without enjoying the satisfaction of securing the condemnation of the men whom he had arrested. He wanted drama and heroics. Marcus Porcius Cato helped him to bring the proceedings to a speedy and bloody end. Cato had already spoken in opposition to Caesar, and for the rest of his life he scarcely ever stopped speaking in opposition to Caesar. Now he backed Cicero, proposed the death penalty, and the senators finally agreed. The five Catilinarians, including Mark Antony's stepfather Lentulus Sura, were executed immediately, while the Senate was still in session.

The question may be asked, if Crassus and Caesar were hand-in-hand with Catiline, what could they hope to gain?

Cancellation of debts, one of the items on Catiline's agenda, would have helped Caesar but he would not risk everything simply on that count, and since much of his debt was most likely to be owed to Crassus, the proposed cancellation would have deprived Caesar's greatest benefactor of his profit. If Crassus and Caesar were deeply involved with Catiline, did they initially attach themselves to a man they thought they could use to pave the way for the elimination of their enemies at his hands, followed by their own takeover of the state? If so, it could not have been long before they realised that he had got out of hand, so were they involved at the start, but then dropped him like a hot potato? Would they have set up Catiline to fail, then stepped in to prevent him from taking power by force of arms, and saved Rome, as Cicero claimed he had done? This all seems unlikely. Crassus preferred to work in the background, influencing people by buying them with cash or other rewards and favours, and both he and Caesar were shrewd enough to realise that armed revolution is a highly unsophisticated method of changing the government. Such a method requires the utmost wariness afterwards, because it creates factions, all aiming at opposition to the leaders but not necessarily in the same ways. Civil war, in other words. Sulla had managed to create the government that he wanted, but many lives were lost while he reached the pinnacle, and his rule was based on fear and intimidation. After his death, most of his legislation was annulled or modified. Just after Sulla died, there was a slight glitch when Aemilius Lepidus tried armed revolution, but it hardly got off the ground before it was quickly nipped in the bud. Did Catiline think he could do better?

Catiline left no personal record and all reports about him are hostile, so the extent of his association, if any, with Caesar and Crassus is not elucidated. The whole business of Catiline's activities did not end until his defeat in 62 BC, but the aftermath continued for much longer. Caesar was never to free himself totally from suspicion that he may have been involved in the conspiracy, and Cicero was to pay a high price for saving the state.

6

Praetor and Propraetor,
62–60 BC

From the late 60s BC, the accounts of the historians, such as Suetonius, Plutarch, Appian, and Dio, are supplemented by the letters of Cicero to Atticus, and to his other friends. These give an invaluable insight into the contemporary political scene, and of course Cicero's personal opinions about events and personalities. The letters begin in 61 BC, and become more abundant for the following years. The correspondence provides a massive amount of day-to-day detail, quite a lot of it concerning Caesar, from his praetorship to his assassination in 44 BC.

Caesar entered his praetorship on 1 January 62. Marcus Porcius Cato was tribune for the same year, 10 December 63 to 9 December 62. The prospect of what Caesar might accomplish once he was in office alarmed the senators. Plutarch relays a story that before Caesar was about to become praetor, which narrows down to the end of December 63, Cato persuaded the Senate to establish a monthly grain dole for the urban poor, costing the state 7.5 million drachmas. It was hoped that by this means the populace would be pacified, and Caesar's influence would be undermined, or at least the corn dole would remove the possibility of food riots, which Caesar could have exploited.[1] This shows how far the Senate was willing to go to undermine Caesar's *popularis* tendencies, and to ensure that he did not gain any credit for instituting the corn dole on his own initiative.

On the very first day as praetor, Caesar put forward a bill aimed at discomfiting Quintus Lutatius Catulus, who had been entrusted with the restoration of the Temple of Jupiter on the Capitol Hill. The temple had been burned down in 83 BC, and Sulla had started the rebuilding work. In 78 BC the ongoing reconstruction was awarded to Catulus and funds had been allocated to this task. Progress had been slow. The temple had been consecrated in 69 BC, though it was in an unfinished state, much as medieval cathedrals could be consecrated before they were complete and religious services could take place without the benefit of an entire building. Seven years after the consecration Catulus had still not completed the Temple of Jupiter. Caesar summoned him to a *contio*, or public meeting, in the Forum, to give an account of the building work and also to explain what had happened to the money, which Caesar said had been embezzled. Catulus was allowed to speak, but not from the elevated platform of the Rostra where speeches were normally made. Caesar deliberately humiliated Catulus by making him speak from the ground. The humiliation was rounded off by the proposal that the responsibility for finishing the temple should be given to another man.[2] This could only mean Pompey, who was on the point of returning home after a series of successful campaigns in the East.

While Caesar was busy cutting Catulus down to size in public, the new consuls, Decimus Iunius Silanus and Lucius Licinius Murena, commencing their term of office on 1 January, were making sacrifices on the Capitol, in accordance with tradition. The consuls were usually accompanied by their friends and presumably clients, and were escorted back to their homes after the sacrifices had been made. When these crowds appeared in the Forum, displaying hostility to the treatment of Catulus, Caesar had to abandon the proceedings. Suetonius explains that Caesar withdrew the proposal because he was overwhelmed by the throngs gathering around him, intent on obstinate opposition. Caesar's lack of success did not matter. He had killed two birds with one stone, achieving the humiliation of his enemy Catulus, and identifying himself as the champion of rectitude in public affairs.

Though Rome was now free of the danger of Catiline and his army, military action was still taking place in Italy. After the execution of the conspirators in Rome at the end of 63 BC, there had been desertions from Catiline's two legions which were based in Etruria, but Catiline and his troops still posed a threat. There was also the worry that further uprisings might be instigated in other parts of Italy, either in sympathy with Catiline, or independently because of some other cause. Groups of people with grievances against Rome could take advantage of the preoccupation with Catiline to make trouble, so praetors were sent out to try to prevent this. Cicero's consular colleague Gaius Antonius Hybrida had been sent against Catiline, but he suffered an attack of gout and withdrew, leaving his deputy Marcus Petreius, a more experienced soldier, to take charge. Catiline had been forced by Metellus Celer to abandon his plan of retreating northwards, and chose to make what turned out to be his final stand at Pistoria, where Petreius defeated him. Catiline and his deputy Manlius were both killed. There would have been no point in surrender.

Before it was clear that there would be no further danger from Catiline, the tribune Metellus Nepos proposed that Pompey should be recalled from the East, together with his army, to restore order in Italy. Nepos had been serving with Pompey, and had been sent back to Rome to look after the great man's interests, but the proposal that Pompey should return at the head of his army to wipe out Catiline and his rebels is unlikely to have been instigated by Nepos alone. Cato blocked Nepos' proposal, delivering a somewhat histrionic speech in the Senate that while he lived, Pompey would never enter the city with soldiers behind him – in other words, 'over my dead body'. A general entering Rome at the head of an army was too recent an occurrence, and at this stage it was not certain whether Pompey would emulate Sulla or submit to senatorial authority.

Caesar supported Nepos when he came to read out the bill on the steps of the Temple of Castor and Pollux. He positioned his chair next to Nepos, but the tribunes Cato and Quintus Minucius Thermus, deliberately insulting the two men, seated themselves between Caesar and Nepos, and prevented Nepos from the customary preliminary reading of the bill. Cato tore it from Nepos' hand, and then when Nepos continued to recite the clauses of the bill from memory, Thermus clamped his hand over Nepos' mouth.[3] If Cato and Minucius Thermus considered it necessary to resort to such crudely violent methods of stopping the bill from being presented to the public, they presumably thought that it stood a good chance of success and Pompey would soon be coming home to save Italy, commanding an army, and sanctioned by law. The shenanigans on the podium of the temple would have been comic but for the seriousness of the riot that ensued. Nepos had foreseen trouble, and had distributed a number of gladiators among the crowd, who at his signal subjected Cato and Thermus to a fierce stoning. Cato, the professed Stoic, endured it stoically, until the consul Murena dragged him away to safety. Nepos called his gladiators to heel when his opponents had fled, then prepared to have the vote taken on his bill. Before he could do so, the supporters of Cato returned, having armed themselves. The bill was never made law.[4]

Nepos went back to the East, after making a somewhat hysterical speech accusing Cato and his friends of plotting against Pompey, ending his oration with the sentiment that they would soon regret their behaviour. It would have been better if he had kept silent and simply taken ship, even though as tribune he was not supposed to leave the city without permission. Caesar also made a speech, justifying the actions of Metellus Nepos and his own part in the proposal. The text survived until Suetonius' day, so he was able to read it, but he adds that in the opinion of Augustus the text was not a polished, published version of Caesar's speech, but a shorthand account of it, in which the writer had not kept up with Caesar's delivery.[5] The attempt to justify himself by means of this speech did not help Caesar.

The Senate was called together and passed the *senatus consultum ultimum*, or last decree, to empower the consuls to dismiss Nepos and Caesar from office. It was decided to strip Nepos of his tribunate, but Cato prevented this from happening. Caesar retained his post, but was forbidden to exercise his functions as praetor. At first he defied the ban and carried on as normal, but it soon became clear that the Senate was willing to use force, so he dismissed his lictors, went home, and stayed there. The first indication that he had a significant following among the populace was revealed at this point, because either the next day or the day after that, the mob gathered outside his house threatening to riot if he was not reinstated. Was this a spontaneous demonstration of the will of the people on behalf of a praetor they knew and liked? Caesar knew how to pull whatever strings were necessary and had by now built up good contacts, so he may have organised the whole demonstration. At any rate, the Senate took it seriously enough, and a meeting was called to decide what to do about the mob gathering outside Caesar's residence. Regardless of whether or not Caesar had engineered the gathering, it could easily have escalated and got out of hand. He quelled the riot, and earned the gratitude of the senators. He was invited to return to the Senate and was soon reinstated.[6]

The shadow of conspiracy still hung over Caesar even after the battle at Pistoria and the deaths of Catiline and his deputy in February 62 BC. According to Dio, sometime later Lucius Vettius, who had joined Catiline, turned informer on a promise of immunity from prosecution, and gave a list of names of men who had been members of the conspiracy.[7] Dio does not mention a story found in other sources, alleging that Caesar had written to Catiline, and Vettius promised to produce a letter in Caesar's own handwriting that would confirm his complicity in the plot. Vettius was backed by Quintus Curius, who was eager to earn the customary reward for informing the authorities, so he was probably convinced that Vettius had a good case. Another man was involved, Novius Niger, the president of the court for dealing with violent crimes, to whom Vettius had brought his information, and Novius had agreed that there was a case for prosecution. Caesar defended himself to the Senate, protesting that he had not supported Catiline and had in fact revealed information to Cicero in advance of the discovery of the plot, and Cicero backed him up.[8] The people too supported Caesar, and Vettius was beaten up in front of the Rostra, then thrown into prison on Caesar's orders. His property was destroyed. Curius lost his expected reward, and Novius Niger was imprisoned because he had presumed to hear a case against a higher-ranking magistrate. Caesar's swift reaction in punishing the men who accused him was within the law. He had made it clear that he would not tolerate such allegations against him, though rumours never ceased. Vettius turned up again during Caesar's consulship, babbling once again about plots, which are equally impenetrable.

Towards the end of the year, in December, Caesar as Pontifex Maximus hosted the festival of the Bona Dea, the Good Goddess, in his house.[9] Only women were allowed to attend this celebration. Caesar's mother Aurelia and his sister Julia presided, though strictly speaking the hostess ought to have been his wife Pompeia. Nothing is known of Caesar's relationship with Pompeia. There were no children from this marriage, which ended in divorce after the festival had been interrupted by the discovery of the quaestor elect Publius Clodius Pulcher, who gate-crashed the proceedings dressed as a woman. It was assumed that he had been having an affair with Pompeia, since he was noted for such behaviour, but what he had to gain by ruining the Bona Dea celebrations is not known. The whole affair could have been quietly brushed aside, dismissed as a puerile prank. Instead it became a public issue, largely because Clodius had several enemies who wished to see him brought down, and this incident could have provided the means of doing so.

Clodius had to be charged with some misdeed, but it was not immediately clear what the charge should be. He had not physically harmed anyone, he had not stolen anything or wrecked the house, nor damaged Caesar's reputation, except in so far as he may have seduced Caesar's wife. The college of *pontifices* and the Vestals were consulted, and it was decided that Clodius had committed sacrilege, an offence against the gods, but there was no standing court that could deal with the charge. The Senate passed a decree to empower the consuls to put a bill before the people to constitute a special court, or *quaestio extraordinaria*, but then there were problems with the jury. Normally the jurors would be chosen by lot, but this case was not normal, and it was proposed that they should be hand-picked. This caused trouble among Clodius' supporters, and the tribune Quintus Fufius Calenus pronounced his veto on the whole decision, especially the hand-picked court. The lawyer Hortensius calmed everyone down, persuaded Fufius to withdraw his veto, and to accept the provisions of the bill. He suggested that the jury should be chosen by lot.[10] The case was becoming a momentous problem. And Caesar's part in all this? He refused to bring a charge against Clodius, even though his mother and sister had given evidence against the offender in his house. His only definite action was to divorce Pompeia, and when asked why he did so, he said that members of his family should be above suspicion. Caesar made no move to stop the prosecution from going ahead, but by refusing to prosecute Clodius, he could keep up relations with him in the future, and, more importantly, Clodius owed him something. The case was still going on when Caesar left for his province of Further Spain in 61 BC.

Caesar was supposed to wait in Rome until the Senate had confirmed his appointment as provincial governor, and had voted him the funds to carry out his allotted tasks. But his debts had reached astronomical proportions, and his creditors were getting restless, so he left early without waiting for confirmation of his post or the allocation of funds. Caesar's debts were legendary, and as yet he had not had much opportunity to amass a fortune to pay them off, except for a short term as quaestor in Spain. Plutarch alleges that he already owed 1,300 talents before he had even taken up any public office, which amounts to 31,200,000 sesterces.[11] Appian reports that Caesar said he needed 25,000,000 sesterces, just to have nothing at all, but as he was about to depart for his province, he settled with his creditors as best he could, which means that Crassus paid off the more pressing debts, as Plutarch asserts. Crassus stood surety for 850 talents, a considerable sum. Plutarch adds that Crassus needed Caesar's energy and his abilities to assist him in his struggle with Pompey.[12]

Suetonius says that Caesar's hasty departure for Spain was contrary to precedent and law, and gives two alternative reasons for it.[13] The most likely reason was his fear of prosecution by his creditors. While he was in office as praetor he could not be prosecuted, but if there was any delay between stepping down from the praetorship and taking up his post as propraetor he could have been classed as a *privatus*, and prosecuted like any other individual without office. He needed to step seamlessly from his office as praetor to his term as propraetor, but there was a delay in assigning provinces in 62–61 BC. This was because the trial of Clodius was holding everything up. On 25 January 61 Cicero wrote to Atticus, with the throwaway line embedded in his other news that 'the praetors have not drawn their provinces yet'. In another letter dated 13 February, Cicero complained that the Senate had decided that no action was to be taken on the distribution of the provinces among the praetors, or the hearing of legations, or on anything until the measure on the formation of the jury to hear Clodius' case was passed.[14]

In connection with Caesar's early departure for Spain, Suetonius adds the cryptic comment that perhaps there had been appeals for help from the allies of Rome, and this may have been why Caesar was in such a hurry to get there.[15] If this was correct, and there had been internal troubles in Spain, it would provide Caesar with an excuse to leave Rome, and then to attack certain tribes within his province when he arrived there, under the heading of peacekeeping. Caesar's term as provincial governor attracts little notice in the sources. In his chronological section, Suetonius dismisses his tenure with the bald statement that he restored order in his province, which provides some support for the earlier comment that the communities in Spain may have asked for Roman assistance. Suetonius then says that Caesar left his province early, without waiting for his successor to arrive. Plutarch says that as soon as he arrived in his province Caesar raised extra troops, as many as ten cohorts, to add to the troops already in the country.[16] These extra soldiers were presumably raised from the natives of the province, who may have joined him willingly if there was internal unrest. It is not known if they equipped themselves, or if Caesar paid them out of the funds allocated to him by the Senate.

With his augmented troops he attacked the tribes of the Callaici and Lusitani. He subdued all the tribes that had not previously submitted to Rome, as far as the outer sea, implying that he arrived at the western coast and the Atlantic. He had covered the same area when he was quaestor, so he was not in entirely unknown territory. Much of the military action was against the bandits who infested the country. Caesar ordered them to come out of their mountain strongholds and settle in the lower lying areas to live there in peace and quiet. This meant submitting to Roman rule, so the bandits refused, giving him the excuse that he needed to attack and defeat them. Some diehards fled to an island off the west coast of Spain, where they managed to repel Caesar's attempted landing from rafts. After a short delay Caesar brought ships from Gades and captured the bandits. He followed up his victory with a display of naval and military strength to other cities, notably Brigantium on the northern coast.

Not all accounts of the ancient authors are laudatory. Dio sneers that although the brigands undoubtedly caused trouble in the province, Caesar knew very well that his demands that the bandits should leave their homes and settle in the plain would not be met, and so he provided himself with an excuse to make war. In reality he could quite easily have cleared all of the bandits away and kept quiet about it, but chose instead to inflate his achievements in his desire for glory.[17] Dio is consistent in his opinion that Caesar was an opportunist, that he created excuses for war so that he would appear to be the avenger not the aggressor, and that he made much of his achievements in Rome for his own self-aggrandisement.

Plutarch acknowledges that Caesar made his fortune in Spain, and in the process he also enriched his troops, who hailed him as Imperator, a great honour.[18] According to Suetonius, Caesar begged for money from the provincials in order to pay his debts, and took booty from towns that he sacked, even after the inhabitants had opened their gates to him.[19] Caesar had obviously won over the soldiers, and had not neglected them, since the promise of booty was what motivated most of them. These skills, and his understanding of the psychology of the provincials and of the soldiers, enabled him to persuade men to follow him, and were to bring Caesar to the summit of his career. Caesar also earned prestige and respect for solving the provincials' problems, mostly concerning debts (and Caesar ought to know how to deal with debts) and arranging peace between different communities. He arranged that debtors should keep their property, but should then pay two thirds of their income every year, keeping one third for themselves, until the debts were cleared. Appian has a different version of Caesar in Spain, alleging that he neglected his civilian duties and the administration of justice because these matters did not serve his purpose, which Appian implies was the conquest of independent tribes and making them tributary to Rome. Appian adds that Caesar made sure that he despatched money to the treasury.[20]

Somewhere between these extremes there is probably more to Caesar's credit, but he emerges as wholly concerned with his own prestige and reputation and determined to extract as much wealth as possible to pay off his debts and accumulate financial resources in preparation for his next political step, the consulship. The fact that every provincial governor, with the notable exception of Lucius Licinius Lucullus, seemed to regard the provinces as fair game does not excuse Caesar, but Caesar did it differently. He was careful to ensure that some of the wealth was distributed among his soldiers, and no doubt among the friends he had taken with him, and he also enriched the treasury in Rome, but not on the same scale as Pompey had done from his eastern campaigns. In arranging peace between tribes and communities Caesar placed them morally in his debt, and perhaps he conciliated the most prominent provincials with assurances that he would represent their interests in Rome. In this way he would gain not only money but loyal clients to add to those he already had in Italy. Some of his financial gain may have come to him in the form of gifts. A law of the late third century BC forbade the acceptance of gifts in return for acting as an advocate in trials, but far away in Spain the rules were perhaps relaxed, and there were other ways of helping people apart from acting on their behalf in legal matters.

There would be grateful men and women who appreciated Caesar's activities in suppressing bandits, bringing peace to the settled areas, hearing cases in court, and so on. Perhaps he restored stolen property to those who had been robbed by the bandits, and the response may have been along the lines of 'How can we ever thank you?', and Caesar would have thought of something that circumvented the laws on provincial government. The character of Caesar as we now understand it, with all its accrued heroism over the centuries, makes it difficult to imagine that he would have stooped to begging for money, as Suetonius says.[21] Gifts freely given, on the other hand, would have been more acceptable. There would have been gifts from people whom he had helped, and perhaps he dropped hints, without actually begging for money, from those who asked for his help and therefore hoped to be grateful to him in the future. It was not strictly legal, but others got away with it.

When Caesar was governor, the provincials living in both Spanish provinces were still emerging from the aftermath of the war against Sertorius which Pompey had brought to a conclusion. Pompey had become patron to some leading Spanish nobles, and Caesar could emulate him. As a patron Caesar was loyal and supportive, but no doubt he chose carefully before engaging in any kind of relationship. One important contact from Spain was Lucius Cornelius Balbus from Gades, whom Caesar probably met when he was quaestor. Balbus had originally become a protégé of Pompey when the general was fighting against Sertorius. Later Balbus transferred his allegiance to Caesar, who benefited greatly as quaestor and then governor in Spain from his association with him. Balbus was extremely wealthy, a factor that probably had a bearing on the association, at least from Caesar's point of view. In these early days it may have been clear to Balbus that Caesar was destined for greater things, and diverting some of his wealth to support the young man was potentially a good investment.

Significantly, although Caesar was accused of sacking places that had submitted to him peacefully, there is no record of any accusation of extortion, and no provincial delegates from Spain arrived in Rome to ask an advocate to take up a case against him because of his behaviour as governor.

Events in Rome had presumably not escaped Caesar's notice. He would have had friends and agents in the city to inform him of what was happening, so he could keep his finger on the pulse of political activity. Pompey had landed at Brundisium with his troops in December 62, and had dismissed his soldiers. He had refused to emulate Sulla by marching on Rome, and though he had expressed a wish to stand for the consulship *in absentia*, he did not force his way to the elections when he was refused permission by the Senate. Almost immediately on his return to Italy, Pompey divorced his wife Mucia, the mother of his two sons Gnaeus and Sextus, and his daughter Pompeia.[22] One of Mucia's alleged lovers was Caesar, but Mucia's infidelity was not the prime reason for the divorce. It meant severing relations with her relatives the Metelli. She was the half-sister of Metellus Nepos, Pompey's former officer. Pompey considered that the time had come to ally himself with the senatorial oligarchy, and he proposed a marriage alliance with a niece of Cato. But Cato rebuffed him, so Pompey was the most eligible bachelor in Rome. When Caesar returned from Spain he would take advantage of this, and offer his daughter Julia to Pompey, thus arranging what seems to have been a happy marriage, which contented both partners and Caesar himself.

Pompey approached Rome as conquering hero, not conquering tyrant, and stayed at his villa outside Rome until he could hold his triumphs, in the plural. Until then he was not allowed to cross the *pomerium*, or boundary of the city, because he was still technically a general in command of troops. His triumphs were not held until September 61, over the pirates, Mithridates, and Tigranes of Armenia. Naturally they were splendid.

In the spring of 61, Clodius was eventually tried in the special court that had been set up. Cicero reported on it to Atticus in June, deploring the fact that Clodius had been acquitted.[23] It was a fairly narrow margin, thirty-one votes for acquittal to twenty-five against, but it still let Clodius go free. Cicero blamed Hortensius for smoothing the problems of the hand-picked jury and persuading Fufius to propose a jury to be selected by lot. Hortensius never imagined that any jury could possibly fail to condemn Clodius. Hortensius was perhaps just naïve, but Crassus was the real villain, according to Cicero, because he had summoned the jurors to his house and bought most of them with ready cash, promises of favours in the future or introductions to young men of good family, and certain ladies, for purposes that do not need to be explained. In his letter to Atticus, Cicero's spluttering disbelief and rage can still be heard. Twenty-five brave individuals had dared to go against Clodius, but thirty-one of the most worthless scoundrels had blotted out right and justice, for cash, and a third criminal had been let loose on the country by a jury, the two others from the past being Lentulus Sura and Catiline who had stood trial and likewise been acquitted.[24] Clodius was free, but he came out of the court with a grudge against Cicero. He had tried to prove that he was not in the city on the date when the offence at the Bona Dea festival had been committed, and he had persuaded a friend to testify that he had been at his house all the time. But Cicero had destroyed his alibi by attesting that he had seen Clodius in Rome on the relevant date. A short time later, Clodius would have his revenge.

Meanwhile, Cicero attached himself to Pompey, though the great man was never sufficiently effusive about the fact that Cicero had saved the state in 63 BC. However, the association was noticed by the people, who by June 61 were calling Pompey 'Gnaeus Cicero'.[25] Since the trial of Clodius, Cicero had been out of favour, but in the shadow of Pompey he was no longer hissed at in public.

For Pompey himself, affairs were not going well. Undoubtedly successful as a general, political success was denied him. Pompey had won bigger and better victories than any Roman before him and enriched the city on a massive scale, greater than any other general even after the most brilliant campaigns. He had been thwarted of his wish to stand for the consulship *in absentia*, but he still had an unassailable reputation and a wide circle of agents and clients. His influence ought to have been preponderant, and he could have expected that the settlement of his veterans and the ratification of his arrangements for the eastern provinces and allied states would be a brief formality. But the climate in Rome had changed; the aristocrats had gathered strength and a few of the leading members closed ranks against him. His main opponents were Cato and Lucullus, the latter still smarting under the humiliation of being wrested from the eastern command and then watching from Rome as Pompey went from victory to victory. Now he persuaded the Senate that Pompey's settlement of the East should be dissected clause by clause. Cato supported him, using his particular talents for talking ideas to death in debates.[26]

The settlement of Pompey's veterans was also dragged out. The tribune Lucius Flavius had proposed a land bill to provide for Pompey's soldiers, and also to alleviate the pressure on the city by removing the urban poor to the countryside. In January 60, Cicero dismissed the bill as unoriginal, and compared it to the weak law proposed by Plotius, or Plautius, in 70 BC, when Pompey and Crassus were consuls. By March 60 Flavius' land bill had still not been passed, and Cicero explained to Atticus that the only popularity it enjoyed was derived from its supporter, meaning Pompey himself, who had set his heart on having his veterans settled by means of the bill. The main problem, as always, concerned the landowners who might be dispossessed, so Cicero rejected all the clauses that might impinge on private rights, except the one advocating the purchase of land using the revenues accruing from Pompey's eastern conquests, which would enable the urban poor to leave the city and farm lands of their own. The Senate opposed the entire bill, mostly because the senators feared that Pompey was angling for special powers.[27] By June 60 interest in the bill had waned, so Pompey and his veterans were still in limbo.

There were other interesting features of political life in Rome that will have given Caesar food for thought while he was in Spain. There had been trouble in Transalpine Gaul at the turn of the years 62 to 61 BC, when Gaius Pomptinus quelled a rebellion by the Allobroges.[28] The tribesmen had failed to find solutions for their various problems when they had sent ambassadors to Rome just before Catiline's conspiracy had been unveiled, and they had finally resorted to war. Pomptinus held a triumph for his victories. Trouble broke out again, when the Gallic tribe of the Aedui, allied to Rome, were attacked and defeated. Cicero calls them our brothers, *fratres nostri*.[29] Fear of a major war was the main topic of conversation, and the two consuls were to cast lots for Cisalpine and Transalpine Gaul instead of going to the provinces originally assigned to them. It was proposed to send ambassadors to the other Gallic tribes to pacify them and prevent them from taking sides, and names had been chosen by ballot: Quintus Metellus Creticus and Lucius Flaccus. The trouble was that nothing could be done at the moment, because the Senate had been forced to suspend all other business until another problem had been settled. This was the plight of the tax collectors, or *publicani*, who were in the embarrassing situation of having put in an excessively ambitious bid for the tax farm of Asia, and now, finding that they would be out of pocket, wanted it rescinded. At the beginning of December 61 Cicero had arranged a hearing for them, but the matter was still not solved in January 60, largely because Cato was being particularly obstructive. Cicero expressed impatience to Atticus, saying that Cato displayed more consistency and honesty than judgement or ability.[30] In another letter he says that Cato, despite his honesty and good intentions, was doing a lot of harm.[31] Another snippet from Cicero, in January 60, concerned Clodius. The tribune Gaius Herennius was trying to convert the patrician Clodius to a plebeian, so that he too could stand for election as a tribune. It was proposed that the people should vote on the matter in the Campus Martius.[32]

In June 60 Cicero reported to Atticus that Caesar was due to arrive in Rome in a few days' time. Cicero was hopeful that he would be able to influence Caesar, to persuade him to be a true patriot and put the state first.[33] The senators had formed their opinion of Caesar as a *popularis* and no doubt feared what he would try to achieve if he became consul in 59 BC, as he obviously intended to do. So far there had been some consistency in his career, and some principles that he had adhered to. He was not a rabble-rouser just for the sake of making a point. Cicero had said that the speech he had made advocating imprisonment instead of summary execution for the Catilinarians showed that Caesar was not a demagogue, but a man with a true appreciation of the interests of the people.[34]

Caesar had associated himself with popular causes, but had chosen more carefully than most which causes he adopted and how he went about trying to solve them. He had prosecuted provincial governors for extortion at the behest of provincials or on his own behalf, but the men were usually blatantly guilty. The fact that they escaped condemnation did not harm his career because he had been seen to be associated with oppressed or powerless individuals against a jury composed of biased individuals whose acquittals went against all reason, except for their own interests and those of their cliques. Caesar had supported the legislation to restore the rights of tribunes that Sulla had destroyed, and he also advocated the restoration of civil rights to the exiled followers of the rebel Aemilius Lepidus, and later in the mid-60s he supported the restoration of citizenship to the sons of the men whom Sulla had proscribed. He had championed the award of citizenship to the Transpadane colonies which had only Latin rights, and made himself popular by speaking in favour of the bills of Gabinius and Manilius to bestow special commands on Pompey, the first of which, for a command against the pirates, would release pressure on the food supply. As aedile he had thrown himself and lots of his borrowed money into games and shows, and either then or two years earlier he had also thrown money at the improvement of the Via Appia, so at least some part of the population will have been grateful for the entertainments and the improved transport facilities. Consistently, he had taken action against the execution of citizens without trial, though his prosecution of the aged Rabirius in order to make his point does not redound to his credit. It is to be hoped that he never intended to have the old man condemned and executed, having previously arranged with Quintus Metellus Celer to stop all proceedings by raising the flag on the Janiculum, thus putting a halt to the trial. There was a ruthless streak in Caesar that makes it permissible to believe that he would have condemned and killed Rabirius, and this is what the senators probably feared.

The cultivation of popular causes may have endeared him to the people, but it frightened the Senate. No one could be certain if Caesar acted according to strict principles, like Cato, or whether he was just a clever opportunist who saw advantages for himself in certain situations, while judiciously avoiding potentially detrimental occasions. This is the clever, ambitious, devious, calculating politician who was coming back to Rome in summer 60 BC. Since he had to be in Rome in time for the consular elections for 59 BC, Caesar left Spain before his successor had arrived. There was much to think about as he was journeying to Italy. The tax collectors had still not found satisfaction, Clodius was still a patrician, the Gauls were not pacified, Pompey's eastern organisation had not been ratified, and his soldiers were still awaiting their allotments.

Caesar had been voted a triumph for his achievements in pacifying the Lusitanian bandits and restoring order in his province. Until he held the triumph he was still in command of his troops, and as a general with troops at his back he could not enter the city to stand for election as consul for 59 BC. He had set in motion the preparations for his triumphal entry into the city, since a procession with all the spoils of war could hardly be arranged at the last minute. After all, Pompey had just held three triumphs, more splendid than anyone had ever seen before, so Caesar had to make his triumph as magnificent as possible. Unfortunately, here was a slight problem. According to the law, candidates for office had to be present in Rome, in person, to canvass, so Caesar asked permission from the Senate to be allowed to campaign for election *in absentia*, so that he could continue with the organisation for his triumph at the same time as he conducted his electoral campaign. Pompey had been refused permission to stand for election *in absentia*, so it was unlikely that the Senate would decide in Caesar's favour, but it was still worth asking. It was principally Cato who blocked this request, making it clear that Caesar must make his choice. He must resign his command and forfeit the triumph to be able to enter the city and become a candidate for the consulship, or he could hold the triumph and give up any idea of becoming consul for the following year.[35] It was a great honour to be awarded a triumph, not an honour to be cast lightly aside.[36] Did Cato and his small band of intransigent adherents in the Senate imagine that Caesar was so vain that he would prefer the triumph over the chance of becoming consul? Surely they knew by this time that he was intent on obtaining the highest office as soon as possible, so he was hardly likely to choose to hold the triumph and then stand for election in 59 for 58 BC. It is difficult to ascribe to Cato and his friends any motive other than spite. Did they thwart Caesar to prove to themselves and to others that he was so intent on power that he disregarded the honour that had been bestowed on him? Whatever they hoped to gain, history shows that Caesar abandoned the preparations for the triumph, and entered the city to begin canvassing for election as consul.

The Senate had gone even further to thwart him in his future career after his consulship. Anticipating that he might become consul, the Senate utilised the law of Gaius Gracchus passed in 123 BC, that stipulated that consular provinces should be allocated before the elections, and the senators made sure that there was no territorial province to be assigned to the retiring consuls of 59 BC. The Gracchan law, or a supplementary law, forbade any tribunician veto on these measures.[37] The main responsibilities for the retiring consuls of 59 BC were to be the care of the woodlands and paths, and the eradication of bandits who infested them. This is closer to the term 'province' in its original sense, meaning a task of any description, not necessarily indicative of a territorial command, but it was applied to the first territories that Rome acquired and was then always used to describe them. This lowly task of administration of woods and pathways for the retiring consuls of 59 BC was meant to be the Senate's safeguard if Caesar did become consul, since the senators had no doubt guessed correctly that he would succeed in being elected.[38] The intransigence of the Senate in opposing Pompey and frustrating his wishes for two years, and in churlishly making Caesar choose between pomp and circumstance and real power, merely set the stage for a momentous year, involving the Senate's humiliation and the launch of the conquering hero who would bring the whole of Gaul within the Roman Empire. In the last act, the whole of the Roman world would be brought under the control of a single man.

7

Consul, 59 BC

The elections for the two consuls of 59 BC were conducted by polarised groups, canvassing for Caesar on the one hand and Marcus Calpurnius Bibulus, the son-in-law of Cato, on the other. Cato was morally opposed to electoral bribery, but it was vitally important to him to have a member of his own circle in power and in opposition to Caesar, so Cato fully endorsed the large-scale distribution of cash as a persuasive measure to influence the voters to choose Bibulus. As for Caesar, both Crassus and Pompey lent their support for his electoral campaign, but their association became more than just two individuals helping a third to canvass for the consulship. Appian describes in simple terms the inception of the coalition of the three men, beginning with the hostility of Lucullus to Pompey. Lucullus thought that he had defeated Mithridates and left him so weak that all Pompey had to do was to finish the job, but now Pompey was claiming all the credit. Appian's version is that Crassus, always opposed to Pompey, sided with Lucullus, which annoyed Pompey, so he made friends with Caesar, and promised to support him for the consulship of 59 BC. Then Caesar approached Crassus, and brought him into the circle, thus creating what was popularly termed *Tricaranus*, the title of a pamphlet written by Varro, meaning the Three-Headed Monster.[1] The text of this pamphlet, and the date when it was published, are not known. Suetonius also places the formation of the compact between the three men before the election of Caesar as consul, asserting that Caesar patched up the quarrel between Pompey and Crassus.[2]

The formation and development of the Three-Headed Monster was probably not quite so straightforward, nor so immediate. In modern terms it is the First Triumvirate, but this is a misleading concept, implying that the three men had joined together in an officially authorised political organisation, but it was never a formal compact and was never officially recognised by the state. Each of the three joined the other two simply to further his own ends. The title First Triumvirate is a modern convenience, based on the somewhat tenuous similarity with the so-called Second Triumvirate (actually the first official version) when another three men, Octavian, Mark Antony and Aemilius Lepidus, joined forces in the aftermath of Caesar's assassination. The only real similarity is that three men got together and organised the state for their own ends, but the Second Triumvirate was not remotely comparable to the so-called First. Octavian, Antony and Lepidus were very careful to have their alliance officially recognised, sanctified even, by law. They operated under the title *IIIviri* (or *Tresviri*) *rei publicae constituendae*, literally three men empowered to reconstruct the state. This was prefigured by Sulla's appointment as Dictator with a similar purpose and title, although it was a little more specific, *Dictator legibus faciendis et rei publicae constituendae*, proclaiming Sulla's authorisation to make laws and to restore the Republic. As Triumvirs, an English version of the Latin title, Octavian, Antony and Lepidus were granted powers equal to the consuls for a term of five years. They were empowered to command armies, promote legislation and raise taxes. Caesar, Crassus and Pompey had none of these advantages. They were quite outside the state machinery, having joined forces for the achievement of certain goals, and to achieve anything they had to operate by ordinary, traditional methods, that is by supporting some of their associates and seeing them installed in important posts, or by becoming consuls themselves. Their association was reinforced in 56 BC, at the so-called conference at Luca (modern Lucca), which is described below in its chronological context.

Although Caesar's candidacy for the consulship of 59 BC was backed by Crassus and Pompey, this does not mean that his two supporters were acting in unison. The exact date for the beginning of the coalition of Caesar, Pompey and Crassus is disputed, largely because there is simply no evidence for a specific start date. It is not even feasible to seek for such a narrowly confined date, since the agreement was informal and personal, and probably unrecorded in any form. They did not give themselves and their association a proper title, with a set of rules and regulations, and presumably did not call formal meetings and take minutes, though Dio says that the three men ratified their agreement with oaths.[3] The coalition was more likely a gradual process rather than a sudden decision, arrived at by debating around a conference table. The Second Triumvirate was formed in this more formal way, when Octavian, Antony and Lepidus met on an island in the middle of a river, most probably at Bologna (ancient Bononia), but another suggestion is that their meeting was at Mutina.

As Goldsworthy points out, the coalition of Caesar, Pompey and Crassus probably began by letter.[4] Before Caesar's election campaign, there would probably have been an exchange of tentative suggestions, probing to discover the temperament of each of the future partners. It may have been Caesar who made the first move while still in Spain, or at least on his way back to Rome, perhaps by approaching Pompey, writing something like 'sorry to hear your *acta* for the eastern territories and your hopes for veteran settlement have been so long delayed, perhaps if I become consul I can be of use to you?' This is more acceptable than suggesting that Pompey wrote to Caesar asking when he was coming back and perhaps he would appreciate some assistance in the consular elections. The driving force, according to Suetonius, was Caesar, who associated himself with Pompey and then reconciled Pompey with Crassus, after which he made a compact with both of them.[5] It would seem logical to the later ancient authors to attribute the compact between Caesar and Pompey to the need for ratification of Pompey's eastern settlements. This is how Appian viewed the situation, saying that Pompey made friends with Caesar because the Senate would not ratify his arrangements for the eastern territories, and then it was Caesar who brought in Crassus and persuaded the two men to sink their differences.[6] Plutarch does not venture to suggest when the union of three began, but passes judgement, in the biographies of both Caesar and Pompey, that it was not the quarrel between Pompey and Caesar that led to the civil wars, but their friendship, during which they collaborated to overthrow the aristocracy and only then began to fall out with each other. In the biography of Pompey, Plutarch credits Cato with this observation, labelling the association of Pompey and Caesar as the greatest evil that befell Rome.[7] The Three-Headed Monster is ignored by Plutarch, and he does not describe Crassus as the partner of the other two men, except in so far as he is acknowledged as a supporter of Caesar in his bid for the consulship.

Velleius Paterculus, writing in the early Empire, summarised what each of the three hoped to gain from their association, which he pronounced damaging to Rome, the rest of the world, and ultimately to the participants themselves. He says that Pompey needed Caesar to push through the legislation to settle his veterans and ratify his eastern arrangements, while Caesar, by making a concession to the prestige of Pompey would increase his own. Caesar was content to increase his own power, while all the odium for assuming great power was thrown on Pompey. As for Crassus, Velleius thought that by using the influence of Pompey and the power of Caesar, he could achieve the prominence that he could not gain on his own account.[8] The ancient authors do not mention that Caesar would benefit greatly from the fact that Pompey and Crassus were extremely wealthy, and an election campaign was an expensive business.

The union of the three can probably be traced back to the election campaigns in 60 BC or even before then, but this does not mean that in this early stage it deserves the modern appellation as the First Triumvirate.[9] It has been argued that even at the end of 60 BC, some months after the elections had been held, there was no evidence of total unity between the three men. Cicero wrote to Atticus, probably in December, explaining how he had received a visit from Caesar's friend Cornelius Balbus, who relayed the message that Caesar would take advice during his consulship from Pompey and from Cicero. Balbus also promised to try to reconcile Pompey and Crassus, which implies that they were still estranged from each other.[10] An alternative suggestion, interpreting this letter from Cicero in a different light, is that the Three-Headed Monster was already formed, but the three men still wished to keep their association secret, most especially from Cicero, using their front man Balbus to keep up the deceit. Two opposing theories have been suggested to support these alternative viewpoints. Taking Cicero's letter at face value, it is affirmed that Caesar could survive the election campaigns with Crassus and Pompey each supporting him on an individual basis, but when he became consul it would be more advantageous to have them working together, because then all their clients and adherents would be singing from the same song sheet. According to this theory, Caesar probably waited until he was in power to work on the two men to sink their differences and pool their resources to enable him to put through his intended legislation.[11] On the other hand, a counter argument runs that the three men deliberately deceived Cicero and the senators, but in fact they were already working together before and during the elections in 60 BC, because it would be damaging if Pompey and Crassus were not reconciled and their clients and their followers would therefore be working against each other for the elections. Dio asserts that if Caesar befriended one without the other, he would incur the enmity of the neglected one, and in a separate passage, Dio says that the clients of all three were in harmony with each other.[12]

Modern authors suggest that Caesar used all his charm to reconcile Pompey and Crassus before the elections, and that the three were united in 60 BC, but their association was not widely known until January 59, which is corroborated by Dio, who says that the three men concealed their association deliberately, even going so far as to pretend to be in opposition to each other on certain issues.[13] Canfora puts a different interpretation on Cicero's letter, cited above, concerning the visit of Balbus in December 60, suggesting that the 'pact' between the three men was due to start on 1 January 59 when Caesar took up his consulship.[14]

As consul Caesar was already perceived as a clever and potentially ruthless politician. He had successfully pursued the middle path between the Marian and Sullan factions, and was clearly intent of forging a successful career for himself. The consulship was not going to satisfy him as the summit of this envisaged career. He would always want more, and ultimately this would probably mean supreme power, and on this count, he was feared. The senators foresaw that his relentless accretion of power would depend upon a prestigious provincial command after his consulship, and the Senate had already made feeble attempts to prevent Caesar from obtaining what he wanted by declaring the post-59 BC consular provinces as the care and protection of forests and roadways. This arrangement could only be validated if the retiring consuls of 60 BC, Metellus Celer, chosen by lot to be governor of Transalpine Gaul, and Lucius Afranius as governor of the Cisalpine province, successfully countered the threat of tribal warfare by the end of 59 BC. If war was looming in the north of Italy and in the Gallic provinces, the retiring consuls of 59 could hardly spend the whole of 58 BC caring for woodlands and paths and combatting banditry.

Before Caesar's consulship began, Cicero wrote to Atticus that he hoped that he might be able to influence Caesar to adopt a more patriotic stance, in other words to act for the good of the country and not simply for his own ends.[15] Clearly Cicero and other senators feared disruption, but they were probably unable to predict the details of Caesar's policies and just how the disruption would make itself felt. It was obvious that Caesar would introduce a new land bill, and there were several loose ends still not tied up since the return of Pompey from the East, so it was probably clear to contemporaries that there would be some kind of wheeling and dealing between the two of them. All Pompey's efforts to install his own candidates in significant offices had come to nothing. His supporters Marcus Pupius Piso, who was consul in 61 BC, and Lucius Afranius, consul the following year, were ineffective, and the tribune Flavius had introduced a land bill that met with the usual intransigence and defeat. The result was that the settlement of Pompey's veteran soldiers and the ratification of his eastern conquests seemed as far away in 59 BC as they had been in 61 BC.

At the consular elections Caesar and Calpurnius Bibulus were voted in, Caesar with a large majority over Bibulus, which gave him priority to introduce his legislation first when each consul took up his post in January. Suetonius lists two measures which Caesar probably dealt with at the earliest opportunity, one of which would need to be in place before any serious state business began. Caesar's first enactment, according to Suetonius, advocated the compilation of a daily record of the debates in the Senate and of matters laid before the people. The record was to be made public so that everyone, not just the people who had been present and had heard the debates, would be able to find out what had been said and done, and more importantly, by whom.[16] No senator would be able deny the opinions that he had expressed. The publication of records may have discouraged some men from giving their true opinion, at least for a short time.

Caesar's next measure was designed to placate Bibulus. Each alternate month, the *fasces*, symbols of authority, were carried before the presiding consuls, and as a mark of respect to Bibulus as well as to gain popularity, Caesar revived an old custom which had lapsed, by declaring that during the months when Bibulus held the *fasces*, he himself would have his lictors walk behind him, with only a clerk in front of him, so that his display of power would be muted.[17]

The land bill was probably ready for presentation to the Senate on 1 January. As Goldsworthy points out, Caesar held the *fasces* that month, and in February Bibulus would be the holder, so there was every need to have the bill ready very quickly in order to observe the obligatory twenty-four day interval before presenting the bill to the people.[18] In December 60 Cicero wrote to Atticus discussing his options when the expected land bill was introduced. At this stage Cicero could not have known precisely what Caesar was going to propose, except in so far as there would be a continuous thread running through all land bills, which could differ only in their details. But a land bill was imminent, and Cicero, without knowing what it entailed, debated what he should do. He had three main choices. He would have to oppose the bill very strongly, bringing upon himself a political struggle by which he might or might not earn some prestige, or he could choose to stay out of the fray and keep silent. Alternatively he could support it, and he understood from Caesar's secretary Cornelius Balbus, who visited him in December, that this is what Caesar expected him to do.[19] In the end Cicero decided not to support the bill, thus depriving Caesar of his oratorical skills that may have persuaded senators to vote for it.

The text of Caesar's land bill was most likely a product of collusion between Caesar and his friends, probably including some input from Pompey and Crassus. The collaboration in compiling the new bill would have to be done in the last months of 60 BC, even if Caesar had already made a start independently, possibly even before he was successfully elected. Gelzer says that he probably worked on the bill and its provisions for most of 60 BC.[20] Caesar could not have produced the bill entirely unaided. He and his friends presumably made an intensive study of the previous land bills, proposed by other tribunes, perhaps going back as far as the Gracchi and Livius Drusus, and definitely studying the bills put forward by Servilius Rullus and Lucius Flavius. Caesar and his friends would not only study the clauses of these bills, and thereby decide which of them was relevant to the present circumstances and therefore worthy of inclusion in the new bill, but also would no doubt have examined precisely why the previous bills had been defeated, identifying which clauses would be likely to incense certain senators and making efforts to pre-empt such criticism, or to package the inevitable unpalatable suggestions in a more subtle and persuasive manner. Caesar could not have been ignorant of the perpetual need for land among the urban poor, and for the veterans of various wars who needed lands to cultivate when they were discharged. There were potentially inflammatory problems in the redistribution of land if people already settled had to be uprooted. Caesar wished to avoid the thorny problem of confiscation of land and the eviction of farmers, which had been one of the main objections to Flavius' bill.[21] Fortunately there were uncultivated lands in Italy that could be exploited.[22]

The promoter of the bill would be Caesar as consul, so he had to be well-versed in the clauses to be able to defend them with conviction and fluency. In presenting the land bill himself, Caesar departed from custom. Plutarch sneers that it was to be expected that such a bill would have been presented by a most radical tribune, but not by a consul.[23] All the tribunes who had tried to promote a land bill in the last decades had met with defeat, no matter how carefully they drafted their bills. One major problem with the land question was the lack of any co-ordinated long-term plan. Land bills were usually reactive rather than pro-active, formulated only in response to a crisis that had actually occurred, or to one that was looming, and there had been no officials of greater weight than the tribunes on the front line to present legislation.[24] Caesar decided to promote the bill in person, with greater authority behind him in the Senate than the tribunes could achieve. He could have decided to select or even bribe a likely candidate to be elected tribune and take up office in December 60, and then put him to work in promoting a land bill, standing by while the tribune either got it right or made a mess of it, without being able to control it directly. It was too important to risk using someone else who may not possess highly polished oratorical skills or the fortitude to stand up to a hostile Senate.

In presenting the bill for the first time, Caesar attempted to keep within the accepted parameters of the law, going through the proper channels, approaching the Senate, hopefully reaching agreement with the senators, and then presenting the bill to the people for ratification and conversion into law. He presumably did not expect that the bill would be passed into law without argument escalating into tumult, but he had tried to smooth over all the stumbling blocks of the earlier bills. There were to be no compulsory purchases of land, and therefore no compulsory evictions. Only the men who wished to sell would be approached, and the price to be paid for their lands was to be based on the last census ratings so that no one would be able to make a quick profit from inventing new prices more compatible with their own estimation of what the land was worth. The cash for the purchase of land was already available, derived from the profits of Pompey's eastern conquests. The settlement of veterans could therefore be paid for from the proceeds of the victories that the soldiers had helped to win. There was to be no disruption to the earlier settlements of Sulla's veterans, so no one should feel under threat. Unjustly evicted farmers could be used by Caesar's opponents, especially if landless people were forced into Rome, adding to the urban mass. All that would be achieved was to remove one set of people from Rome and replace them with a different set, only this time it would be the urban poor with grudges.

The bill was primarily aimed at the creation of allotments for the urban poor so that the pressure on the city's resources would be alleviated. Some, if not all, of Pompey's veterans would be settled, but only one ancient source mentions veterans. Dio creates a speech for Pompey in which he says that he can honour the promises made to his soldiers, who had been waiting for lands for two years, during which time Pompey's plans were repeatedly thwarted in the Senate.[25]

One of the major stumbling blocks of previous land bills concerned the fertile land of Campania, especially the areas around Capua. The *ager Campanus* had come under direct Roman control after the war with Hannibal, when the states which had sided with the Carthaginians had their lands confiscated as punishment. Under Roman control the land was declared to belong to the public, and had been occupied mostly by squatters, including some senators, whose estates usually covered a large acreage. The farmers were supposed to pay rent to the state, but this was not strongly enforced. The well-watered agricultural lands of Campania were often targeted as sites for settlement of the urban poor or for veteran soldiers, but this usually involved the eviction of people who had been farming it for years and regarded it as their property. Caesar promised that Campanian lands would not be touched. There was to be a commission of twenty men to oversee the reorganisation of the land and the distribution of the allotments, and Caesar deliberately excluded himself from membership of the commission so that he could not be accused of seeking power and prestige.

He also promised that as he presented each clause, if senators objected strongly he would withdraw the offending section. Even Caesar's enemies had to acknowledge that his bill covered almost everything and was well drafted. Modern authors agree that the bill was well-constructed, sensible and necessary, and that there could be no serious objections to it except that Caesar would gain far too much popularity from it.[26] Meier says that it did not rob anyone.[27] Some senators of Cato's and Bibulus' factions objected on principle, and discussion went on and on. When Cato was asked for his opinion of the bill in the Senate, he held the floor for a long time. This would be towards the end of the debate, because senators were usually asked to speak in descending order of rank, and Cato had not reached the praetorship. Cato talked *ad infinitum*. This was one of his usual ploys to delay proceedings, or on occasion to talk a bill into an early death. He had been asked for his opinion, so it was not proper for anyone to stop him, and he had only to continue speaking until dark, in which case the session had to be ended without the opportunity for votes to be taken on the topic under discussion. Cicero refers to a different occasion in December 61, in which Cato was due to speak, but the day ended before he got his turn.[28] During his vocal marathon concerning the land bill, Cato did not object to it outright. He admitted that there was some merit to the bill, mostly because the other speakers had eagerly supported it and it would have seemed churlish to disagree with the majority opinion. Instead, Cato suggested that this was not the most appropriate time to introduce such a bill. He did not round off his speech by using that conclusion as the finale, but just went on talking.

Caesar's response was the wrong one. He probably foresaw that Cato would do everything in his power to delay proceedings at every meeting of the Senate, so he silenced him on this occasion by ordering his lictors to take Cato to prison.[29] This merely played into Cato's hands, because Caesar was now seen as a man who would get his own way by force; not quite another Sulla, but with the potential to behave like the Dictator. It may have seemed to some senators that Caesar's affable mask had slipped.[30] The soldier Marcus Petreius, the nemesis of Catiline at Pistoria, began to march out of the Senate, and when Caesar asked why he was leaving, he said he preferred to be in prison with Cato than in the Senate with Caesar.[31] The story has accrued a few extra and sometimes contradictory versions. An alternative to the lone stand of Petreius is that many of the senators trooped out to join Cato, but this may be a conflation with the imprisonment of the consul Metellus Celer, when the senators held their meetings at the prison with Metellus. Plutarch does not specify the context, merely relating how Cato objected to some of the laws that Caesar proposed, and as he was taken off to prison the people followed him looking dejected, so Caesar quietly asked one of the tribunes to release him.[32] Suetonius places the story of Cato's arrest in a separate context, together with other examples of Caesar's strong-arm tactics, including his harsh treatment of Lucullus, and his revenge on Cicero by helping Clodius to become a plebeian, and then tribune, bringing about the exile of the famous orator.[33]

The inconclusive end of that day's business was no doubt a depressing time for Caesar. He had to relent and let Cato go free. Meier suggests that Cato's obstruction was spun out because of a fear that the bill would pass, and he also questions whether Caesar wished to carry on the debate after Cato was taken away, hoping to get the bill passed without him.[34] Before business could be resumed in the following days, the senators would have time to think about each clause of the land bill, and they could mull over whatever Cato had said in opposition to it. There could be endless debate all over again. This is what the Senate had done to Pompey's bill for the settlement of the East, until it wilted. Caesar had no intention of letting this happen; there was so much else he wanted to do in the rest of the year. He rallied quickly, perhaps the very next day, by calling a meeting in the Forum, to speak to the people from the Rostra outside the Senate House. He asked Bibulus to give his opinion of the land bill, but the consul would not approve it. He did not have any valid objections, but gave the same reasons Cato had delivered in the Senate, that the bill should not be made law at this particular time, which implies that the two of them had conferred to decide what stance they would take against a bill that was reasonable, highly sensible, and desired by the people. Bibulus was being manipulated into revealing his stubborn intransigence, because all the time, as Caesar repeatedly tried to persuade him to have the bill approved by the Senate and then presented to the people for ratification, he was making it clear to the audience that the bill could pass if only Bibulus would give his consent, thus portraying his consular colleague as the single obstacle to having the land bill made law. Bibulus persisted in his opposition, finally making a mistake in bursting out with the ill-advised remark, 'You shall not have it this year, even if you all want it'.[35] This was a highly provocative action, displaying pure aristocratic disdain for the populace, and more importantly it thwarted people's expectations of the new land law.[36] There may have been some violence after this demonstration of ill-will by Bibulus. There were fisticuffs in the Forum, but it is not always clear which of Caesar's measures provoked the violence, nor is the chronology elucidated. Appian's description of rioting in the Forum probably belongs to the day when voting was to take place on the land bill, and is described below in that context.[37] Suetonius laconically puts the blame on Caesar, for being the first to resort to armed conflict to drive Bibulus from the Forum, but he does not explain the context.[38]

Perhaps it was at this meeting in the Forum, after order had been restored and Bibulus and Cato were out of the way, or at another meeting arranged later, that Caesar summoned Crassus and Pompey to give their opinion of the bill.[39] They both supported it; Pompey resorting to soldierly terms, declaring that if anyone took up the sword against it, he was ready with his shield. Plutarch reports that Pompey said he would bring his swords *and* shields to the defence of the bill.[40] Pompey would probably have been wiser to have used a less militant metaphor, given that violence had become a recent feature of Roman politics.

If contemporaries had not yet realised that Caesar, Pompey and Crassus were working in collusion, there can have been no doubt about it when Caesar began to introduce his legislation and called upon his two colleagues to support it. The three men cannot have been taken by surprise when the land bill did not have a smooth passage through the Senate, and had presumably discussed what to do when their opponents made it clear that they were determined to block the passage of the bill. They had to plan an alternative route.[41] Caesar had tried to have his legislation passed by the Senate by the traditional methods, at least at first. Then he resorted to other means. Plutarch dramatizes this decision, with Caesar almost flouncing out of the Senate, crying that the senators had forced him, against his will, to take his bills to the peoples' assemblies.[42] Gruen blames Cato's tactics for forcing Caesar and Pompey to resort to violence and extremism.[43] Violence was nothing new in Roman politics, nor was presenting bills direct to the people. Tiberius Gracchus had passed his legislation in this way. It was the old story all over again, the Senate versus the *populares*. Caesar was able to cast his opponents in the roles of intransigent, uncaring, narrow minded, selfish oligarchs, and the senators were given enough fuel to cast Caesar as a power-hungry despot. The relatively small group of senators who seriously opposed Caesar objected to his methods, not necessarily his legislation. Caesar's policies may have been beneficial for the state, for the government, for the administration, or for the individuals who made up the state, but the threat of dominance by one individual weighed more heavily than the intent and purpose of the proposed laws.

On the day set for voting on the agrarian law, Caesar prepared for trouble. There were plenty of Pompey's veterans who could be called upon to demonstrate solidarity in Rome. They and the tribune Publius Vatinius between them made it clear how serious Caesar and Pompey were about the land bill and their other measures. When everything was ready for voting, Bibulus and his retinue of three tribunes arrived, perhaps with the intention of using the tribunician veto on the whole proceedings. Appian describes a skirmish involving Caesar's and Bibulus' followers, without specifically relating the turmoil to the day of the voting on the land bill, but this is the most likely context for it. He says that Bibulus burst into the Forum while Caesar was still speaking, and fighting ensued, in which Bibulus' *fasces* were broken, and Bibulus himself melodramatically bared his neck to Caesar's followers, so that if he were to be killed, Caesar would have his death on his conscience ever afterwards. Then Cato appeared, only to be physically ejected, but he found another way into the Forum and the same thing happened again.[44] At some point during the fracas, Bibulus was covered with the contents of a chamber pot, and possibly nearly killed, but friends saved him from becoming a martyr to the cause by dragging him into a temple. Caesar's land bill became law, and the committee of twenty men could be appointed to oversee its operation. Pompey and Crassus were the most eminent members of this committee, and as mentioned above, Caesar was not part of it.

The people swore an oath to observe the law, and Caesar instructed all senators to do the same. Sulla had administered an oath as a means of securing the legislation he had made in haste, in the short interval between driving out Marius and his supporters, and setting off for the Mithridatic War. But Sulla had merely asked the two consuls elect to take the oath, not all the senators, and he can scarcely have expected them to keep the oath. Caesar went further, by proposing the death penalty for anyone refusing to take the oath, and the people converted this into law. Cato and the ex-consul Metellus Celer held out for a while, but were persuaded by Cicero that there was little to be gained by refusing to take the oath, because they could not help the Roman state by being executed or going into voluntary exile; it was much better to take the oath, and stay in Rome to help whenever possible.[45]

Bibulus called a meeting of the Senate the day after the riots at the voting session, probably in the hope that a state of emergency could be declared, and then he could be appointed Dictator. If such was his plan, no one supported him eagerly enough to propose the measure, so without support from the majority of senators he was powerless. From now onwards Bibulus retired to his house, and did not venture out in public for the remainder of his term of office.[46] Plutarch says that Bibulus was not achieving anything by obstructing Caesar, except for putting himself in danger of being killed in the Forum.[47] Suetonius describes how Bibulus retired to his house and issued proclamations announcing adverse omens.[48] Cicero also refers to Bibulus watching the heavens for bad omens.[49] 'Watching the skies' was a religious ploy, open to augurs and to magistrates, who could stop all public business if the omens were bad. In theory, this nullified all Caesar's acts that were passed while his colleague was gazing at the heavens and proclaiming that the omens were not favourable; presumably whenever the assemblies were to be held. This would theoretically make it easier to overturn all the legislation at once when Caesar was no longer consul, but this could have been achieved anyway by proposals in the Senate, even though it would have taken longer and each law would have to be tackled individually. The date when Bibulus retired and his reasons for doing so are variously reported. Suetonius places Bibulus' withdrawal just after the stormy passage of the agrarian law, while Appian connects it to the plot to kill Caesar and Pompey, as revealed by Vettius, (described below), after which the people provided a bodyguard for Caesar, and Bibulus abstained from all public business.[50] Bibulus was certainly watching the heavens for adverse omens by early May 59, when Cicero praised Bibulus' firm stance in continually impeding the *comitia*, but he considered that ultimately it did nothing to improve the state of affairs.[51] By removing himself from political activity, Bibulus left the way clear for Caesar to act alone, probably putting through all his legislation much more rapidly, ignoring the adverse omens. The Romans customarily dated each year by citing the names of the two consuls, but in 59 BC the people labelled the year as the consulship of Julius and Caesar, because no one remembered anything achieved in the consulship of Bibulus.[52]

It is not possible to produce a strict chronology of all the bills that Caesar presented in person and those that were promoted by his adherents, such as the tribune Vatinius, who did nothing gratis and demanded a high price for his services, but apparently Caesar paid up.[53] The sources sometimes gloss over the specifics of the legislation. Suetonius mentions that laws were passed, but cites only the agrarian bill, while Appian also devotes attention to the land bill, and for the rest, he says that Caesar brought forward laws that would please the people.[54]

After the agrarian law had been passed, and the committee of twenty men had been selected to oversee the distribution of the land, the land grants for the urban poor and the settlement of Pompey's veteran soldiers could at last begin. Soon it became apparent that there would not be enough land to cater for all the eligible settlers, so the Campanian lands, which Caesar had promised were not to be affected, were included in the programme by means of another act. The ancient authors do not distinguish this from the first act. Allotments were to be offered to men who had at least three children, and the sources agree that 20,000 individuals came forward.[55] Towards the end of April, Cicero wondered, in a letter to Atticus, how Caesar could possibly solve the problem of land distribution without meeting with opposition, then on the last day of the month he received correspondence from Atticus informing him of the new law about the Campanian lands. Cicero said that he was taking a nap when the letter arrived, and was then kept awake by thinking about the problem. He considered that there could not possibly be enough land, even Campania could not sustain more than 5,000 farmers, and this at the cost of upsetting the rest of the people who were not selected.[56]   Another problem was that the settlement programme would abolish the taxes that were currently levied, so all that would be left to the state was the five per cent tax on the manumission of slaves.[57] Then Cicero launched into a condemnation of Pompey for allowing himself to get involved in all this, and then distancing himself from everything, refusing to commit himself on any topic, merely saying that he approved of Caesar's laws but it was up to Caesar to administer them.[58] Gruen suggests how the settlement may have been organised, by allocating units of ten *iugera* to each settler, so that there would be sufficient space for all. The allocated plots were inalienable, not to be sold for twenty years, which would discourage unscrupulous men from receiving lands and trying to sell them immediately to make a financial profit. Although some farmers may have lost a part of their lands, there is no evidence for outright evictions, and no record of disturbances except for some possible boundary disputes.[59] If there had been serious disturbances, surely Caesar's enemies would have made much use of them.

An important piece of legislation still to be effected was the ratification of Pompey's eastern arrangements, hopefully avoiding protracted senatorial debates. Lucullus was the main opponent, still bearing a grudge against Pompey for replacing him in the Mithridatic war. It is said that when Lucullus tried to oppose the arrangements for the East while Caesar was consul, Caesar rounded on him, threatening to prosecute him for his conduct during the Mithridatic War. Though Lucullus had done much to win this war, a prosecution by one of Caesar's friends or by Caesar himself was not out of the question. Lucullus then fell on his knees and begged for mercy.[60] It may have been a display of abject cowardice, or it may have been an ironic gesture, to reveal to the world that Caesar was the one man to be feared in Rome. Perhaps this display of naked force by Caesar silenced any further opposition, but if anyone else was bold enough to object to Pompey's eastern settlement, Caesar may have reminded the Senate that the Manilian law, which bestowed on Pompey the command against Mithridates, contained clauses that also granted him the power to make war and peace, to arrange treaties, and forge alliances. Prolonged quibbling about the details was uncalled for. Pompey had been authorised to make whatever arrangements he wished to make, and the custom of the earlier Republic of sending out commissioners from Rome to organise new territories had lapsed, therefore what Pompey had done should be allowed to stand. Especially in the East, the distances were too great and the time delay too long for the governor or commander on the spot to send back to Rome for instructions or approval of their organisation, so other commanders had often made their arrangements without waiting for a commission of senators to be sent from Rome. All their measures were then ratified in retrospect. While Lucullus had been in command, he too had organised the provinces and allied states without consulting the Senate. The ratification of Pompey's *acta* in the East became law thanks to Caesar, but it does not receive much attention in the ancient sources. Suetonius, Plutarch and Velleius ignore the event; Appian says that Caesar caused all of Pompey's acts to be ratified, as he had promised.[61]

Other legislation concerned the *publicani*, the equestrian tax collectors, who were compromised because their original bid for the tax farm of the province of Asia had been too high, so their profits were not what they had expected. Crassus had tried to alleviate the position, but it was Caesar who finally pushed through the necessary legislation to relieve them of one third of their self-imposed burden, cautioning the tax gatherers not to make the same mistake again.[62] Appian points out that on this account Caesar gained much support from the equestrian class.[63] The Egyptian question still required attention. Ptolemy Auletes at last gained official recognition from Rome, though at a price. He was already in debt to Roman money lenders, but disregarding the plight of his people, he could draw on the seemingly inexhaustible resources of Egypt, especially if he was secure on his throne, endorsed by the power of Rome. Pompey and Caesar made fortunes out of the arrangement.

Caesar also passed a law to improve provincial administration. His *lex Julia de repetundis* remained in force throughout most of the Empire, and some of its clauses and provisions were preserved in the

Digest, one of the compilations of law drawn up by the Byzantine Emperor Justinian in sixth century AD. Such laws dealing with extortion had been necessary throughout the Republic, to ensure that provincials could bring about a prosecution of those governors who had misused their powers to cheat and rob them, as well as mistreating the people. Caesar's new law was a synthesis of some of the clauses contained in previous laws, but this does not mean that he had simply read through the legislation and quickly compiled a list so that his law would gain a modicum of popular support for him. He drew on a body of Roman and provincial experience, putting together a complex law that tried to take into account all possible scenarios. It encompassed more than the acts of extortion by governors, but included all the peripheral features aimed at preventing extortion and maltreatment of the provincials by the lesser officials and the members of each governor's entourage. The clauses of the law included each type of offence and the measures for dealing with them. Clearly some governors had been claiming far too much in the way of expenses, both from the Roman treasury and from the provincials, so a limit to such claims was specified, and governors were made responsible for strict accounting for all financial aspects of provincial administration. Their accounts had to be published in two major cities of each province, and a set of accounts was to be sent to Rome. Everything concerning the accounts had to be sealed to prevent anyone from tampering with them. In vernacular terms, cooking the books was probably one of the most lucrative ways of making a fortune in the provinces. There were two aspects contained in the regulation of the behaviour of provincial governors; the protection of the inhabitants of the provinces was one aspect, and the other was the offence against the Roman state itself. Governors could be prosecuted under the laws for *maiestas*, or treason, for leaving their provinces, crossing territorial boundaries, or for making war, without permission from the Senate. The law did not stop at defining the offences and the relevant punishment, but it also included measures to tighten up procedure of the courts when prosecutions were conducted.[64] This law was extensive and well drafted, possibly with considerable input from colleagues of Caesar and possibly from senators specifically invited to participate in its formulation, and as such it ought to have occasioned more attention from the ancient authors, but probably because it was sensible and necessary, and did not occasion riotous opposition, and was thus largely ignored in the sources.

In late April or early May, Caesar married Calpurnia, the daughter of Lucius Calpurnius Piso Caesininus, who was to be one of the consuls in 58 BC, and therefore bound closely to Caesar while he was absent from Rome as governor of his province, which was probably not yet decided. Another marriage strengthened the association of Pompey and Caesar. Pompey had divorced his wife Mucia when he returned from the East. It was rumoured that among Mucia's lovers was Caesar. Pompey's subsequent attempts to ally himself by marriage to the family of Cato had been spurned. Caesar nullified the betrothal of his daughter Julia to Caepio, and arranged her marriage with Pompey. The consensus of contemporary and modern opinion is that this marriage was much more than a political expedient, and that Pompey fell head over heels for his new wife. Cicero did not approve of what to him was a sudden marriage contract, and accused Pompey of setting up a tyranny. Cato went around proclaiming that the state had become a matrimonial agency, and that arranged marriages had become the new currency by which the official posts could be bought and sold.[65]

In the summer, probably in May or June, the mysterious and probably insoluble case of Lucius Vettius flared up briefly and sputtered out. The ancient authors give different versions of this episode. Appian sets the events just after he describes how the oath was administered to all senators to observe Caesar's laws.[66] Vettius already had a shaky reputation after giving information on the men who were associated with Catiline.[67] Vettius now re-emerged. According to Appian he ran into the Forum with a dagger, which he said had been given to him by one of Bibulus' lictors, and he was acting on behalf of Bibulus, Cato and Cicero to murder Caesar and Pompey.[68] The tale was probably even more garbled with the passage of time. Dio does not mention Vettius running into the Forum with a dagger, but reports that it was Cicero and Lucullus who wanted Vettius to kill Caesar and Pompey, but his case fell apart when he named Bibulus as party to the plot, because Bibulus had warned Pompey in May to beware of such plots.[69] Cicero's contemporary report, in a letter to Atticus in mid-October 59, is more reliable.[70] He says 'Vettius promised Caesar, as far as we can see, that he would get some criminal suspicion thrown on young Curio'. He planned to do this by making Curio's acquaintance and then telling him that he was determined to attack Pompey with the help of his slaves. Curio told his father, who reported the matter to Pompey. Vettius was hauled before the Senate, denied ever meeting Curio, then changed his story, making Curio the ringleader of the plot, and naming others who were involved. He said that Caius Septimius, Bibulus' secretary, had given him a dagger. As Cicero says, the idea of Vettius not being in possession of a dagger unless Bibulus sent him one is preposterous, and on 13 May Bibulus had got wind of a plot and warned Pompey against it. Caesar put Vettius on the Rostra the next day, and when he was questioned the list of names of guilty parties had been changed, some not being mentioned, and some added. Vettius was to be tried on a charge of violence by Crassus.

According to Appian, Caesar intended to question Vettius the next day, but Vettius was killed during the night.[71] Suetonius says that Caesar had him poisoned, while Plutarch drops hints that he was strangled; either way, his death was passed off as suicide.[72] The motives and objectives of the main actors in this strange scenario will probably never be explained. Suetonius assumed that Caesar was behind it all, accusing him of bribing an informer to declare that he had been persuaded to murder Pompey. No name is provided by Suetonius, but he must be referring to Vettius. Taking the lead from Cicero, some modern authors take it for granted that Caesar had tried to use Vettius to silence the young Curio, who had spoken against him and sided with Cato and Bibulus. Cicero reported to Atticus that Curio was the only voice that could be heard speaking out against Caesar, and he was becoming more and more popular. At the games in honour of Apollo, there were cheers for Curio, but when Caesar appeared there was a lack of enthusiasm.[73] Vettius as an agent of Caesar is hardly credible, especially since he had tried to implicate Caesar in the conspiracy of Catiline. He was more likely Pompey's man than Caesar's, because Vettius had served in the army under Pompeius Strabo, Pompey's father, but then it is just as incredible that Pompey would attempt to hatch such a far-fetched scheme to discredit some of his opponents.

Caesar required a provincial command that would bring military glory and popular approval. He intended from the first that it should be a long-term command, and since the East was quiescent after

Pompey's campaigns, Caesar had to look to the West or towards the Danube for his military campaigns. Gaul was his ultimate choice, which as Suetonius says was the most likely command to bring him triumphs and profit.[74] There had already been warning signs of potential trouble in this area. In 62–61 BC Caius Pomptinus had campaigned against the Allobroges in Transalpine Gaul, whose legitimate complaints against Rome had been ignored, provoking them to rebel.[75] In March 60, Cicero reported to Atticus that the consuls of 60 BC, Quintus Caecilius Metellus Celer and Lucius Afranius, were to draw lots for the governorship of Transalpine and Cisalpine Gaul, that recruiting was to begin for the army, and ambassadors were to be sent to the other Gallic states to prevent them from joining the Aedui.[76] The chief of the Aedui, Diviciacus, appealed to Rome for help against the Sequani. The war threatened to escalate because in their struggle against the Aedui the Sequani had called upon the German Ariovistus, chief of the Suebi, and he had gladly given assistance but in return demanded lands to settle some of his tribesmen within the territory of the Sequani. Everything appeared to be in turmoil. Whole peoples were displaced, and the Helvetii, who had migrated to Switzerland from the Rhine and Main region, now wanted to move again. Their route would probably take them through Roman territory.

By-passing the Senate, the tribune Vatinius proposed a new law in the people's assembly, that Caesar should become governor of Cisalpine Gaul and Illyricum.[77] With control of Cisalpine Gaul, Caesar would be well-placed to observe what was happening in Rome and Italy, but a command in this province alone would not allow him to achieve very much in the military sphere, so the addition of Illyricum gave him wider opportunities. At this stage it was not certain whether he would concentrate on Gaul, or whether he would perhaps be called upon to fight in Dacia, where the tribal leader Burebista was growing powerful. The command in Illyricum would allow him to turn rapidly towards Dacia with his troops. The situation changed when Metellus Celer died. He had been destined to govern Transalpine Gaul, in view of the fact that the Gauls were in turmoil and a war was looming, but unfortunately for him, and fortunately for Caesar, Celer died before he took up his command. Thus the second member of the clan of the Metelli died conveniently for Caesar to obtain a post that he desired: a potential case for crime novelists to exploit. Pompey proposed in the Senate that Caesar should be given the province of Transalpine Gaul, with one legion. The senators granted the command because it was obvious that even if they refused, the people would bestow it on Caesar anyway.[78] The command was to commence on 1 January 58 for one year, so unlike the command in Cisalpine Gaul and Illyricum, it would have to be renewed annually. Thus Caesar obtained his proconsulship of Gaul in two stages, first Cisalpine Gaul and then Transalpine Gaul.

The command in Cisalpine Gaul and Illyricum gave Caesar three legions. There was to be a fixed term of five years. This was unequivocal; there was a specific terminal date before any other arrangements could be made for these provinces, specifically 1 March 54. The necessity for continuity of command and a reasonable term in which to achieve anything had been a lesson learned from previous experience; the tremendous power that could accrue from such a command had not been lost on Caesar. He was to receive the provinces with immediate effect, in the early summer of 59 BC, which meant that he held a military command while still consul, with potential access to troops that would give him a slight edge in anything he proposed during the remainder of his office. Transalpine Gaul in its wider sense indicated the whole of Gaul beyond the Alps, as the name suggests, but in the narrower sense of Roman territory, it comprised the old province formed in 121 BC to protect the Greek colony and port of Massilia (modern Marseilles), and also the land route from Italy to Spain. The capital was at Narbo (modern Narbonne), which gave the province its later name of Gallia Narbonensis. In Caesar's day, the area under Roman control was referred to as the Province, *Provincia*, a name that still survives today as Provence. Beyond the Province, the Romans labelled the rest of the country Gallia Comata, which means Long Haired Gaul. It was to be this area where Caesar would fight his battles. These commands represented all he wished for, and according to Suetonius he gloated in the Senate, boasting that he had obtained his greatest desires to the detriment of his enemies, and then he resorted to vulgarity, exclaiming that from then on he would mount on their heads.[79] J. C. Rolfe, the translator and editor of Suetonius' work in the Loeb edition, adds a note to explain that this has a double meaning, the second quite unmentionable.

When Caesar's consulship came to an end, the situation in Rome would change unless he could find some means of protecting his legislation, and also some means of influencing political events from a distance. He needed friendly allies in the Senate and in important magistracies while he was away from Rome, and he cultivated people with this end in view. For the consulship of 58 BC he promoted and supported his father-in-law, Calpurnius Piso, and Pompey's man Aulus Gabinius. He used a variety of means to bind people to him or put them under obligation to him, but he helped only those who would defend him in his absence, not shrinking from extracting an oath from his chosen men, or occasionally a written contract.[80] Swearing an oath was a religious act, set about with all sorts of penalties if the oath were broken. An irreligious man may have disregarded this if he made an oath to an ordinary individual, but swearing an oath to the Pontifex Maximus, who was also consul, may have given the matter a little more weight. Like Crassus, Caesar bought up debtors, loaning money at low rates of interest, and he extended assistance to those who were in difficulties with the law. Others he bought with lavish gifts. Cicero lamented to Atticus that there was no hope of ever having free magistrates again.[81]

Caesar made considerable efforts to cultivate Cicero. In June or July he offered Cicero a place in his entourage in Gaul, together with a free travelling pass which he could use at any time, and when this offer of a post was refused, he then tried to tempt Cicero to become a member of the commission of twenty men in charge of the land settlements, to replace Cosconius, who had died.[82] Cicero admitted that becoming one of Caesar's lieutenants would be a more honourable method of keeping out of danger than running away, because he already knew that Clodius was a threat to him, frequently mentioning the problem in letters to Atticus throughout the summer. How different Cicero's life would have been if he had accepted Caesar's offer. But having refused, he was obviously intent on remaining in Rome where he would not be able to keep silent or prevent himself from opposing Caesar.

Caesar decided to find a way of ensuring that his opponents could not speak against him while he was absent. He made a start on silencing or controlling potential opponents while he was still in office. In the spring of 59 BC, Cicero took the opportunity at a trial to make a speech lamenting the current political situation. This is generally assumed to be the defence of Antonius Hybrida, who had done Cicero a favour and extracted a promise from him to defend him after he returned to Rome from his province of Syria. Appian adds information about what Cicero was supposed to have said, namely that the union of the three men was verging on monarchy.[83] Having failed to win Cicero over, Caesar now laid the foundation for his political embarrassment and eventual exile. According to Suetonius, it was on the same day that Cicero spoke out in court that Caesar gratified Clodius' long-term wish to become a plebeian.[84] Caesar as consul and also as Pontifex Maximus, and Pompey as augur, presided over a ceremony whereby Clodius was adopted by the plebeian Publius Fonteius, a man younger than Clodius, simply to facilitate the transformation from patrician to plebeian. Fonteius backed out of the arrangement once the formalities were over, and Clodius continued to call himself Clodius, and not, as he should have done, Fonteius Clodianus, indicating that his origin was with the Claudian family, but his adoptive family was that of Fonteius. Plutarch labels this piece of chicanery Caesar's worst act, asserting that Clodius was made a plebeian with the specific purpose of becoming a tribune so that he could get rid of Cicero.[85]

As a plebeian, Clodius successfully stood for election as tribune, taking up office on the traditional date of 10 December 59. He started to agitate immediately, passing a law which outlawed anyone who had executed Roman citizens without a trial. Cicero knew precisely where Clodius' political and legal manoeuvrings were leading, and after his consulship ended Caesar lingered near Rome until March 58, long enough to witness the gradual wearing down of the consul of 63 BC who had executed the five Catilinarians without trial. Caesar presumably felt some smug satisfaction when he pointed out in a debate that he had warned of the consequences of such a peremptory act – a speech that could be summed up as 'I told you so and you didn't listen'. He reminded people that he had spoken against the death sentence at the time, but he also added that he did not approve of retrospective legislation such as Clodius had introduced. A lost cause, Cicero turned to Pompey for help, even going so far as to visit him at home, but Pompey exited through the back door as Cicero was shown in the front. Voluntary exile was the only noble option before he faced trial, so Cicero packed up and left. His house in Rome was pulled down.

Cato was the next to be removed. Clodius decided to annexe Cyprus, wresting it from the rule of the Ptolemies. It was said that Clodius held a grudge against Ptolemy Auletes because when he was held to ransom by pirates, and Ptolemy undertook to pay, he did not send enough cash. This cannot have been the only motive for annexation; trading and shipping interests predominated. The new province required a governor, and Cato was sent out to oversee the conversion of Cyprus into a Roman acquisition. As Caesar entered his command in Gaul, two of the most persuasive speakers in Rome, who patently did not have his best interests at heart, had been removed. Clodius was active in other spheres. He introduced the free distribution of corn rations to the urban poor – always a politically motivated measure to pre-empt food riots and gain popularity. He also forbade the observation of the skies as a means of obstructing political business. At some point, he and Caesar had probably been to the same dinner party and talked earnestly for a while.

During the rest of Clodius' tenure as tribune his street gangs controlled Rome and could be met only by more street gangs. Clodius had an agenda of his own that at best could be described as erratic and mercurial. If Caesar thought that he could use Clodius to control Rome in his absence then he had reckoned without the unscrupulousness and belligerent nature of his candidate. Clodius was no one's tool and performed only when it suited him. Perhaps Caesar's main aims were the removal of his opponents, and he did not much care about the mayhem he left behind. Like Pompey, who sat back and waited to be asked to do something when there was a crisis, he may have thought that if things got too far out of hand he could return to Rome and quell the troubles, thus making the populace and the Senate grateful. Perhaps as he set off for his Gallic provinces he did not anticipate that he would be absent from Rome for ten years.

8

Caesar, the Gauls, and the Roman Army, 58–50 BC

In writing about any subject, most especially ancient history, there will be one of two problems: a dearth of information, or alternatively far too much. The first problem leads to much speculation to fill the gaps in knowledge and sometimes to flesh out the narrative by describing contemporary circumstances and social and political history. Caesar's account of the Gallic wars falls into the second category, in that Caesar provided far too much detail to be reproduced in its entirety in a single chapter, since it would make it inordinately lengthy.

An additional factor is that while Caesar was in Gaul for the best part of a decade, political life at Rome and in the other provinces was also running its course, and if some events outside Gaul did not affect Caesar directly, towards the end of his term of office developments in Rome certainly did impinge on him. The 50s and 40s BC are among the best documented in Roman history, so Caesar's exploits in Gaul and the political history of Rome during the same period could provide enough material for several chapters or even a small set of encyclopaedias. As the French saying has it, the art of boring people is to tell absolutely everything.

This chapter therefore presents some general points about Caesar's account, and also describes his army, for which so much information is provided by Caesar himself. General information about the *Commentaries* and about the army apply equally well to Caesar's account of the civil wars, and obviate the need to go over the same ground again in those contexts. The chapter following this one covers the campaigns in Gaul up to the time when Caesar left his province.

Caesar's *Commentaries*, also known as *The Gallic Wars*, have raised some controversies among scholars, who question when the work or the various parts of it were written, when they were published, in whole or in instalments, and did Caesar use the dispatches that he sent to the Senate as the basis of the work? Did he revise these for public consumption? Perhaps more importantly, the reliability of the books must be examined, as with any book, ancient or modern. It has been suggested that the first seven of the eight books of the *Commentaries* were written in the winter of 52/51 BC, and published in 51 BC. It is known that Caesar did not complete the eighth book, which was written by one of his officers or perhaps one of his friends. This is usually agreed to be Aulus Hirtius, but Suetonius also suggests that it may have been Caesar's secretary Oppius.[1] Whoever the author was, he wrote a preface to the eighth book, addressed to Lucius Cornelius Balbus, Caesar's close friend and secretary. As for the accuracy of the *Commentaries*, was Caesar scrupulously honest, did he suppress information or lie by omission, or did he simply make mistakes? According to Suetonius, the historian Asinius Pollio thought that the work was carelessly written, that Caesar did not sufficiently examine the information that his subordinates reported to him, and that he had somehow perverted the account in places, which he perhaps intended to revise at some time, but never did.[2] If there were inaccuracies by design or by accident in Caesar's work, the situation may have been compounded by the possible miscopying of the manuscripts over the centuries. The earliest extant manuscripts date from the period between the ninth and the twelfth centuries, which leaves a gap of about ten to thirteen centuries since Caesar published the work, a long time in which losses of parts of the work could have occurred, and copying errors could have found their way into the various manuscripts that were handed down, largely through the monasteries. The errors or omissions would probably concern only individual words, which may or may not have altered the sense of some sentences, but would not have been too detrimental to the description of events.

Caesar was writing to impress his Roman audience, so he would naturally have tailored his work to this end. The work is interesting, vigorous, almost pictorial in its representation of people and events. The books would be designed to be read aloud to an audience, so they would take on the quality of a performance, and would keep Caesar in the public eye. Since self-promotion was the prime purpose of the work, there is all the more reason to suggest that the first seven books were published while Caesar was still in Gaul, bolstering his political and military reputation as part of his preparations for the consular elections when he returned to Rome.

Perhaps because Caesar's *Commentaries* dealt with the Gallic wars so completely, some of the ancient historians chose to summarise events, rather than analyse the ten-year conquest. Suetonius says that Caesar chose the Gauls as his province after his consulship because they seemed the most likely to yield profit and furnish victories worthy of a triumph. Trouble was already brewing in Gaul before Caesar's consulship, and military action had already taken place against the Allobroges under Gaius Pomptinus in 62–61 BC. As for Caesar's campaigns, Suetonius devotes a short chapter to the most important of Caesar's achievements, relating how Caesar made all the territory between the Pyrenees, the Alps, the Cevennes, the Rhine and the Rhine into a province, and designated as allies all those states which had helped him. He was the first to bridge the Rhine, and invaded Britain, where he met hitherto unknown peoples. Financially, the new province yielded 40,000,000 sesterces every year. Then Suetonius lists three disasters: the loss of the fleet on the British coast, the destruction of a legion at the Siege of Gergovia, and the deaths of two of Caesar's officers on the borders of Germany.[3] In a later passage Suetonius accuses Caesar of pillaging temples and shrines, and attacking cities and towns for the sake of plunder.[4] The damage that Caesar did is partially offset by the fact that he embellished cities in Gaul and Spain, but this is not the reason why Suetonius includes this information. He places it in a passage outlining similar activities to illustrate how Caesar acted independently without consulting the Senate.[5] In other ways, too, Caesar showed his independence of the Senate by sending enslaved prisoners as gifts for his friends, and he also lent his auxiliary forces to allied rulers without much consultation.[6] In merely presenting a synopsis of Caesar's achievements, Suetonius was not being unnecessarily negligent, because in his day, the *Commentaries* were still extant, and so were some of Caesar's letters to the Senate, so his audience would have no need of a reiteration of what Caesar had written.

Plutarch, on the other hand, fleshes out his summary of Caesar's conquest of Gaul, and was clearly using Caesar's own work, but he does not confine himself to strict chronological order. He takes examples of Caesar's characteristics in warfare and diplomacy from the accounts of the Gallic wars and the civil wars, rather than giving a strictly year by year narrative. Plutarch pronounces Caesar's conquest of Gaul as a fresh start in life. His achievements were unprecedented, and after the conquest of Gaul, he entered upon a new life. Plutarch's account is adulatory, stating that Caesar was a better general than any of the other Romans, resorting to superlatives to explain the reasons: Caesar operated over more difficult terrain, fought more battles against fiercer enemies, inflicted more casualties on his foes, taking 800 cities by storm, subduing 300 tribes, and killing a million people out of a total of three million, and took as many prisoners.[7] The concept of what constitutes glory has been modified a little since Caesar's day. The ghosts of generals such as Pompey and Sulla might have quibbled about the more difficult terrain, and the fiercer enemies, but Plutarch compared his Romans with Greek heroes, and he paired Caesar with Alexander, so his work would have suffered if he had not been able to show that Caesar was the equal of Alexander in every way. By means of anecdotes derived from all the wars that Caesar fought, Plutarch illustrates Caesar's special talents, such as his ability to inspire loyalty in his soldiers and his friends.

Appian's account of the civil wars, reproduced in the Loeb edition in the volumes of his *Roman History*, contains very little about the Gallic wars because he dealt with them in greater detail in his *Celtic History*, so in his history he deals with political developments at Rome while Caesar was absent in Gaul. Velleius Paterculus is even more adulatory than Plutarch, but then he was writing in the reign of Tiberius, not long after Caesar's lifetime, and without Caesar, neither Augustus nor Tiberius could have become head of state. Velleius says that Caesar's Gallic wars constituted an enormous task which could scarcely be covered in many volumes. Velleius comments that Caesar even crossed the sea into Britain, twice, as though he was adding another world to the Empire, and as for the Siege of Alesia, an ordinary man would not have attempted it, and no one could have achieved it except a god.[8] Stirring stuff, but then when Velleius wrote his history, Caesar had been declared *Divus Julius*, expressed in English as Divine Caesar, during the supremacy of Augustus, so Velleius' words would not strike a contemporary audience as a bit over the top.

Caesar's own literary works had no need for the hyperbole that accrued after his death. He tells the story in clear language, his style praised by Cicero himself, and even the criticisms of Asinius Pollio did not extend to a condemnation of Caesar's style. The written works give some idea of his clarity in his speeches, keeping to the salient points, presenting facts in a logical order without too much embellishment, sometimes perhaps witty and entertaining, and bitterly brief and acute in others. Caesar begins his account with the now famous observation that Gaul is divided into three main parts, occupied by the Belgae, the Aquitani, and the Celtae, known to the Romans as Galli. The divisions were actually much more numerous than this, with several smaller tribes constituting the whole, some of which Caesar names in the *Commentaries*. Some of these tribes would be subordinate to the larger ones, perhaps even tributary to them, or at least under their protection. Larger and more powerful tribes sometimes allied with smaller ones and protected them, without taking them over entirely. When the tribe of the Bellovaci rebelled against Caesar, Diviciacus of the Aedui pleaded for mercy on their behalf, since this tribe had long been a dependency of the Aedui, who helped and protected them.[9] Tribal names and groupings, and their territorial boundaries, were not fixed for all time. The Romans were not the only empire builders. Some tribes were led by power-hungry rulers, and encroached on others to expand their territory. Other tribes were compelled to move because of pressures beyond their lands, or within them, but movement into another area most often involved displacing or annihilating other tribes. Another way of reducing the influence of a tribe was to wean their dependencies away from them, which is how the Sequani, originally a less powerful tribe than the Aedui, managed to weaken the stronger tribe by absorbing their dependent peoples.[10] For a variety of reasons and in a variety of ways, whole tribes could be absorbed by larger ones, and their names disappeared from the record. A multiplicity of tribal names in Gaul, Britain or Germany is not indicative of the actual number of tribes in a given territory at any period of their history. It is significant that some of the tribes listed by Caesar in his expeditions into Britain were no longer in evidence nearly a century later when the Emperor Claudius embarked on the conquest of the island in AD 43.

The territorial names Gaul, Germany and Britannia used in Roman contexts create a false impression of unity, but there was no strong sense of nationhood among the tribesmen, whose loyalties were primarily to their tribe and their leader, and only secondarily to the concept of being a Gaul or a German or a Briton. The lack of unity among the tribes was their greatest weakness. Not only were there quarrels and open warfare between the tribes, but there was also a lack of unity even within a tribe, where ambitious warriors could strive for leadership at the expense of the existing ruler. A stronger power could exploit this disunity, allying with some tribes against their common enemies, or if the existing tribal leader could not be won over, there was usually an ambitious rival all too eager for supreme power, frequently within the family of the king or chief. Such individuals could be cultivated with the promise of assistance in gaining power in their own right, and also the promise of continued support thereafter to ensure their leading position. This is how the powerful Orgetorix of the Helvetii gained the confidence of other tribal nobles. He was not the ruler of the Helvetii, but he was backed by many supporters. He knew enough about the Aedui and the Sequani to realise that he could utilise the divisions in their ruling houses to set son against father, and brother against brother, then perhaps establish the ambitious relatives as new chiefs, and put them under obligation to him in his quest for supreme power among the Helvetii. He therefore went on a diplomatic tour of other tribes, and targeted Casticus of the Sequani, persuading him to overthrow his father Catamantoloedes, and Dumnorix of the Aedui, offering support if he wished to supplant his brother Diviciacus. Both Catamantoloedes and Diviciacus had been designated friends of the Roman people by the Senate, as Caesar was careful to note in the *Commentaries*. As friends of Rome, the leaders of the tribes could have appealed for help if civil wars broke out at the instigation of Orgetorix, but in the end his plans were foiled by his own people. He evaded trial by gathering his thousands of supporters, but shortly afterwards he conveniently died. It was probably suicide, said the Helvetii.[11]

What Orgetorix had attempted could have been emulated by Caesar, but he did not deliberately foster civil wars among the tribes. Instead he selected rulers who were favourable to Rome and cultivated them, the most important of these being Diviciacus of the Aedui, whom Caesar describes as the one man in whom he had absolute confidence.[12] In cases where he could not promote one individual from the beginning, he settled internal tribal disputes and installed rulers of whom he had formed a good opinion. One example was Tasgetius of the Carnutes, who had been of great help to Caesar in the previous campaigns. The family of Tasgetius was descended from the rulers of the tribe, so Caesar chose him as ruler, but after two years the people rose against their new chief and assassinated him. Caesar responded quickly, because he foresaw that if the assassins took power, the Carnutes might rebel against Rome. He sent Lucius Munatius Plancus to winter in the territory of the Carnutes with a legion, and to seek out and send to Caesar the men who had killed the chief.[13] On a later occasion, the Aedui found themselves in difficulties because two men, Convictolitavis and Cotus, both claimed that they had been elected as ruler of the tribe for a year, so they appealed to Caesar, who was anxious to keep the peace within the tribe. He decided in favour of Convictolitavis, ordering Cotus to give up the power he had claimed. The Aedui were bound to the Romans by ties of friendship, and more pertinently, Caesar was backed by his armies, so it was wise to do as he said.[14]

The Gallic and German tribes were not unsophisticated savages. They had developed their own political systems and social hierarchies to try to keep order among their own people and to organise their defence against other tribes. Their civilization and organisation differed from the lifestyles of the Romans and Greeks, because although there were important central places where justice was dispensed, or places of religious importance, there were no city states or townships comparable to those of the Greek and Roman world. Some tribes were moving towards statehood as Rome extended her influence into the Celtic west, and the Romans applied the term *civitas* (plural *civitates*) to the tribes, indicating states. They termed their settlements as *oppida* (singular *oppidum*) translated as towns, but while these were not like the Greek and Roman cities with regular street plans lined by stone buildings, they signify corporate organisation and administration.

There was one important difference between tribal society and the Roman world, in that while Romans went to war, made peace,

Statue of Caesar, a modern
replica of the marble statue
in the Capitoline Museum.
It is situated on the Via dei
Fori Imperiali in Rome, near
to the excavated remains
of the Forum Julium. It is
one of a series of replicas
depicting the Emperors
Trajan, Augustus and Nerva
on the opposite side of the
Via dei Fori Imperiali, in
front of Trajan's Markets,
the Forum of Augustus
and the Forum of Nerva.
(© Patricia Southern)

Portrait bust identified
as Caesar, showing him
at a mature age and with
a receding hairline, at
the Capitoline Museum.
(© Patricia Southern)

Green slate bust of Caesar from Egypt, one of the liveliest portraits of Caesar of unknown date from Berlin Museum. It may be an idealistic and later portrait. (© David Brearley)

Another green slate portrait from Egypt, but not as realistic as the previous example. (© David Brearley)

Above: Silver denarius minted in 44 BC, showing the head of Caesar and the abbreviated IMP, standing for Imperator, the title awarded to him by the Senate as a personal name. Until Caesar's Dictatorship, Roman coins customarily depicted the heads of gods and goddesses, not living individuals, though ancestral portraits were considered valid. In 54 BC Quintus Pompeius honoured his two grandfathers, Pompeius Rufus and Sulla, and in 46 BC Gnaeus Pompeius issued coins, probably from the mint at Corduba in Spain, bearing the portrait of his late father Gnaeus Pompeius Magnus. Until the beginning of 44 BC Caesar's coinage carried his name but no personal portraits, then he began to depict himself. (Drawn by Jacqui Eden)

Below: Head of Caesar as Dictator for the fourth time, on a silver denarius of 44 BC. He wears his laurel wreath, one of the several honours awarded to him by the Senate. The format of the portraits and legends around the coins was copied by Augustus and succeeding emperors. (Drawn by Jacqui Eden)

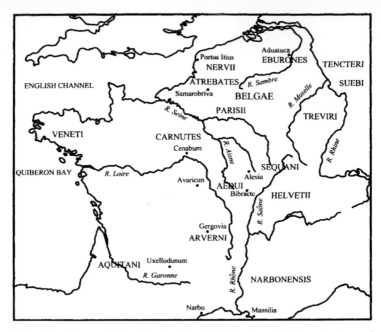

Above: Sketch map of Gaul showing the principal tribes and their territories, and the area of Gallia Narbonensis, or *Provincia* (the Province), which survives in the modern name Provence. Caesar's province of Transalpine Gaul did not originally include all of the country, but he interpreted it widely and subdued all the tribes. (Drawn by Jan Shearsmith)

Below: Plan of the siege of Alesia showing its position on a hill between two rivers, and Caesar's lines of circumvallation. (Drawn by Jan Shearsmith after Fuller)

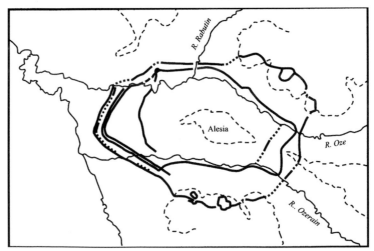

Above left: The Arverni issued their own coins bearing the head of Vercingetorix, presumably a stylized likeness, but acknowledging his leadership. His great achievement was in persuading the different tribes to work together for a long period to oppose Caesar. He gave himself up to Caesar to save his people from further harm, spent six years in prison, walked in Caesar's triumph, and was then strangled. (Drawn by Jacqui Eden)

Above right: Silver denarius of Julius Caesar, *c*.47–46 BC. The reverse shows Aeneas carrying his father Anchises. The Julian family traced their descent from Aeneas' son Iulus (The Metropolitan Museum of Art)

Above: Gold aureus of Julius Caesar, 46 BC, celebrating Caesar's third consulship, and showing the head of Pietas. (The Metropolitan Museum of Art)

Right: Silver denarius issued by Caesar in 49 BC, either in Gaul before the crossing of the Rubicon, or in Italy after Caesar had gained control of the country. The image of an elephant stamping on snakes implies that this is how Caesar intended to deal with his enemies. The reverse shows religious artefacts of the college of priests, specifically the Pontifex Maximus, which Caesar had held since his election in 63 BC. (Drawn by Jacqui Eden)

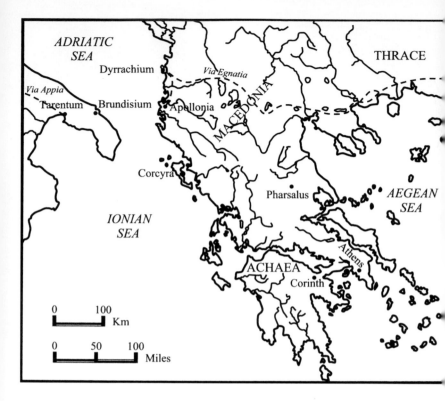

Above: Map of Greece with the sites of the main events in the civil war between Pompey and Caesar. (Drawn by Jan Shearsmith)

Left: Coin bearing the portrait head of Pompey the Great with the abbreviated title Imperator. It was issued posthumously by his elder son Gnaeus in Spain in 46 BC. In the following year after the Battle of Munda, Gnaeus was killed. (Drawn by Jacqui Eden)

The earliest known coin portrait of Mark Antony, on a silver denarius dated to 44 BC. It shows Antony bearded and veiled, with religious implements, the *lituus* and a jug, identifying him as augur. Caesar backed him for the priestly office as well as election as tribune of the plebs in 50 BC. The reverse shows a rider and galloping horses, associated with the Games of Apollo, but the significance in connection with Antony is unknown. (Drawn by Jacqui Eden)

Portrait bust of Marcus Porcius Cato, Caesar's perennial opponent. Cato committed suicide at Utica after Caesar destroyed the Pompeians at Thapsus in 46 BC, and this bust comes from Volubilis (modern Oubili) in North Africa. (From Rabat Museum, photo © David Brearley)

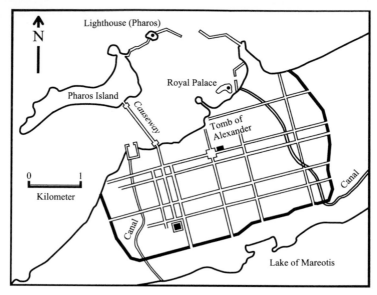

Above: Plan of Alexandria and the Pharos Island where Caesar fought the army of the Egyptians and the young Ptolemy XIII under Achillas and then Ganymede. Legend had it that in burning some of the ships in the harbour Caesar also burned the great Alexandrian library, but this is now refuted. Another legend, that during a battle he had to swim for his life in the harbour while holding papers above his head, may be true. (Drawn by Jan Shearsmith)

Below: 'The Head of Pompey Presented to Julius Caesar', by artist Giovanni Antonio Pellegrin. (The Metropolitan Museum of Art)

Cleopatra VII portrayed on a silver coin from Alexandria. Her hairstyle is consistent on several of her portraits, drawn back and contained within a headband. Cleopatra was not beautiful, as this unflattering portrait shows, but she was said to have possessed a mellifluous voice, great charm and intelligence, as well as speaking several languages. (Drawn by Jacqui Eden)

Cleopatra VII and her son Caesarion portrayed in Egyptian costume as Isis and Horus, on the wall of the temple at Dendera. It was said that Caesarion resembled Caesar, and Cleopatra always claimed that he was Caesar's son. Whether or not this was true, the boy represented a threat to Caesar's legal heir Octavian, and was killed after the fall of Alexandria in 30 BC. (© David Brearley)

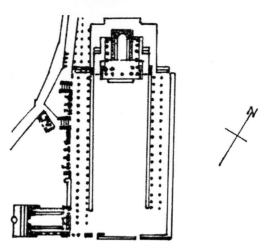

Plan of the Forum Julium, attached to the rear of the Senate House. The building was dedicated in 46 BC but it had not been completed. One of the reasons for the delay was that the Senate House, in ruins since the fire at the overzealous funeral of Clodius in 52 BC, had to be moved to make space for the projected Forum. In 46 BC the senators had not yet given permission to relocate the Senate House a short distance from its original site. Caesar did not live to see the finished building, which was achieved by Augustus. Inside the Forum was the Temple of Venus Genetrix at the north-western end. (Drawn by Jacqui Eden)

The rectangular podium and the foundations of the Temple of Venus Genetrix in the Forum Julium, dedicated along with the Forum in 46 BC. Caesar had vowed to build and dedicate a temple to Venus Victrix if he won the Battle of Pharsalus. When he began the building he changed his mind and dedicated the temple to his divine ancestress, Venus Genetrix. The temple was surrounded on three sides by columns, but the three resurrected examples seen here date from the reconstruction by the Emperor Trajan in the early second century AD. (© Patricia Southern)

Drawing of the Forum Julium as seen today, showing the aisle flanked by columns and the side of the Temple of Venus Genetrix. (Drawn by Jacqui Eden)

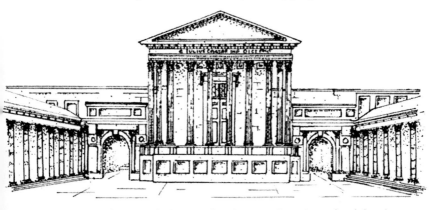

Reconstruction drawing of the Temple of Venus Genetrix enclosed by the porticoes of the Forum Julium. The side facing the modern Via dei Fori Imperiali is still buried under the pavement and the road, where it joins the buried sections of the Forum of Augustus. (Drawn by Jacqui Eden)

Part of the ruins of the Basilica Julia, showing the arches of the western end. There was a previous Basilica on the site, originally built by Tiberius Sempronius Gracchus in 169 BC, and underneath that there was a house. Caesar replaced the existing Basilica on the same site and dedicated it in 46 BC while still unfinished. It was one of the several projects completed by Augustus. The Roman basilica usually housed the legal courts and the administrative personnel associated with them, and such buildings are found in most of the towns and cities of the Empire. The Basilica Julia lies parallel to the open space of the Forum Romanum, and the administrative offices belonging to it probably lie on the unexcavated side, under the shadow of the Palatine Hill. Caesar's original building was completed by Augustus, but burned down, and was rebuilt. The visible remains date from the later third century, when the Basilica was destroyed by a fire once again. (© Patricia Southern)

The western end of the Basilica seen from the slopes of the Capitol Hill. Only the stumps of the columns of the aisle on the northern side remain, parallel to the Forum Romanum. The Basilica extended eastwards to the Temple of Castor and Pollux, of which three tall columns can be seen in the distance. A road called the Vicus Tuscus separated the end of the Basilica from the temple. (© Patricia Southern)

The Rostra of the Augustan period in the Forum Romanum, where speakers addressed the people. The name derives from *rostrum*, a ship's prow or beak, which the Romans took from defeated enemy vessels and hung from the front of the platform, hence Rostra in the plural. Behind this platform are the remains of the curved Rostra built by Caesar. The eight columns to the left belonged to the Temple of Saturn, originally founded in the early fifth century BC. It housed the treasury. Whilst Caesar, Cicero and others did not deliver speeches from the version of the Rostra shown here, they did so in the immediate vicinity. (© Patricia Southern)

Part of the façade of the Theatre of Marcellus and the columns of the Temple of Apollo Medicus Sosianus, situated between the Tiber and the southern end of the Capitoline Hill. The Temple of Apollo was originally founded in the later fifth century BC and rebuilt at least three times, the last occasion being contemporary with the theatre. Caesar had planned to build a theatre to rival Pompey's in the Campus Martius, but never completed it, so Augustus took over and named the theatre for his sister's son Marcellus. The entire semi-circular theatre façade has not survived, but the building still exists because it was fortified by the Pierleone family in the eleventh and twelfth centuries. It is still inhabited. The arches to the right in darker stone were built in the 1920s. Caesar's plans for the reconstruction of Rome surely encompassed many new buildings never started, and one can speculate what the city would have looked like if he had lived to old age. It was Augustus who found a city built of brick and converted it to marble. (© Patricia Southern)

Remains of the Temple of *Divus Julius* facing the south-eastern end of the Forum, showing the semi-circular recess in the visible remains of the base. The recess was originally open, but later blocked off by the paler stones across the entrance. The temple was founded by the three men of the second Triumvirate, Mark Antony, Octavian and Marcus Aemilius Lepidus, and was built over the site of Caesar's funeral pyre, where a short-lived altar was set up by Caesar's supporters. The temple was not dedicated until 29 BC. The building has been extensively robbed and is hardly recognisable as a temple, so the imagination has to be employed to visualise it clad in marble, with probably six columns rising from the podium to support a triangular pediment. (© Patricia Southern)

Inside the recess of the Temple of *Divus Julius* is the stump of a round monument that may have been a replacement for the altar that was originally set up after Caesar's death and then removed. In modern times visitors still place offerings on this structure, usually flowers, coins and candles. (© Patricia Southern)

The reverse of a silver denarius issued in 42 BC by Quintus Servilius Caepio Brutus, Caesar's assassin. It commemorates the Ides of March, depicting two daggers flanking the cap of Liberty. Most of Brutus' coinage was issued in Macedonia when he and Cassius took over the eastern provinces, raising troops and gathering resources to fight against Antony and Octavian. In the same year that this coin was issued, the Battle of Philippi was fought, Cassius committed suicide, and Brutus was killed. (© Patricia Southern)

The date of this coin is not established. It shows Octavian sporting a beard, and the legend proclaims him *divi filius*, indicating that he is the son of the now deified Caesar. The reverse, not shown here, bears a portrait of Caesar with the legend *Divos Julius*. If the coin was securely dated it would help to establish when Octavian decided to use this title, which he could have begun to use shortly after his return to Rome and his acceptance of the inheritance that Caesar had left him, but this is disputed. (Drawn by Jacqui Eden)

Above: The Temple of Mars Ultor, Mars the Avenger, in the Forum of Augustus in Rome. Octavian had declared his intention to avenge the death of Caesar and he vowed to build the temple to Mars before the Battle of Philippi in 42 BC. The building was finally dedicated in 2 BC, and the Forum in which it stands joins up with the side of the Forum Julium, but the remains are hidden under the Via dei Fori Imperiali. (© Patricia Southern)

Left: Bust of Julius Caesar by the artist Andrea di Pietro di Marco Ferrucci. (The Metropolitan Museum of Art)

and arranged alliances in the name of the state, tribesmen usually made alliances in the name of the ruler. The state was embodied in the king or chief; treaties and alliances were made on a personal basis between the king or chief, and the Roman who arranged the treaties and alliances on behalf of Rome. The loyalty of the tribe and its leader was therefore to the Roman individual rather than to the Roman state as a corporate entity, which meant that on the death of the native ruler, or of the Roman official, especially during the Empire, the alliance or agreement was null and void. The Romans needed to monitor developments among their native allies to keep their alliances up to date.

They also needed to understand tribal society and how it was organised; who held power, who dispensed justice, and how the tribe was policed. There was not necessarily a template for social, military or religious customs across all of the tribes, but there were certain features to which the Romans could readily relate. The tribal nobles usually gathered a group of followers, similar to the *clientes* of a Roman noble. Caesar uses different terminology to describe these retainers, sometimes labelling them as *familia*. In the case of Litaviccus, who rebelled against Rome and joined the Gauls at Gergovia, he calls the followers *clientes*, and Litaviccus as their *patronus*.[15] In another instance, he calls the retainers of other tribal leaders *ambacti clientesque*, meaning *ambacti* and clients.[16] *Ambacti* may be a Latinised Celtic word, and may be distinguished from ordinary clients, signifying a deeper and stronger relationship with the patron. In this context, Caesar is describing the knightly class, which he calls *equites*, adding that the number of their dependents is their one source of power and influence.

There were some parallels between Roman and tribal society in that there were appointed officials, such as those of the Helvetii. The Aedui elected their officials to hold power for one year, as mentioned above in connection with the two rival candidates for the position of tribal chief, Convictolitavis and Cotus. The chief official of the Aedui was the Vergobret. Caesar says that this individual held the highest magistracy (*summo magistratui praeerat*). The Vergobret was the supreme judge, with powers of life and death over the people, holding power for one year. At the outset of his governorship, Caesar met the Vergobret called Liscus, who told him that there were some men of the Aedui who had accrued tremendous influence so that they were more powerful in their private capacity than the magistrates. In a private session with Caesar, Liscus went on to name Dumnorix, brother of Diviciacus, as the main culprit. Dumnorix was accumulating power, property and wealth. He had for years in succession contracted for the customs dues and the taxes of the Aedui and no one dared to bid against him. With his increased wealth he could distribute gifts to bind people to him, and to bribe others, and he had even increased his influence among other tribes by marriage alliances, offering his mother, his half-sister and his female relatives to other rulers, to cement his personal association with them.[17] Just like being in Rome, then, but dressed in a different costume and speaking a different language. The acquisition of wealth and its uses, and private associations with other states, could just as easily be applied to Crassus and Caesar himself, or indeed Pompey the Great and any other ambitious Roman politician.

Factionalism was another aspect of Gallic society that was paralleled in Rome. Caesar explains that such divisions were rife among the Gauls, from entire tribes down to the individual households.[18] The danger of such factions was that they could foment civil war, the last thing Caesar wanted among any tribe while he was busy making a name for himself in subduing them all.

In his account of the events in Gaul Caesar frequently explains situations via the speeches he puts into the mouths of his allies and enemies, a device that other ancient historians used. It lightens up the narrative, which would otherwise consist of explanations in indirect speech, such as 'the king told Caesar that...', or 'the chief explained how...'. Direct speech has a sense of immediacy and would lend authenticity to the performance when the account was read aloud to an audience in Rome. Whether the speeches are a faithful rendering of what was said is perhaps doubtful, because some editing was probably done, and some suppression of facts may have been necessary. But Caesar portrays the natives as intelligent, thinking people, even though his opponents, such as the German Ariovistus, are made to reveal their arrogance and hatred. Caesar expresses only the Roman point of view, of course. In general, Caesar respects the tribesmen for their intelligence, even if it emerges in the form of duplicity and deceit. The Romans were not the most scrupulously honest in dealing with their enemies, so duplicity is intelligence in inverted form, and as such it is to be admired. All's fair in love and war. Caesar acknowledged the skills of the natives, and their ability to learn, as for instance when the Nervii erected a rampart and ditch around Quintus Cicero's camp to invest it, learning by observation from the Romans and from some soldiers they had captured. But they had no proper tools for this work, and had to resort to cutting turves with their swords, and extracting the blocks by grasping them in their cloaks. Nevertheless, they built a fortified line around the Roman camp in only three hours. They then constructed siege-towers and shelters within their rampart, just as the Romans would have done.[19] There is a hint of admiration in Caesar's description, but he could afford to be generous because he catastrophically defeated the Nervii in the end. Naturally, the skills and accomplishments of the Gauls and Germans must be acknowledged, because there would be no credit for Caesar if he spent nearly a decade subduing people who were ignorant idiots. Caesar knew that the Gauls were patently not idiots. The German leader Ariovistus could speak at least two languages, his own Germanic tongue and that of the Gauls, a skill he had acquired from long practice.[20] When the Helvetii had been overcome, and were persuaded to return to their homes, the written records that they had kept were brought to Caesar. They had used Greek lettering for a census of their own people and of the tribes who accompanied them.[21] These records divided the populace into those capable of bearing arms, then old men, women and children, and the allied tribes were numbered separately. The total was 368,000 people, of whom 110,000 survived, according to a census that Caesar organised when the tribes had been resettled. This does not mean that the entire tribe was literate, but perhaps a few of the elite tribesmen could read, or they employed scribes for producing the census figures and other types of records, revealing a sophistication that belies the false image conjured up by the terms 'barbarians' and 'tribesmen'. 'Barbarian' derives from a Greek word used to describe anyone who could not speak Greek, and made unintelligible bar, bar, bar noises instead. In Gaul, the use of Greek lettering, if not the language, had probably been learned from the Greeks of Massilia (Marseilles), which had been founded *c*.600 BC and was well known to Greek traders even before then. Greek letters were also used by the Druids, for the few records that they needed to set down in writing. Caesar thought that they used Greek to prevent their records from being understood by everyone.[22] He was confident that although some of the tribesmen could understand individual Greek letters, communications written in the Greek language could not be deciphered by the large majority of Gauls, since in 54 BC he sent a message written in Greek to inform Quintus Cicero, whose camp was under siege, that he was on his way to the rescue. The use of Greek was designed to foil the Gauls if the letter happened to be intercepted, which implies that the tribesmen could read Latin.[23] This supposition is borne out by the fact that, according to Suetonius, Caesar sometimes used a cipher for the transmission of messages, using the fourth letter of the alphabet for the real one, D for A, and so on.[24] In the sixth book of his *Commentaries* describing the campaigns against Ambiorix of the Eburones, Caesar devotes a few chapters to the characteristics, customs and religious practices of the Gauls and Germans.[25] This might have been better placed in an introduction to the whole book, but perhaps he could not have produced such an account until he had gained some years' experience of the tribes he was dealing with.

The army that Caesar commanded in Gaul initially comprised three legions in Cisalpine Gaul and Illyricum, and one on Transalpine Gaul, which was added to his original command a short time later. Caesar's legions were soon increased in number. With the Helvetii on the move, most likely intending to pass through the Roman Province, Caesar needed many more troops if he was to stop the migration. He immediately began to raise troops from the Province. This was the first of several recruitment drives to raise legions and auxiliary troops from various sources. After Caesar had built a fortified line, 19 miles long from Lake Geneva to the Jura mountains, to delay the Helvetii, he placed Titus Labienus in command while he dashed off to Italy to raise two more legions.[26] At the outset of the campaign against the Belgae in 57 BC, another two legions were raised.[27] After returning from the second expedition to Britain in 54 BC, with a revolt looming in Gaul, he may have raised another legion, since he refers to a legion recently raised from the peoples living north of the Po.[28] When Pompey and Crassus were consuls in 55 BC, and passed a law to extend Caesar's command for another five years, Caesar raised three more legions.[29] According to

Suetonius, Caesar raised legions at his own expense, one of them being the *Alaudae*, or Larks, raised in Transalpine Gaul, which he equipped and trained himself. The legions were normally recruited from Roman citizens, but this legion, and perhaps others, were Gauls. Caesar enfranchised the men of the Alauda legion later on.[30] Other legions were sometimes given names, but Caesar numbered his legions from VI to XV, indicating a total of ten legions under his command, but he refers to them in his text as the ninth legion, or the tenth, and so on; *legionis nonae et decimae milites*, for instance. In modern accounts initial capitals are the norm, as in the Ninth and Tenth legions.

There would be losses as the campaigns progressed, most notably the disaster that wiped out the troops of Quintus Titurius Sabinus and Lucius Aurunculeius Cotta during the revolt of the Belgae in 54 BC. Both commanders were killed, and Caesar acknowledges a great loss of troops.[31] Recruitment would have been an ongoing concern to fill gaps in the ranks, as well as to constitute new legions and auxiliary troops. Fatalities would have resulted from battles, but there were probably large numbers of men who died from disease and accidents. Where modern statistics are available, such as for the American Civil War, many more men died of disease than from their wounds. Caesar admitted that legions were never at full strength.[32]

The legions did not operate as single cohesive units at all times. Detachments were sent on special missions, and sometimes cohorts from different legions could be grouped together, placed under the command of an officer detailed for special tasks, not all of them involving fighting. Food supplies had to be gathered and transported, if the natives who provided supplies were not instructed to bring them to a designated camp or depot. Reconnaissance and policing duties were also part of the army's duties, and could be conducted by detachments from legions, sometimes accompanied by auxiliaries.

The structure of the legions and auxiliaries of Caesar's command was not quite as fully developed as it would become during the Empire under Augustus and his successors, but was well on the way. Although legions could remain under arms in war zones for long periods, there was no standing army until Augustus began to create it by degrees between 30 BC and AD 14, when he died. In the first century BC legions were enrolled for specific campaigns and then discharged when the wars ended, as they had always been raised from the beginning of the Republic. Hence there were always problems in finding lands for discharged veterans returning home at the end of campaigns. The problem had been alleviated by setting up Roman citizen colonies of veterans in the provinces and in Italy, but there were still more and more ex-soldiers who required land crowding into Rome. Augustus created a pension scheme for veterans, initially financed from his own funds and then by specific taxes, but Caesar's men could only hope for an allotment to enable them to provide for themselves, after discharge. The best hope for soldiers who were still young and fit was to re-enlist in another army and continue to receive pay, supplemented from other sources, such as donatives from their commanders, and booty. It was difficult for a commander to prevent looting if a city, town or any settlement had been overrun, and it was acknowledged that the promise of booty was one of the prime incentives for soldiers to join the army. Caesar addressed the issue on one occasion by promising 200 sesterces to every soldier and 2,000 sesterces to each centurion in lieu of booty. The figures may be incorrect, but the principle is the same: keep the soldiers happy, and if they cannot claim booty then reward them anyway.[33] Suetonius says that Caesar doubled army pay, but does not provide a date for when he did so. It was probably towards the end of the Gallic war, when profits were sufficient to sustain such a measure.[34] Alternatively Caesar may have instituted double pay when he was in sole power at the end of the civil wars, and would be able to extend the double pay to all the legions at the same time. It is calculated that after Caesar's pay award, legionaries would receive 225 denarii per annum. There were no further pay rises until the reign of Domitian towards the end of the first century AD. Increased pay would make service in the army more attractive and would facilitate recruitment, which was now necessary all the time because troops were needed in the provinces as well as for specific campaigns. In Caesar's day armies were permanently in existence somewhere in the Empire, but it is worth repeating that there was no permanent standing army with regular terms of service until Augustus gradually developed it.

Republican legions were divided into maniples, literally handfuls of men, usually 120 in each maniple (though the numbers could be increased), grouped around their own standard. The maniples were drawn up in three lines, called the *triplex acies*, with gaps between each maniple, and these gaps covered by the maniples behind the first and second lines. The three-line formation was still used in Caesar's army, and he makes several references to the *triplex acies* in the *Commentaries*. In 58 BC, during the campaign against the Helvetii, he drew up four legions in three lines half way up a hill, with the most recently enlisted legionaries and all the auxiliaries at the top.[35] On another occasion when he was fighting against the Germans under Ariovistus, he deployed in triple line right up to the enemy camp. During the ensuing battle Caesar's right wing was very hard pressed, and Publius Licinius Crassus noticed this and ordered the third line to support the wing.[36] In 55 BC, on the way to the Rhine and fighting the Tencteri and Usipetes, Caesar marched in triple columns, ready to form line of battle.[37] The legions of Caesar's day were divided into cohorts, a term which is first recorded by ancient historians describing the army of the third century BC, but in some cases the term may have been used anachronistically. In 206 BC, on campaign against the Carthaginians in Spain, Publius Cornelius Scipio placed two groups, each composed of three maniples, on his left and right wings, ordering them both to turn inwards towards his centre – the men on the left wing wheeling to the right, and the men on the right wing turning to their left. The Greek historian Polybius labelled the collection of maniples as a cohort. It is not certain if the legionary cohort became a permanent feature from this time onwards. Following Scipio's example, cohorts may have been formed up only for special tasks. The credit for the development of legionary cohort formation belongs to Marius, Caesar's uncle, and by Caesar's day it was the norm. Caesar refers to maniples on two occasions. The first reference concerns the Battle of the River Sambre in 57 BC, when the troops had become too compacted to be able to use their weapons properly, but Caesar dashed in, seizing a shield from one of the soldiers, and called to the centurions by name, giving the order to spread out the maniples (*manipulos laxare iussit*) so that the men could wield their swords.[38] The second occasion belongs to the campaigns against Ambiorix of the Eburones in 53 BC, when the troops gathering food outside the camp were suddenly attacked, and the maniples clustered around their standards. After arguing about what to do, the men broke through the enemy, led by their officer Gaius Trebonius.[39] With only two references to maniples, compared to the number of times that Caesar mentions cohorts, it is clear that cohort formation was fully established in the legions, but maniples were not forgotten. Until the late Empire, ordinary soldiers were still sometimes referred to as *manipulares*.

Each legion contained ten cohorts, which is confirmed for at least one of Caesar's legions in 53 BC. Caesar describes how Titus Labienus had crossed the Seine and was marching towards Lutetia (Paris), but then the revolt of the Aedui and other tribes changed the situation so completely that he had to withdraw. He managed to deceive the Gauls that he was crossing the river in three different places by sending some boats downstream, and then by ordering five cohorts of one of the legions to guard the camp and the other five cohorts from the same legion to march upstream with all the baggage, making a tremendous noise, and accompanied by some men in oared boats rowing upstream, also creating a great din.[40] Each cohort comprised of six centuries, whose complement was not 100 men as the name suggests, but eighty soldiers, commanded by a centurion. The total for the legion would be about 4,800, but there are uncertainties and variables to consider. No source states categorically how many men there were in a legion, save for the figures of 4,000–5,000 given by Polybius for the Republican legions of the second century BC. The numbers may never have been standard. Some if not all legions of the Imperial era had a double first cohort, and another factor is that when campaigns began it is possible that recruitment was stepped up to create over-strength legions, which, by the end of the wars, were probably under strength. The hypothetical figure of 4,800 was certainly not met in 54 BC, when Caesar, marching with two legions and some cavalry, gives the total number of men as just under 7,000.[41]

Another feature concerning legionary cohorts is that there is, as yet, not a shred of evidence at any period of Roman history for a cohort commander in a legion. Neither in the surviving literature, nor in the extensive collection of inscriptions from all over the Empire, is there any mention in the careers of soldiers and officers that any of them commanded a legionary cohort. The lack of evidence strongly suggests that there never was such a post, which implies that the responsibility for receiving and carrying out orders, and giving them, devolved upon the centurions. There was a gradation of seniority for each cohort and each century of the legion, and a corresponding grading for the centurions who commanded the centuries. The most senior centurion, not only in the first cohort but also the moist senior in the whole legion, was the *primus pilus*, literally meaning first spear, a rank which many centurions could aspire to but not many could actually attain. Caesar mentions two centurions, Titus Pullo and Lucius Vorenus, who were approaching the first class of their rank (*primis ordinibus appropinquarent*).[42] Promotion would be achieved by a variety of means: occasionally after election by the soldiers, or by performing well and coming to the notice of the senior officers or the commanders. Promotion from the ranks usually meant that the new centurions would serve in a different legion. Recounting the attack of the Germans on a Roman camp in 53 BC, Caesar mentions centurions who had been promoted from the lower ranks of other legions into the higher ranks of the recently recruited Fourteenth legion.[43] Another means of promotion was by filling dead men's sandals. The newly promoted centurions mentioned above fell fighting the Germans, and in 52 BC, at the Siege of Gergovia during the revolt of Vercingetorix, there was a disastrous battle in which no less than forty-six centurions were killed.[44] Many hopeful legionaries would have achieved higher rank after losses on this scale. Most if not all of Caesar's centurions were known to him, probably because he made a point of learning their names, even if he merely selected a few names to learn by heart to impress the army. During the battle against the Nervii in 57 BC, when the troops were in trouble, he dashed into the ranks, calling to the centurions by their names. Perhaps he did not remember all of the names correctly, but the fact that he recognised some of his officers in the heat of battle cannot be overestimated as an attribute of a general, engendering not only affection and loyalty in the troops, but also total confidence.[45]

Although Caesar's legions were similar to those of the Imperial standing army, there was an important difference in command structure. Caesar sometimes appointed his quaestor to command a legion, or sometimes more than one legion, with responsibility for different missions. In the expedition to Britain command of the ships was shared out between the *legati*, the *praefecti* commanding the auxiliary troops and the quaestor, who is not named.[46] He was probably Marcus Licinius Crassus, son of the colleague of Caesar and Pompey, who is mentioned as quaestor and commander on different occasions. Later, Mark Antony, a late arrival in Gaul, became quaestor, and in 51 BC he was placed in command of the army in winter quarters.[47] In Imperial times, the quaestor was not usually placed in command of military units.

Each of the legions of the Empire was commanded by a *legatus legionis*, who would be appointed by the Emperor and would remain in post for a couple of years before receiving further appointments. Ranking below the legate were the six military tribunes, one of them of senatorial rank, and five of equestrian rank. These officers had always been commanders of the Republican legions, serving under the consuls. Caesar frequently refers to *legati*, but his legates were not permanent legionary commanders. They were men who had been delegated for particular tasks, mostly short-term, and could be placed in temporary command of a single legion, or of three or more legions, or of collections of troops from different legions, sometimes accompanied by auxiliaries. They would serve in this capacity for as long as necessary, and then go on to different tasks with different troops. Caesar names several of his *legati*, and describes their various accomplishments, and sometimes their mistakes. In 54 BC he split up his army into smaller units to put them into fortified winter quarters over a wide area because of the scarcity of food caused by a prolonged drought, and he lists the *legati* and their locations for that winter, most of them commanding one legion: Gaius Fabius was in the territory of the Morini; Quintus Cicero, brother of the orator, with the Nervii; Lucius Roscius was with the Esubii, in the quietest part of Gaul; Titus Labienus was in the lands of the Treveri and the Remi; the quaestor Marcus Crassus, together with Lucius Munatius Plancus and Gaius Trebonius, were all in the territory of the Belgae; Quintus Titurius Sabinus and Lucius Aurunculeius Cotta were in command of the most recently recruited legion and five cohorts in the land of the Eburones.[48]

The most frequently mentioned *legatus* was Titus Labienus. His career in Gaul illustrates what was required in a *legatus* of Caesar. He had to possess enough experience to command troops while on separate missions away from the main army. He also had to possess relentless energy, resourcefulness, quick thinking and determination. Labienus had been tribune in 63 BC, when he co-operated with Caesar when he was praetor in the same year. Labienus was an ideal second-in-command, and on one occasion Caesar calls him *legatus pro praetore*, meaning that he deputised for Caesar as governor and as army commander.[49] At the outset of the campaign against the Helvetii, Caesar put Labienus in command of the rampart and ditch that he had built along the border between the Helvetii and the Sequani, while he went to Italy to recruit more troops.[50] In 54 BC, during the second expedition to Britain, Labienus was left in command in Gaul, controlling three legions and 2,000 cavalry, with instructions to guard the ports, to secure the food supplies, and to keep watch on events in Gaul. For all else, Labienus was given free rein to make his own plans as occasion and circumstance demanded.[51] When many of Caesar's ships were destroyed or damaged during a storm on the British coast, Labienus was ordered to construct as many ships as possible with the help of his legionaries.[52] Versatility and a capacity for organisation were two of the other desirable qualities that Caesar demanded from his *legati*.

During the course of the Gallic war, Labienus was sent to the territory of the Treveri four times, so he could be regarded as something of a Treveran specialist. This tribe was noted for its aversion to Rome, and its affinity with the Germans, sometimes appealing for help from tribes across the Rhine. In 56 BC Labienus took command of the whole of the cavalry, with the task of keeping the Treveri and the Remi loyal to Rome, and to hold back the German tribes from whom the Treveri had asked for help.[53] Two years later he wintered with his troops in Treveran territory.[54] He was attacked by the tribesmen in 53 BC. Labienus knew that the Treveri had summoned help from the Germans, so he was eager to bring about a battle before the German allies could arrive on the scene. He had been put in charge of the baggage of the entire army, so he ordered five cohorts to guard it, and with twenty-five cohorts he broke camp with a lot of activity as if he was going to make a hasty withdrawal. The Gauls took the bait without waiting for the Germans, chasing after what they thought was a beaten army, only to be faced by troops who were ready for the fight. On the previous night, Labienus had outlined his plan to the military tribunes and the centurions, so they knew what to do when the order came to wheel and deploy into line, and to place the cavalry on the wings. The battle turned into a rout, and the Treveri submitted.[55] In 51 BC, Labienus was once again in Treveran territory when Ambiorix rebelled, and he fought a cavalry action in which he captured some Gallic chiefs.[56] In 53 BC, during the revolt of Vercingetorix, Caesar divided his army into two unequal parts and gave an independent command to Labienus with four legions and some of the cavalry, to operate in the territory of the Senones and Parisi, while Caesar took the other six legions and the remaining cavalry towards Gergovia, where the Gauls had concentrated. Labienus aimed for Lutetia (modern Paris) and having tried and failed to cross the marsh which drained into the Seine, he commandeered fifty ships and set off downstream, but he was interrupted by the news that Caesar had been forced to abandon the Siege of Gergovia and had to retreat. His operations have been described above in connection with the number of cohorts in a legion, but to recap briefly he deceived the Gauls into thinking that he was crossing the river, in three places, and brought about a battle. He placed the Seventh legion on the right and the Twelfth on the left, which was attacked with determination, but the tribunes of the Seventh ordered their troop to the rear of the enemy and killed nearly all the Gauls.[57] On this occasion Labienus had no hope of help from Caesar, and had to fall back on his own resources to get his troops safely back to base. On another occasion in 53 BC, he was ordered to take six cohorts to the assistance of troops which were in difficulties. His instructions were to hold at all costs, or break through if he could not. The Gauls were not held back by the ramps and ditches that the Romans had built and Labienus sent a message to Caesar to inform him of what he considered the best plan, and Caesar rode to join the battle.[58] Labienus was one of the most efficient and effective of Caesar's *legati* throughout the Gallic wars. He was from Picenum, Pompey's territory, and towards the end of the wars his loyalty wavered. This is reported in the eighth book of the *Commentaries*, written by Aulus Hirtius, who records that in 50 BC Caesar heard from several sources that Labienus was being influenced by his enemies, but he refused to believe the rumours.[59] It must have been deeply wounding when Labienus went over to Pompey at the outbreak of the civil war and became one of Caesar's most bitter enemies.

The legions were as far as possible self-sufficient and contained a number of specialists, who were soldiers who fought and marched with all the others but possessed particular experience and skills, such as carpenters, blacksmiths, metal workers, and artillerymen, among others. Weapons would need to be manufactured and repaired, and temporary workshops established, probably while the army was in winter quarters. There was an officer in charge of legionary workshops called the *praefectus fabrum*, and Caesar gathered various *fabri* together from his legions when he needed to repair the ships damaged by a storm in 54 BC off the British coast.[60]

The army did not consist solely of legions, but auxiliaries of different kinds were raised from the native population. Not much is known about how they were organised. Even the regular auxiliary units of the Empire were not fully formed until the mid-first century AD. The auxiliaries of Caesar's army were commanded by *praefecti*, who were probably Roman officers in long-term command of the units, unlike the *legati*, whose commands were temporary and varied. The auxiliary units were usually established for the campaigns being fought in their territory and then disbanded, and even during the later Republic some auxiliary forces were commanded by their native chiefs. Caesar's auxiliaries accompanied the legions on foraging expeditions and sometimes in battle, but they were not always considered reliable, probably because they were only recently recruited and had not been properly trained, and also because their loyalties were not always certain. When Caesar met with Ariovistus in person in 58 BC, he complied with the German leader's request that he should be accompanied only by a small cavalry guard, but he did not trust his life to the Gallic horsemen that he had recruited, so he put men of the Tenth legion on the Gallic horses instead.[61] In 56 BC, when Publius Crassus was operating independently in Aquitania, he decided to draw up in battle formation in two lines (*omnibus copiis in duplici acies constituta*) with the auxiliaries massed in the centre, but when the Gauls did not offer battle in return, he advanced to their camp, crossed the enemy trenches and started to build a ramp to get his troops near the fortifications to drive away the defenders. He used the auxiliaries to carry turves to build the ramp and to hand up missiles and stones, so that they would look like fighting troops, but he was not sure of their conduct in battle.[62] Caesar's auxiliaries were not always drawn from the Gauls. Late in the campaigns, he recruited Germans from across the Rhine. Only 500 horsemen came, but the Germans were valued for their versatility, combining infantry with cavalry.[63] In addition to auxiliaries raised from the Gallic and German tribes, Caesar also mentions Numidian and Cretan archers, and Balearic slingers (*funditores*), all three peoples recognised as the very best in their field, the Numidians also being skilled horsemen. They were probably not formed into units like the Gauls, and there is no mention of commanders in charge of them. Caesar used the archers and slingers as skirmishers, and to drive off enemy defenders from their ramparts. He sent some of them across a river with the cavalry, and during the invasion of Britain he used them on board ships that were rowed up close to the shore to fire at the exposed flank of the Britons on the coast.[64] Like all armies, Caesar's troops were accompanied by a collection of non-combatants. The officers and some soldiers would have slaves, and there may have been slaves corporately owned by the army for menial tasks. A few slaves were killed in a skirmish while out foraging in 51 BC, with the loss of some draught animals. The loss was labelled insignificant in the *Commentaries*. Another group was called *calones*, distinguished from slaves, variously translated as sutlers or camp-followers, but they may have been personal servants of the soldiers. They were just as interested in booty as the soldiers were. In 57 BC during the campaigns against the Belgae, instead of remaining safely in camp, the *calones* observed that the Romans seemed to be winning the battle and dashed out to plunder, only to find that the Gauls had entered their camp and everyone else was in flight, so they fled too. Their ultimate fate is not recorded.[65] *Calones* were probably free men, but were under military command, as demonstrated when Quintus Cicero was ordered by Caesar to keep everyone in camp, including the *calones*, during the revolt of Ambiorix. After a few days Cicero decided to send out a forage party, and gave permission for the *calones* to accompany it, but shortly afterwards the German horsemen appeared, scattered the foragers and tried to enter the camp. The *calones* dashed for higher ground, were quickly repelled, and crashed headlong into some of the Roman troops, causing even more confusion, but they were eventually saved by the soldiers.[66]

Caesar's *Commentaries* provide the best source for the operation of a Roman army on campaign, because he gives details about practicalities and organisation as well as racy accounts of battles. He names individual centurions and soldiers who had performed brave deeds, possibly not without bias, but these individuals would have otherwise gone unrecorded. Caesar paid attention to the details, especially logistics and supplies, always securing his food stocks before campaigns and when putting troops into winter quarters. He was presumably not the only commander to take care over these essentials, but there is no better source for how a late Republican army worked than his *Commentaries*. Already described is the winter when he had to split up his forces because of food shortages caused by drought and the consequent poor harvests. The winter camps on this occasion were not more than 100 Roman miles distant from each other.[67] Winter quarters were usually placed in tribal territory, in a fortified camp if necessary, but not in permanent forts which form such an important feature of the Imperial provinces. On the march, unless the area was friendly, the soldiers usually built a fortified camp at each halting place, which would consist of an earthen bank formed from cut turves surrounded by an outer ditch. Soldiers had to carry entrenching tools and they probably felt that they were doing more digging than fighting, but usually the entrenching parties were rotated so that the same men did not have to do it all the time.

The size of a camp would give some indication of the number of soldiers that it contained, but in order to deceive the Gauls during the revolt in 54 BC, Caesar deliberately made the camp smaller by narrowing the streets inside and cramming the soldiers together, hoping that the Gauls would think that there were fewer men than there actually were, and could be induced to attack. Scouts were sent out to find the best routes to cross the nearby valley, and having established his exit strategy, Caesar ordered the troops to pretend to be afraid, calling back the cavalry, which was attacked outside the camp, and then making the ramparts even higher. The Gauls took the bait, attacked the camp, and were routed.[68] A particularly well-fortified camp is described in book eight of the *Commentaries*, belonging to the end of the Gallic revolt in 51 BC. The camp had ramparts 12 feet high, and a breastwork on top in proportion to the rampart, though no dimensions are given for this. Outside, a double ditch was dug, 15 feet broad and with straight sides, which would obviously make it difficult to climb up. At intervals on the ramparts, there were timber turrets three storeys high, each of them connected by a bridge, which may mean that the rampart top was planked over, or alternatively that they were connected by timber walkways higher up. Whatever the exact meaning of this passage the *Commentaries* implies that the soldiers would not become isolated in a single tower but could move from one to the other without having to return to ground level inside the camp and then climb up to the next one. At the gates the towers were even taller. It was proposed to put soldiers on the *vallum* nearer to the enemy, possibly indicating that not all the earth that was dug out was used to build the ramparts of the camp, but was also used to build a mound of earth and turf on the lip of the ditch. A second row of defenders was placed in the towers on the ramparts of the camp, much higher up, so there would be two lines of defence, one higher than the other, on the same principle of the medieval concentric castles.[69] Perhaps the most famous of Caesar's entrenchments is not a temporary camp to house and protect the soldiers, but the siege works around Alesia (Alise Saint Reine), which he describes in sufficient detail to allow for attempts at reconstruction. When completed, his lines of circumvallation enclosing Alesia were 11 miles long, with four camps for cavalry and four for infantry spread around it, accompanied by smaller forts. The lines were further strengthened by fire-hardened stakes with sharpened points embedded horizontally and facing outwards. In front of the lines, pits were dug containing more sharpened stakes pointing upwards, covered over with branches and leaves. They were 3 feet deep, and arranged in alternate rows, with the gaps in the middle row covered by the pits in front and behind. These were called *lilia*, because they resembled the shape of lily flowers, and were deadly if anyone failed to notice them and fell in, to be fatally impaled. The circumvallation was further strengthened by ditches on the western side. Two rivers flow past the hill on which Alesia sits, the Ose to the north and the Oserain to the south, both of them joining the River Brenne to the west. Between his lines of circumvallation and the town, Caesar dug three separate trenches. The first was a ditch 20 feet wide with perpendicular sides, joining the two rivers, to prevent the Gauls from breaking out at that point. Behind this obstacle he dug two more ditches, 15 feet wide and 15 feet deep, also joining the rivers. The one closest to the 20-foot ditch was filled with water diverted from one of the rivers, and behind this was an earthen rampart, 12 feet high, with a palisade on top and timber towers spaced 80 feet apart. The fortifications were completed by another line 14 miles long, enclosing the first lines and facing outwards to oppose the Gauls, who were on their way to relieve Alesia.[70]

Reconnaissance was not a strong point of earlier Republican armies, leading sometimes to disasters where the commanders were taken by surprise, but according to Suetonius, Caesar was conscientious about carefully reconnoitring, making enquiries and never leading his army where an ambush was possible, which stretches the truth a little.[71] In the *Commentaries* there is frequent mention of scouts, *exploratores*, or *speculatores*, which may indicate slightly different types of scouting parties, or alternatively could perhaps be synonyms, used simply to avoid repetition of the same word in one paragraph. Caesar describes the scouts of the Gauls and the Germans as *exploratores*. Sometimes when Caesar's scouts reported that the enemy was on the move or had taken up a position, a reconnaissance party was sent out to verify the reports and to gather more information.[72] But in describing a battle during the revolt of Vercingetorix, Caesar does not mention scouts, presumably because he did not send them out in advance of his army, and he was surprised while on the march. His account of this battle is sketchy, leaving the impression that he left a few details out.[73]

There were interpreters attached to the army, one of whom was Gaius Valerius Procillus, the son of Gaius Valerius Caburus, a Gaul who had been enfranchised by Gaius Valerius Flaccus, and, as was customary, had adopted the family name of his benefactor. Procillus is described as a leading man of the Province, and Caesar's personal friend, in whom he placed the greatest trust. He preferred to use the skills of Procillus in talking to Diviciacus of the Aedui. The regular interpreters were dismissed on this occasion, indicating that there were usually several of them. Procillus was sent to parley with Ariovistus, who had learned the Gallic speech, but Ariovistus accused him of spying and imprisoned him. During a battle while Caesar was pursuing the Germans with the cavalry, he came upon

Procillus being dragged along in chains, and rescued him. Caesar expressed his pleasure that his friend had been spared.[74] Procillus was probably quite pleased too. He had faced death three times when the Germans had drawn lots to see if he should be burned alive immediately or saved for another occasion.

It remains to give an account of the years that Caesar spent in Gaul, and his campaigns. They were bloody and aggressive, and mostly aimed at augmenting the reputation of Gaius Julius Caesar. He could afford to admire certain traits in the Gallic and German tribes and to respect their intelligence, but nevertheless he killed thousands of them. Perhaps he had not envisaged that the Gauls would prove so difficult to subdue, and that he would need an extra five years after his original command expired to achieve the conquest. Modern thinking tends to recognise the awfulness of it all, the bloodshed and cruelty, the stubborn resistance of the tribesmen in a war that need not have been waged. This is the subject of the next chapter.

9

Gaul and Britain, 58–50 BC

When Caesar embarked on the conquest of Gaul, it was the first time that the tribes had faced a common enemy who was determined to subdue them all, but they still could not unite completely to combat the Romans. Inter-tribal rivalry was too deep seated for that, and it must not be forgotten that the Gauls and the German tribes could be as cruel to each other as Caesar was to the conquered peoples. Caesar packaged the campaigns as vitally necessary for the defence of the Province, or for the defence of another tribe, or for the defence of his troops, so that all the battles would be justified in the eyes of the Romans. It was a long tradition in Rome that the wars they fought were just wars, not simply with regard to the people, but also in the eyes of the gods. The Gauls who struggled and died between 58 and 50 BC could not have known that a couple of generations later, their country would become one of the most Romanized and peaceful provinces of the Empire.

The campaigns are described in Caesar's *Commentaries* in chronological order. If readers require the details, no better recommendation can be given than to read the original, for which translations are readily available. What follows here is a summary of the main events.

The campaign against the Helvetii is described in the first book of the *Commentaries*.[1] The tribe had settled in what is now modern Switzerland, where they had begun to perceive a threat from the Germanic tribes across the Rhine. They planned to move westwards to the territory of the Santones, who lived around modern Saintonge. The Romans likewise perceived a threat if the tribe passed through or nearby the Province. Caesar dashed northwards in March 58, having waited in Rome to see the outcome of the activities of the new tribune Clodius, who brought about the exile of Cicero. Caesar had tried to save Cicero by offering him a post on his staff, or on the land commission, but Cicero had refused.[2]

The Helvetii had built a bridge across the Rhône. Caesar destroyed it and then erected a fortified barrier along the river valley to prevent the passage of the tribes. The effect was to turn the Helvetii to a different and more difficult route, this time through the territory of the Sequani. Whichever route the Helvetii chose, their migration could not be stopped with only the legions voted to Caesar in Vatinius' law, so Caesar left Titus Labienus in command on the Rhône, and enrolled two new legions in Cisalpine Gaul. Soon the Aedui and Allobroges appealed for protection against the Helvetii who had passed through and damaged their lands, which provided the justification for the war that Caesar was about to wage.

The leader of the Aedui, Diviciacus, was at odds with his brother Dumnorix, who disrupted the food supplies intended for the Roman army. When he found out, Caesar put Dumnorix under guard, and marched for the Aeduan capital at Bibracte (Mount Beuvray) to secure his supplies. The Helvetii followed him and attacked, together with the Boii and Tulingi. The fighting lasted until nightfall, and ended with the defeat of the Helvetii. Survivors fled towards the territory of the Lingones. Caesar warned the other tribes not to assist the Helvetii, as this would be construed as an act of war. About one third of the Helvetii survived and these people were sent back to their homes, charged with the task of keeping the Germanic tribes beyond them at bay.

In the meantime, the Sequani were pursuing their war with the Aedui, and now approached the Germanic Suebi and their leader Ariovistus for help.[3] Protection for the Aedui, allies of Rome, was the main reason for Caesar's going to war with Ariovistus, despite the fact that only a year had elapsed since Caesar had persuaded the Senate to proclaim the German leader a friend and ally of the Roman people. This was one reason why Caesar did not go to war immediately, resorting first to diplomacy, ostensibly to discover whether it might be possible to reach a peaceful compromise. It looked good in the Roman equivalent of the newspapers. Caesar reminded Ariovistus that the Aedui were under Roman protection, and asked Ariovistus to abandon the territory that he had overrun, and return to the previous boundaries. Ariovistus said that the lands were his by right of conquest and naturally he refused to give them up. After all, as Ariovistus pointed out, the Romans were intent on the same thing. Dio's opinion is that Caesar made demands that he knew would not be met so that he would not appear to be the aggressor.[4] Secondly, Caesar absolutely forbade any further movements of the Suebi across the Rhine. Diviciacus had informed Caesar that the German tribesmen had been infiltrating Gaul for some time, and there were now 120,000 German settlers. Lapsing into hyperbole, Diviciacus said that eventually all the Gauls would have to migrate as the Helvetii had done, to get away from the Germans.[5]

Caesar moved to the capital of the Sequani at Vesontio (modern Besançon), but already the reputation of Ariovistus and the Suebi had spread fear among the legions and the auxiliary troops. Caesar's non-military friends and hangers-on were thinking of going home. Caesar rallied everyone by means of a speech, which may bear some resemblance to what is reported in the *Commentaries*, but the clincher was his promise to face the enemy alone with the Tenth legion, which he trusted with his life.[6] An understanding of the psychology of the soldiers was to work in Caesar's favour more than once. A very long speech appears in Dio's account, incorporating some of the points raised in the speech in the *Commentaries*, and Dio also uses it to illustrate Republican history and ethics, using up ten chapters of his work to express all this. If Caesar had actually delivered this speech he would have been hoarse and the soldiers may have become a little restless.[7] One telling remark in Dio's version is that Caesar says that 'no one can dispute that we go to war justly'.[8]

Six days later the Roman army was drawn up within about a day's march of Ariovistus' camp. The two leaders met, and Caesar inserted their speeches into the *Commentaries* as a means of furthering the narrative. Caesar's main point was that the infiltration of the Germans was to cease and that if anyone was going to conquer Gaul it would be him, not a Germanic chief from across the Rhine. After failed attempts to arrange more talks, Ariovistus placed his warriors behind Caesar's camp, threatening the Roman supply lines, so Caesar built a smaller camp a short distance from the first to protect communications. On the seventh day the real battle commenced, progressing so rapidly that the two sides closed before the Romans had a chance to throw their spears. Instead they drew their swords and went straight in. The Germans were scattered, and no more Suebi crossed the Rhine. Ariovistus escaped, according to Dio, by boat.[9] Thus ended the first of Caesar's campaigns.

For the winter, Caesar returned to his headquarters in Cisalpine Gaul, to attend to civil government and the court cases that had accrued. Titus Labienus was in command of the army. Caesar needed to maintain awareness of what was happening in Rome, which for the present was under the thumb of Clodius, who had turned against Pompey, allegedly plotting to assassinate him, and almost besieging him in his own house. He tried to annul all Caesar's acts during his consulship, which is what Bibulus had hoped for when he spent his consulship watching the skies and announcing bad omens, making it easier for anyone to declare invalid all public business that had been conducted under these conditions. Clodius' adoption into a plebeian family was not a law passed via the Senate or the people, but if he had succeeded in his aim of obliterating all Caesar's acts, his plebeian status may have been annulled as well.

In Gaul, Labienus' agents reported that the various groups of the Belgae of north-western Gaul had formed a coalition.[10] Caesar began to move in early spring with the Twelfth and Fourteenth legions raised in Cisalpine Gaul. Diviciacus and his Aeduan cavalry and infantry were sent to prevent the Bellovaci them from joining the main group of the Belgae. Caesar made for the territory of the Remi, around modern Rheims and Châlons. The tribe joined with the Romans, and gave hostages as Caesar demanded, and came under Roman protection.[11] When the Bellovaci attacked the Remi, the Romans beat them off. The Belgae followed Caesar to the River Aisne, where he built a bridge, and crossed to the northern bank. The tribesmen crossed the river some distance away with the intention of coming up behind Caesar, but a Roman cavalry attack drove them off. Caesar had secured his food supplies, but the tribesmen had not, so it was only a matter of waiting until they were forced to move. When they did so, Caesar thought it may have been a ruse to draw him in pursuit, but he soon realised that it was not, and sent the cavalry to harass the tribesmen while he occupied the native towns of the Suessiones and Bellovaci to keep them quiet.

The next encounter took Caesar by surprise. He reached the River Sambre and came face to face with the Nervii, the Viromandui and the Atrebates, who had joined the federation of the Belgae. While the legionaries of the vanguard were setting up camp near the river, with the rest of the army still on the march, the tribesmen attacked. There was only a cavalry screen protecting the builders of the camp, and the horsemen were quickly dispersed, but the legionaries were disciplined enough not to waste time trying to form up with their proper units, and simply ran to the nearest standards. The Viromandui and the Atrebates were forced back across the river, but on Caesar's right, the Nervii were about to come round behind the Romans. Caesar's reputation was at stake, not to mention the lives of his soldiers. He rose to the challenge with panache, rushing to the scene, borrowing a shield and somehow pushing his way to the front, calling to the centurions by name, then sounding the charge. Then Titus Labienus commanding the Tenth legion managed to sandwich the Nervii between his own legion and the two legions who were at the end of the line of march. The remaining Nervii had to come to terms. The tribesmen were to keep their lands, and other tribes were warned not to attack them.[12] Caesar's victory was well received, and even his enemies had to admit that it was a momentous achievement. Where the army had gone, there would be opportunities for trade. Both Cicero and Pompey spoke in favour of Caesar in the Senate, voting him an extraordinary fifteen days of thanksgiving for his victories.[13] Pompey had merited only ten days for his eastern campaigns.

Meanwhile in Rome, Pompey had organised a gang under Titus Annius Milo to curb the wilder activities of Clodius by meeting violence with violence.[14] Pompey had also arranged the recall of Cicero from exile. In the autumn, Caesar went to Illyricum. He now had only two more seasons in which to conclude his conquest of Gaul, and events in Rome were slightly worrying. There had been food riots in the city. Clodius had instituted a corn dole to the urban poor, but it had placed a great strain on the supply system. Pompey had been given an extraordinary command to regulate the corn supply, with powers for five years and a staff of fifteen legates. With a command such as this, close to the interests of the populace, Pompey might soon eclipse Caesar, who was far away and dealing with problems that did not directly affect the lives of ordinary people. He had to rely on his agents to place suitable candidates in positions of influence. The Three-Headed Monster was no longer influential enough. Already at the end of

57 BC the tribune Publius Rutilius Rufus had set about dismantling Caesar's agrarian law, and Lucius Domitius Ahenobarbus, a cousin of Catulus and the brother-in-law of Cato, was seemingly intent on obtaining the consulship for 55 BC, and then getting himself made proconsul of Gaul and thereby removing Caesar from his Gallic command.[15] Caesar required more support in Rome. In the spring of 56 BC he went to Ravenna, on the very edge of his province, and met up with Crassus. He then moved on to Lucca in April to meet Pompey. The so-called conference at Lucca is described more fully in the next chapter, but the main provisions which resulted from the meeting are outlined here. Pompey and Crassus were to be consuls for 55 BC, and thereafter arrange provincial commands for themselves. Most importantly for Caesar was that his Gallic command was to be extended for another five years. This would allow him to settle affairs in Gaul to his own satisfaction, so that he would gain all the credit for the conquest. He had no intention of succumbing to the fate of Lucullus, who had to step down from his campaigns against Mithridates, and then watch while Pompey became the conquering hero. Caesar's future plans had presumably crystallized by this time. These plans entailed the retention of his army and his command while he stood for the consulship so that he could glide seamlessly and unassailably from military command to consul designate, then to consul, without an interval as a private citizen, when he would have been exposed to prosecutions under various headings that his enemies were probably already drafting clause by clause. But this was in the future. For the present, Caesar was no doubt gratified by a decision of the Senate to take up and maintain the cost of the four legions that he had raised and sustained himself. He was also awarded ten *legati* who may have been designated as military commanders, though Dio says that they were to administer the affairs of the new Gallic province.[16]

Assured that Pompey and Crassus as consuls would extend his command, Caesar had managed to defer any discussion about when he should be recalled until a future date, and he would now have more time to carry out long term plans in Gaul, which included an expedition to Britain. Publius Crassus was sent to win over the Veneti and other coastal tribes in what is now Normandy and Brittany. Friendship with the Romans was agreed and hostages were given, but when Roman envoys arrived to organise the food supplies for the army, the Veneti imprisoned them, demanding the return of their hostages. In Roman eyes this was a just cause for war. The Veneti were expert seamen, so this war would involve battles at sea as well as on land. Caesar built warships on the Loire, giving the naval command to Decimus Brutus. The ships of the Veneti were well adapted to the low tides and frequently rough seas, and Brutus achieved nothing until he developed grappling hooks on long poles, used to drag down the yardarms of the Veneti ships. The tribe was subdued, and Caesar took revenge for the imprisonment of the Roman envoys. He executed the leading men of the Veneti, and sold the rest of the tribesmen and women as slaves.[17] Caesar then marched to flush out the smaller coastal tribes nearer to the Rhine, but they fled into the forests. Winter was coming on, so the campaign was put off until the spring.

Meanwhile the Suebi had displaced other tribes on the Rhine, among them the Usipetes and Tencteri, who crossed the river in the winter in search of new lands. They sent representatives to explain why they had been forced to leave their homes, and requested settlement in Gaul. They promised not to advance beyond a certain boundary. It was feasible that the tribes could be allowed to enter the lands of the Ubii, who lived close to the Rhine and who had submitted to Caesar. A truce was arranged, and Caesar promised to meet with representatives of the Usipetes and Tencteri, advancing towards them and making camp close by. But then the truce was broken. Some of the German cavalry attacked Caesar's Gallic cavalry. Without negotiation Caesar received the tribal leaders next day, imprisoned them, and attacked the Germans still in their camp. Survivors fled, chased by the Romans to the banks of the Rhine, where they were killed, or drowned trying to escape.[18] Caesar followed up this massacre by building a timber bridge over the river, in only ten days. He describes the bridge in some detail, but not enough to clarify everything, so up to the present time no definitive reconstruction has been made, though there have been some practical experiments from which much has been learned.[19] The tribes prepared for war as the Roman army crossed into German territory, but no war was waged. Caesar had made his points only too well. Roman military and engineering ability had been demonstrated, and tribal incursions across the Rhine would not be tolerated. Caesar destroyed the bridge so that the Germans would not be tempted to use it, and the casual destruction of a work that had been speedily erected further demonstrated that the Romans could build any amount of bridges if they wanted to enter German territory.

The projected invasion of Britain now looked as though it would have to be postponed, because it was late in the year for further campaigning on the scale that the expedition demanded. But a quick reconnaissance was not out of the question. As an excuse for the expedition, Caesar claimed that the Britons had sent help to the Gauls, and had provided refuge for some of the Gauls who had fled. Before the army set sail for Britain Caesar sent a reconnoitring party under a trusted officer, Gaius Volusenus, to find suitable landing places in Britain. Volusenus did not identify Richborough as a suitable site, where the invasion under the Emperor Claudius landed in AD 43, but it is possible that the coastal features in 54 BC were not as convenient as they were nearly a century later. Another mission was undertaken by Commius, who had been installed as King of the Atrebates in Gaul. There was a branch of this tribe already settled in Britain, and it was hoped that Commius would be able to persuade this tribe and others to submit to Caesar. The southern parts of Britain were not uncharted territory. Traders regularly crossed the Channel, and the tribes within reach of the coast had developed a taste for Roman goods, as shown by archaeological finds in their lands. Caesar questioned as many traders as he could find, but their information was limited to the coastal areas.[20]

The expedition set off from two separate ports, almost certainly Boulogne, and perhaps also from Ambleteuse. Caesar used the ships that he had built for the war against the Veneti, and those that he had commandeered from other coastal tribes. He took two legions, the Seventh and the Tenth, and some cavalry, but the horse transports were unable to land in the stormy weather, so it was with infantry alone that Caesar faced the British opposition. The tribesmen marched along the coast, following the Roman ships. The first battle may have been at Deal. Wherever it was, the soldiers were reluctant to disembark, until the standard bearer of the Tenth legion leapt into the shallow water, and the men followed rather than allow their standard to be captured.[21] The Britons still used chariots in battle, carrying the charioteer and a warrior. According to Caesar, not without some disbelief from modern authors, the charioteers first drove rapidly around hurling weapons, then approached the battle lines, and the warrior was deposited to fight on foot, while the chariots withdrew, ready to collect the warrior and flee if the battle went badly. Caesar admired the skills that the Britons displayed in this antique form of warfare, long abandoned in Gaul.[22] The Britons were defeated, and submitted to Caesar and sent hostages. Shortly afterwards, the British weather proved to be the ally of the warriors. The horse transports still could not come in to land, and since the Roman ships had not been beached, the wind and rough tides wrecked twelve of them and damaged the rest. Witnessing this disaster, the Britons attacked a forage party of the Seventh legion, but were driven off. Caesar knew very well that he should have taken more precautions and ought to have found out about the tides on the British coasts, but disarmingly he could afford to recount the near disaster, which only emphasized his own and his soldiers' skills in overcoming them. In calm weather, Caesar sailed back to Gaul.

As his troops were disembarking, some men of the Morini tribe attacked them, initially only a few but then, according to Caesar, their numbers grew as another 6,000 joined in. The soldiers formed up and withstood the attack for four hours, until help arrived. The Morini ran away and eventually surrendered. Caesar's response was to devastate the lands of the Menapii, for reasons which he does not make clear.[23] No other Roman general had been to Britain, so Caesar's reputation in Rome would be enhanced, despite the lack of real achievement. Dio comments that Caesar had not accomplished anything for the country or for himself, but he magnified it in Rome, having made known what was hitherto unknown. The Senate voted him twenty days' thanksgiving.[24]

The year 55 BC had been a good one for Caesar. By defeating the German tribes and making his Rhine crossing, as well as carrying Roman arms to the furthest known island, he probably felt that he had earned the twenty days of thanksgiving voted to him by the Senate. But fame is short-lived, especially when opponents in Rome began to agitate against him. Marcus Porcius Cato had returned to Rome from governing Cyprus. He had hoped to be elected praetor, but by means of bribery, Pompey and Crassus, the consuls for 55 BC, had thwarted him. Cato now embarked on a series of speeches against Caesar. He took up the cause of the Germans, not because he felt sympathy for the tribes but because Caesar had gained the kudos and self-advertisement that he desired. The war against the Germans could be classified as a necessary war, given that the incursion of the tribes could have affected Rome if left unchecked, and the memory of the Cimbri and Teutones had not yet faded. The British war, however, had not been militarily necessary, since the tribesmen hardly represented a threat to Roman interests. At this moment, probably only a few people listened seriously to what Cato was saying. Pompey and Crassus had been placing their own adherents, and some of Caesar's, into as many official posts as they could, and via the tribune Gaius Trebonius they each secured provincial commands to be taken up after their consulships. They also honoured Caesar's wishes and organised the extension to his command in Gaul for five years.

Caesar determined to undertake a second expedition to Britain in 54 BC. Dio says that the pretext was that the Britons had not sent the hostages, as agreed after the first expedition, but even if they had done so, Caesar would have found some other reason to justify his second campaign in the island.[25] However, before Caesar could make a start, several of the Gallic chieftains allied, led by the hostile Aeduan, Dumnorix. The Treveri had appealed to the Germans, but since there were two rival leaders, Cingetorix and Indutiomarus, Caesar pronounced in favour of one of them, choosing Cingetorix, who submitted to him. Indutiomarus was forced to renounce his ambitions and send hostages. Once this was settled, Caesar embarked his troops at Portus Itius (Boulogne). He summoned the Gallic chiefs to meet him there, then he kidnapped all those whom he did not trust, intending to carry them to Britain where he could keep a close watch on them. Dumnorix tried to escape, but he was captured and killed.[26]

The second British invasion started in July, with about 800 ships, including some private vessels which had been built by members of Caesar's army and entourage.[27] On landing, there was no enemy to fight. The Britons had retreated to high ground, waiting for the Romans to come to them. Caesar left his ships at anchor in order to disembark the troops and march to battle with the Britons, without beaching the ships, because to do so would waste valuable time. He drove the Britons off the higher ground, but then found when he pursued them into the woods that they had felled trees to block all the entrances. Some men of the Seventh legion formed the *testudo* or tortoise, raising their shields above their heads and storming the fortifications. Caesar intended to chase the tribesmen the next morning, but then bad news arrived. He had considered that the ships would be safe because they were on a sandy open shore, but he was mistaken. After the battle, there was another storm, and the anchored ships crashed against each other. Nearly forty of them were irretrievably damaged, but the rest could be repaired. Caesar had to spend ten days beaching the ships, organising their repair and building a fortified line all around them attached to the camp where the contingent guarding them was housed. He wrote to Labienus in Gaul to instruct him to build more ships.[28]

The Britons sank their differences and selected a leader, Cassivellaunus, chief of the Catuvellauni, overcoming for the time being the disunity that could lead to defeat in piecemeal fashion. Caesar marched cautiously inland, until he met the Britons at the Thames, where they had fortified the river bank with stakes. The Romans managed to get across the river and drive the Britons from their fortifications. It was a victory, offset by the fact that Cassivellaunus roused the Kentish tribes to attack the troops who were repairing the ships at the naval base. Caesar turned his attention to the Trinobantes, who had no cause to love the Catuvellauni. Cassivellaunus had killed their king, whose son Mandubracius had found refuge with Caesar in Gaul. The Trinobantes submitted willingly, followed by other smaller tribes. Cassivellaunus would soon find himself isolated and without support, and unless the tribes united they could not hope to defeat the Romans. He asked for terms. It was a strategy to get Caesar out of the way, not an ignominious defeat. He was shrewd enough to realise that since Caesar had not yet pacified all the Gallic tribes he could not stay in Britain for long without endangering what he had achieved so far. Total conquest of Britain was not part of Caesar's agenda, so if peace was made, he would most likely return to Gaul, and the Catuvellauni could get on with their own empire building ambitions unmolested. Caesar was content to demand tribute and hostages. He had to convey his troops to Gaul in two instalments because he had too few ships. The ships dropped off the first instalment and returned to pick up Caesar himself and the remaining troops, but some of them were driven off course, and Caesar and his men had to cram themselves into what ships they had to hand, and got back safely to Gaul.[29]

The achievements of 54 BC were marred by the death of Julia, Caesar's daughter and Pompey's beloved wife.[30] She died after giving birth prematurely to a son, and the infant died soon afterwards. Only Dio says that the child was a daughter, while other sources affirm that the infant was a boy.[31] The people of Rome showed their respect for Julia by escorting her body to the Campus Martius, insisting that she should be laid to rest there, rather than outside the city. Strictly, senatorial approval ought to have been sought before the funeral took place, but protests were in vain and the people got their way.[32] It was an honour for Caesar, and he acknowledged it as such.[33] Caesar may have made plans to reaffirm his connections with Pompey. He sent his secretary Cornelius Balbus, who had accompanied him to Britain, to Rome. Balbus had been Pompey's friend initially, so if there was a personal overture to Pompey from Caesar, Balbus was the best choice of messenger. The purpose of Balbus' visit to Rome is not elucidated, but there were rumours of a proposed marriage alliance. Caesar was to divorce his wife Calpurnia and marry Pompey's daughter, and Pompey was to marry Caesar's great niece Octavia.[34] If the proposal was ever conveyed to Pompey, it came to nothing. Pompey eventually married Cornelia, the daughter of Quintus Metellus Scipio, who was noted for his opposition to Caesar. This need not mean that Pompey had renounced his association with Caesar. If Julia had lived, or even if her son had survived, it is possible that Caesar and Pompey would not have found themselves on opposite sides of the political scene some years later, but scholarly opinion is divided on this issue. Without affirming his earlier statement that Julia had given birth to a daughter, Dio says that this child was the only thing keeping Pompey and Caesar on friendly terms, but he inserts this passage in the context of 50 BC, four years after the baby died.[35] In 54 BC, and for some time afterwards, there were no signs that the partnership was starting to break up.[36]

The harvests of 54 BC had been poor, and the troops in Gaul had to be placed in dispersed winter quarters at the end of that year. The fragile peace was soon to be shattered. The Treveran chief Indutiomarus resented his deposition by Caesar in favour of his rival Cingetorix. He persuaded Ambiorix, chief of the Eburones, to attack the Romans encamped at Aduatuca. The Eburones had provided food for the Romans in their territory, and Caesar's messengers had regularly made contact with Ambiorix. For this reason, perhaps, the Roman commanders Quintus Titurius Sabinus and Lucius Aurunculeius Cotta trusted him more than they ought to have done. Rather than attempting to besiege the Romans, Ambiorix deliberately made a feeble attack, and then requested a meeting with some representatives from the Roman camp. He persuaded the Romans that he was obliged to attack as part of a plot that had spread among the Gauls to launch an assault on all the Roman camps at once. He convinced the Romans that the German tribes were also involved and that some tribesmen were en route for their camp at that very moment. He advised Sabinus and Cotta to attempt the two-day march to join Quintus Cicero, camped near the modern town of Namur. This they did, despite the objections of Cotta and some of the centurions, and they were slaughtered. A small number of survivors reached Labienus' camp. Caesar recounts all this at considerable length, together with speeches made by Ambiorix and the Roman commanders.[37]

The Gauls now knew that the Romans could be defeated, and other tribes joined in the rebellion. The Nervii, who had already suffered a disastrous defeat at Caesar's hands in 57 BC, negotiated with Quintus Cicero, attempting the same ruse that Ambiorix had used to persuade Cotta and Sabinus to leave their winter quarters. The Nervii said that all the Gauls were in revolt, and Caesar was hard pressed, but Cicero and his troops were guaranteed safe passage if they marched out now. Cicero said he would not negotiate with an enemy under arms, and stayed put. The Nervii then put his camp under siege, using Roman methods to build a fortified line around it. They had learned a lot since their earlier defeat. In the context of this siege, Caesar inserts a vignette concerning two rival centurions, Titus Pullo and Lucius Vorenus. Pullo came out of the camp to tackle the Nervii close to the fortifications, and not to be outdone, Vorenus followed. Pullo went down, Vorenus rescued him, then he went down too and Pullo rescued him, and both men got back to the camp without wounds. Pullo had been struck by a missile, but it stuck in his belt and did not injure him. This escapade was probably reported to Caesar by Cicero, and it would make for a lively conversation piece among the officers and soldiers.

Cicero strengthened his fortifications and built more towers, knowing that he could not hope to hold out indefinitely. He sent messages to Caesar at Amiens, but some of them were caught, and then brought back and tortured in sight of Cicero's camp. Only one messenger reached Caesar, a slave who had been promised freedom by a Nervian called Vertico, loyal to the Romans, who had fled to join Cicero when the hostilities began. The slave carried a message attached to a spear, probably hidden inside the shaft. Caesar rapidly gathered troops from other camps, but not as many as he would have wished for. Indutiomarus had successfully pinned down Labienus, so Caesar had to do without his lieutenant and his soldiers. One of Caesar's Gallic horsemen was persuaded to take a message to Cicero, written in Greek letters, to let him know that help was on the way. The Gaul attached the message to a spear, and Dio says that the horseman aimed the spear at the ramparts as if he was part of the attacking force. But it stuck fast in one of the towers and remained there for two days until a soldier found it.[38] As Caesar approached Cicero's camp, the Nervii broke off the siege to meet him. Cicero sent the loyal Nervian Vertico to inform Caesar that the tribesmen had raised the siege and were coming to intercept him. The Nervian host was about ten times stronger than the Romans. Caesar built a small camp, narrowing the roads inside it to give the impression that he had even fewer men than he really had, and he ordered the legionaries to pretend to panic. The Nervii were deceived, and attacked. Caesar's men rushed out from all the gates, supported by the cavalry, and the tribesmen were scattered and many of them were killed.[39]

Caesar marched to Cicero's camp. When Indutiomarus heard how the Nervii had been defeated, he raised the siege of Labienus' camp and fled to the Treveri. He tried to entice the Germans to come to his aid, promising money, but none of the tribes crossed the Rhine. But the Senones and Carnutes joined Indutiomarus. It was decided to attack Labienus' camp. Forewarned by Cingetorix, who had been deposed by Indutiomarus, Labienus had time to assemble cavalry forces from nearby tribes. He brought these horsemen into his camp one night, and concealed them from the Gauls. Indutiomarus approached the camp each day to taunt the Romans, but Labienus did not respond until one evening when the Gauls were departing, unaware that the Roman and native cavalrymen were poised at two gates to launch an attack. They were instructed to find Indutiomarus and kill him, not waste time on any other Gauls. This they did. The Nervii and Eburones went home, and there was a brief lull in hostilities.[40]

Then the Treveri allied with the Eburones. Smaller tribes also started to arm themselves. Caesar raised two more legions in Cisalpine Gaul, and he borrowed another from Pompey, who was technically governor of Spain, but still in Rome. The three new legions were with him by the end of the winter. In the early spring of 53 BC, Caesar summoned the Gallic chiefs to a conference, but the Senones, Treveri and Carnutes were conspicuous by their absence. There was a danger that other tribes, even those which had submitted to Caesar, might be beguiled by thoughts of independence and join forces to try to rid themselves of the Romans. But unless the tribes could unite, they were not strong enough to stand against the Romans. Caesar transferred his base to Lutetia (modern Paris) and marched towards the Senones, but he did not have to fight. The Senones and the Carnutes submitted.[41]

Caesar now focussed on Ambiorix and the Eburones, and their allies the Menapii and Treveri, supported by the loyal Aedui and the Remi. Caesar first attacked the Menapii at the mouth of the Rhine, in order to isolate the Eburones by depriving them of allies or any place to find refuge. It remained to deal with Ambiorix, and Caesar had evidently lost patience. The campaign against the Eburones was callous and cruel. The Romans were spared from bloody battles because Caesar laid waste to the land, crops and homes of the tribe, and gave rival tribes free rein to attack the Eburones, kill as many as they liked, to pillage and steal, and to destroy the territory. Caesar was unconcerned about the Eburones or the tribes who attacked them. He considered, callously, that it was better for the Gauls to risk their lives in the wooded terrain, rather than the soldiers.[42] Only a few of the Eburones survived. Ambiorix was never captured. The invitation to pillage encouraged the German Sugambri to cross the Rhine, but instead of raiding the Eburones they attacked the Roman camp at Aduatuca, where Caesar had left Quintus Cicero with the all the baggage, the Fourteenth legion and 200 cavalry. The attack launched by the Sugambri caused panic among the Roman troops, and cut off a foraging party. Inside the camp a wounded soldier called Publius Sextius Baculus, already cited by Caesar for his acts of bravery, emerged from his sickbed, rallied the centurions of the cohort guarding the camp, and held the gate until he fainted, but the fort was not penetrated.[43] Some of the soldiers who had been cut off decided to charge the Germans and managed to break through into the Roman camp, but another party of soldiers and camp followers had taken refuge on high ground, where the centurions held off the Germans for long enough to allow many of the soldiers to reach the safety of the camp, however, many others perished before they could escape. Then the Germans gave up their attempt to storm the camp and headed back across the Rhine, and finally Caesar arrived. He remarked that instead of pillaging the territory of Ambiorix as the Germans had originally intended, they assisted him by drawing off Roman troops.[44]

Caesar summoned the Gallic chiefs to Rheims. He punished the Senones by executing their leader Acco and stationing in their lands six of his ten legions in winter quarters from 53 to 52 BC. The soldiers could watch them closely, and as further punishment the Senones would have to bear the heavy burden of supplying the troops.[45] Battles had been won, but the war had not ended, and Caesar was to learn that brutal treatment did not induce the Gauls to capitulate. Instead it did more to unify the tribes than any other event of the last few years. All that was required now was a charismatic leader who could persuade the tribes to act together.

While Caesar was dealing with revolts in Gaul, the year 53 BC was also turbulent in Rome. The elections for the consulship of 53 BC had been delayed, and it was only in the seventh month that Domitius Calvinus and Valerius Messalla were appointed.[46] There were riots, and rumours spread that Pompey was to be made Dictator to pacify the city and restore order. He said that he did not desire the office, which was just as well because Cato made sure that he did not get it. The Three-Headed Monster lost one of its heads when news arrived in summer 53 that the Parthians had defeated and killed Crassus and his son. It is questionable whether the loss of Crassus had a deleterious effect on the alliance. In 53 BC there were no definite signs that Pompey and Caesar were at odds with each other, and later, with or without Crassus, Caesar would still have to find some means of stepping from his proconsulship to his second consulship without a break. If he laid down his powers as proconsul and lost command of his armies, and then stood for election as consul for a second time, he would have to endure a short interval as a vulnerable *privatus*, and would almost certainly face prosecution on one charge or another, whether the charge was justified or not. It has been suggested that no one would dare to convict him, but this was not the most important point. If he was brought to trial he would not be allowed to stand for the consulship.

In 52 BC, the government of Rome and the provinces was virtually non-existent, because the magistrates and officials had no successors. Eventually Pompey was made sole consul, an anomalous position, but it avoided the title Dictator and it also avoided the need to appoint a colleague until the state was more settled. Writing more than two centuries after the events, Dio detected a change in Pompey from this point onwards, when he stopped pleasing the people and started to do everything for the Senate.[47] While Rome was in turmoil, Caesar faced the strongest challenges to his command in Gaul. In the political arena he had enemies who were determined to recall him, and on the military front he became better acquainted with a Gallic chief called Vercingetorix. The war with Vercingetorix takes up all of the seventh book of Caesar's *Commentaries*; it is covered briefly by Dio.[48] The rebellion starting early in 52 BC did not involve all the tribes, but notably even some of the tribes which had been friendly to the Romans now turned against them. Groups of tribesmen met to champion the cause of freedom for the Gauls. The first move was made by the Carnutes, who secured a promise from the tribesmen, under oath, that if they began the campaign then the other tribes would not abandon them. They then massacred the Roman traders at Cenabum (modern Orleans). There were two potential leaders for the united tribes, Commius of the Gallic Atrebates, and Vercingetorix of the Arverni. Both had been cultivated as friends of the Roman people by Caesar. They could persuade their allies and friends among the tribes to join them.

Caesar had not yet joined his army, and realised that it would be difficult to do so. With some new recruits and a provincial militia he made for Narbo (modern Narbonne) immediately after hearing that some tribesmen were closing in on the town. This meant that the rebellion affected the peaceful Romanised parts of Gaul as well as the northern parts. Caesar learned that Vercingetorix was not with his people, the Arverni, but was with the Bituriges, trying to persuade them to join him. Hoping to draw Vercingetorix back home, Caesar decided to attack the Arverni, and then when he heard that the plan had worked, he rode to join the two legions based near Langres. He could now set about gathering his army.

The war became a matter of rapid movements and sieges rather than violent decisive battles.

Vercingetorix was besieging Gorgobina, a settlement where Caesar had placed the tribesmen of the Boii as dependents of the Aedui. If Caesar failed to come to the aid of the Boii it would appear that he was not powerful enough to protect his friends, and the Aedui would lose faith in him, possibly leading to the defection of this loyal tribe, followed by the spread of the rebellion to the whole of Gaul.[49] He set off to bring aid to the Boii and on the way he took one of the strongholds of the Senones, and then Cenabum, chief town of the Carnutes, where the Roman traders had been killed. After this he crossed the Loire, marching towards the lands of the Bituriges, and prepared to besiege Noviodunum, one of their strongholds. The town was just about to capitulate, but Vercingetorix was approaching, so they thought they would be relieved and closed their gates. But Caesar's German cavalry, a legacy from his defeat of Ariovistus, drove off the warriors of Vercingetorix, and Caesar was then free to march on the wealthiest and most important settlement of the Bituriges, Avaricum (modern Bourges).[50]

Vercingetorix adopted a scorched earth policy, ordering his allies to fortify their towns, or to burn everything if the settlements could not be defended. All food supplies were to be denied to the Romans. His leadership was strong enough to give such an order and be obeyed. The Bituriges burnt twenty settlements in one day, according to Caesar, but would not sacrifice Avaricum.[51] Caesar laid siege to it, but the disruption of his supplies was so effective that he almost abandoned the siege. The legionaries would not hear of it, despite their lack of food. Vercingetorix camped nearby, then left the scene temporarily, so Caesar took advantage of his absence to attack the camp, which failed because the defences were too strong. Caesar then started to build a ramp to reach the defences. It was presumably timber-framed and flammable, and was set alight by the Gauls who dug a shaft under it. The troops that Caesar had posted on permanent guard duty were able to cut a fire break, and beat off the Gauls who rushed out of the gates to the attack. From inside the town the defenders threw pitch and grease, and anything that would ignite, onto the ramp so that it would burn more thoroughly. Next day Caesar noted the determination and bravery of the Gauls on the ramparts, throwing balls of flaming pitch.

One man was killed by Roman missiles, and another stepped into his place, until he too was killed, and so on, one man after another, until the fighting ceased. Caesar was impressed with the pertinacity and self-sacrifice of the Gauls, and perhaps he appreciated for the first time the depth of the extreme hatred of Roman rule.[52]

One day, there was heavy rain, and the Gauls did not man the ramparts strongly. The Roman siege towers were brought close to the walls, the troops attacked and Avaricum fell. The Romans massacred everyone inside, including women and children. It was labelled as revenge for the traders who had died at Cenabum. Caesar reckoned that out of the 40,000 people who had been in the town, only around 800 reached Vercingetorix. The disaster did not diminish the support for Vercingetorix. Instead he gained more allies, and even the Aedui were beginning to waver. Caesar had to work hard to regain their trust and friendship, relying as he did on the Aedui for the greater part of his food supply.[53]

In the north the Senones and Parisi were restless. Titus Labienus was despatched to their territory with four legions while Caesar and the rest of the army marched alongside the River Allier towards the Arvernian settlement of Gergovia, a naturally strong settlement on a high plateau. Vercingetorix destroyed all the bridges across the Allier, and posted some of his men to prevent the Romans from building a bridge, but Caesar still managed to build one. He concealed two legions near to one of the crossing points where only the bridge piles remained, then sent out the other legions with their cohorts spread out to give the impression that all the legions were marching together. Caesar gave them time to reach the place for their next encampment, then, using the two legions left behind, he constructed a bridge on the old supporting piles. Dio, however, says that Caesar crossed by rafts.[54] Vercingetorix realised that the Romans had succeeded in crossing the Allier, and he and Caesar raced for Gergovia. Caesar needed only a cursory glance at the site of Gergovia to understand that he could never take it by storm, so he decided to attack Le Roche Blanche, a nearby hill where Vercingetorix had posted some of his tribesman to secure the water supply and the pasture. Caesar made camp, constructed a smaller camp to the south-east, and took the hill during the night. He stationed two legions on it and joined the small camp to the large one by two parallel ditches.[55]

While Caesar was concentrating on Gergovia, the Arverni concentrated on detaching the Aedui from the Romans. They offered bribes to the Aeduan chief Convictolitavis, who contacted a young noble called Litaviccus and his followers, fomenting rebellion. Eporedorix, a loyal Aeduan who was with Caesar, told him that it was believed that Caesar had executed the Aedui serving in the Roman army, including Eporedorix himself and Viridomarus. In response, the tribesmen had killed all the Romans in charge of one of the supply convoys. Caesar left a small garrison in the camps at Gergovia, and marched to meet Litaviccus and the rebels. Observing that Eporedorix and Viridomarus were alive, the tribesmen surrendered, realising that they had been duped.[56]

Anxious to return to Gergovia, Caesar did not punish the Aedui. The Gauls had attacked his camps while he was absent. It was not a disaster, but he decided to abandon the blockade of Gergovia, although not before he had made a demonstration of strength. The plan did not work as he had intended. He feigned an attack on an undefended hill south-west of Gergovia, sending a legion towards it, with his baggage men mounted on their mules as fake cavalry. When the Gauls were about to counterattack, he suddenly launched his troops on the camp that Vercingetorix had built to the south of the town. According to Caesar, the original plan was to pull back once the damage had been done, but in their ardour the troops pressed on, oblivious to the signals to retreat. They forced their way through the camp until they came up against the town defences, where they met with determined opposition. The cost was high: 700 soldiers and forty-six centurions killed, and many wounded. The next morning, Caesar assembled the whole army in battle formation, confident that Vercingetorix would not attack. His main purpose was to praise the soldiers for their enthusiasm, but also to underline the point that discipline and obeying orders were vital to the success of any mission. Is this account true, or was it tweaked to disguise the fact that an assault had been disastrously beaten back?[57]

Moving off from Gergovia, Caesar made his headquarters at Noviodunum in Aeduan territory. He had not dealt decisively with the rebel Aedui, and now, without warning, Eporedorix and Viridomarus changed sides, encouraging the Gauls of the entire area to rebel. It was imperative for Caesar to assemble his whole army, so he marched to join Labienus, who knew that Caesar had abandoned Gergovia. Thinking that he was cut off, and that Caesar was miles away, he set off southwards with his four legions, aiming for the Roman Province. The Gauls tried and failed to stop him from crossing the Seine, while Caesar marched rapidly and crossed the Loire without opposition. The two armies met up, but were still not secure. Caesar was fortunate that the Remi refused to be influenced by Vercingetorix and remained loyal, as did the Lingones, and the Allobroges of southern Gaul. Vercingetorix was experiencing problems because the rebel Aedui wanted to take over, but then the tribes voted for him as leader, and he continued his policy of cutting off food supplies to the Romans. He knew that his best policy was to avoid pitched battles, and to wear down Caesar's army by guerrilla tactics and denying them supplies, and waiting. He probably knew that in Rome there were movements to recall Caesar, and in any case, his extended command of five years would surely expire soon. Another winter might see the end of hostilities. This was true; however, the Romans had almost unlimited manpower, and could go on recruiting soldiers and training armies, and if the Senate decided that the total conquest of Gaul was necessary, then commanders would be appointed and the war would continue.[58]

Vercingetorix encouraged the Aedui and other tribes to attack the Province. Caesar appointed one of his relatives, Lucius Caesar, to its defence. Twenty-two cohorts were recruited and strung out along the borders of the Province, and the Allobroges blocked the passage of the Rhone. This was inadequate, but Caesar's troops were exhausted, he was cut off from Italy, and he needed reinforcements. He sent for contingents of German horsemen, but when they arrived he found their horses unsuitable, so he made his officers give up their riding horses for use as cavalry mounts. Then he set out for the Province, through the lands of the Sequani.[59]

Vercingetorix set up his headquarters at Alesia (modern Alise-Sainte-Reine), a settlement in the territory of the Mandubii, situated on a plateau surrounded on three sides by rivers, the Ose and Oserain to the north and south, both flowing into the River Brenne on the west. He decided to surprise Caesar on the march, and succeeded. Caesar's troops were attacked at the head of the column and on both flanks, but they withstood the Gallic cavalry, allowing him time to bring up his own cavalry and order his legions to form up, protecting the baggage. On Caesar's right, the German cavalry drove off the Gauls, and then the tribesmen fled from the scene.[60]

When Caesar arrived at Alesia, where Vercingetorix had fortified the stronghold, he reconnoitred, concluding that the only option was a blockade, since a siege was not viable. He started to encircle the whole area with banks and ditches, distributing the troops in camps along the fortifications. Vercingetorix attacked Caesar's cavalry on the west side of the town, and the Romans were in difficulties until Caesar sent in the German horsemen. The Gauls turned and made for their camp, but the German cavalry slaughtered them, and when the survivors tried to escape to the town Vercingetorix shut the gates. From then on he kept firmly within the defences, sending his horsemen away during the night, with orders to assemble a relief party from other tribes. The absence of the horses would ease the problem of feeding them, but he left himself without the means of harassing the Romans. He began to ration food. Caesar heard of this from deserters and immediately tightened the cordon around the town, building two sets of defences, one facing inwards and the other facing outwards to protect the Roman troops against the relieving force that was certain to arrive. The siege works are more fully described in the previous chapter.[61]

Food supplies for the besiegers were soon exhausted. After one or two days, foraging became more difficult because the soldiers had to go further and further out to find food. Fortunately, Vercingetorix did not attempt to attack the foraging parties. The Gauls were assembling to relieve Alesia. The Aeduans contributed about 250,000 infantry, led by their chiefs Eporedorix and Viridomarus, and a relative of Vercingetorix called Vercassivellaunus. Commius, chief of the Atrebates and formerly Caesar's ally, joined them. The Gauls occupied the high ground south-west of Alesia, and the next day deployed the cavalry to face Caesar's outer defences. They had communicated with the Gauls inside the town, so these attacked the inner defence works at the same time. Caesar manned both lines and once again it was the German horsemen who performed well, scattering the Gauls of the relieving force. As these sped back to their camp on the heights, Vercingetorix withdrew his men from the inner lines and retired. Next, the Gauls attacked the inner and outer lines by night. They failed to breach them, but they discovered that north of the town, where the River Rabutin joined the Ose, two legions guarded a gap in the defences. The relieving army marched round to this point, while from inside Vercingetorix mounted a number of assaults at different points to keep the Romans pinned down so they could not form up en masse to assist the two legions. Caesar had to take command himself when the Gauls began to tear down the inner line. Labienus was sent with six cohorts to the aid of the two legions guarding the gap in the outer line, but he was soon in difficulties, so Caesar gathered some cavalry and infantry and set off to join him, sending another force round the outside to come up behind the Gauls. This attack from the rear surprised and disconcerted the Gauls, and they began to give way when they recognised Caesar's red cloak. This last point may be true, but it was probably still dark, and red would be hard to distinguish. A modern jury would question Caesar's statement, and attribute it to self-importance. Nonetheless, after Caesar and his troops gained the upper hand, the Gauls were heavily defeated, and many of them were killed.[62]

This battle abolished any hope of victory for Vercingetorix. There would not be enough time to raise another relief army before his food supplies ran out. Vercingetorix assembled his chiefs and offered to surrender himself to the Romans. It must have been a bitter moment. He had made a determined stand against the Roman Imperialist advance, but his policy of guerrilla warfare involved patient waiting while the tribes suffered. Immediate and continued successes might have welded the Gauls together, but freedom from Roman domination was uncertain and nebulous. Vercingetorix could offer no rewards, only hardship, hunger, perhaps death for a cause, and years of recovery afterwards. Blood, toil, tears and sweat are noble sentiments, certainly, but they lack the pulling power of cart-loads of portable wealth.

Caesar prepared to receive the Gallic leaders. He demanded the surrender of all weapons. Vercingetorix rode in, dismounted, and knelt before Caesar. Dio says that Vercingetorix arrived unannounced.[63] Vercingetorix could have fled from Alesia to continue to fight somewhere else. He could have died gloriously in battle, or perhaps at the hand of another Gallic chief who saw a quick way of ending the war. Instead he survived for six years in a Roman prison, walked behind Caesar's chariot in one of his triumphs, and was then strangled. When his country became a nation, he became a national hero, as the gigantic statue at Alise-Sainte-Reine attests.

The fall of Alesia did not signify the end of the revolt. Caesar tried to tone down his hitherto merciless policy. Aeduan and Arvernian prisoners were returned to their tribes. The Aedui resumed their former status as friends of the Roman people, and he left their internal organisation untouched. He put his troops into winter quarters, and remained at Bibracte in Aeduan territory.[64] He anticipated further trouble, which came from the Bituriges at the beginning of 51 BC. Before he marched against them, Caesar gave Mark Antony command of the winter camps. Antony had been with Caesar for some time, but this is the first mention of him by name in the *Commentaries*.[65]

After the defeat of the Bituriges, Caesar did not punish them, confining himself to a demand for hostages. Perhaps he considered that leniency would persuade the Gauls that there was more to be gained by cooperation with Rome than by risking a battle against his armies.[66] The policy worked, because instead of attacking the Romans, the tribes started to fight each other. The Carnutes raided the Bituriges, and Commius – the arch rebel and dedicated survivor – encouraged the Bellovaci to attack the Suessiones. It required an energetic Roman campaign to reduce the Bituriges and Bellovaci, whose chief was Correus. The Bellovaci encamped on high ground in the forest of Compiègne. Caesar camped opposite them, and started to enclose them. Remembering what happened at Alesia, the Bellovaci clearly saw the parallel and made efforts to get away. They did so eventually, by retreating behind a massive smoke and fire screen at night.[67] Correus made another camp and attacked the Roman foraging parties. Caesar discovered that Correus planned an ambush for the next foraging party and its escort. He sent out cavalry, as was usual when foraging was to be done, but interspersed these with light-armed auxiliaries, and followed with the legions as closely as possible. Instead of ambushing the Romans, Correus was ambushed himself. Correus was killed, and resistance crumbled. Caesar adopted his lenient policies once more, and other tribes submitted to him voluntarily.[68]

The Romans had failed to capture Commius, who had not renounced his fierce anti-Roman attitude. He may have been the force behind the other chiefs who determined to resist the Romans, using the memory of Ambiorix to stiffen the resolve of the tribes. Labienus was sent against the Treveri, and other officers were sent on operations in the north-west of Gaul. The remnants of the Eburones, Ambiorix's tribe, were massacred and their lands destroyed for the second time. Caesar could not capture him, so he made the name of Ambiorix hated throughout his own country. But the revolt stumbled on.[69] Two leaders called Drappes and Lucterius occupied Uxellodunum (modern Puy d'Issolu), where they had amassed quantities of food and stores to last them and their army through a siege, but the one vital element that the Gauls were unable to protect or to store was water. Caesar sent his engineers to cut off the water supply, and the inevitable consequence was the surrender of Uxellodunum.[70] Leniency did not enter into Caesar's response this time. He assembled all the men who had taken up arms against him and cut off their hands, to ensure that they did not have an honourable death and would be visible reminders of the power of Rome. In Roman opinion this action was perfectly justified, but in modern eyes it brings him little credit.[71]

The last of the Gauls to surrender was Commius. He gave himself up by sending deputies to Mark Antony, promising to go wherever he was directed, provided that he did not have to come anywhere near a Roman.[72]

Caesar began to court the friendship of the Gauls by relaxing the burdens imposed upon them, and by giving prestigious gifts. As Hirtius states, it was of the utmost importance to Caesar to avoid any further outbreaks of fighting so near to the end of his governorship.[73] The controversy over precisely when Caesar's proconsulship was to end still causes the flow of much ink and pounding of keyboards without resolving the problem, and is the subject of the next chapter.

10

The Road to War, 58–50 BC

As this chapter title suggests, this section is taken out of chronological sequence, back-tracking to take into account events in Rome which were only briefly mentioned while describing what Caesar achieved in Gaul. Since it takes two to tango and at least two to make a war, whether it is people, factions or nations, the civil war that broke out in 49 BC was as much Pompey's war as it was Caesar's, and involved all their associates, friends, and enemies. Was the civil war that saw the elimination of Pompey and the brief but packed supremacy of Caesar inevitable? Why could Caesar, Pompey and the Senate not reach a satisfactory compromise at some time before January 49? Is there an identifiable point at which it can be said that the seeds of the civil war had been irrevocably sown? Was it gradual and predictable, or sudden and unexpected?

The antecedents of the split between Pompey and Caesar are debatable. The starting point could be stretched as far back as the beginning of their association, as Plutarch thought. It was not their quarrel that caused the civil war, he wrote, but their friendship, because they collaborated to overthrow the aristocracy, and only then did they quarrel.[1] This could be disputed as an over simplification, and to take the story so far back would involve repeating much that has already been described in previous chapters. This chapter provides an overview of events in Rome while Caesar was absent, and describes some of the significant events that have been suggested as the cause of the rift, though these are not necessarily conclusory.

As Caesar departed for Gaul in spring 58, the main activities in Rome centered on the tribune Clodius, who was determined to see Cicero prosecuted for putting to death Roman citizens without trial. Caesar lingered near Rome until March, outside the *pomerium* because he had taken up his command, watching what happened. Apart from Cicero's fate, a more compelling reason for Caesar to linger was the proposal of the praetors Lucius Domitius Ahenobarbus and Gaius Memmius to have his consulship discussed in the Senate, with the intention of invalidating all the acts of his term of office.[2] Caesar published speeches against the praetors, but could do very little more himself. Clodius took up the cause, and he also arranged a meeting of the people in the Circus Flaminius, outside the city boundary so that Caesar could attend. The subject was to be the executed Catilinarians. The two consuls, Lucius Piso, Caesar's father-in-law, and Aulus Gabinius, an adherent of Pompey's, objected to the procedure that had brought about the deaths of the so-called conspirators. Caesar supported the objections, reminding the people that he had also objected to the death penalty in 63 BC, and now he advised against passing any law about the execution of Roman citizens and then applying it retrospectively to past events. Clodius did exactly that, via the *lex Clodia de capite civis*, which made it illegal to put Roman citizens to death without trial.[3] Cicero went into voluntary exile before it was forced upon him, and then Clodius passed another law declaring him an enemy of the state. Neither Caesar nor Pompey did anything to stop the law from being applied. It was suspected that the deal was that Pompey would be left alone if he took no action to save Cicero.

Cato was the next to be removed from Rome. The kingdom of Cyprus was to be annexed, and its king, Ptolemy, brother of Ptolemy XII Auletes of Egypt, was to be deposed. Clodius, via the Roman people, bestowed this honour on Cato, who did not want it.[4] The annexation of Cyprus could upset the eastern settlements Pompey had fought so hard to have ratified, and the deposition of the King of Cyprus could have repercussions on the arrangements that Caesar and Pompey had made with the King of Egypt. Clodius then kidnapped the younger Tigranes, son of the King of Armenia, one of the hostages whom Pompey had brought to Rome. Pompey and the consul Gabinius protested, and were attacked by

Clodius' gangs.[5] Pompey then devoted his energy to the recall of Cicero.[6] The first bill on Cicero's behalf was proposed by a tribune, but was vetoed. The proposal was shelved until 56 BC.

The relationship between Caesar and Pompey in 58 BC was probably as cordial as possible, but there are insinuations that all was not well. Caesar's influence has been detected behind an alleged plot to assassinate Pompey. It has not gained much credence, mainly because it was all so ridiculous. On 11 August one of Clodius' slaves, lingering nearby just as Pompey was about to enter the Senate, extracted a knife that he had concealed in his clothing and ostentatiously dropped it.[7] Caesar would not need to remove or intimidate Pompey at this stage, so the episode, if true, may have been a warning to Pompey to leave Clodius alone, a warning that was reinforced when the great man was besieged in his own house by Clodius' gangs.[8] The rumours that Caesar tried to have Pompey assassinated may have been fostered by parties in Rome who wanted to separate the two men. It may have been now that the tribune Quintus Terentius Culleo urged Pompey to divorce Julia and cut his ties with Caesar, but this only proved that Pompey was happily married, and had no intention of breaking with Caesar.

In January 56 Messius and then Fabricius proposed to recall Cicero, but Clodius blocked them in a violent bloodbath. Cicero's brother Quintus escaped death only by hiding under a pile of corpses. Since all Rome had now witnessed how far Clodius was prepared to go in stopping the recall of Cicero, Pompey gave a free hand to the gangs formed by the tribunes Sestius and Titus Annius Milo to combat Clodius. It took six months to pass the law recalling Cicero, who arrived back in Rome early in September.

Clodius instigated a riot on the score of the corn supply. As tribune, he had instituted a free corn dole, which Cicero claimed had cost the state one fifth of its revenue.[9] Clodius blamed the grain shortages on Pompey, because he had filled the city with his own supporters when he promulgated the bill for Cicero's recall. But problems with the corn supply were unpredictable because of the dependence on weather, good or bad harvests, shipping, storage, and greedy middlemen. The consuls Spinther and Metellus Nepos proposed that Pompey should be allocated the task of *cura annonae*, care of the corn supply, with proconsular powers and fifteen legates for five years. The tribune Messius suggested a much wider command, with far greater powers, but the bill was never passed. Pompey chose Cicero and his brother Quintus as two of his legates; the others are unknown.[10] The powers and privileges that Pompey was granted in this command were once again anomalous, placing extraordinary powers in the hands of one man. Clodius objected to the appointment of Pompey for precisely this reason.[11] But Pompey's position while he attended to the corn supply was secure with the Senate and with the mob in Rome, since he was rendering an essential service. Would it have given Caesar pause for thought if Pompey had accepted the wider powers proposed by Messius? Cicero wrote to Atticus, explaining that 'the law that the consuls propose is now considered quite moderate; that of Messius perfectly intolerable. Pompey says he prefers the former; his friends that he prefers the latter'.[12]

Since Pompey was given control of the whole of the corn supply from the sowing of the seeds through harvesting to transport, storage, and distribution, he had to travel around the Roman provinces and negotiate with landowners, farmers and growers, dealers and merchants, shippers and harbour masters. He would also have to be present in Rome itself on occasions, but since he commanded troops, special dispensation to enter the city was granted to him on each occasion when he needed to return. Pompey instituted a census to discover who was entitled to the corn dole. It is not clear whether this was a complete count, or whether Pompey was merely planning ahead by counting up new names which would be included in the future, after the full census due in 55–54. There were many potential new recipients, because people had been freeing their aged slaves in anticipation of the reorganisation of the corn dole. The only source for the numbers of recipients of the corn dole comes from Suetonius' life of Caesar, who is said to have reduced the number from 320,000 to 150,000.[13]

At the same time, there was a problem in Egypt. Ptolemy XII Auletes retained his throne by paying a fee to Pompey and Caesar, and the Egyptian tax payers who paid for the privilege rioted. Auletes had fled to Rome in 57 BC, living at Pompey's Alban villa. He offended prominent Romans and quietly murdered his opponents who had come to Rome for redress. Pompey arranged for Rabirius Postumus to advance a huge loan to Ptolemy, and later Rabirius went to Egypt to become in effect Ptolemy's finance minister. Pompey may have hoped to combine his administration of the corn supply with a commission to restore Auletes to Egypt, but in the end, the Senate blocked all proposals for restoration of Ptolemy by Roman agents.

In 56 BC, prosecutions were brought against Pompey's and Clodius' associates alike. Clodius himself prosecuted Milo in February, and his gangs shouted Pompey down when he tried to speak in Milo's defence. Clodius had prepared well. 'Who is starving the people to death?' he asked, and the crowd shouted 'Pompey!' Then Clodius asked, 'Who wants to go to Alexandria?' and the mob shouted 'Pompey!' 'Who do you want to go?' and the mob answered 'Crassus!' Then there was a serious fight, but Pompey's men, most likely veteran soldiers, threw Clodius off the Rostra. A meeting of the Senate was immediately summoned, and the next two days were spent discussing the riotous proceedings, but only as an excuse for Caius Cato to make a scathing speech about Pompey, whilst praising Cicero, in a thinly disguised attempt to drive a wedge between them. The trial of Milo was adjourned until 17 February, and a prosecution was arranged of Pompey's man Sestius, who was to be defended by Cicero. Pompey brought in clients from as far away as Picenum and northern Italy, so that he would be much stronger than Clodius.[14]

Pompey was losing popularity after the rioting, neither a favourite of the people nor the leader of any strong faction in the Senate. There was a marked lack of men of consular rank or political influence among his friends.[15] His relationship with Crassus, never brilliant, had deteriorated, and cash was getting short for the adminstration of the corn supply. Pompey turned to the Campanian land settlements. state revenues had been lost by selling allotments, but if these lands were returned to the control of the state, the revenues would be restored, and the Senate would have no excuse for not voting to Pompey the funds he needed to attend to the corn supply. His own veterans would not be affected, because they had been settled elsewhere. While Pompey was absent from Rome, the tribune Rutilius Lupus introduced a bill concerning the Campanian lands, explaining that he did not wish the senators to vote immediately because he did not wish to act without knowing what Pompey's wishes were. The result was that the senators deferred to Pompey, who did not explain everything properly, and nothing was done. Cicero revived the matter in the Senate in April 56.

The proposals for the Campanian lands signalled potential conflict with Caesar, who may have dissuaded Pompey from pursuing the matter when they met at Lucca in 56 BC. During that winter Caesar stayed at Ravenna, at the very edge of his province, and Crassus went to meet him there. Then Pompey, ostensibly setting off for Sardinia to look into the corn supply, travelled to Lucca to meet Caesar. This meeting, labelled by modern historians as the conference at Lucca, has become part of the lore of the later Republic, but the three men may not have met together at Lucca at all. Crassus had already seen Caesar at Ravenna, and since he and Pompey were not well disposed towards each other, Crassus may have returned to Rome without meeting Pompey. The earliest source for the meeting is Cicero's letter to Spinther, written two years later in 54 BC.[16] Appian says that Caesar had come to the Po valley, and then Pompey and Crassus met him, but he does not name Lucca and he does not say that all three met together. What he does say is that 200 senators and 120 lictors gathered around Caesar.[17] Gelzer suggested that the numbers are exaggerated, and Gruen assumes that Crassus' supporters and clients made up a large crowd at Lucca.[18] Some scholars interpret the meeting, combined with Cicero's proposal concerning the Campanian lands, as a panic attack on the part of Caesar and Crassus because Pompey was gaining too much influence, and that Crassus hastened to Ravenna to explain the latest moves to Caesar. Suetonius suggests that Caesar feared the designs of Domitius Ahenobarbus.[19] As praetor, Domitius had already tried to replace Caesar in Gaul, and if elected consul for 55 BC he would no doubt try again to remove Caesar from his command, and take over Gaul for himself as proconsul. Therefore, according to Suetonius, it was Caesar who arranged the meeting at Lucca, and Caesar who compelled Pompey and Crassus to stand for the consulship of 55 BC, and to do everything they could to block Domitius' candidacy for the office. One result which could possibly be attributed to the meeting with Caesar is that when Pompey went to Sardinia in connection with the corn supply, he talked with Cicero's brother Quintus, with a clear message that Cicero should drop the matter of the Campanian lands. He reinforced the message by sending his agent Lucius Vibullius Rufus to see Cicero.[20]

The agenda at the so-called conference of Lucca is not known, but the ancient authors who describe the agreement of 56 BC assume that the consulship of 55 BC for Pompey and Crassus, and the extension of Caesar's command for another five years, were discussed and arranged on the spot, largely because this is what actually happened. Appian names only these goals in describing the meeting.[21] Pompey and Crassus were also to receive proconsular commands equal to Caesar's, and some modern scholars suggest that the provincial commands were the most important features of the arrangements, because this ensured the future careers of Pompey and Crassus, and the potential to earn greater glory. It is not certain if Caesar limited his request to the extension of his command or whether he discussed his longer term plans, namely to gain a second consulship, without having to relinquish his military command, thereby risking prosecution. If he did mention this to Pompey and Crassus, he may have kept silent about the time frame, not specifying the year in which he intended to stand for the consular elections. The law that Sulla had passed stipulating a ten-year gap between consulships was still in force, so technically Caesar would have to wait until 49 BC before he was allowed to stand for the consulship of 48 BC. But Caesar did not allow laws to stand in his way if they could be circumvented, so Pompey may have been prepared for Caesar to stand for election in 50 BC, which may explain some of the features of his interaction with Caesar during that year.

Meier asks whether the triumvirs were concerned for the wellbeing of the Republic or only for themselves.[22] Probably they thought of themselves and their futures first and the Republic second, hoping to be able to cater for their security while remaining loosely within the legal and political framework.[23]

Back in Rome, Pompey and Crassus achieved their election by subterfuge, intimidation and bribery. They delayed putting their names forward as candidates and somehow they blocked the consuls of 56 BC from staging the elections.[24] At one point when the consul Marcellinus attempted to hold the elections, Caius Cato declared that the omens were unfavourable and the proceedings had to be stopped. He had been bought by liberal distributions of cash from the coffers of Pompey and Crassus. In the absence of legitimate elections, special arrangements had to be made. The regulations stated that if there were no elections within the consular year, an *interrex* had to be appointed to oversee the elections, so it was then necessary to ensure that a pliable appointee was chosen for this task. All other candidates for the consulship had to be removed, and dissuading them was heavy handed. Domitius was wounded in a riot, and one of his supporters was killed. Thus did Pompey and Crassus commence their second joint consulship amid violence and mayhem.[25]

The immediate concern of the new consuls for 55 BC as they entered office in late January, was to hold the elections for the other magistrates and to have as many of their supporters immediately placed in post as praetors, aediles and tribunes, without any time lapse during which prosecutions could be brought against them. A suggestion that there should be a gap of sixty days before the new magistrates entered office was squashed by the new consuls, unequivocally revealing the tenor of their year of office. The next most important feature was the legislation designed to give both men long term proconsular commands, and to extend Caesar's command in Gaul.[26] These commands for Pompey and Crassus were probably not worked out in minute detail at Lucca. Cicero visited Pompey at Naples in April and reported that nothing definite had been arranged then, though Pompey was never as forthcoming about his plans as Cicero would have liked, and may simply have been prevaricating.[27] The tribune Gaius Trebonius presented the bill to give Crassus and Pompey provincial commands for five years. Extraordinary commands like these would always rouse opposition, and in this case opposition was violent but not of prolonged duration, and not successful. Cato voiced his objections and was imprisoned briefly. Two tribunes objected, Caius Ateius Capito and Publius Aquillius Gallus, and were forcibly silenced. On the day of voting, Cato and company were barred from entering the Forum, and it was not a peaceful process. Amidst violence and intimidation, the bills became law. The territories in question, the two Spanish provinces and Syria, were allocated by lot, the Spanish provinces falling to Pompey, and Syria to Crassus. The law also furnished the two men with the right to levy troops and to make peace or war as necessary. Pompey and Crassus insulated themselves against senatorial interference by setting a definite terminal date for their commands, before which no discussion was to be permitted – that date was 1 March 50.

Crassus was determined to start a campaign against the King of Parthia, and if Pompey had to go to Spain instead of remaining in Rome, he could still have been able to keep watch on events in Rome and the West, just as Caesar did from Gaul.[28] But Pompey chose not to leave Italy, and Dio says that he sent his legates to Spain immediately after his appointment was ratified, and Crassus also sent legates to Syria, where Gabinius was still technically in command.[29]

The next law perhaps came as no surprise, to extend Caesar's command in Gaul and Illyricum for another five years.[30] According to Dio, Caesar's command was for three years, but this is not correct.[31] The extension to Caesar's command was probably one of the topics arranged between the three men in northern Italy, possibly in a three-way discussion between Caesar and the other two. Caesar could not come to Rome to arrange it himself, but his allies could push through the necessary legislation for him. The extension of Caesar's command may or may not have come into force as soon as the law was passed in 55 BC, but it is equally possible that the start date was January 54, which would have an impact on the date when it was to terminate. Another point is that in the original allocation of Caesar's provinces, he received Cisalpine Gaul with Illyricum for five years, followed by the allocation of Transalpine Gaul for one year, to be renewed annually. The new law may have lumped all three provinces together for the extension of five years. A third unknown factor is that although the provincial commands of Pompey and Crassus had a definite terminal date of 1 March, it is not known if the same arrangement also applied to Caesar's extended proconsulship of Gaul. If these points should ever be clearly elucidated, it would put an end to a great deal of scholarly debate concerning the attempts to recall Caesar from 51 BC onwards, and the problems that arose in 50 and 49 BC, when the controversy over the recall of Caesar reached critical mass.

For the time being, the future of the Roman world for the next half a decade was divided up between three men, who exercised most but not all of the political influence at Rome, while also commanding the most important provinces and about twenty legions between them.[32]

The consulship of Pompey and Crassus was not noted for sweeping reforms, except for the institution of laws designed to tidy up electoral procedures, including a law to curb bribery at elections.[33] This was somewhat ironic considering how the two men had reached the consulship themselves. These measures may have been aimed at reducing the power of Clodius and his gangs, but during this period of Pompey's ascendancy, Clodius was quiescent.[34] He was perhaps neutralised when Pompey's elder son Gnaeus married the daughter of Appius Claudius, Clodius' brother, probably in 55 BC, or perhaps in the following year.

The personal position of the so-called Triumvirs was almost unassailable, but that of their associates was open to attack. Trials proliferated of the adherents of the three men, beginning in 56 BC with Cornelius Balbus, who was accused of unlawfully assuming the Roman citizenship granted to him by Pompey. Crassus and Pompey spoke on behalf of Balbus, and Cicero made a concluding speech. The jury confirmed Balbus' Roman citizenship. Trials continued in 55 BC. Much of Pompey's time was occupied with them, making speeches in defence of his adherents. Pompey regained some prestige in August 55, when his theatre was inaugurated, the first permanent stone theatre ever built in the city, with colonnaded walks and a park that became a famous meeting place. In its grounds there was a new meeting house for the Senate, the *curia Pompeii*, close to Pompey's new residence. The theatre and house were outside the city boundary, so Pompey could attend meetings without crossing the *pomerium* and having to extract concessions from the Senate.[35] The meeting house was a fortunate addition to the building, since the Senate House in the Forum was destined to be destroyed by fire in 52 BC, and it was still not rebuilt in 44 BC. It was in Pompey's building that the Senate met on the Ides of March in 44 BC, when Caesar fell dead at the foot of Pompey's statue.

Pompey and Crassus now ceased to try to engineer or block the election of their successors for 54 BC, or possibly they were unable to influence proceedings quite so easily. The Lucca conference and especially the consulships of 55 BC strengthened the resolve of their opponents, who began to manipulate public opinion against the unofficial triumvirate 'with consummate skill'.[36] Their sworn enemy Domitius Ahenobarbus was a consular candidate. Perhaps because they were secure for the time being, Pompey and Crassus could afford to allow politicians free rein.[37] There was an absence of violence during the electoral campaigning, but there was still a delay in holding the elections, for reasons unknown. Domitius was duly elected along with Appius Claudius Pulcher. If the marriage of Pompey's son to Appius' daughter had already taken place, the alliance did not mean that Appius was to be a mouthpiece for Pompey, nor for Caesar.

Crassus left for Syria towards the end of 55 BC, ignoring the violent opposition to his projected attack on Parthia. An aggressive war was not catered for in the law assigning Crassus to Syria, but everyone knew what was planned. Appian points out that the Parthians had done no harm to Rome.[38] The tribune Ateius Capito tried to block Crassus by arresting him, but Pompey supported Crassus, and accompanied him out of Rome. Ateius had to content himself with solemnly cursing the general and the Parthian war. Perhaps he was as surprised as anyone else at the effectiveness of his curse when Crassus met with complete disaster in 53 BC.

Since Pompey was still in charge of the corn supply, he did not take up his post as governor of the two Spanish provinces, continuing to govern through his legates, Lucius Afranius and Marcus Petreius. Appian says he governed through friends, while Dio says that he governed though lieutenants, without naming Afranius and Petreius.[39] This was an important precedent, underlining his pre-eminent position. Appian points out that Pompey was the first of the consuls who controlled two of the greatest provinces, an army, and public money, while at the same time holding supreme power in the city.[40] This was the basis upon which the Emperors, beginning with Augustus, governed the whole Empire, via well-chosen *legati*, while holding supreme power and influence over the whole Empire. Pompey's extraordinary commands were not permanent, but always had a specified number of years to run, or a precise terminal date attached to the law that gave him special commands. Domination was less frightening when chopped up into potentially terminable chunks, and Augustus made a point of not accepting any powers in perpetuity.

Probably in the summer of 54, there was personal tragedy for both Caesar and Pompey, when Julia died as a result of the premature birth of her son. Pompey had been involved in a riot at the elections for the aediles, and his clothing had been splattered with blood. When Julia saw her husband's bloodstained outer clothing being brought home, she collapsed before it could be explained that he had not been injured.[42] Dio thought that Julia had formed a strong bond between Caesar and Pompey, but Velleius Paterculus thought that the alliance had been held together only with difficulty even when Julia was alive.[43] For modern authors, it can be said that while Julia was mourned by her husband and father, her absence did not lead directly to a split between them. There was no detectable animosity, and no noticeable political change in either Caesar's or Pompey's attitude to each other, as attested by the fact that Caesar had already made a will leaving his estate to his son-in-law, and he did not alter it at this point.[45] The two men were still co-operating politically in 50 BC.[46] It may have been at this juncture that Caesar offered new marriage ties with Pompey, but the only source is Suetonius, who does not provide a chronological context.[47] Caesar suggested that Pompey should marry his great-niece Octavia, and he himself should marry Pompey's daughter, Pompeia. This would have meant that Caesar should divorce Calpurnia, Octavia should divorce Marcellus, and Pompeia should break off her betrothal to Faustus Sulla. Pompey refused the offer, but there is no firm indication that he intended to turn away from Caesar after the death of Julia.

As consul in 54 BC, Domitius Ahenobarbus lost no time in attacking the followers of Caesar, Crassus, and Pompey.[48] If it were not possible to prosecute the great men directly, their enemies focussed on their associates instead, to undermine support for the magnates, since if a great man was powerless to protect his followers, then he would eventually lose support. Most of the accused were acquitted, but this did not compensate for the hassle and time spent in organising their defence.[49] Cicero was persuaded to defend Caius Messius, who had proposed wide-ranging powers for Pompey as controller of the corn supply. Messius had also supported the recall of Cicero from exile, so defence of this individual was not so onerous to Cicero, but he was also asked to defend Vatinius, Caesar's tribune of 59 BC, and praetor in 55 BC. Cicero had virulently attacked Vatinius in the past, but agreed to defend him, despite the fact that Vatinius had left himself wide open to prosecution.[50] The trials did not abate during the rest of 54 BC. When Pompey's man Aulus Gabinius returned home in September 54, he was immediately prosecuted on more than one count. Cicero informed Atticus that because it was rumoured that Pompey was to be made Dictator, the jurors were frightened to do anything other than acquit.[51] When Gabinius' trial for *repetundae* came up, Pompey forced Cicero to defend him, but despite the attentions of the best defence that could be procured, it was this trial for extortion that finished Gabinius' career. Dio suggests that the condemnation of Gabinius was a surprise to Pompey.[52]

The question of a Dictatorship for Pompey had been circulating since 54 BC when there was an extremely prolonged delay in holding the elections for the consulships of 53 BC. Pompey's cousin Lucilius Hirrus announced his readiness to present a bill making Pompey Dictator. Hardly anyone believed Pompey's rejection of such tremendous responsibility. Even Cicero was not sure. In the end nothing happened. In 54 BC the consular candidates for 53 BC were not friendly to either Caesar or Pompey, with the exception of Caius Memmius, previously hostile to Caesar but now reconciled. Pompey gave modest support to Marcus Aemilius Scaurus, who had married Mucia after Pompey divorced her, but Scaurus was undergoing prosecution for extortion in his province of Sardinia. The other candidates were Marcus Messalla and Domitius Calvinus, neither of whom were acceptable to Pompey. Electoral bribery was so rampant that there were debates about it in the Senate, and the elections for the consuls of 53 BC did not take place until the middle of that year, almost exactly one year later than they should have been held.[53] At last, Pompey presided over the elections, and Messalla and Calvinus were elected for what remained of the year 53 BC. It has been suggested that Pompey obstructed the proceedings to create a situation in which he could be called upon to save the state, and that consequently this indicates the beginning of a split between Caesar and Pompey, but this has been refuted.[54]

If the death of Julia in 54 BC cannot be earmarked as the beginning of the rift between Caesar and Pompey, some authors, ancient and modern, have interpreted the removal of their third partner Crassus as a potential loosening of the ties between them. When Crassus and his son were both killed in Parthia in 53 BC, the quaestor Gaius Cassius Longinus rounded up the survivors and organised the defence of Syria in case the Parthians followed up their victory.[55] The question of sending either Pompey or Caesar to Parthia was raised some time later, but came to nothing. The only change in the political sphere was that some of the clients of Crassus turned to Caesar to swell the ranks of his followers. But it was not yet a step towards civil war simply because there were only two men instead of three who wished to control the Roman world.[56]

Electoral bribery and violence in Rome continued exponentially in 53 BC and into the following year.[57] The candidates for the consulships of 52 BC were Plautius Hypsaeus, Metellus Scipio and Titus Annius Milo. Clodius was standing for the praetorship. He seemed to be more or less reconciled to Pompey and Caesar, so Pompey began to withdraw his support for Milo, going so far as to block his candidacy. As events turned out, Milo unintentionally removed himself from any chance of gaining the consulship. In January, he and his gangs met up with Clodius outside Rome on the Appian Way, and a serious fight ensued, in which Clodius was wounded. He was carried to a nearby tavern, but it was said that Milo's men dragged him out and finished him off, probably aware that if Clodius survived there would never be an end to the matter, but if he was killed there would be only the charge of murder. Clodius was given a splendid send-off by the people of Rome, who cremated him in the Forum, using the Senate House as his funeral pyre.[58]

The mob laid siege to the houses of Milo, but support for him increased a little after the destruction of the Senate House and the attack on Lepidus, so he returned to the city. The violent incidents polarised the Romans; the enemies of Clodius such as Cicero, Cato and the tribune Marcus Caelius Rufus supported Milo, while the tribunes Munatius Plancus and Quintus Pompeius Rufus opposed him. The state of affairs demanded extraordinary measures; the Senate passed the last decree, the *senatus consultum ultimum*, empowering the tribunes and Pompey to see that the state came to no harm.[59] Pompey already held *imperium* as part of his command to regulate the corn supply and to govern Spain, and he was now authorised to recruit more soldiers in Italy and to conscript all young men of military age. Caesar heard of the Senate's decree, and began to recruit soldiers in Cisalpine Gaul.[60] The tribunes Plancus and Pompeius Rufus alleged that Milo was scheming to assassinate Pompey, who increased his bodyguard, living with the soldiers in his gardens as if he were on campaign.

It was high time that somebody restored law and order. Republican Rome did not possess a standing police force, so firm measures would be necessary, but despite the violence a Dictatorship was still not proposed in the Senate. A compromise was reached when it was suggested that Pompey should be appointed consul without a colleague. Appian says the proposal was Cato's, Dio that it was Bibulus who suggested it.[61] These two men would in any case be working together. Pompey as Dictator would have been immune to tribunician veto, and would not have been accountable for his measures, but as consul, both these restrictions would apply. On the other hand he would not be limited to the six-month period of the Dictatorship.

The concept of a sole consul was anomalous and unprecedented, but the title excluded the possibility that Caesar should become Pompey's consular colleague, which helped Cato and Bibulus form a wedge between the two men, and then attach Pompey to themselves. Their plans were almost upset when the ten tribunes presented a bill to recall Caesar and appoint him as colleague to Pompey. This would have enabled Caesar to move straight from his Gallic command into the consulship, retaining his *imperium* and avoiding a short time as a *privatus*, open to prosecution. Bibulus and Cato were spared from shrieking their opposition from the rooftops, because Caesar was not ready to leave his province without concluding the conquest, which would annihilate all credit for his achievement.[62]

Writing retrospectively, ancient authors detected a turning point in Pompey's attitude to Caesar in 52 BC. Previously, according to Appian, Pompey had been the friend of Caesar, the Senate, and the people, but in considering the events of 52 BC, both Velleius Paterculus and later Dio thought that this was the moment when Pompey changed. Velleius says that he was reconciled with the *optimates* and began to turn away from Caesar, and Dio agrees that in 52 BC Pompey started to please the Senate instead of the people.[63] If he had begun to turn against Caesar as early as this, he still co-operated with him, helping to push through another law promulgated by the ten tribunes to allow Caesar to stand for election as consul *in absentia*, so that he could retain his command in Gaul and not appear in person in Rome to canvass for election.[64]

Pompey was now free to tackle the violence and the bribery and corruption that attended elections. He passed a law authorising any citizen to demand an account from any magistrate, backdated to Pompey's own first consulship in 70 BC. This was seen as an attack on Caesar because his consulship fell within the specified period, but Pompey replied that he had gone back as far as his own consulship in order to cure once and for all the problems of the state.[65] Attending to the problems of the legal processes, Pompey streamlined court hearings and made it almost impossible to bribe the juries. Firstly he set a limit on the timescale for court hearings, which were to be completed within four days. Three days were allowed for the examination of witnesses, and on the fourth day the prosecution was allowed two hours for speeches and the defence three hours. For the juries he selected a total of 360 jurors, made up of 120 men from each of the three classes eligible for jury service, as proposed by Aurelius Cotta in 70 BC. All the 360 jurors were to sit through the first three days of the trials while witnesses were examined, and then eighty-one of these would be selected for the jury on the final day. The large number of jurors ensured that no one could possibly bribe them all, and the short timescale between the appointment of the final jurors for the last day of the trial gave no one sufficient opportunity to tamper with them. As part of these legal reforms, character witnesses for the accused were forbidden to appear, since more often than not they made irrelevant time-wasting speeches that were nothing to do with the case, and more importantly, if they were sufficiently persuasive, men who were clearly guilty were acquitted.[66] Then Pompey broke his own rules about banning the appearance of character witnesses by rescuing Metellus Scipio from prosecution. He also sent a written statement on behalf of Milo, and supported Munatius Plancus when he was prosecuted for violence in December 53. The historian Tacitus describes Pompey as the maker and breaker of his own laws.[67]

The projected multiple trials of Milo began and ended with his prosecution for using violence. His accusers were Clodius' two nephews, and his defence was conducted by Cicero, who was heckled and intimidated by Clodius' supporters. Cicero was aware that Pompey wanted Milo removed, even though he probably did not consider him guilty. As Milo said before the trial, the death of Clodius was an accident, since no one plans a murder and then sets out encumbered with his baggage and his wife, hoping to meet his enemy on the road.[68] It was a sign of the times that Pompey lined the court with his soldiers, and gave Cicero a bodyguard.[69]

Milo went into exile at Marseilles. When he received the written version of Cicero's speech, he remarked that it was fortuitous that Cicero had never delivered it, because he would have been acquitted, and therefore he would never have experienced the delights of the excellent red mullet of Marseilles.[70]

For what remained of the consular year, Pompey chose as his colleague Metellus Scipio, his father-in-law. He had married Scipio's daughter Cornelia, a widow since her first husband Publius Crassus was killed in Parthia. This new alliance forged by Pompey need not mean that he was about to turn against Caesar, but viewed in retrospect, with the outbreak of the civil war following on so closely, the marriage alliance could be interpreted by contemporaries and by later historians as the beginning of the split. But Pompey was still co-operating with his colleague in 52 BC, though his legislation seems to belie his co-operative attitude. Before his command in the Spanish provinces had expired, he extended it for a further five years, and he was voted money for the upkeep of his troops, securing his own position for the immediate future, but this was not intended to diminish Caesar's position.

Two of Pompey's laws of 52 BC, concerning the government of the provinces and the election of magistrates, represented an attempt to put right what had been wrong with the system for some time, but the laws seemed to impinge on Caesar, specifically on the law of the ten tribunes that Pompey himself had helped to push through, allowing Caesar to stand for the consular elections *in absentia*.[71] Pompey's subsequent legislation seemed to contradict this law. The *lex Pompeia de iure magistratuum* stipulated that candidates for election to any of the magistracies must present their names in person and remain in Rome for canvassing. The law was inscribed on bronze and deposited in the treasury, but immediately caused trouble for Pompey. Suetonius accuses him of forgetfulness, in that he ought to have included a clause naming Caesar as exempt from the law.[72] Some scholars describe Pompey's actions as those of a blundering incompetent who could not make up his mind as to whether he opposed Caesar or not, and others have said that he was absent-minded and forgot that he had recently helped to pass a law giving Caesar the right to stand for election *in absentia*. Yet others explain that the laws were part of a programme of administrative reform from which Caesar was specifically exempted. Pompey was probably highly exasperated by the nit-picking that attended this legislation. Meier says that Caesar's friends were slow to pick up on the possible implications of Pompey's new law, and when they did, they claimed that Pompey had invalidated the law that allowed Caesar to be a candidate *in absentia*.[73] Pompey added a codicil to the *lex de iure magistratuum* exempting Caesar from its provisions. It has been pointed out that the codicil had no validity in law.[74] Despite this disadvantage the codicil demonstrated that Caesar had been legally entitled to stand for election *in absentia*, and that there was no change to this circumstance, but Caesar was to be the final candidate to whom the privilege could be granted. Thereafter all candidates had to be in Rome for the canvassing and the elections for magistracies. It was as straightforward as that. Pompey was not absent-minded, nor was he forgetful or incompetent, nor had he resorted to deceitful subterfuge in the hope that he could quietly annul the law of ten tribunes concerning Caesar's right to stand for election *in absentia*. Perhaps Pompey heaved an exasperated sigh and patiently explained through gritted teeth that when he passed his new law stipulating personal appearance in Rome for canvassing, there was an existing law specifically granting exemption to Caesar, and, crucially, *this law had not been repealed*.

Pompey's other law on provincial government seemed more directly threatening to Caesar. It had been proposed in 53 BC but not drafted until 52 BC when Pompey re-assembled it and presented it to the Senate.[75] Its origins lay in the rampant bribery that attended elections, a theme already dealt with in part by Pompey and Crassus when they were consuls together in 55 BC. Candidates for office spent mostly borrowed fortunes, in the hope of obtaining a lucrative province and reimbursing themselves and their creditors at the expense of the provincials. In order to prevent this, Pompey's *lex de provinciis* interposed a compulsory gap of five years between a magistracy in Rome and a promagistracy in a province.[76] Both Meier and Gelzer take the view that Pompey, probably deliberately, undermined Caesar's legal privilege and therefore his whole political standing, and that this is evidence of Pompey's unfriendly attitude towards Caesar.[77] Caesar himself interpreted the law as hostile in intent, and it made a useful tool in justifying his actions in the civil war, because it played into the hands of those who agitated for his recall.[78] After the new law was passed, the retiring magistrates could not go out to a province for five years, so the government had to draw upon the pool of ex-consuls and praetors who had never governed provinces, or had done so five years earlier. In turn this meant that existing provincial governors could be superceded immediately, because the new governors did not have to wait until their year of office had expired. Caesar's enemies could move in as soon as possible to have him recalled and replaced. One of the casualties of Pompey's law was Cicero. Since the magistrates currently in office could not govern provinces, the government had to choose men who had held the relevant offices but had not been governors for at least five years. Cicero was well qualified in this respect, and had to fill the gaps in available personnel. He had to go out to govern Cilicia, much against his will.

Just after he took Metellus Scipio as his colleague, Pompey held the elections for the magistracies of 51 BC, and Marcus Claudius Marcellus and Servius Sulpicius Rufus were elected consuls. Marcellus took the stance that the Gallic wars were now finished, so there was no need for Caesar to remain in Gaul at the head of troops.[79] He ignored the law passed by Pompey and Crassus to extend Caesar's command. The extended term cannot have expired yet, but it is worth reiterating that no one knows if that law contained a specific terminal date, and if so, what that date may have been.[80] Both Suetonius and Hirtius assert that Marcellus' attempts to replace Caesar were made *ante tempus*, before the term had expired.[81] Marcellus' colleague Sulpicius did not support the suggestion that a magistrate who had done no wrong should be removed in the middle of his term as governor.[82] Thwarted, Marcellus tried another tack, claiming that the *lex de iure magistratuum* had negated the special dispensation granted to Caesar to stand for election *in absentia*. In the Senate in March 51 Pompey made a speech opposing Marcellus.[83] It was proposed that there should be a discussion specifically on Caesar's provincial command, perhaps in August, but it was postponed until September, and then Metellus Scipio suggested that it should be put off until 1 March 50. This may have been the original terminal date specified in the law passed by Pompey and Crassus to extend Caesar's command. Marcus Caelius, the tribune of 52 BC, wrote to Cicero, explaining that there was to be no discussion of Caesar's command before 1 March 50, and the agenda for that day was to be cleared so that full attention could be devoted to the matter.[84] Whether or not this date had been specified when Caesar's command was extended by Pompey and Crassus in 55 BC, the new ruling afforded a short time for Caesar to watch events and plan ahead.

Marcellus now resorted to petty and ultimately useless annoying tactics. He proposed that the colonists of Novum Comum, granted Roman citizenship by Caesar, should have their citizenship retracted, and to prove the point he flogged one of the men from the colony.[85] Flogging of Roman citizens was illegal. Marcellus' action was a direct challenge to Caesar's authority. It gained nothing on the political scene except to help to precipitate the civil war.

The question of Parthia was raised from time to time, where threats seemed to be emanating from the Parthian Royal House. It was rumoured that Pompey would be sent to the East, especially after Calpurnius Bibulus, governor of Syria, detected an impending Parthian invasion. It was also suggested that Caesar should be sent to Parthia.[86] The removal of either one of the great men would have postponed, or possibly even prevented the civil war. But Caesar remained in Gaul and Pompey remained in Italy. Pompey travelled to Ariminum, coming close to Caesar's province of Cisalpine Gaul, and though the two could not have met in person because Caesar was concentrating on war against the Eburones, there may have been some contact by letter or messenger. Pompey may have been concerned to find out whether the Gallic war was nearing completion, and whether Caesar really needed more time to organise the provinces, and if so, how much time would he need?

The consuls for 50 BC were Gaius Claudius Marcellus, a cousin of Marcus Marcellus, consul of 51 BC, and Lucius Aemilius Paullus, neither of them likely to be sympathetic to Caesar. Potentially more worrying was the election of the staunchly anti-Caesarian Scribonius Curio as tribune, holding office from December 51 to December 50.[87] Curio was a teenage friend of Mark Antony, whose debts he had offered to pay until his father stopped him. He had also been a friend of Clodius, and he had married Fulvia, Clodius' widow. Curio's automatic inclusion in the camp of the anti-Caesarians was taken for granted.

Pompey was asked whether he would condone Caesar holding the consulship without disbanding his armies, and he said he would not tolerate it. He was doing just that himself, but he probably thought that Caesar would disband his troops when he finally became consul. When he was asked what would happen if Caesar did command armies while consul, Pompey indicated that he did not think this likely, by making the famous reply, 'What if my son were to take a stick to me?' He said this with the utmost gentleness, according to Caelius, who reported the incident to Cicero.[88] Perhaps war was not yet inevitable. But whatever Pompey had tried to convey, people now began to think that there was a split between him and Caesar.

11

Escalation: The Outbreak of the Civil War, 50–48 BC

The beginning of the year 50 BC was not as tendentious as may have been expected. Curio began his career as tribune with multiple schemes designed to appeal to the people. He put forward proposals to divide the Campanian lands among the poor of the city, to annexe the kingdom of Numidia, to build roads, to distribute grain to the people.[1] It was the usual paraphernalia of the *popularis* tribunes, but his schemes were perhaps never intended to be seriously fought for. The Senate rejected all the proposals that Curio put forward, including his suggestion that the priests should insert an intercalary month at the end of February. It was necessary to do this from time to time because the Roman calendar was based on a lunar reckoning and had gradually slipped out of synchronisation with the seasons. Curio's suggestion was squashed because it was interpreted as a means of putting off the discussion about Caesar's provinces by moving the agreed date of 1 March forward one month. Gruen suggests that up to this time Curio was acting on his own initiative, and it was at this point that he went over to Caesar. According to this scenario Curio and the Marcelli were operating independently of each other, but were dedicated to the same ends, to destroy the alliance of Caesar and Pompey.[2] But it was also suspected that Curio had been purchased by Caesar before he became tribune, and had kept his association under wraps for a while. It would not have been easy for Curio to refuse an offer to settle all his massive debts, which is apparently how Caesar purchased his allegiance.[3] Curio showed his hand when the consul Gaius Marcellus, emulating Marcus Marcellus, opened a discussion about sending a successor to Gaul to replace should be chosen to take over his provinces. Curio countered by suggesting that Pompey should also give up his provinces. He would continue to block proposals to replace Caesar unless Pompey also disarmed, and earned great popularity for his consistent stance.[4] Pompey was in a more precarious position now. He lost popularity because in putting an end to rampant bribery at the elections, the people were displeased because they were far from averse to a little bribery, and had become accustomed to receiving the cash.[5]

The crucial date of 1 March 50, when the matter of Caesar's provinces had been scheduled for debate, came and went. Lucius Aemilius Paullus was presiding consul for March, and no discussion of Caesar's command took place. Marcellus could only wait until he was presiding consul in April to raise the subject again. Paullus did not support him. It was widely supposed that Paullus' silence had been purchased by Caesar, who was perhaps financing his building projects, one of them being a basilica in the Forum.[6] When the discussion about Caesar and his provinces did begin, Pompey proposed that Caesar should be allowed an extension of his command until the Ides of November, which fell on the thirteenth day of that month.[7] The reason for the choice of this date is not known, and it has been argued that it did not go far enough to ensure Caesar's seamless transition from proconsul to consul. Pompey's motives in suggesting this November date are not clear.[8] It may have been an attempt to appear to be treating Caesar reasonably, without giving him any advantage, in other words gaining the Brownie points while not risking anything. Much depends on the year when Caesar intended to stand for the consulship. As already mentioned, the Sullan law placed a statutory interval of ten years between consulships, which would prevent anyone from holding successive consulships such as Marius had enjoyed. By the terms of this law Caesar would have to stand for election in 49 for 48 BC. The law of ten tribunes exempting him from appearing in person in Rome presumably did not specify the date of his candidacy, and it is possible that Caesar's original intention was to stand in 50 BC for the consulship of 49 BC, so this may be what Pompey and his colleagues expected Caesar to do.[9] If this was the case at the time when Pompey made his offer, it was a perfectly reasonable suggestion, since Caesar could have become consul elect in 50 BC, while still in command of his army, and then could disband his army by 13 November 50. But in the month and a half between then and 1 January and the commencement of his consulship Caesar would still be at risk. Besides, if Caesar had wished to stand in 50 BC, he ought to have asked for a dispensation to the ten-year rule, and there is no record that he did so, possibly because he thought it would be refused.[10] Having already secured exemption from appearing in Rome in person for the elections, seeking yet another dispensation would have fallen into the category of give an inch and he takes a yard; where would it all end? Gelzer says that Pompey's offer to postpone discussion of Caesar's command until 13 November was made in the knowledge that it was of no practical use, since it would leave Caesar unprotected.[11] This is to assume that Caesar had always intended to stand for the consulship in 49 BC, in which case the termination of his command in November 50 would render him vulnerable to his enemies who had no doubt already prepared cases for prosecution, and the interval would allow sufficient time to fight and win in court.

In the end discussion is merely academic because Curio blocked Pompey's proposal. Caesar may have interpreted it as a trap, since he would be at the mercy of the great man to keep his options open for him at Rome. What if Pompey decided to postpone the elections? Or perhaps when the time came to stand for election, Pompey and his friends would refuse to accept his candidature. Then there was the possibility that Caesar would not be successfully elected, despite the flow of cash that streamed from him to virtually everyone in Rome.

It is possible that even at this stage Pompey was absolutely sincere, hoping to find a way to retain his own supremacy side by side with Caesar. But it is just as likely that Pompey calculated that he could make this ostensibly reasonable offer to Caesar, anticipating that it would be refused. His own accommodating attitude would then highlight Caesar's uncompromising obstinacy. It is impossible for modern scholars, knowing with hindsight that the civil war was not averted, to discern clearly who intended to wrong-foot whom in the spring of 50 BC. The blame for the civil war cannot be placed wholly on either one or the other. Velleius Paterculus, whose bias towards Caesar reaches sycophantic proportions, tries to skirt the issue by throwing all the odium on Curio, who 'applied the flaming torch which kindled the civil war'.[12] Velleius avoids having to acknowledge that Caesar did not wish to embark on the next stage of his political career as Pompey's subordinate or in his debt, and Pompey did not wish to be overshadowed or even equalled by Caesar.

In the summer, Pompey fell dangerously ill. The cause is not known and has been attributed to malaria, and also to stress, but whatever it was, the illness was severe, perhaps life-threatening. Prayers were offered for his recovery, and when he finally emerged in better health, there was great rejoicing. Cicero reported to Atticus that the people had offered prayers for Pompey's recovery, but later, with hindsight, he considered it had all been insincere.[13] Plutarch reports that after the public rejoicing at his recovery, Pompey thought that the population was solidly behind him.[14] It probably contributed to his boast that he had only to stamp his foot and troops would rise up in Italy.

While he was ill Pompey wrote to the Senate, recounting his services to the state, praising Caesar's activities, and using his old ploy of suggesting that he was weary of command. He offered to lay down his command and affirmed that Caesar would be willing to do the same. In the Senate when he returned to Rome, Pompey repeated these sentiments.[15] He may genuinely have intended to renounce his claim on the Spanish provinces, relying upon his pre-eminence to maintain his position. Unfortunately not all of his audience could believe this. In a meeting of the Senate, Curio suggested that Pompey was a potential tyrant, that Caesar's armies were necessary in order to keep him in check, and therefore Pompey should be the first to disarm. Pompey swept out of the Senate House, flinging threats at Curio as he went. According to Appian, Curio proposed that unless both Pompey and Caesar laid down their commands at the same time, they should be declared public enemies, and military forces should be assembled against them.[16] Pompey was perhaps heartened later that day by the news that the Senate had thwarted Curio. Fear of Caesar prevailed, and Pompey was needed to counter him.

Caelius wrote to Cicero in August 50 while he was governor of Cilicia, explaining that he could not foresee a peace settlement that would last for a year, and there was bound to be a struggle (*contentio*), not yet naming it as a war, but in a subsequent paragraph he suggested unless Pompey or Caesar went to fight the Parthians there would be violence, only settled by the sword.[17] The Parthian problems were sufficiently serious to warrant an assemblage of troops. It was decreed that both Pompey and Caesar should each contribute one legion to the war effort. Pompey had lent one of his legions to Caesar in Gaul, and since his own legions were far away in Spain, and the Gallic war was apparently over, he recalled that legion. Caesar handed it over without protest, as well as one of his own.[18] Pompey kept both the legions in Italy, near Capua.[19] Caesar blamed Marcellus and the Senate, not Pompey, for retaining the legions within call, but he also said that the armed tyranny of Pompey was causing alarm in the Forum.[20] Talk of civil war began to circulate.

Curio consistently proposed that the two generals should lay down their commands simultaneously, so Marcellus tried to demonstrate how the Senate really felt by proposing two separate motions to be put to the vote: should a successor be sent to replace Caesar, and should Pompey's command be terminated? Appian says that the majority voted that Caesar should give up his command, but none voted that Pompey should give up his. Dio corroborates this, adding that only Caelius and Curio voted against the motion that Caesar should lay down his command.[21] On the strength of this vote, the Senate decreed that Caesar should be replaced. Curio countered with his usual suggestion that Caesar and Pompey should both lay down their commands simultaneously, and this motion was passed by 370 votes to twenty-two.[22] This demonstrates that the desire for peace was very strong. Marcellus dismissed the Senate, without putting this vote into effect.

Rumours began that Caesar was marching on Rome, so Marcellus proposed that the legions at Capua should be mobilised. Curio tried to reassure the Senate that the rumours were false, but Marcellus decided that if the Senate would not pass a decree to mobilise, then he would act on his own authority as consul, and he appeared at the door of Pompey's Alban villa to place a sword in his hands, charging him with the defence of the state, and empowering him to take command of the two legions that had been destined for the Parthian war, and of any other troops in Italy. He could also recruit further troops as he wished. Pompey replied that he would take command if nothing better could be achieved.[23] He was confident that he had the people behind him, because they had prayed so ardently for his recovery from illness, and he had heard from the soldiers of the two legions that Caesar had sent for the Parthian war that Caesar's army was disaffected, and could be persuaded to join Pompey and the Senate. At this stage it is possible that negotiation could have settled the immediate difficulties, and it is probable that Pompey imagined that a display of force would be sufficient to persuade Caesar to back down. Appian says that since Curio's term as tribune was due to end on 9 December, and he saw that nothing further could be achieved on behalf, he left Rome to join Caesar.[24]

When Curio ceased to be tribune, Caesar required a replacement. Someone must be found who could continue to work in Caesar's favour. Mark Antony was the favoured candidate, and he travelled to Rome for the elections. He was elected tribune of the plebs along with Cassius Longinus, so Caesar had two men who could look after his interests in Rome.[25] Antony also stood for election to a religious post, as augur. The death of the orator Hortensius had created a vacancy in the college of augurs that must be filled. Caesar canvassed vigorously on Antony's behalf, and his influence ensured that Antony defeated the main rival Lucius Domitius Ahenobarbus, who belonged to Cato's faction. Cicero was not impressed, and reiterated his feelings later, after Caesar's death.[26] It was useful for Caesar to have a friendly augur in Rome, since one of the duties was to watch for omens, specifically in the flight of birds, which is the origin of taking the auspices to assess the will of the gods. The term *auspicium*, or *avispicium* derives from *avis* (bird) and *specio* (I look), hence watching birds, though not in the modern sense of a twitcher. No magistrate in Rome or the provinces would undertake any serious business without first taking the auspices, so an augur could assist in declaring that the omens were favourable, or obstruct business by declaring the omens unfavourable. Caesar decided to attempt further negotiation to defuse the situation, directing his friends in Rome to declare that he would give up his provinces and his troops, retaining only Cisalpine Gaul and Illyricum with two legions, until he should be elected consul. Pompey accepted the deal, but the Senate did not.[27]

Cicero came home from governing Cilicia in November 50, but he did not arrive in Rome until the beginning of January 49. He found a gloomy situation, and was torn between friendship for Pompey and an ardent wish for peace. He was at Formiae on 17 December when he reported to Atticus that he had not met anyone who did not think that it would be preferable make concessions to Caesar rather than go to war.[28] Probably on the next day or slightly later he wrote to Atticus again, labelling Caesar without actually naming him, as the one source for all the evils currently besetting the state. 'We ought to have resisted him when he was weak,' said Cicero, but acknowledging that it was too late, because Caesar was a leader of influence and daring, too strong because he controlled eleven legions, cavalry, the northern tribes across the Po, the city mob, the tribunes of the plebs, and the young profligates. It really was too late, because Marcellus had charged Pompey with the safety of the state. Cicero now realised that the only options were to fight Caesar or allow him to stand as a candidate for the consulship according to the law.[29]

By the end of December, in Cicero's opinion, Pompey did not want peace, because he had come to the conclusion that Caesar's intentions were revolutionary, and he would achieve what he wanted by force, even if he gave up his provinces and his armies. Pompey was severely provoked by Caesar's newly elected tribune Mark Antony, who attacked him and his policies in a speech in the Senate on 20 December. But Pompey merely pointed out that if this was how one of Caesar's officers behaved, it would be much worse when Caesar was consul.[30]

Distrust of Caesar was complete. He had held a province for ten years, not one that had been allocated by the Senate, but obtained by force. He had arranged the term of office to suit himself. Cicero did not want war, but was convinced that if 'the right party' were defeated, Caesar would act like Cinna in slaughtering the nobility and like Sulla in robbing the rich.[31] Cicero met Pompey on 25 December. They journeyed to Formiae together, where they talked all afternoon. Cicero concluded that Pompey did not want peace, but he thought that when Caesar heard of the preparations for war against him, he would give up the idea of standing for the consulship, preferring to keep his province and his army.[32]

The consuls for 49 BC were Lucius Cornelius Lentulus Crus, who was no friend of Caesar, and Gaius Claudius Marcellus, the third Marcellus to hold the consulship. In January 49 Caesar wrote to the Senate via Curio, who gave the letter to the consuls only when they were about to enter the Senate so that it should be witnessed in public and not easily suppressed. The tribunes Mark Antony and Quintus Cassius insisted that the consuls should read the letter, in which Caesar reminded the senators of all the benefits that he had conferred on the state, and proposed that he and Pompey should lay down their commands simultaneously.[33] He refused to give up his own command while Pompey retained his. Metellus Scipio then made the proposal that Caesar should give up his armies by a specified date, and it would be deemed a hostile act if he refused.[34] The Senate was willing to adopt this proposal, but Antony and Cassius vetoed it. Pompey summoned the senators to his house after the meeting, and continued the debate. An embassy to Caesar was suggested and volunteers were found, but this idea was not followed through.[35] The consul Lentulus, with Cato and Metellus Scipio, advocated a policy of resistance to Caesar, refusing to allow Caesar to keep Cisalpine Gaul and Illyricum with two legions, or Illyricum with only one legion. Pompey was in favour of the proposal to allow Caesar to retain Illyricum with one legion, but Lentulus and his friends would not condone the idea.

In his account of the run up to the civil war, Caesar tries to exonerate Pompey, not putting blame on him directly but insisting that he had been influenced by his friends who were eager to see Caesar defeated.[36] The *senatus consultum ultimum* was passed on 7 January, to authorise the consuls, praetors, tribunes and all the men of proconsular rank near the city to take steps to ensure that the state came to no harm.[37] Significantly the decree did not name Pompey as supreme commander, and he was not named as such until much later. The consuls threatened the tribunes Antony and Cassius with violence if they interposed their vetoes; some sources say that they were ejected from the Senate.[38] Tribunes were sacrosanct, and to threaten them was tantamount to sacrilege. Caesar was in Cisalpine Gaul, close to the border with Italy, when he heard that Antony, Cassius, Curio and Caelius were on their way to his camp. In the account of the civil wars Caesar nonchalantly mentions that he was waiting at Ravenna for replies to his 'very lenient demands', hoping that a peaceful agreement might still be reached.[39] Naturally he portrays himself as willing to compromise even at this late stage, thus transferring the blame for the war to the Senate and Pompey.

Caesar had one legion with him, the Thirteenth. The rest of his army was still in Gaul. Addressing his single legion, Caesar presented the soldiers with a catalogue of all the wrongs that had been done to him in the past.[40] He mentioned that the tribunes' right of veto had been crushed. Caesar pointed out that in the past the *senatus consultum ultimum* had been passed only in cases of extreme danger, such as a serious riot of the people, or the seizure of temples and the like. Nothing of this nature had actually occurred in this instance to warrant such a measure. According to Appian, Caesar and his army were declared *hostes*, enemies of the state, while Pompey and his troops were the protectors.[41]

Whether or not Caesar actually relayed all this to the troops does not matter; the written account of the beginning of the civil war was designed to remind his audience that he had not made the first aggressive move. Whatever Caesar said to the soldiers he whipped them up into a frenzy of righteous indignation on behalf of their wronged commander, and the fact that despite having serving on Rome's behalf for so long they were now deemed enemies of the state. They were ready to follow him wherever he went.

Plutarch says that the expulsion from the Senate of the tribunes Antony and Cassius gave Caesar the excuse to make war.[42] The order of events has been distorted in some modern accounts, making it seem as though Antony, Cassius, Caelius and Curio arrived at Caesar's headquarters, and were shown to the soldiers immediately, to stir up their enthusiasm for the war, and only then did Caesar invade Italy. Suetonius makes it clear that Caesar had already crossed the Rubicon before he welcomed the tribunes.[43] Neither Appian nor Dio mention the Rubicon, and nor does Caesar in his account of the opening moves of the civil war. The name of the River Rubicon derives from Suetonius and Plutarch, and no one knows for certain which river or stream it is.[44] Caesar did show Antony and the others to the soldiers just as they were, probably still disguised as slaves, but their appearance and the account of their treatment was not the catalyst that precipitated the war, which technically had already begun when Caesar crossed from Gaul into Italy. Appian says that Caesar crossed the Alps with 5,000 infantry and 300 cavalry, arriving at Ariminum, now Rimini, the last town inside his province, and contiguous with Italy.[45] Dio relays the same information, but he also adds that for the first time, Caesar stepped outside his province, and it was only after he had done so that he asked Curio to tell the soldiers what had happened in Rome.[46]

Suetonius and Plutarch both set the scene for high drama. Plutarch says that Ariminum, or Rimini, lay just across the border from Gaul, then he paints the traditional picture of the night of 11 January, when Caesar halted for a while at the River Rubicon, debating the enormity of what he was about to do. Behind this river, Caesar was a legally appointed governor authorised to command troops. Crossing the river at the head of an army, without permission from the Senate, he was committing treason against the state. Suetonius relays an epic tale, explaining how Caesar was encouraged by the apparition of a wondrous being who played on a reed pipe; it then seized a trumpet from one of the soldiers, sounded it, and crossed the river to the opposite bank. Caesar declared that he and his followers should take the course pointed out by the gods and the false dealing of his foes, concluding with the famous phrase, 'the die is cast'.[47] Plutarch does not mention apparitions, but in the biographies of Pompey and Caesar, he reports a similar phrase 'let the die be cast'.[48] The historian Asinius Pollio was present at the scene, and he may be the source for the phrase reported by other historians, namely a quotation from the Greek poet Menander, 'Let the dice fly high'. Whatever Caesar said, crossing the Rubicon is an iconic scene that would readily lend itself to the modern fashion in film, where the current phrase, repeatedly heard when heroic groups prepare for action, is 'Let's *do* this!'

In his account of the civil wars, Caesar more than once makes a point of justifying his actions and casting blame for the war on Pompey and the small group of intransigent senators who were determined to block his path to the consulship for 48 BC. In his first paragraphs he outlines the opinions of the more moderate senators who were spokesmen for a peaceful settlement and the avoidance of war, and the contrary opinions of the opposition who squashed their suggestions. Caesar had previously maintained that his enemies had led Pompey astray, and while reiterating this, he now adds that

Pompey could not contemplate anyone being on the same level of authority as himself, and had consequently withdrawn from Caesar's friendship.[49] Using his speech to his soldiers to convey all the wrongs done to him, Caesar complains about the suppression of the tribunician veto, referring obliquely to the treatment of Antony and Cassius. He reminds his audience that even Sulla had not suppressed that privilege, but Pompey had done so. In Caesar's rhetoric Pompey is now the enemy, not the senators who had influenced him. Caesar then enumerates his own achievements and his service to the state, claiming that he and his army had pacified all of Gaul and Germany.[50] This a slight exaggeration, since the Romans never did conquer Germany, but Caesar was nothing if not his own best press-agent. At other points in his narrative of the civil wars, Caesar uses the same ploy, reporting speeches he made, in various circumstances, to justify his actions. In the early stages of the war, dealing with Lentulus Spinther who had come to him to ask for mercy, Caesar interrupts him to say that he had not left Gaul with evil intent, but to defend himself against the insults of his enemies (*a contumeliis inimicorum*), to restore the position of the tribunes of the plebs, and to assert for himself and the Roman people the freedom that had been oppressed by a small faction.[51] In a later passage, when he addressed the Senate convened outside Rome, Caesar reports a longer speech, bitter in tone, reminding the senators that he had not sought any extraordinary office except the consulship in due course. He emphasised that a law had been passed to grant him the privilege to stand for election *in absentia*, not forgetting Cato's opposition by 'spinning out the days in obstructive speech'. Then he highlights Pompey's dubious attitude and asks if Pompey disapproved of the law, why did he allow it to be passed, and if he did not disapprove of it, why he prevented him from taking advantage of the law? The wrongs done to him and the suppression of the tribunes are mentioned again, as well as the reasonable terms he had offered, which had been refused. He concludes in somewhat threatening mode, asking the senators to help him administer the state, but if they are too afraid, he says, he will administer it himself.[52] Perhaps he should not have said that, since it was what the senators had always feared he would do.

Characteristically, beginning his invasion of Italy, Caesar did not wait until he had assembled all his forces before he crossed the Rubicon. The longer he delayed, the more time Pompey would have to recruit soldiers, but in reality Pompey's recruitment was not going as well as expected. He had been initially buoyed up by the support of the populace while he was ill, and also by the rumours of discontent in Caesar's army, and he had claimed that he only had to stamp his foot and troops would spring up in Italy. Appian tells how Favonius asked Pompey to stamp and see what happened, and Pompey replied, 'You can have them, if you are not horrified at leaving Rome, and Italy as well'.[53] The tale is probably an invention, and Pompey probably never did announce his intention to leave Italy so clearly at this stage. But unspoken comments about foot-stamping probably occurred to several people. Pompey stationed the two legions, that had been given up by Caesar for the Parthian war, in Apulia. These were trained and experienced troops, but even though one of them had originally been his own, Pompey could not trust them. It was these troops who had spread the rumours that some of Caesar's soldiers would probably join Pompey, so by now it may have been clear that this had been deliberate misinformation.

In haste on 7 January the Senate had appointed provincial governors, breaking all the rules that Pompey had made to insert a five-year gap between city magistracies and provincial pro-magistracies. The provinces of Syria and Transalpine Gaul were designated as consular, and lots were drawn for them; Lucius Domitius Ahenobarbus was appointed to Transalpine Gaul, and Syria was allocated to Pompey's father-in-law Scipio, who had been consul in 52 BC and ought to have waited three more years for a province according to Pompey's law on provincial government. Caesar hints that not all the names of eligible men were included in the draw. The praetorian provinces included the corn rich areas of Sicily, Sardinia and Africa, and these went to Cato, Cotta and Tubero. Troops were levied throughout Italy, cash was collected from towns and temples, and the consuls left Rome, which Caesar says had never happened before.[54] The city was without its chief magistrates for the first time, but the abandonment of Rome and the removal of its government preserved the city, since there was nothing to fight over and therefore no damage was done.

Cicero had embraced the principle that if Caesar invaded with hostile intent it might be necessary to withdraw from Rome, to deny him access to money and supplies of food. In December 50 he spoke with Ampius Balbus and Pompey himself, and discussed the possibility of leaving Rome and also Italy. He discussed with Atticus and his friends, by letter, the alternative strategies that were open to Pompey, including the possibility that Pompey might choose to leave Italy, and hoping that he would not do so.[55]

On 17 January Pompey left Rome for Capua, his main recruiting ground.[56] In March 48, at Formiae, Cicero wrote to Atticus, recalling Pompey's mood: 'I saw on 17 January that he was terrified'.[57] Pompey realised that many senators would worry about losing their possessions, and might prefer to go over to Caesar, so he declared that anyone who did not follow him would be classified as an enemy. The consuls and several senators trailed after him. On 22 January, Titus Labienus joined Pompey. He deserted Caesar after ten years of good service in Gaul, and some years of service as tribune in Rome. Allegedly he was jealous of Mark Antony, whose advancement had been rapid once he came to Caesar in Gaul. Labienus may have felt more loyalty to Pompey because they both came from Picenum; or perhaps he was high minded enough to refuse to follow Caesar in rebellion against the state. Dio says that Labienus had become too haughty, and Caesar had ceased to be fond of him.[58] Cicero reported to Atticus that it was almost certain that Labienus had deserted Caesar, then when he knew that the rumour was true, he called Labienus a hero.[59] It is not known what Caesar called him, but he sent all Labienus' baggage after him.[60]

Pompey had sent Lucius Caesar (not a close relation to Caesar, despite the name) as envoy to Caesar, to explain that it was not personal enmity to Caesar that motivated him, but as always he thought of the welfare of the state. Now Caesar returned the messenger to Pompey with suggestions as to how the deadlock might be broken. He may have been sincere, or perhaps he simply wanted to present himself as the rational, reasonable party who did everything he could to make peace. Caesar proposed that he and Pompey should meet in person, and he suggested that both he and Pompey should abandon their armies, Pompey should go to Spain, arms should be laid down in Italy, and elections should be held.[61] Pompey replied that Caesar must give up Ariminum and return to Gaul, and Caesar complained that this was unfair because he would have to give up what he had gained.[62] Cicero's report is slightly different. He says that Caesar's terms were accepted, with the proviso that he should abandon the cities that he had occupied outside his province; then the government would return to Rome.[63] Did Pompey or Caesar intend to abide by the peace terms they proposed, or were they each trying to be the appeaser in the face of the other's intransigence? There was no positive result from this attempt at negotiation. Pompey and his allies could not seriously expect Caesar to put himself at a disadvantage, and Caesar presumably did not trust Pompey and his allies to leave him unmolested.

Caesar pressed on into Italy, sending Mark Antony to Arretium (Arezzo) with five cohorts, and Curio to Iguvium with three. From Auximum, Caesar traversed all of Picenum, gratified to find that towns were willing to open their gates and contribute troops to his army.[64] He marched to Corfinium, where Domitius Ahenobarbus had stationed troops to try to stop him. Pompey wrote to Domitius, rebuking him for not keeping him informed, and trying very hard to explain that with split forces they could never hope to resist Caesar. He had written to Domitius more than once to ask him to bring his troops to Luceria, and now he advised Domitius to make a start before it was too late. This was not the first or the last occasion where Pompey had to deal with colleagues who thought they knew better than he did how to fight the war, and it is important to remember that he had not been appointed as supreme commander. That came much later, when the Pompeians faced Caesar in Greece. On 16 and 17 February Pompey wrote again to Domitius, having heard from him that he intended to march to join the main army if Caesar made a move in its direction, but if Caesar remained nearby he would try to resist him. Pompey tried to get his point across politely: 'I think you are acting with courage and high-mindedness, but we must be careful to avoid the situation where we are divided and therefore no match for the enemy since he has large forces and will soon have larger.' Domitius presumably knew how many legions Caesar could call up from Gaul, but perhaps thought that he could bring about a swift victory before the whole of the Gallic army had assembled. Domitius had perhaps overestimated his own abilities or underestimated Caesar's, and when Caesar encamped outside Corfinium, Domitius was soon writing to Pompey to ask him to come to his rescue. Pompey replied that he could not rely on his untrained troops and had no intention of risking the fate of the Republic on one pitched battle in the north.[65] It dawned on Cicero with disbelief that Pompey was not going to rescue Domitius.[66] Two days later Pompey confirmed Cicero's worst fears, by giving the order to march to Brundisium. Domitius was forced to surrender to Caesar, but was allowed to go free, along with his colleagues Vibullius and Attius Varus. He was even allowed to keep his treasury, worth six million sesterces, which had been voted to Pompey by the Senate. This was a studied display of reasonable and merciful treatment. Domitius' troops, however, swore an oath of loyalty to Caesar, and were absorbed into Caesar's army.[67]

When Caesar heard that Pompey had started for Brundisium he sent a message to him via one of the prisoners he had captured, a man called Magius, Pompey's *praefectus fabrum*, or chief engineer. He was instructed to ask for a meeting with Pompey.[68] Caesar was surprised that Pompey did not send Magius back to him with an answer, but according to Cicero, Pompey had in fact sent a reply via Magius.[69] Cicero wrote to Atticus, enclosing a copy of a letter from Caesar to Oppius and Cornelius Balbus, referring to the capture and release of Magius and another of Pompey's prefects, in which Caesar said, 'If they have any gratitude they should exhort Pompey to prefer my friendship to that of the men who were his bitterest enemies both to him and to me'.[70] But Pompey refused to meet Caesar, who then sent Caninius Rebilus, a personal friend of Scribonius Libo, who was a member of Pompey's entourage. Libo was persuaded to repeat the request to Pompey for a personal interview. Pompey replied that he could not accede to this request in the absence of the consuls, who had not yet joined him.[71] Caesar may have been sincere in wishing to arrange peace, and Pompey may have refused to meet him because he knew that Caesar's charm offensive might persuade him to agree to lay down his arms. But it is equally possible that the request for a personal interview was a delaying tactic. At this stage it is doubtful that either Caesar or Pompey could have made peace, or even wanted to.

There has been considerable modern debate about Pompey's original intentions, and even the ancient authors did not know what he had planned. The contemporary sources are limited to Caesar's narrative of the civil war with its self-justificatory propaganda, and Cicero's correspondence, which gives much detail but insufficient military insight. Later ancient sources have to indulge in speculation, just as modern historians do. History records only what Pompey did, not what he intended to do at any given point. While Pompey was still collecting troops, it was not known whether he intended to make a stand in Italy, or take his army elsewhere. He may have arrived by degrees at the decision to evacuate Italy, because he had underestimated his own ability to raise and train troops, and had not fully appreciated Caesar's determination and speed of action. Dio says that Pompey changed his plan when he heard that Caesar was advancing on Rome, because he had not enough troops to resist, and there was a lack of popular support for the war. Unfortunately Dio does not explain what the plan was before it was changed, but the general tenor of Dio's account is that Pompey originally planned to fight in Italy. In the next paragraph, Dio describes how Pompey set out for Campania, thinking that he could more easily carry on the war there.[72] In a later passage, Dio says that Pompey had no further hope of Italy, and resolved to cross into Macedonia and Greece.[73] Even Caesar was not certain of Pompey's original plans. After Pompey had sailed away from Brundisium, Caesar says that he was unsure whether Pompey was alarmed by the siege works around the town and chose to escape by sea, or whether he left because he had always planned to do so from the beginning of the war.[74] As far as can be known Pompey did not declare his intentions to anyone, but this is hardly surprising if he had decided to withdraw from Italy from the very beginning, because it would not have been sensible to announce this in advance to all the senators, or to the recruits that he was trying to assemble. Better to keep silent and spring the idea on people at the last minute, then the panic would have been short-lived and easier to deal with.

Caesar had by now approached Brundisium. He had not been able to prevent the departure of most of Pompey's army and the two consuls, who had gone to Dyrrachium in Greece. Caesar could not be certain whether Pompey, with his remaining twenty cohorts, intended to follow his army, or whether he planned to hold Brundisium, so that he could control the Adriatic and the coasts of Italy and Greece.[75] It was a feasible choice, and Caelius wrote to Cicero wondering whether Pompey had decided that it was better to make a stand at Brundisium.[76] Caesar invested the city on the landward side and attempted to block access to and from the harbour, by building floating walls from each side. He anchored rafts covered with earth to create a sort of pier, which he protected with screens and towers. Pompey responded by using merchant ships in which he installed towers that were higher than Caesar's towers.[77] Then Pompey's ships returned to take him and his remaining troops off to Greece.

On 17 March Pompey himself broke out of Brundisium with his remaining troops. His evacuation was a masterpiece of organisation, and even Caesar admired the measures that Pompey had taken to ensure that he was not pursued too soon. He had installed light-armed troops on the defences facing Caesar's siege works, and taken off the heavy armed ones with orders to embark in strict silence. When they had boarded, at a pre-arranged signal the defenders left the ramparts and followed their companions onto the ships. Caesar's men were then able to storm the defences to enter the town. In his account of this part of the proceedings, Caesar could not resist the temptation to cast Pompey as the villain, describing how the inhabitants were embittered because of the wrongs done to them by the Pompeian troops, and the insults of Pompey himself, so they warned Caesar that Pompey's men had dug trenches across the main streets, and concealed pits with sharpened stakes embedded in them, to delay the pursuit.[78] Some streets had been barricaded, and huge palisades guarded the route to the harbour. Caesar's troops had to spend valuable time circumventing them, and by the time Caesar reached the harbour, Pompey had set sail. Two ships were captured by the Caesarians, but that was all. It must have been a tremendous anti-climax for Caesar, and a great relief for Pompey, for he was now committed to his course of action, with no going back.

12

The Civil War, 48–47 BC

Caesar had hoped to prevent an evacuation of Italy, because if Pompey escaped intact to another province, the war would be prolonged and there could be no settlement at Rome while Pompey's troops were present in Spain, or wherever else he chose to go. When Pompey sailed off to Greece, where the consuls and the rest of his army had already arrived, he then controlled armies on either side of Italy, and he also had the larger and better fleet. With hindsight, the appointment of Pompey's father-in-law Scipio as governor Syria suggests that Pompey was planning ahead and intended from the first to go to the East to fight the war. The province of Syria, always a key area at the best of times, would be even more important if Pompey was to control the eastern provinces, so it was necessary to allocate it to someone he could trust. Pompey was well established in the eastern provinces, where he had many clients and wealthy investments, and kings and rulers who owed their positions to his influence would contribute troops for his struggle against Caesar. In addition he had good knowledge of the terrain and its potential for maintaining an army. It is at least feasible that as war with Caesar became a reality Pompey had decided from the beginning that he would have to fight it in the East.[1]

After Pompey left Italy, Caesar could not follow him immediately. There were no ships to be found because Pompey had collected all the available ones, and it would take a long time to build more, so Caesar would have to wait. He ordered the municipal towns of Italy to find ships and despatch them to Brundisium, and ordered the building of two fleets, one in the Adriatic and another in the

Tyrrhenian Sea, with Hortensius and Dolabella appointed as admirals while the building was in progress.[2] He probably did not even consider marching overland to try to find and defeat Pompey, because that was an even more arduous and time-consuming business than building ships, and while he was absent he could not control what was happening in Rome. It was more important to return to Rome immediately, where there was no official government.

Caesar made arrangements to secure the corn-producing provinces, which Pompey had initially tried to take over via legates. Caesar won back control of Sardinia, and despatched Curio to Sicily, which he won without a fight because Marcus Porcius Cato, the governor whom Pompey had wanted to send out some months earlier, had refused to go immediately, and when he did finally take over, he had to start recruiting and training troops, but too late. When he heard that Curio was on his way, Cato abandoned the island on 23 April. He took with him all the soldiers that he had raised, and a number of requisitioned ships, to join Pompey in Greece.[3] Appian has an alternative story, in that before Curio was sent to Sicily, Asinius Pollio was despatched, and Cato asked him if he had brought with him an order from the Senate, but in the next chapter, Appian covers the same ground, saying that Curio was sent to replace Cato. Moving to Africa, Curio soon drove Attius Varus, the unofficial governor, into the city of Utica, but his army was attacked by Juba and his Numidians, and was defeated, almost to a man. Curio was killed.[4]

Urgently needing cash to pay his soldiers, Caesar appropriated the funds in the treasury, not without opposition from the tribune Lucius Metellus, who tried to bar the doors, to no avail. Plutarch says that Caesar shouted him down and threatened him, and ordered the soldiers to break the doors; Dio says that the soldiers cut the bolt in two.[5] Caesar also appropriated funds which had never been touched, but had been set aside after the disastrous invasion of the Gauls in the fourth century BC. A curse had been laid on anyone who removed the money, unless it was for the purpose of fighting the Gauls, but Caesar said that since he had conquered the Gauls, there was no danger of invasion, so the curse had been lifted.[6]

Intending to deal with Pompey's army in Spain, Caesar made arrangements to secure Italy and the provinces that were open to him. He appointed Marcus Crassus, the son of his erstwhile colleague, as the governor of Cisalpine Gaul, and he enfranchised the Gauls of that area who had helped him. Northern Italy was secured. Marcus Aemilius Lepidus was appointed prefect of the city, so Rome was also secured. Mark Antony was given command of all the troops in Italy, and his brother Gaius Antonius was sent to Illyricum. Caesar does not mention Gaius Antonius in this context, but his defeat in Illyricum is recorded at a later time.[7] Setting off for Spain, Caesar apparently announced that he was going to fight the army without a leader, and then he would return to fight the leader without an army, referring to Pompey in Greece.[8] On his way to Spain he found that the city of Massilia would not open its gates to him. The citizens said that they owed debts to both Caesar and Pompey, and were friendly to both of them, but would receive neither of them in war. After a failed attempt to take the city by storm, Caesar decided not to waste any more time, and left Gaius Trebonius in charge of the siege works, while he himself pressed on to Spain.[9]

Pompey's legates in Spain were Lucius Afranius, Marcus Petreius and Terentius Varro, with a total of seven legions under their command. Caesar brought six legions and a complement of auxiliary troops, 6,000 of which were cavalry, most of them highly experienced after ten years of wars in Gaul. Whilst Varro held Further Spain with two legions, Afranius and Petreius joined forces in Nearer Spain. By the time that Caesar's first troops arrived under the command of Fabius, they were encamped on a low hill near Ilerda (modern Lerida), on the River Sicoris (modern Serge). At first, Afranius performed well against the measures that Fabius and Caesar employed to dislodge him, beating off an attack by the Fourteenth legion, and attacking one of Caesar's convoys. Eventually he was driven off when Caesar began to create a man-made ford across the river, which would enable him to bring troops across it and prevent the Pompeians from foraging and gathering supplies. Afranius and Petreius moved off towards the River Ebro; Caesar chased them, managed to overtake them and cut them off from their objective, and forced them to turn back. They made for Ilerda, but on the march they were trapped on a hill without access to water, and finally surrendered.[10]

In battles at sea, Decimus Brutus had defeated a Pompeian fleet, but in turn the Pompeians defeated Caesar's naval commander Dolabella.

Gaius Antonius was forced to surrender to the Pompeians in Illyricum. In the north of Italy Caesar's legions mutinied. There was little profit in civil wars, and the soldiers were tired. The Ninth legion was the most seriously disaffected. Caesar ordered its decimation, meaning that every tenth man should be killed, but this was a threat to bring the men to their senses. He listened to their protests, and then sought out 120 of the ringleaders and executed twelve of them, putting an end to the mutiny. One of the twelve men was able to prove that he had not been present when the mutiny began, so Caesar executed the centurion who had accused him.[11]

Meanwhile in Greece, Pompey had profited from the time granted him while Caesar was in Spain. Caesar records that Pompey gathered a large fleet by requisitioning ships, presumably with able crews on board, from Egypt, Phoenicia, Cilicia, Syria, Bithynia, Pontus, Athens, Corcyra, and Asia. In coastal areas Pompey set about building more ships. He also raised more troops. He had taken five legions with him from Italy, and raised two more from veterans who had settled in Cilicia, Greece and Macedonia. The consul Lentulus raised two legions from veterans in Asia. In all Pompey had nine legions of Roman citizens, and was expecting two more to come from Spain. Pompey called upon the allied kings whom he had installed after his campaigns, who all contributed troops. He raised auxiliary troops from Thessaly, Boeotia, Achaea and Epirus, and took over the legionaries who had surrendered with Gaius Antonius. Pompey also recruited specialist troops, such as Cretan archers, and two cohorts of slingers. His son Gnaeus brought ships and 500 men from Egypt, who were among the men left there by Aulus Gabinius when he mounted his expedition to reinstate Ptolemy Auletes on his throne.[12]

Pompey excelled in the organisation and administration that this build-up of troops required. He also trained his troops, taking part in the exercises himself, aged fifty-eight according to Plutarch, and able to outshine most of the men in his exercises.[13] More importantly, Pompey was belatedly made supreme commander by the senators who had accompanied him. According to Appian, Pompey made a speech comparing himself and his followers with those who had abandoned Athens and then regained it when the city was under threat, and those who abandoned Rome when the Gauls invaded. This may arise from Appian's imagination and knowledge of history, but it makes the point that Pompey's strategy was theoretically correct.[14]

Returning to Rome at the end of 49 BC, Caesar was made Dictator, which gave him legal entitlement to hold the consular elections. He held the Dictatorship for only eleven days, and then was elected consul with Publius Servilius Isauricus as colleague. The other magistrates such as praetors and tribunes were appointed, and the vacant priesthoods were filled. Pre-empting any possibility of riots connected to the food supply, or to debts, Caesar passed laws designed to alleviate these major problems.[15] The food supply was the most crucial issue, because Pompey's supremacy at sea, and his control of Africa, which supplied much of Rome's grain, meant that he could blockade Italy. Caesar distributed corn to the people and used his warships to guard the sea lanes and the ports of Sardinia and Sicily.[16] The Roman world now possessed two sets of magistrates, those whom Caesar appointed in Rome, and in Greece the consuls and praetors continued in office as pro-magistrates, since it could hardly be claimed that they had been elected by the people of Rome.[17]

At Brundisium, Caesar's troops were assembling, but they had not all arrived when Caesar came there himself. The soldiers who came later would have had to wait in any case because Caesar did not have enough ships to transport the whole army to Greece. Antony was put in charge of bringing over the remainder, while Caesar set sail with 15,000 legionaries and 500 cavalry. He managed to avoid the Pompeian fleet under Calpurnius Bibulus, and came ashore 80 miles of south of Dyrrachium. Bibulus captured thirty of the transports as they headed back to Italy to pick up Antony and the rest of Caesar's troops. Bibulus burnt the ships with the crews on board, in direct contrast to Caesar's studied policy of letting captives go free, and thus playing into his hands in terms of propaganda.[18]

Pompey did not think that Caesar would set sail from Italy in winter, so he left Scipio in Macedonia with two legions, and marched to put his troops in winter quarters at Dyrrachium, Apollonia, and in other towns on the coast of the Adriatic.[19] On the march he learned of Caesar's arrival. Then he heard that the inhabitants of Oricum, where he had based his supplies, had opened their gates to Caesar, and Apollonia had also fallen.[20] Pompey had lost two cities that he thought were loyal, and much of his supplies. He now hastened to Dyrrachium, because Caesar was marching there too. Arriving there, Pompey made camp near the city. Dyrrachium was well stocked and could also be supplied by sea, facilitated by Pompey's naval supremacy, which was fortunate because Pompey had more mouths to feed than Caesar. Pompey had nine legions, and Scipio was marching from Macedonia with two more, but numbers perhaps did not count for much since none of Pompey's men were as experienced as Caesar's.

Caesar's troops were battle hardened, but he was outnumbered and short of supplies. In order to hold off Scipio and the two legions from Macedonia, Caesar detached two legions under Domitius Calvinus to march against him, with the result that Scipio did not join Pompey. Caesar camped on the south bank of the River Apsus, the boundary between the territory of Dyrrachium and that of Apollonia. Caesar says that he decided to winter there and wait for the rest of his troops to arrive under Antony.[21] Impatient for Antony's arrival, and beginning to suspect that Antony might be adopting a neutral stance, waiting upon events to see which side was winning, Caesar went to find a boat and crew that would take him, in disguise, across the sea to Brundisium to find out what was happening there, but there was a high wind blowing onshore and strong currents, and the helmsman wanted to turn back. Caesar threw off his disguise, telling the crew not to fear, since they carried Caesar, and good fortune sailed with him. But this time fortune deserted him, and the boat had to return.[22]

Near the River Apsus, the two armies faced each other but neither commander was in a position to offer battle. The sources tell of cavalry encounters, and hint that Pompey tried to cross the river, which may have been an attempt to cut Caesar's supply lines.[23] Caesar made the best of a bad situation. The Pompeian fleet-base was on the island of Corcyra, so Caesar occupied a strip of coastline opposite the island, to prevent Pompey's ships from coming inshore for fresh water. Antony was blockaded at Brundisium and adopted the same tactics, preventing the Pompeian commander Libo from obtaining water. Caesar records that Bibulus and Libo tried to arrange a truce with him, but he refused their request.[24]

Caesar tried once more to open negotiations with Pompey, sending a message by Vibullius Rufus, captured at Corfinium by Caesar and released, and captured again in Spain. Pompey did not listen to the terms, replying that he had no wish to reach old age courtesy of Caesar. He knew that Caesar was in a precarious position, and would soon be short of supplies; and he also knew that one of Caesar's motives in proposing peace was to cast Pompey and the Senate in the role of warmongering fanatics.[25] Caesar utilises the escalation of hostility to his own advantage. He tells how his troops began to fraternise with Pompey's who were camped nearby, but Labienus put a brutal stop to it, saying that only the delivery of Caesar's head would end the war.[26]

Dio says that Antony had not dared to try to set sail from Brundisium while Calpurnius Bibulus was alive, but when Bibulus died, overwhelmed by the hardships he had endured, Antony succeeded in breaking out with his transports.[27] Antony crossed the Adriatic to land at the harbour of Nymphaeum.[28] He began the march southwards to join Caesar. According to Dio, Pompey immediately retired to Dyrrachium, but this is to anticipate events.[29] In reality Pompey planned to trap Antony at a narrow pass over the Genusus river, but the Greeks living nearby warned Antony, so he made camp and waited for Caesar, who marched round to the east and joined up with him, threatening to trap Pompey between his two armies. Pompey decided not to risk battle and made for Asparagium, travelling westwards along the Egnatian Way, to protect the route to Dyrrachium.[30] Caesar followed him, camped opposite him on the route, and the next day drew up his army in battle order. Pompey refused to be drawn, and on the following morning Caesar moved off. Pompey's scouts reported that Caesar was heading towards Dyrrachium so Pompey would have to follow to avoid being cut off from the town, but he was nearly too late because he allowed his men to rest before marching. He camped near Dyrrachium on a hill called Petra, ordering part of his navy and his supply ships to assemble in the large bay.

Caesar camped to the north of Pompey. Not having command of the sea, he could scarcely interrupt the supplies for Pompey's army, so he could only prevent him from foraging, which would gradually make life very difficult for the cavalry and their mounts. He occupied the hill tops running in an arc to the east of Pompey's camp, building small forts on them and joining the hills with a series of trenches. Caesar describes how his main concern was to confine Pompey, and Pompey's was to occupy the widest possible circuit, and in exercising these two conflicting aims there were several small battles.[31] Pompey built an inner ring of lines, enclosing as much territory as he could, from his camp at Petra to the River Lesnikia (modern Gesnike) to the south. Caesar was forced to extend his own lines, stretching his troops to the limit to guard them. Caesar ordered Antony to occupy and fortify a hill, from where he might have been able to turn his trenches westwards to the coast, thus enclosing Pompey within a much smaller area, but Antony was forced off the hill, and Pompey carried on extending his lines southward.[32]

Caesar's problem was in finding food. He tells how his soldiers were very patient in enduring hunger, and found a root called 'chara', which they mixed with milk and made loaves, which they defiantly hurled into Pompey's camp.[33] Plutarch says that Pompey did not let the main body of the army see these loaves, since his soldiers already thought that they were fighting wild animals and their morale was very low.[34]

Pompey's problem was with his officers. Plutarch documents the petty internal squabbles among Pompey's staff.[35] Pompey knew that inactivity was the best policy while Caesar starved, but his subordinates were restive, demanding action. Cicero describes the majority of Pompey's officers as completely selfish, thinking only of ways in which to get rich quickly from plunder and pay off their debts.[36] Caesar describes how the officers and senators argued about who should fill all the vacant magistracies and priesthoods in Rome once the war was over.[37]

Pompey's strategy was correct, but despite his enclosure of land for foraging, he was losing cavalry horses and baggage animals. The problem was made worse when Caesar cut off his water supply by blocking the streams running from the mountains towards the sea. Pompey's men had to dig wells in the strip of land near the shore, but it was high summer and the wells dried up, so this shortage of water combined with the lack of forage decided Pompey to remove the cavalry to Dyrrachium, where the horses could be properly fed and watered.[38]

Pompey sent to Caesar a false message, to the effect that the city of Dyrrachium was ready to surrender to him. Caesar took a small force by night, expecting someone to open the gates, but Pompey had ferried troops along the shoreline and ambushed Caesar, who almost lost his life. While this was going on, Pompey's men attacked Caesar's lines in three separate places, but were repulsed. Caesar insists that he had few casualties in these engagements, and that Pompey sustained at least 2,000 dead. This is probably a cover-up to save face.[39]

Eventually Caesar managed to cut off Pompey's cavalry from their foraging grounds, and the horses had to be ferried back by sea to the limited ground enclosed by Pompey's lines. It was only a matter of time before Pompey would be in desperate straits, so he had to try to break out. Two Gauls who had deserted from Caesar's camp told him that at the southern end of Caesar's double lines there was a gap by the sea, because Caesar had not joined up the two lines by digging a trench parallel to the coast.[40] He had merely put Lentulus Marcellinus in command of the Ninth legion in a camp some distance from the sea. Pompey sent light-armed troops by night to sail down the coast and land in two groups, one in the gap between the two lines, and one to the south. His troops rolled back the Caesarians caught in between the two lines, so that in retreat they clashed with the fresh troops that Marcellinus brought up. The Pompeians were eventually driven off by the arrival of Mark Antony with twelve cohorts, and then Caesar himself with thirteen cohorts. Pompey was driven off but he occupied a camp outside Caesar's lines, to the south near the coast, so he could bring his cavalry to forage in safety, and protect his ships as they approached the coast. Caesar attempted to take this new camp by storm, before Pompey had moved the whole garrison into it. While it was still defended by only a few men, Caesar attacked, broke through the ramparts and herded the Pompeians together in a corner of the camp, but then Pompey arrived with five legions. Caesar's troops panicked and tried to flee, but their route was blocked by the rampart they had just broken through. Many were trampled to death, and Caesar records that he lost thirty-two standards, thirty-two tribunes and centurions, and 960 men. Plutarch and Appian record that Caesar said there could have been a complete victory for the Pompeians if only they had been led by a victor, but Caesar does not include this anecdote in his own account.[41] Pompey did not follow through after mauling Caesar's troops, possibly because he expected Caesar to capitulate, and he wrote in this vein to various kings and cities, insisting that

Caesar's army was oppressed by hunger and his defeat.[42] Pompey was correct. The recent action signalled the end of the blockade, and Caesar decided that the time had come to move off in search of food and forage. Dio says that he destroyed all his fortified lines before he left.[43]

As soon as he knew that Caesar was moving off, Pompey followed. There was a skirmish where Pompey's cavalry caught up with Caesar's rearguard at the River Genusus, but after this the two armies peacefully occupied their old camps, facing each other at Asparagium,Pompey's officers decided to return to Dyrrachium to collect their baggage, which they had not had time to pack when they hastily began to chase after Caesar. While this was going on, Caesar moved off, and was some few miles away by the time Pompey could gather his troops. Pompey pursued for a few days, then returned to the Egnatian Way, possibly back to camp at Asparagium.

He held a council of war, to discuss his options, while still advocating his policy of attrition. Afranius recommended that the Pompeians should prolong the war in the hope of wearing Caesar down. Another alternative was to decamp without delay and invade Italy, where it was supposed that Caesar's foothold was tenuous. Pompey may have considered this, because just before the final battle he sent part of his fleet to blockade Brundisium and to attack Sicily, which could be interpreted as preparation to invade Italy. But he was reluctant to abandon Scipio, because Caesar was marching to join Domitius in Macedonia, and therefore Scipio would be faced by a larger Caesarian army.[44] Pompey decided to march to join Scipio. There followed a series of marches and counter-marches in Thessaly. Caesar approached the city of Gomphi and found its gates closed against him. Pompey had announced a great victory, so the inhabitants of Gomphi thought that Caesar had been defeated, and to open their gates might bring Pompey's wrath on their heads. The unfortunate town was soon apprised of Caesar's true status, and he sacked it. Thereafter, none of the city-states of Thessaly, except Larissa where Scipio was camped, dared to defy Caesar.[45]

Caesar arrived in the fertile territory near Pharsalus and made camp. There are two settlements close together with the name Pharsalus, one being Old Pharsalus and the other a later town with the same name. It is not known precisely where Caesar's camp lay. By the calendar it was August, but it was out of synchronisation with the season, which was actually midsummer, and the crops were nearly ready for harvest.[46] Pompey and Scipio marched to find Caesar, and made camp on a hill, in a naturally defensive position. Caesar drew up his troops in battle order, each day a little closer to Pompey's camp, but Pompey merely paraded his men in an inaccessible position on the hillside, continuing his policy of starving Caesar out.[47] It nearly worked, despite the fact that in a short time the crops could be harvested and Caesar's problem would be temporarily solved. Caesar had decided to move off to find supplies, then to return and harass Pompey wherever he encamped. On the very day planned for Caesar's departure, Pompey brought his army out and advanced much further than usual down the hill. Why did he choose to offer battle when he had so steadfastly refused to do so before? Plutarch says that Pompey was overly concerned with his good reputation and did not want to seem disrespectful to those who advised him to fight.[48] These advisers accused him of prolonging the war unnecessarily, exulting in giving orders to consulars. He was nicknamed Agamemnon, and king of kings.[49] Possibly he had grown tired of his insubordinate subordinates and their continual carping, and simply wanted to end the war one way or another. Appian considers that some of his officers were also tired of the war and wanted a quick decision.[50]

Pompey outlined his battle plan in a council of war held some days earlier. His cavalry, of which he possessed a large force, was to wait until the two armies had drawn near to each other, then attack Caesar's right wing in flank, and work round to the rear to encircle Caesar. All this was to be done rapidly so that Caesar's army would be routed before the main assault with the rest of Pompey's troops had even begun, thus sparing the legionaries from damage.[51]

While he was preparing to march, Caesar's scouts reported that Pompey's troops were drawn up further from his camp than usual, so he stopped his preparations to break camp and arranged his troops in battle order. He observed that on Pompey's left there were the two legions that he had given up towards the end of the Gallic war, and also Pompey himself. Scipio commanded the centre, and the troops brought over from Spain by Afranius and the Cilician legion were stationed on the right wing, which was protected by a stream with difficult banks. The whole army numbered about 45,000 men, and there were 2,000 reservists from Pompey's former armies, and seven cohorts guarding the camp.[52] Caesar had 22,000 men in the battle lines, the Tenth legion on the right, where he stationed himself with Publius Sulla in command, and Mark Antony commanded the left, where the Ninth legion, much depleted, was brigaded with the Eighth legion, the combined forces still only about the size of one legion. Gnaeus Domitius Calvinus commanded the centre. Observing the movements of the horsemen on Pompey's left, Caesar guessed what was about to happen. Accordingly he detached some cohorts from the third battle line to make a fourth line, explaining that the outcome of the battle depended on them.[53]

The first clashes of the infantry proved the mettle of Pompey's men, who stood firm and received the attack of the Caesarians without flinching. Plutarch says that Caesar ordered his soldiers to aim their spears at the faces of the Pompeians, but Caesar does not mention this.[54] When Labienus ordered the Pompeian cavalry to attack Caesar's right wing as planned, Caesar brought out his extra troops from his fourth line, hurled them against the flank of the attacking Pompeians, and panicked them so badly that some of them turned and fled. Although the centre and the right wing of Pompey's line were holding out, Caesar's men were now encircling the Pompeian left. A Pompeian victory was impossible. It should be noted that Caesar's account of the Battle of Pharsalus differs from that of Plutarch and Appian, who may have derived their information from the historian Asinius Pollio, who was present at Pharsalus.[55] Dio's account is wordy but vague, with phrases such as 'it was a very great battle and full of diverse incidents'.[56] He attributes the defeat of Pompey to the composition of his army, the larger part of which was composed of Asiatics, who were untrained, as opposed to Caesar's army, which as he described in another passage composed the largest and most genuine Roman portion of the state legions.[57]

Knowing that the situation could not be retrieved, Pompey rode back to camp, and when Caesar's men broke in he mounted his horse and rode away. A small number of the Pompeian troops made a last stand on a hill near to the battlefield, but had to surrender when Caesar cut their water supply.[58] Caesar reports 15,000 Pompeian dead, and 24,000 surrendered, at a cost of thirty of his own centurions and 200 soldiers. As ever, these figures are disputed.[59]

After the battle was over, Suetonius reports that Caesar said, 'They would have it so. Even after so many great deeds I would have been found guilty if I had not turned to the army for help.'[60] Plutarch phrases it slightly differently. Caesar blames his enemies for bringing this outcome on themselves, because 'they forced me into a position where if I had given up my forces I would have been condemned.'[61] The story derives from Asinius Pollio, who was probably in Caesar's presence when he spoke the relevant words. The emphasis is always on the necessity of keeping his army together to prevent his enemies from prosecuting him. Caesar was not the first to do so, and after him command of the armed forces would become the mainstay of Imperial rule. It was quickly discovered that the armies could make or break Emperors, starting with Nero and the three men who followed him in quick succession, until the third of these, Vespasian, became Emperor and remained in power until he died ten years later.

There were skirmishes between the Pompeian and Caesarian fleets, until the news of Pompey's defeat reached the Pompeian commanders.[62] In the meantime, Caesar decided that it was of utmost importance to follow Pompey, rather than attend personally to everything else. If Pompey gathered another army, the war would go on. Caesar did not know where he had gone and what he intended to do. Pompey had sent his cousin Hirrus as an envoy to the Parthian court, and it was rumoured that he intended to go to Parthia for aid. Plutarch and Appian both explain that Pompey discussed three choices of where to turn, claiming that he did not want to go to Africa or Egypt because he did not trust King Juba or Ptolemy, but that his preference was for Parthia.[63] Caesar does not mention this tale, and Dio rejects it, but in an earlier passage he had described how Pompey had approached allied states and kings for contributions of money and troops, among them Orodes, King of Parthia, who said he would ally with Pompey if he could have control of Syria, which Pompey did not even consider giving to him.[64] The embassy of Hirrus may have been nothing to do with seeking aid after defeat, but to ensure the neutrality of Parthia in order to protect Syria and the Roman provinces from attack.

Pompey's greatest need now was for men and money as well as more ships, even though his command of the sea was not as yet diminished. After a brief dash to Cyprus, Pompey tried to go to Syria, but found that the Roman citizens in the towns and cities had decided to deny him access.[65] Though he did not trust the Ptolemaic regime of Egypt, in the past he had been instrumental in securing the throne for the late Ptolemy Auletes, and Egypt was a wealthy country where he could perhaps find troops and money in order to build up another army to continue the war. He set sail for Egypt, landing at Pelusium, to seek an audience with the young Ptolemy, who was engaged in a civil war with his sister Cleopatra VII. Ptolemy's advisers, Achillas, commander of the Royal army, Pothinus, the finance minister, and Theodotus, Ptolemy's tutor, all decided that it would be better to appease the victorious Caesar than to harbour the defeated Pompey in their midst. 'Dead men don't bite,' said Achillas.[66] Thus the greatest Roman of his day met his ignominious end on the Egyptian shore. The Egyptians took his head, leaving the body on the shore, to be burned by Philippus, his freedman.[67]

Caesar had by now heard that Pompey had been seen in Cyprus, and guessed that he would aim for Egypt.[68] When he arrived in Alexandria, only three days after Pompey, he was presented with Pompey's head and signet ring, whereupon, says Plutarch, Caesar burst into tears. Pompey was, after all, the husband of Caesar's only child, his daughter Julia.[69] Dio accuses Caesar of hypocrisy when he shed tears over Pompey. Not mincing words, Dio goes on to say that Caesar had always hated Pompey, and had waged war with no other purpose than to secure his rival's ruin.[70] This opinion is decisive, but debatable, and would probably make for a good exam question: discuss Dio's statement and its relevance to the causes of the civil war of 49 BC. Caesar ordered Pompey's head to be buried in a plot of ground near the city, which he dedicated to Nemesis. According to Appian the plot was destroyed in Trajan's reign, when he was fighting the Jews in Egypt.[71]

The civil war had not ended. There were other Pompeians still at large, though Caesar was probably not yet certain about where they had gone. The Pompeian fleet was still a major force to be reckoned with. But for the time being, Caesar remained in Egypt, with very few troops. He had summoned a legion from Thessaly, and another from Achaea, together with 800 cavalry and warships from Rhodes and Asia. In Egypt he was immediately embroiled, perhaps deliberately, in the internal wars between Ptolemy and Cleopatra. There were two other surviving children of Ptolemy XII Auletes, a young boy also called Ptolemy, and another daughter, Arsinoe, but only the eldest son, the young Ptolemy XIII, and the eldest daughter, Cleopatra VII, had been named in the last will and testament of Auletes as his joint heirs. Neither of them wished to share power with the other, and both of them had an entourage and an army with which to fight it out. Cleopatra had been driven out of Alexandria, and was with her army somewhere near the city. It would be worthwhile attempting to arbitrate, so that the established rulers would be grateful to Rome, and specifically to Julius Caesar. He wrote that the struggle in Egypt affected the Roman people and himself as consul, because of the alliance with Ptolemy Auletes. Therefore he ordered Ptolemy and Cleopatra to lay down their arms and settle their dispute by law instead of armed force.[72]

Pothinus summoned the army under Achillas to come from Pelusium to Alexandria. Caesar had not enough men to risk a battle outside the city. Achillas had 20,000 soldiers, some of whom were Romans from Aulus Gabinius' army, long since settled in Egypt after Gabinius had dashed from Syria to shore up the Egyptian throne. They had gone native from long association with the country and the people.[73] Caesar's account of the civil wars ends with fighting in the streets and the attack on the port. Caesar could not allow Achillas to gain control of the ships and the harbour, as that would cut him off from supplies and reinforcements. He needed to gain control of Pharos Island (which gave its name to the famous lighthouse built on it) and attacked it. He appealed to neighbouring provinces for troops, and strengthened important positions in Alexandria.[74] The narrative overlaps with the account of the Alexandrian war, where another attack on Pharos Island is recorded.[75] This may be duplication of the attack described in *The Civil Wars*, or it may mean that on the first occasion he garrisoned only the area around the lighthouse at the eastern end of the island.

The Alexandrian War describes the battles that ensued from Caesar's intervention in the war between Ptolemy XIII and Cleopatra VII. There is scant mention of Cleopatra in *The Civil*

Wars, except the information that she had been expelled from Alexandria.[76] Significantly, Hirtius, the probable author of *The Alexandrian War*, ignored her altogether, except to say that she was made ruler of Egypt before Caesar left to fight against Pharnaces. Later authors embellished the story, influenced by the reputation Cleopatra had gained from the propaganda of Octavian-Augustus, portraying her as a mortal enemy of Rome, immoral, unscrupulous and dangerous.

Cleopatra's entry into history traditionally begins when she rolled out of a carpet at Caesar's feet. Plutarch's version is that Caesar sent for her, and she arrived inside a bag for storing bedding, carried by Apollodorus.[77] Cleopatra could not enter Alexandria openly, with or without her army, because if she fell into the hands of Achillas or Pothinus she would have been killed. Caesar was the most powerful general in the world, and she had to reach him quickly but secretly, banking on being able to persuade him to take up her cause. Plutarch says that Caesar fell for her on the spot.[78] Dio is even more emphatic about her charms. She was beautiful, he says, whereas other sources insist she was not a great beauty but she was attractive, and clever. She had a mellifluous voice, with which Dio agrees. He does not include the story of the rolled-up carpet, but says that she entered the palace without alerting Ptolemy, and since Caesar was susceptible to women, having slept with all the ones he encountered, he was captivated by her.[79] This is retrospective. In Dio's era, the separate histories of both Caesar and Cleopatra, and their brief association, had passed into legend.

All four children of Ptolemy Auletes, the two brothers Ptolemy XIII and his younger sibling Ptolemy, and the two sisters Arsinoe and Cleopatra, were cooped up in the Royal Palace with Caesar when Achillas brought up Ptolemy's army to Alexandria. Caesar began to fortify the area under his control. His soldiers were spread over two regions of the city and needed to be brought under a single command. He barricaded some streets and built mobile towers, to be drawn by draught animals. He ensured access to food and fodder, collected arms brought in by the Egyptians, and established arms factories. At the outset of the war he summoned ships from Rhodes, Syria, Cilicia and Nabataea, together with artillery engines and supplies of grain.[80] He also sent for reinforcements to be brought in by sea, and had contacted his ally Mithridates of

Pergamum, sending him to Syria and Cilicia to recruit more troops, but it would be some time before these reinforcements reached Alexandria.

Pothinus was executed because he had exhorted Achillas to make war on the Romans.[81] Arsinoe escaped to join Achillas and the army, with one of her main supporters, Ganymede, who assassinated Achillas and was made commander of the army. Ganymede dug trenches to allow seawater to flow in and spoil the fresh water supply of the areas controlled by Caesar, first closing off and protecting the channels which brought water to the other parts of the city. The Romans dug wells, and survived, but they could not do so indefinitely.[82] Supply ships arrived from Domitius Calvinus who commanded the eastern provinces, but they could not enter because of contrary winds. Caesar boarded a ship and ordered the others to follow him to get the supplies, but did not take troops with him because they were needed to guard the fortifications, so he could not risk a naval battle. Nonetheless, one of the Rhodian ships was attacked and Caesar had to rescue it, but he caused considerable damage to Ganymede's fleet. Then the supply ships were towed in.[83] Control of Pharos Island was paramount, together with the causeway and its two bridges connecting the island to the mainland. While he was fortifying the island Caesar's men were attacked, and many were drowned. Caesar had to make for his own ship to escape, but with the press of soldiers trying to get on board he realised that it would capsize, so he dived into the sea and swam towards other ships.[84] While he was swimming, he apparently held important papers above his head to keep them dry. This may be a later embellishment, and it is not mentioned in *The Alexandrian War*.[85]

Help was on its way. Mithridates was marching from Syria, and the Egyptians heard the news before Caesar. Just before his arrival, the Alexandrians had asked Caesar to send Ptolemy XIII to join the army outside Alexandria because they were disenchanted with 'the girl', meaning Arsinoe. Caesar agreed, and Ptolemy shed a few crocodile tears before he left, then immediately launched himself into the war.[86] When Mithridates took Pelusium, east of Alexandria, Ptolemy led the army out against him. Caesar followed, to find that Ptolemy had made a strong camp, with a branch of the Nile, with high banks, between him and Caesar's line of march. Caesar's troops managed to cross the river, despite the difficulties. German cavalrymen swam across, and the legionaries felled trees – scarce in Egypt – long enough to span the gap between the high banks and make a causeway. After a hard fight Caesar overwhelmed Ptolemy's fortifications and routed the Egyptians. Ptolemy fled to the Nile and was taken on board a ship, but too many Egyptian soldiers tried to come aboard. The ship sank and Ptolemy was drowned.[87] According to Egyptian lore this conferred divinity upon him. Caesar had his body fished out and put on display to demonstrate that he was mortal and dead.

Cleopatra was made Queen of Egypt with her young brother Ptolemy XIV as consort.[88] Her true consort for the time being was Caesar himself. They went on a pleasure trip down the Nile, with 400 ships.[89] There were rumours that Caesar had married Cleopatra according to Egyptian rites, scandalous if true, because he could not legally marry her for two reasons: he was already married to Calpurnia, and in Roman law it was illegal for a Roman to marry a foreigner. It is doubtful that Caesar made their association official.

Around June, or at some time in the summer of 47 BC, Caesar left Egypt, and shortly afterwards Cleopatra gave birth to a son whom she called Ptolemy Caesar, and whom the Alexandrians nicknamed Caesarion (Little Caesar). This boy combined Egypt and Rome, and Cleopatra hoped that he would be able to maintain independence for Egypt, avoiding absorption and annexation by Rome. Caesar acknowledged him, and after Caesar's assassination, Antony vouched for the boy's parentage, possibly because it was useful to him.[90] But there was room for doubt about who the father was, and later it was useful to Octavian, Caesar's heir, to portray Cleopatra as a scheming individual who slept with whoever she fancied, so that anyone could have fathered Caesarion, who was a serious rival to Octavian. As Caesar's legitimate heir, albeit with dubious legality because he had been adopted by means of a codicil attached to Caesar's will, Octavian was determined that there should be no other heirs, and therefore Caesarion had to be killed.

On leaving Egypt, Caesar did not return to Rome, but first marched to quell the Empire-building activities of Pharnaces, the son of Mithridates whom Pompey had defeated. More than half of the narrative of *The Alexandrian War* is devoted to this war, first providing the justification for it, when Deiotarus, King of Galatia, came to Domitius Calvinus, governor of Asia and neighbouring territories, to ask him to prevent Pharnaces from taking over Lesser Armenia and Cappadocia, respectively or his own kingdom, and that of Ariobarzanes. If this takeover came about, Deiotarus said that he would not be able to pay the sums he had promised to Caesar.[91] The narrative outlines what Pharnaces had done while Caesar was involved in the civil war, chasing Pompey to Egypt, and then establishing Cleopatra as Queen. There is also an account of events in Illyricum, and a longer description of the antics of Quintus Cassius Longinus in Spain, setting the scene for the final act of the civil war against the Pompeians, commanded by the sons of Pompey.[92]

The war against Pharnaces had to be waged because Roman provincial and allied territories were threatened, and Romans were killed. Domitius sent a delegation to Pharnaces, to ask him to withdraw from Armenia and Cappadocia. He assembled troops at Comana in Pontus, and Pharnaces withdrew from Cappadocia, but not Lesser Armenia, because he said it was his by right of the conquests of his father, Mithridates. Domitius countered this with the statement that he was recovering the kingdoms of Rome's allies. The result was a battle near Nicopolis, in which Domitius was defeated with considerable losses. He collected the troops and marched into Asia through Cappadocia – leaving Pharnaces unopposed as he entered Pontus – killed Romans and took their property.[93]

On leaving Egypt, Caesar knew that his presence was demanded in Rome because of the state of affairs in the government, but he considered it more important to settle the eastern provinces. Hirtius expresses Caesar's aims rather grandly: he wished to organise the governments of the provinces and allied states to ensure their protection from internal unrest and external aggression, and induce them to accept a legal constitution. He was confident that he could achieve this in Syria, Cilicia, and Asia, because there were no wars threatening these areas. To this end, Caesar spent some time in the most important cities in Syria, giving judgements in long-standing disputes and exhorting kings and rulers of allied states to protect their territories. Then he made the same arrangements in Cilicia, giving judgement in court cases and receiving Pompeians who surrendered to him.[94]

Having secured these territories, he set out across Cappadocia and collected troops from Deiotarus, who had supported Pompey and was now eager to ingratiate himself with Caesar. Pharnaces was at Zela in Pontus, encamped near to the town and in occupation of the heights nearby. He tried to draw out proceedings by negotiating, hoping that the problems in the Roman world would force Caesar to return to Rome. But Caesar was not willing to be drawn into this game. Instead he occupied the high ground close to Pharnaces' camp but separated from it by a deep gully and well protected by the steep slope to the summit. Caesar's troops marched out at night, encumbered by their entrenching tools, and erected fortifications on the hill top. Caesar could not quite believe his eyes when Pharnaces launched a frontal attack on this camp, sending his troops across the ravine and up the steep side of the hill. Caesar had to draw up his troops in haste. The soldiers were not formed up in line of battle and might have been overwhelmed had not the VI legion managed to force the enemy back down the hill. The Romans chased Pharnaces and his troops all the way down the hill, up the opposite one and into their camp. But they did not capture Pharnaces.[95] Caesar left two legions in Pontus to prevent Pharnaces from occupying the area. He wrote to his friend Gaius Matius, summing up his achievement, with its emphasis on the lightning campaign and its total success: *veni, vidi, vici*, I came, I saw, I conquered.[96] Caesar was so pleased with the phrase that he used the slogan again in his triumph. He left Domitius Calvinus in command in the East, and started back to Italy, extracting from kings and rulers the money that had been promised to Pompey for the war effort, or collecting fines from the communities which had helped Pompey. He justified this accumulation of wealth by explaining that there were two things that created and protected sovereignty: money and soldiers.[97]

13

Africa and Spain, 47–45 BC

During his stay in Egypt and in the war against Pharnaces, Caesar was kept informed of what was happening in Rome. Hirtius devotes a few lines in *The Alexandrian War* to explain that when Caesar arrived in Syria, he had heard from various sources that the government was far from efficient, that the tribunes of the plebs were at loggerheads with each other, and that military discipline was falling apart because the military tribunes and legionary officers were too lax.[1]

Before Caesar followed Pompey to Egypt, he had sent Antony back to Rome, and in the autumn of 48 BC, the Caesarians had procured Caesar's appointment as Dictator for one year, though the normal term was for six months. Antony was made *magister equitum*, or master of horse, the usual deputy for each Dictator. He had control of military and political matters, and since Caesar was Dictator for one year, Antony was likewise to retain his post for a year, but this caused some grumbling among the senators, until it was pointed out that Caesar's appointment was abnormal in any case, so quibbling about Antony seemed irrelevant.[2] In the absence of regular consuls and praetors, Antony convened the Senate, and upset the senators by wearing a sword when he attended meetings, and men began to distrust Caesar as a result of the behaviour of his subordinate.[3] There was trouble from Marcus Caelius Rufus, who took up the perennial problem of the debt-ridden masses of Rome, and joined forces with Titus Annius Milo, who had returned from exile. They were both men with grudges and could have made even more trouble, had they not been killed, Milo in Apulia and Rufus in Bruttium. The cause of the debtors was taken up by Cornelius Dolabella. Cancellation of all debts was a frequent request in Rome, usually accompanied by violence, and in this case there was a riot in the Forum. The Senate authorised Antony to restore order.[4] He brought up his troops but the crowd did not disperse, leaving him only two choices: backing down, or using his soldiers. He chose to attack the mob, and there were several deaths. Even after this there were disturbances, which did not cease until Caesar at last returned to Rome.[5] He did not punish anyone, but Caesar could not be seen to condone Antony's actions, so he disassociated himself for a while, and Antony was unemployed.[6]

It was autumn by the calendar when Caesar arrived in Rome, but high summer by the seasons. He was made Dictator for the second time. He took measures to alleviate the debt problem, and held the consular elections. His officers Fufius Calenus and Publius Vatinius became consuls for the short time that remained of the year. Several senators and equestrians were promoted. Caesar's great-nephew Gaius Octavius, now aged about sixteen, was appointed as *praefectus urbi*, or city prefect, during the festival of the *Feriae Latinae*. This was an honorary post, often bestowed on young members of upper-class families at the time of the festival, when all the magistrates left Rome in the hands of the priests, to travel to the Alban Mount to conduct religious ceremonies in memory of Roman conquest of Alba Longa, so early in Rome's history that no one could remember it in detail. The post of *praefectus urbi* had little resemblance to the duties of the later city prefects, but Gaius Octavius was technically head of state for a few days. Since he was very young and always ill with one complaint or another, he did not attract much notice.

After the continual disturbances of the last few years most people were content to allow Caesar to organise the Roman government as he wished. Besides, as Dictator he was unassailable. On the political front all was relatively calm, but the Pompeians had gathered in Africa and it was necessary to fight another war before they became too strong. Some of Caesar's soldiers chose this moment to mutiny. They were tired and wanted rest and, most of all, the pay that had been promised them. The soldiers had driven off Caesar's representative Gaius Sallustius Crispus, otherwise known as the historian Sallust, and had killed the praetors Cosconius and Galba.[7]

They came to Rome and camped outside the city, where Caesar met them to listen to their demands. The soldiers said that they wanted to be discharged, expecting that Caesar would make them tempting offers to persuade them to remain under arms. But Caesar did not comply. Instead of addressing them in his usual way as *comilitones* (fellow soldiers), he called them *Quirites* (citizens), as though they had been discharged.[8] Appian has a different version, where Caesar first says 'I discharge you', which reduced the troops to embarrassed silence, and after an interval he addressed them as *Quirites*.[9] Caesar said he would fight the war in Africa with other troops. Knowing him well, the soldiers realised that he probably would do exactly what he said, and if they did not go with him there would be no plunder or pay. There was no more talk of mutiny.

Plutarch covers Caesar's victorious African war briefly in three chapters.[10] Dio's account is longer, but more details are found in the anonymous *African War*, which for convenience is attributed to Caesar.[11] While Caesar was in Egypt and the East, the Pompeians in Africa had congregated at Utica where the governor Atius Varus was replaced by Cato. Juba, King of the Numidians, joined them with his horsemen, archers and infantry. Since the citizens of Utica favoured Caesar, Metellus Scipio planned to massacre them, but Cato protested, successfully avoiding a bloodbath. Scipio was chosen as overall commander, and Cato acquiesced, because Scipio was the more senior and more experienced. By the time that Caesar prepared for war, the Pompeians had assembled fourteen legions, masses of cavalry and light-armed troops, a number of elephants, and several fleets.[12]

Against this force, Caesar gathered six legions and 2,000 cavalry. Part of the army sailed from Lilybaeum in Sicily just as the winter season was beginning, and a storm blew up and scattered the ships, so that even if there had been a pre-arranged rendezvous, the ships could not have reached it. Caesar had no intelligence reports about which harbours and coastal towns were in Pompeian hands. He landed with no more than 3,000 men and 150 cavalry, near Hadrumetum (modern Susa).[13] As he disembarked he fell, but came up again with handfuls of sand and earth, proclaiming, 'I hold you, Africa'.[14] By thinking on his feet, or rather his knees, he converted a potentially bad omen into a positive statement of intent.

Hadrumetum was held by the Pompeian general Considius Longus, and Caesar did not attempt to take it. As he was breaking camp, he was attacked by troops from the town and Juba's cavalry, who had come to collect their pay. He managed to beat them off and he marched south-east down the coast and camped near Ruspina. The first operations of the war centered around this area. Various towns sent representatives offering food supplies and help in whatever way Caesar needed. On 1 January Caesar marched to Leptis Minor (modern Lemta), where he was welcomed, and fortuitously some of his transports arrived.[15] But Caesar still did not have an adequate campaign army, and some of the ships were still unaccounted for. He sent the transports back to Sicily to bring over the rest of the troops, and put Vatinius in command of warships to look for the lost fleet.

After only one day at Leptis, Caesar left six cohorts there and marched back to Ruspina, He went to the harbour, 2 miles away, where part of his fleet lay. He spent the night on board ship, and the next day some of the missing ships arrived. Once these were in port Caesar returned to Ruspina. Immediately, he led out a forage party with thirty cohorts, but they ran into troops commanded by Titus Labienus, Caesar's erstwhile deputy in Gaul.[16] Caesar drew up in a single line, with archers in front and cavalry on the wings. Labienus' cavalry started an encircling movement, so Caesar's cavalry extended their line and consequently thinned out, but Caesar's infantry drove off the light-armed Numidian infantry. Labienus' cavalry completed their encirclement, and came close enough to Caesar's troops to exchange insults, until one of Caesar's legionaries thrust a javelin into the chest of Labienus' horse. Appian says that Labienus was thrown and had to be carried off the field, but this is not mentioned in the *The African War*.[17] Fighting now in completely new circumstances, Caesar ordered his own line to extend and every other cohort to turn round, so that his small army faced in two directions.[18] This manoeuvre could easily have gone wrong in the heat of battle, but Caesar managed to split Labienus' forces into two groups and kept them apart with his cavalry. Maintaining battle formation, Caesar fought his way almost back to his camp, but then Marcus Petreius and Gnaeus Piso arrived with Numidian troops. Night was coming on, so Caesar encouraged his surrounded troops to make one last supreme effort and drive the enemy off, and to gain possession of the high ground nearby. They succeeded and remained there for a few hours, until Caesar led them back to camp in battle formation in the dark.[19] Petreius had been wounded, and according to Appian, Labienus was out of action as well, so this is probably why they did not try to prevent Caesar from getting back to camp, but Appian also says that Petreius called off his troops because he wanted the credit to go to Scipio, who was due to arrive soon. This sounds unlikely as a motive for not following through. Scipio probably was approaching, as Dio reports that Caesar was worried that after being mauled, he would have to face the joint forces of Scipio and Juba, in a disadvantageous position without supplies.[20] Plutarch and Appian include an anecdote about Caesar during an unspecified battle, for which the context is not established beyond doubt, but they associate it with the attack by Labienus and Petreius. The Caesarian troops were running away, and Caesar manhandled some of them back into line, grabbing a standard bearer and turning him round, explaining that the enemy was in the opposite direction.[21]

After this battle several Pompeian soldiers deserted to Caesar, and from these he learned of their battle plans.[22] Caesar's position was precarious. Supplies of all kinds had to be imported; food because the area was already depleted, timber because there were few trees in the country, and with his small number of troops, he had not brought enough equipment and weapons. Besides these commodities, safe entry for incoming troops was necessary. Caesar built two lines of entrenchments from Ruspina to the sea so that he could bring in supplies from his ships. He badly needed reinforcements, the more so because if he failed to send troops to aid the towns nearby which asked for his protection, the inhabitants could so easily declare for the Pompeians, just to save themselves and their property from attack. The war between the Caesarians and Pompeians involved innocent civilians. Towns opened their gates to one side or the other, or were seized by force, and then sometimes besieged by the opposing troops. Food supplies were seized, territories laid waste, convoys intercepted, the aim being either to feed the soldiers and animals, or to deny supplies to the opposing side. Either way, civilians suffered.

Caesar's problems were increased when Scipio at last arrived to join Labienus and Petreius, and made camp only 3 miles from Caesar's.[23] In the meantime King Bocchus of Mauretania, and a Roman called Publius Sittius who had served as one of Bocchus' generals, took Cirta (modern Constantine), the wealthiest city of Numidia, forcing Juba leave the Pompeians to fight his own battles.[24] Dio represents Sittius as Caesar's saviour, acting on his own initiative, even though he did not know Caesar personally.[25]

Scipio drew up his forces in battle array every day, but Caesar did not engage with him, waiting for his second convoy to arrive.[26] The much-needed reinforcements for Caesar arrived at the end of January 46, comprising the Thirteenth and Fourteenth legions and 800 Gallic cavalry, and 1,000 archers and slingers.[27] Deserters from Scipio's camp also reached Caesar, some of them being Gaetulians who claimed association by inheritance from their ancestors with Gaius Marius from the time of his African campaigns. According to Dio, Caesar distributed leaflets among Scipio's troops, promising the native soldiers that they would not be harmed and the Romans that he would give them the same rewards as his own soldiers. Scipio tried to subvert Caesar's troops with no success, because, as Dio points out, he merely asked them to preserve the liberty of the Roman people, and made no mention of rewards.[28]

With his enlarged army, Caesar marched his troops towards the town of Ruspina, which he had garrisoned, and began to fortify the ridge near the town, where a line of hills enclosed the plain, forming a sort of natural amphitheatre on the coast.[29] There were old towers on these hills, and Scipio had posted soldiers on the tower nearest to his camp. Caesar's men started work on the fortification, and Scipio and Labienus drew up their cavalry in battle line, with their infantry in a second line near their camp. Caesar stopped the work on the fortifications and ordered his Spanish troops to dislodge the enemy's Numidians occupying a hill. When they succeeded, Labienus came up with all his cavalry from his right wing to help the Numidians as they retreated. A gap opened up between Labienus' cavalry and the rest of Scipio's forces, and into it Caesar sent out the cavalry of his left wing to cut the enemy off. A farmhouse with four towers screened this manoeuvre from Labienus, who only realised what was happening when his men were attacked from the rear.[30] The result was almost a rout, and Labienus' and Scipio's troops fled back to camp. Now it was Caesar's turn to draw up in battle formation in the plain on the next day, but Scipio did not take the bait, until Caesar's troops slowly approached his fortifications, and then he brought out all his forces. But this was not to offer battle, because Scipio had resolved to march to the defence of the town of Uzitta about a mile away. Scipio had garrisoned it, as his main source of water and supplies, and he stationed his forces outside the town. Both sides remained facing each other all day, but no battle was fought.[31]

Caesar's men were now suffering from the effects of the weather, because they were moving every second or third day, closer to the enemy forces, and building camps each time they stopped. They had no personal baggage, no tents and hardly any food, and then a rain storm broke and spoiled what little they did have.[32] Scipio's army was reinforced by king Juba, who had been summoned from his kingdom by letter. He brought three legions, light-armed infantry, thirty elephants, 800 bridled cavalry, and hosts of Numidian cavalry who did not use bridles, but nevertheless could accomplish feats of horsemanship and riding that other cavalry could only dream of.[33] Caesar decided to bring about a battle. First he needed to take control of the high ground near to Scipio's camp, but Labienus got there before him, and laid an ambush for him in the ravine that he would have to cross as he approached the hill. But it went wrong, because Labienus' cavalry and light-armed infantry did not co-ordinate their movements, and the element of surprise was lost.[34]

If Caesar was to gain anything from a battle at Uzitta he would have to attack Scipio's army and the town as well. He constructed two fortified lines from his own camp, converging on the left and right corners of one side of the town. The lines would protect his soldiers from cavalry attacks and prevent encirclement, and also would enable potential deserters to speak to his troops and gain the safety of his camp.[35] Naturally Scipio's troops skirmished around the works, and then at dusk, as Caesar led his soldiers back to camp after working on the fortifications, Scipio, Juba and Labienus attacked in force, but Caesar turned his legions around to face the enemy and beat them off so decisively that it was said that he could have captured Juba and Labienus if nightfall had not ended the encounter. When the fortified lines were completed, just out of missile range, Caesar made another camp, bringing five legions from the old camp to man the new one.[36]

Scipio's forces were gradually depleted. Several deserters left his camp, most of them going to Caesar.[37] A short time later, Juba had to detach some of his forces to deal with more trouble at home, fomented by Caesar. Two Gaetulians had been sent as spies to Caesar's camp, but they had gone over to him. Caesar had persuaded them to go home and try to start a rebellion in Juba's kingdom, and now they had been successful.[38]

Caesar ordered ships from the fleet at Leptis to guard the approaches to Hadrumetum, and also Thapsus further along the coast, to enable ships to land safely, but transports bringing the Ninth and Tenth legions heading for Ruspina at first mistook Caesar's ships for the enemy, and remained at sea, only coming to land some days later.[39] There was fighting outside Uzitta, which began with Scipio drawing up his battle line and Caesar responding, drawing up about 300 paces away from Scipio's army. They faced each other all day, until Caesar began to lead his troops back to camp. Then the enemy cavalry attacked. Without orders some of Caesar's cavalry and light-armed infantry advanced and were cut off, then the horsemen abandoned the foot soldiers and raced back to Caesar's camp. Scipio broke off the action and returned to camp, pleased with the victory, but further cavalry engagements redressed the balance.

The campaign depended on naval actions as well as land battles. The Pompeian admiral Varus set out from Utica with a large squadron to intercept transports bringing the Seventh and Eighth legions for Caesar. A deserter from Caesar's ships informed Varus that the fleet at Leptis was not guarded, so Varus sailed there, burnt the transports at anchor and captured two quinqueremes. As soon as Caesar was informed, he rode straight for Leptis, put out to sea in a small boat, located one of his detached squadrons watching the coastal towns, leapt on board one of the ships to take command, and chased Varus as he made for Hadrumetum. He re-captured one of the quinqueremes with the enemy crew on board, captured a trireme, and fired the enemy transports at anchor.[40]

Scipio started to forage around the town of Zeta. Caesar decided to take the town, but to reach it he had to march past the enemy camp, in which he accomplished successfully. He occupied Zeta and installed a garrison, then on the return journey he was attacked by Labienus and Afranius, with the Numidian cavalry riding in and out, never fully engaging in battle.[41] They could attack from all sides, encircling the Caesarians, without receiving any damage in return, drawing off very quickly after discharging missiles, then just as quickly regrouping for the next onslaught. The temptation when harassed like this was to make camp, but that would have been suicidal. There were no supplies and, more importantly, no water, so if the Caesarians entrenched themselves they would be condemned to a slow death while the Pompeians watched and waited. Caesar doggedly kept on moving, extremely slowly, beating off attacks as the troops plodded onwards. Discipline held, but it was under tremendously exacting circumstances. The soldiers finally got back to camp at night. The experience decided Caesar to meet like with like; he began to train 300 men from each legion to fight as individuals, like gladiators, instead of in the usual solid battle lines.[42] These new formations successfully drove off Labienus when he attacked Caesar on the way to seize Scipio's stores base at Sarsura.[43]

So far Scipio had adhered to the policy of refusing to engage in pitched battles. Caesar's problem was how to make him change this policy, otherwise the war could drag on forever, and the longer it went on the more worn down his troops would become. He required a battlefield where it would seem that he and his troops were at a grave disadvantage, and where the Numidian cavalry could not operate, but where the legions could engage each other. He found it at Thapsus, garrisoned by Pompeian troops under Gaius Vergilius. In the hinterland of the town there was a narrow strip of land running north to south between the sea and an inland lake. Caesar established his main camp near the town, built another camp to the south between the coast and the lake, and began a siege of Thapsus, while his fleet continued to guard the approaches from the sea. Scipio could not afford to lose Thapsus and his commander, so he followed.[44]

The Pompeians camped at the southern end of the corridor between the lake and the sea, but Caesar's camp hampered their movements. Leaving Juba and Afranius this first camp, Scipio took part of the army and marched around the lake to erect a camp at the northern end, west of the town. Caesar was ready for this. He had given orders to the fleet blockading Thapsus to sail round the promontory to the rear of Scipio's army, and at a pre-arranged signal to make a lot of noise to make the Pompeians imagine that Caesar was about to disembark troops.[45] Scipio drew up in battle formation, with elephants on both wings. As at Pharsalus, Caesar formed up extra troops out of sight, but this time he did so on both wings, to deal with the elephants. Scipio's troops for some reason started to mill about in confusion, and the Caesarians, noticing the turmoil, urged Caesar to give the order to engage. He declined, but then a trumpeter on the right wing, without orders, sounded the charge, and the soldiers could not be held back. Caesar had to accept that he could not stop the soldiers, and signalled 'Good luck'.[46] The slingers and archers concentrated their fire on the elephants, and on Scipio's right the animals panicked and ran through the ranks of the Pompeian troops, causing mayhem as they went. The Numidian horsemen were infected with the panic, and they too left the field. The whole Pompeian army collapsed. Juba and Afranius abandoned their camps, but many of the soldiers were killed by the pursuing Caesarians. The town held out, and Caesar blockaded it, leaving the proconsul Caninius Rebilus in command, while he set off for Utica, where Scipio's surviving soldiers were heading. They disgraced themselves by burning the nearby town of Parada, throwing the civilians into the flames, and arriving at Utica they killed many of the inhabitants. Cato stopped the massacre, but he had to resort to bribery to persuade the men to leave the town.[47]

Pompeian resistance was now confined to Thapsus and Thysdra. Cato did not wish to flee to join the remaining Pompeians, who made for Spain. He made the necessary arrangements for the welfare of his family, and committed suicide, as the preferred option to being forgiven by Caesar.[48] Caesar was angry at being denied the distinction of sparing Cato's life, but he spared Cato's son and all who came over to him voluntarily.[49] The other Pompeians were hunted down. Afranius was captured and executed. He had been allowed to join Pompey after Caesar's victory at Ilerda, but anyone who was captured a second time was usually killed. Scipio was drowned trying to escape by sea. Juba and Petreius failed to find sanctuary, fought each other to the death, and the winner of the combat was killed by a slave.[50] Shortly after the Battle of Thapsus, the town surrendered, as did Thysdra. Caesar occupied Utica, Hadrumetum and Uzitta, and took over the kingdom of Juba, some of which he handed over to Bocchus of Mauretania, and the rest was incorporated into the new province of Africa Nova, with the proconsul Gaius Sallustius Crispus (Sallust) as the first governor. Dio has no good words to say about Sallust, whom he accuses of disgracing himself by harrying and plundering the natives.[51]

The Roman officers who had served with Juba had their property confiscated, and fines were imposed on communities which had supported the Pompeians. Thirteen million sesterces were raised from Hadrumetum and Thapsus alone. At Utica, the lives of the men who had contributed funds to Scipio were spared, on condition that 200,000,000 sesterces was paid to the Roman people, in six instalments over three years.[52] Caesar settled some of his veterans in colonies in towns along the coast, where they formed a guard against the Pompeian fleet. The settlements in Africa avoided having to find lands for the veterans in Italy, but Dio represents Caesar's action as getting rid of the older men in case they mutinied again.[53]

Caesar arrived in Rome in late July 46. Cicero hoped that he would restore the Republic after his two year absence, and was eager to give advice. But Caesar was not ready to relinquish his powers. In April 46 he had been made Dictator for the third time, but without the limitation of the normal six months or even one year. This time he was to hold the office for ten years. His *magister equitum* was Aemilius Lepidus, and the two men were also consuls for the year, Caesar's third term. Unprecedented honours were voted to him. Dio says that he includes in his narrative only those honours that Caesar accepted, not the ones that he refused.[54] At least at this stage Caesar was careful enough to reject some honours without causing offence. He was permitted to sit between the consuls, and speak first in debates. Since he was Dictator and consul this privilege might seem a little superfluous, but it would be an important asset in the future if he ever renounced his offices. For his victories in Africa, forty days' thanksgiving had been decreed by the Senate, more than anyone had been voted before. A statue of him was placed in the Capitoline temple facing the statue of Jupiter. At the foot of his statue there was an inscription apparently proclaiming his divinity, but nothing is known of the text of the inscription, except that it caused offence, so Caesar had the words removed.[55] There is scholarly debate about whether Caesar was aiming at the sort of divine monarchy that had firm roots in the East. If so, he had to content himself for the present time with the consulship, the ten-year Dictatorship and the office of *praefectus morum* (prefect of morals) for three years. It is not certain if this entirely new post was simply awarded to Caesar or if it was the result of a popular vote.[56] Caesar accepted the post 'as if the title of censor was not worthy of him,' says Dio, indicating that the office gave Caesar censorial powers.[57] Though he did not hold the actual censorship Caesar was enabled to promote some men to the Senate and demote others. He increased the membership of the Senate to a grand total of 900, but his methods did not meet with universal approval because he promoted soldiers, sons of freedmen, and, according to Dio, he even rescued from the courts men who were currently being prosecuted for bribery, and made them senators.[58] Some feathers were ruffled among the old senatorial class, where snobbery had always ruled, but a united protest was not recorded.

Apart from his new office of *praefectus morum*, Caesar's powers were given a veneer of political respectability by the use of familiar titles, but they were nonetheless extraordinary powers, greater than anything that had been known before. Even Pompey had not achieved such powers or as many honours as Caesar. Pompey kept within the rules where it was possible, and bent them a little if it was not possible. Only in the final years of his career was Pompey seen as a potential tyrant, even though he had avoided the office of Dictator. Caesar now had supreme power for ten years, and it made people afraid of him. He recognised that some of the honours voted to him fell under the heading of flattery, because people dreaded a return to the turbulent times that had preceded the civil wars and tried to pre-empt such a situation by keeping him contented.[59] Caesar's studied policy of *clementia* (mercy) did not influence everyone, because it meant that with such unprecedented political powers, coupled with his command of the armies, everyone was literally at his mercy.

At the end of September 46, high summer in reality, Caesar held four triumphs: for his Gallic conquests, for the campaign in Egypt, the war against Pharnaces, and the war in Africa, which was represented as a victory over Juba. Victory over other Romans was never mentioned.[60] After six years in prison Vercingetorix was paraded through the streets and then executed, and in the Egyptian triumph, Arsinoe also marched as a prisoner, but she was released, only to be killed some years later by Cleopatra and Mark Antony.[61] Caesar put on shows to please the people, including funeral games and a public feast in honour of his daughter Julia, as he had promised when she died in 54 BC.

Caesar attended to the food supply, giving the people grain and olive oil above the usual amounts. He also revised the lists of people eligible for the corn dole, reducing the numbers of recipients from 320,000 to 150,000.[62] Dio does not give the figures, but says that the numbers of claimants had increased unlawfully, so Caesar removed half of them.[63] This is sometimes confused with the census of Roman citizens, which Caesar also undertook as a separate project.

As part of his settlement program for his veterans, Caesar appointed legates to purchase lands, attending personally only to those cases where purchase was not straightforward. The vast amounts of booty brought home from the wars enabled him to pay 400 sesterces to each of those eligible for the corn dole.[64] When the jealous soldiery, already in receipt of 20,000 sesterces, complained about the amounts squandered on the populace, Caesar dealt harshly with them. He executed one man and had two more sacrificed to Mars, displaying their heads at the doors of the Regia, his official residence as Pontifex Maximus. This was more than a little barbaric, perhaps, but he had to rein in the soldiers and, more importantly, he had to be seen to be doing so. All the same, where was his *clementia* now?[65]

Caesar stayed in Rome from late July to November 46, and in that short time he produced a staggering amount of legislation. He enacted various measures designed to control the mob, and sumptuary laws to curb extravagance. Cicero said that he would make the sumptuary law's allowance for one day last him for ten days.[66] Caesar introduced rewards for families with several children, after the census that he undertook showed a reduction of citizens, not surprising in view of the large numbers of casualties of the civil wars.[67]

Without unduly upsetting creditors, he passed laws to alleviate the problems of debtors, short of cancelling debts altogether. The jury courts were to be composed half of senators and half of equestrians, removing the *tribuni aerarii* installed during the consulship of Pompey and Crassus in 70 BC. Provincial government was reformed and regulated. Propraetors were to govern for one year and proconsuls for two years.[68] From now on, theoretically, no one should be able to extend provincial commands as Caesar and Pompey had done.

In carrying out his legislation Caesar avoided senatorial debate. Individuals who would have opposed him, especially Cato, were dead, and there was probably no one who dared to speak as eloquently and as long as Cato did to employ the usual delaying tactics. Caesar communicated everything to the leaders of the Senate, and sometimes to the entire assembled body, says Dio, veering towards admiration.[69] But Dio lived and worked in the Imperial age, when the Emperor was in control of political appointments, the finances, the armies, and the law, and the Senate's power and influence was much diminished. In the late Republic, simply communicating various measures to the senators was not the way it was supposed to work. Significantly, when Dio mentions that Caesar used the tribunes to recall exiles, and when he elevated to the Senate men who were not considered worthy, there were hostile murmurings against Caesar.[70] There ought to have been intelligent debate and a vote on each of the measures that he proposed. In October 46 Cicero wrote to Lucius Papirius Paetus, complaining that 'decrees of the Senate are being drafted at the house of my dear friend who dotes on you'.[71] This may refer to Caesar himself, though some authors have interpreted 'my dear friend who dotes on you', that is on Paetus, most probably refers to Cornelius Balbus. But the distinction hardly matters. To all intents and purposes, the decrees that Balbus drafted would have been Caesar's ideas, and Cicero was correct in inferring that the government of Rome was carried out in Caesar's house. Cicero also explained to Paetus that on occasion Caesar put Cicero's name down as a signatory to the decrees, even though he was not present. As a result of some of these decrees, Cicero received letters from kings of whom he had never heard, thanking him for his part in approving their new-found kingly status.

The reform of the calendar for which Caesar is justly famous was long overdue. It was probably based on the calculations of Egyptian astronomers, and implemented by Sosigenes, one of

Cleopatra's influential courtiers. The Roman lunar calendar had always required regular adjustments, with the intercalation of extra days, and this had already been done in February 46, but the seasons were still out of synchronisation with the calendar. Caesar added two months between November and December.[72] The solar calendar was instituted on 1 January 45, with 365 days to the year and one extra day to be inserted every four years.

One of Caesar's actions caused resentment in Rome. Cleopatra came to stay at his villa across the Tiber, with her young brother Ptolemy, also officially her husband. The Queen was formally recognised as friend and ally of the Roman people.[73] This status had been conferred on her father Ptolemy Auletes. Cleopatra's visit to Rome was a political expedient. Her main concern was the future of Egypt, and long term recognition as friend and ally of the Roman people would support her regime and give her some stability. As Queen, she can hardly be blamed for associating herself and her country with the strongest political and military power in the Mediterranean world. She was trying to ensure the survival of Egypt as a free country beyond her own lifetime, when Caesarion, who blended Egypt and Rome in one person, would succeed her. For the time being, the problem for the Romans was Caesar's relationship with Cleopatra. Rumours circulated that he intended to make Cleopatra his Queen, and that all Romans were to be made subject to her, or that she was going to be made a living goddess as Caesar was to be made a god. At this stage, Caesarion did not feature in the rumours, though Caesar acknowledged the boy as his own son, and after his death Antony presented Caesarion's claims to the Senate. From there it was an easy step for Octavian-Augustus to persuade the people that Cleopatra and Caesarion intended to rule Rome as well as Egypt.

While pushing through his laws and entertaining the people between July and November 46, Caesar was aware that the civil war had still not ended. The surviving Pompeians were congregating in Spain. Gnaeus Pompeius, Pompey's elder son, had arrived first, after recovering from illness when he was subduing the Balearic Islands.[74] He was followed by his brother Sextus, and Labienus, who brought the fleet and the remaining troops from Africa.[75] Dio says that Caesar intended to conduct Spanish operations through his deputies.[76] These were Caesar's nephew Quintus Pedius, and

Quintus Fabius Maximus. But the Pompeians had increased in strength and numbers, by recruiting among the local population. Pedius and Fabius required reinforcements, and most of all they needed Caesar himself.

The war in Spain is documented by an anonymous work, which is not of the same calibre as *The Alexandrian War* or *The African War*. The translator of the Loeb edition of *The Spanish War* describes it as perhaps the most illiterate and exasperating book in classical literature, and the historian Macaulay considered that the author was a retired centurion who was better at fighting than writing. Skirmishes and battles are described, but not necessarily in the correct order and with no distinction given to the most important ones. There is no attention to supplies and logistics, or topographical details and the construction of fortifications, which characterise the works by Caesar and Hirtius. Nevertheless, it is the only source which gives any detail of the campaigns, and some notice must be taken of it. This war was the most brutal and bloody of the civil wars.

In November 46 Caesar left Rome, but with the intercalation of two extra months between November and December, his return to the city in August 45, according to the new calendar, makes the campaign seem shorter than it was in reality. Caesar took with him the Tenth legion, and the Fifth, raised in Transalpine Gaul, and nicknamed *Alaudae*, 'Larks'. He had also planned to take his great-nephew Gaius Octavius with him to give him experience of war, but the boy was ill, so he had to be left behind. In Spain, the whole region around the town of Ulia had declared for Gnaeus Pompeius, except the town itself, so Gnaeus was besieging it.[77] North of this town lay Corduba, which Sextus Pompeius held with two legions. Before Caesar arrived, Pedius and Fabius had made camp east of Corduba, but were unable to offer open battle. Caesar laid siege to Corduba, threatening Sextus, and hoping to draw Gnaeus away from Ulia.[78] The plan worked, but Caesar realised that Corduba could not be taken quickly or easily, and it was clear that Gnaeus was too wise to offer battle. It was not feasible to remain near Corduba because of the lack of supplies, so Caesar broke off operations and made for the fortified town of Ategua, 20 miles south-east of Corduba. It housed stores of grain, protected by a Pompeian garrison. Caesar laid siege to it, cutting off the town by a palisade and ditch.[79] As well as siege works, Caesar established several outposts, occupied by cavalry and infantry to guard against the approach of Gnaeus Pompey, but when Gnaeus arrived there was a thick fog, so he managed to penetrate through the outposts and cut up cavalry and infantry units so badly that only a few escaped.[80]

On two occasions the garrison of Ategua tried and failed to break through Caesar's lines. Before they made a sally they spent most of the night hurling missiles and firebrands form the walls of the town and succeeded in wounding many of Caesar's soldiers, then in the morning they attacked the Sixth legion who were engaged in constructing fortifications lower down the slope from the town, which initially gave the Pompeian garrison troops the advantage on higher ground. They were beaten off by the gallantry (*virtute*) of Caesar's legionaries. The next time the garrison attempted a sortie they were better prepared. The plan was to set on fire the timber towers and fortifications of Caesar's line, which they were to accomplish during the night, then they were to emerge from the town gates equipped with hurdles to fill in the ditches, and hooks to pull down the soldiers' huts thatched with straw, which by this time should have been burning. They were also to bring silver and clothing with them to tempt the Caesarians to break off the fighting and turn their attention to looting. When their plan was put into operation, they were driven off. After this second victory over the Pompeians, a report was brought to Caesar that the garrison had massacred the civilians in the town.[81] The Pompeians offered terms which Caesar rejected. Gnaeus Pompey drew off, leaving the Pompeians to their fate. After some fighting around the fortifications, the town was surrendered on 19 February.[82]

The two opposing armies chased each other from place to place, and the narrative of the Spanish War becomes a catalogue of desertions and executions of captives on both sides. An interesting aside concerns deserters from Caesar's ranks, who were not killed but taken into the Pompeian army as light-armed troops on low pay.[83] There was a clash around Caesar's fortifications near the River Salsum, where Caesar had men on both sides of the river. Once again the Pompeians attacked from the higher ground. Caesar's troops began to waver, but two centurions from the Fifth legion saved the day by dashing across the river to firm up the line. One was killed, and the other tried to escape encirclement by retreating downhill, but slipped and fell, and was killed. While the Pompeians were ripping off his decorations Caesar's cavalry crossed the river and drove the enemy off.[84] The following day there was another skirmish near Soricaria, with the Pompeians holding the higher ground and consequently with the advantage, compelling Caesar to approach them on unfavourable ground. The Pompeians were driven off the hill, and though the text of the Spanish War is not specific, they probably drew off to a different hill, which saved them from complete disaster.[85]

Eventually the two armies arrived at Munda. The site has not been definitively identified, but was probably west of Urso, which Caesar later chose as a site for one of his many veteran colonies. Here Gnaeus offered battle. Caesar had not expected this, so it was a repeat of the Battle of Pharsalus, where he was in the middle of giving orders for breaking camp when he noticed the enemy forming up in battle array. Caesar signalled for action by using flags.[86] The details of this battle are not clear, except that it was hard fought. Gnaeus Pompeius had chosen his site well, and had every chance of winning the battle. The author of *The Spanish War* reports that it was a calm sunny day, perfect for cavalry operations.[87] However, there was a stream and a surrounding marshy area between the two armies, and the Caesarians were delayed when they crossed it, and all the while, Pompey's troops kept their positions on the high ground without advancing. Then battle was commenced. Caesar's Tenth legion on the right wing drove back the enemy left, so that soldiers from Pompey's right had to be transferred to strengthen it.[88]

At one point Caesar had to dash to the front to rally his troops, then the Tenth legion pushed the Pompeians back on their left wing. Gnaeus ordered Labienus to move from the right wing to assist the left, but before he got into position Caesar ordered up his ally king Bogud of Mauretania with his horsemen, and they drove Labienus away. Dio says that Bogud was moving towards the Pompeian camp, Labienus saw what was happening and followed him, but the Pompeians could not see the reason for his movement and thought that he was leaving the field. The Pompeian soldiers started to run away. The battle was won, at a cost. Caesar said afterwards that he had often struggled to achieve victory, but this was the first time that he had fought for his life.[89] Titus Labienus was killed and buried where he fell.[90] Gnaeus Pompeius escaped, but was captured and, like his father, he was decapitated. His end is graphically described in *The Spanish War*.[91] Sextus Pompeius fled from Corduba, leaving his two legions to their own devices.[92] Caesar built fortifications all round Munda, placing Fabius Maximus in command, with instructions to keep on attacking it until it fell.[93] He marched to Corduba and took the town amid tremendous slaughter.[94] Then he went on Hispalis near the River Baetis, and established a garrison in the town under Caninius. A Lusitanian called Philo left the town and met up with Caecilius Niger and his force of Lusitanian tribesmen. He brought this force back to Hispalis, managed to cross the fortifications to gain access to the town and massacred the Caesarian troops, closed the gates and decided to continue the war.[95] Caesar did not besiege the town with vigour because he was afraid that the Lusitanians might destroy it before they would surrender, so he waited until they made a sortie, and his cavalry fought them off. Hispalis was captured intact. He marched to Asta which surrendered without a fight.[96]

Caesar marched from town to town, crushing resistance very harshly. On the other hand there were rewards for those communities which had been loyal to him. Taxes were reduced and lands increased at the expense of communities which had declared for the Pompeians.[97] Dio points out that he did not grant these favours for nothing.[98] Some towns received Latin rights, and Caesar founded several colonies of Roman citizens with the obligation of defending their own territories and performing military service. During the last phase of the Munda campaign, while he settled communities and made his administrative arrangements, Caesar was accompanied by his great-nephew Gaius Octavius, who had made his own way to Spain, with a few companions, among whom was his lifelong friend Marcus Vipsanius Agrippa. He arrived too late for the Battle of Munda, but once he was in Spain he acquitted himself well, taking part in the foundation of colonies, the settlement of veterans and the loyal Spanish troops, receiving embassies from Spanish towns, and speaking on behalf of the men of Saguntum, who were concerned to clear themselves of certain charges laid against them. He travelled back to Rome in Caesar's own litter. On the journey from Transalpine Gaul, Mark Antony turned up to greet them. After his brutality in quelling the debt riots in Rome, he was back in favour, and destined for higher things.

14

Finale, 45–44 BC

Returning to Rome, Caesar as Dictator did not feel the need to seek ratification for his measures in Spain. He had established colonies named after himself whose inhabitants would direct their allegiance to him rather than to the Senate and People of Rome. Preserving the proper forms despite his supreme powers, Caesar as commander of troops remained outside the city until he held his triumph. He went to his estates at Labici, not far from the city, and revised his last will and testament, adding to it a codicil adopting his great-nephew Gaius Octavius as his heir.[1] Triumphs were also awarded to the two generals of the Spanish campaign, Quintus Pedius and Quintus Fabius Maximus. The pretence that the triumphs were over Spain did not disguise the fact that the only conquest was that of the Pompeians. During Caesar's triumph the tribune Pontius Aquila made a personal protest. When Caesar's triumphal chariot passed his seat, Aquila pointedly refused to rise in greeting. Caesar apparently said, 'Make me give up the state, Aquila. After all you are tribune.' He was probably tired, tense, and on a short fuse, but in earlier days he would probably have prudently kept silent. His behaviour brought him little credit, especially as he would not let the matter drop, adding to the end of every decree, the rider 'Provided that Pontius Aquila allows it.'

Honours flowed in his direction, voted by the Senate. Caesar was presented with a dilemma every time honours were voted to him, because to refuse them all might seem churlish, so he accepted most of them and rejected some of the others, but the very fact of his ready acceptance began to upset and irritate people, especially as the honours kept coming all through 45 and into 44 BC. An unprecedented fifty days of thanksgiving were voted after the victory at Munda, and anniversaries of his other victories were to be marked by festivals and games. He was granted the use of the title Imperator, commander, as a hereditary name to be passed down to his sons, if he had any, or adopted any, and even to his grandsons. Dio carefully explains the normal use of this title, when commanders were saluted by their troops for their victories, but in Imperial times all Emperors received the name Imperator initially, and then if they were saluted by the soldiers they distinguished it by the number two, or three or however many times they had received the honour.[2] Caesar was entitled to wear triumphal dress on all public occasions, as well as a laurel wreath, which happily disguised his baldness.[3] He was given the title Liberator, and a temple was to be built to Libertas, Freedom, in his honour.[4] In the games in the Circus an ivory statue of Caesar was to be carried along with those of the gods. Another statue of him was to be set up in the Temple of Quirinus, with an inscription 'to the unconquerable god'. These measures were passed in honour of his victory in Spain. There were more honours and more powers to follow, not necessarily voted all at the same time, but it is convenient to list them all together, following the example of Dio.[5] Caesar was allowed to sit with the tribunes at the games. He was given the right of making offerings to Jupiter, called *spolia opima*, normally granted to generals who had personally killed an enemy leader. This was an important distinction, important enough for Augustus to deny it to one of his generals who claimed the right, and forever afterwards to reserve it for himself and members of the Imperial family, even if the victories to be celebrated were won by other commanders who had been appointed by him. Caesar was given the title *Pater Patriae*, father of his country, and the title was to be included on his coinage. It became an Imperial distinction for the Emperors. The Roman year used to begin in March, and the fifth month, Quinctilis, was to be renamed July, just as, sometime later, the name of August derived from Augustus. Statues of Caesar were to be placed in all the cities of the Empire and in all the temples in Rome, and two statues were to be placed on the Rostra, one representing Caesar as saviour of the citizens, and the other as saviour of the city of Rome from siege, each with the appropriate honorary crowns. He was voted a golden crown beset with precious stones, and a golden chair that was to be carried into theatres like those of the gods.[6] The chair was presumably preserved, since Octavian intended to display it at the games but he was blocked by the consul Mark Antony.[7] A temple to Caesar and his clemency (*Clementia*) was to be built, and Mark Antony was nominated as priest of the cult of divine Caesar (*flamen dialis*).[8] There is some debate about Caesar's divinity whilst still alive, but Antony was not inaugurated as priest, or *flamen divi Julii*, until 40 BC, after a treaty was arranged between him and Octavian at Brundisium, by which time Caesar had been posthumously deified, or as Suetonius expresses it, he was numbered among the gods by decree and by the conviction of the people (*persuasione vulgi*).[9]

The foregoing list is not complete, but the honours that are included among those that Caesar accepted were greater than any hitherto accorded to one man. As well as significant honours, real powers were voted to him, gradually putting most of the state into Caesar's hands. According to Dio it was decreed that only Caesar should command soldiers, and he alone should administer public funds, so no one else should be allowed to use the armies or finances unless he permitted it.[10] He was granted the censorship for life, with no colleague, and given the immunities of the tribunes, so that anyone who harmed him should fall under the relevant penalties; tribunician powers and the sacrosanctity contained within them, divorced from the actual office, became the one of most significant features of Augustus' reign, and of succeeding Emperors. Almost as a throwaway comment, Dio says that all Caesar's future acts were to be ratified in advance.[11] If this was not supreme power it was a very close second.

In 45 BC Caesar was made sole consul, after the precedent set by Pompey in 52 BC. He took up his office immediately, but after a short interval he stood down, and bestowed consulships on Gaius Trebonius and Quintus Fabius Maximus. On the day before his consulship was to end, Fabius Maximus died, and Caesar committed a solecism against custom and etiquette by appointing Caninius Rebilus to the consulship for less than twenty-four hours.[12] It was interpreted by some Romans that he was contemptuous of the consular office, but for others his action provided an opportunity for mocking humour. On the way to congratulate

Rebilus, Cicero commented that he and his followers would have to hurry, otherwise the consulship would have expired before they arrived, and afterwards he said that Rebilus was the only consul who never slept while holding the office.

When Caesar relinquished the consulship and appointed successors, this was the first time such a procedure had been observed, but it paved the way for the Imperial system, where there were often more than two consuls in a year, the first two being the eponymous consuls who gave their names to the year, and the subsequent office holders were *suffecti* or suffect consuls.[13] This allowed more men to reach the consulship and gain experience, thus providing more personnel to govern the provinces or carry out tasks requiring consular rank. Caesar was given the right to nominate half of the magistrates, but in reality he chose all of them, and he appointed provincial governors without resorting to the lottery.[14] A political system devised for a city state had been stretched and adapted to the government of what was in effect an Empire, and it required more officials to cope with the administrative details. In 45 BC Caesar increased the numbers of quaestors to forty, and the praetors to fourteen, later raised to sixteen in 44 BC. A fortunate by-product of the increased numbers of officials was that the rewards that Caesar had promised to so many men could be fulfilled in this way by setting certain individuals on the political career path.

In addition to honours and powers, Caesar was entrusted with various ambitious tasks. He had formulated grandiose building plans for the city, and in 46 BC he had dedicated the unfinished Forum Julium and the temple inside it, originally promised to Venus Victrix before the Battle of Pharsalus, but Caesar now dedicated it to Venus Genetrix, whom he claimed as his ancestress.[15] The rectangular Forum Julium had not been completed at the end opposite the temple, because the plans involved relocating the Senate House, which had been burned down as part of Clodius' impromptu funeral in 52 BC, and was still in ruins. The Senate had been dilatory in giving permission for rebuilding it a short distance away from its original site. When the responsibility for rebuilding was finally voted to Caesar, together with a new title for the building as the Curia Julia, it was too late for him to complete it, so the task fell to Augustus. Likewise Augustus completed the Basilica Julia which Caesar had dedicated in 46 BC, though that too was still not finished. The Basilica lies on the south side of the Forum Romanum, but Caesar's original building burnt down in 9 BC. Caesar planned to build a new temple to Mars, and a theatre in the Campus Martius to rival that of Pompey, but Augustus also completed this project, dedicating the theatre to his nephew Marcellus, the son of his sister Octavia.[16] The visible remains of buildings associated with Caesar represent reconstructions at various periods, including the rearrangements made in modern times, for instance the three columns now visible of the Temple of Venus Genetrix were resurrected after excavation. Other projects given to Caesar included the diversion of the Tiber and the deepening of its channel, and the draining of the Pontine marshes in Italy, so that the area could be settled and farmed. It was planned to cut a canal through the Peloponnesian isthmus.[17] This illustrates the scale of Caesar's vision and ambition, since the ideas were no doubt originally his own, not the Senate's. His projects were not limited to Rome and Italy. He had founded veteran and Roman citizen colonies in Gaul, Spain and Africa, and continued the policy of colonisation after the civil wars were over. He revived Corinth and Carthage, both of them destroyed by the Romans in 146 BC. Corinth became one of his colonies in 44 BC. Gaius Gracchus had attempted to re-establish Carthage, but he was not successful. Caesar planned to create a new colony on the site, but once again the task was completed by Augustus. Though Caesar had rebuilt or founded several cities, he was most proud of having begun the restoration of these two.[18] Both cities flourished after their restoration.

In the last years of his life Caesar combined charisma and arrogance with his absolute power. To meet him personally was to be both overawed and charmed, as Cicero describes when in December 45 Caesar visited the villa of a neighbour of his, Marcius Philippus, who had married Caesar's niece Atia, the widowed daughter of his sister Julia. Philippus had thus become the stepfather of the young Gaius Octavius, who was to be Caesar's heir, though probably no one knew that yet. There were about 2,000 people and soldiers accompanying Caesar, according to Cicero. Being a little unnerved at the presence of so many soldiers, Cicero was provided with a bodyguard, as he explained to Atticus, adding that Caesar was not the sort of guest to whom one says 'Do call in on your way back'. Once was enough for Cicero.[19] Even so, the charisma and charm comes through in Cicero's account. Sometimes at a distance of 2,000 years and centuries of glorification it is difficult to remember that Caesar was a living, feeling human being, as full of contradictions as anyone else.

Rumours that Caesar intended to be king had been circulating widely and wildly, and all sorts of omens were seen or engineered to that end. It may have been enemies who placed laurel wreaths adorned with white fillets or bands (*fascia*), symbolizing monarchy, on his statues on the Rostra, or it may have been his adherents who genuinely wished to honour him.[20] The tribunes Gaius Epidius Marullus and Lucius Caesetius Flavus removed the offending objects.[21] The same pair arrested a man in the crowd who addressed Caesar as *Rex*, or king. Caesar replied that his name was Caesar, not Rex, referring to the ancient families who held that name. Caesar was angry with the tribunes, who had acted on their own authority and made judgements about whether Caesar should be king, and it may have been independent thinking that Caesar objected to rather than the denial of kingship, which he would have preferred to deny himself. The tribunes responded to his anger with the statement that they were being prevented from exercising free speech and the rights of their office, so that they could not protect the people.[22] Caesar declared his dissatisfaction with the two tribunes to the Senate and allowed the senators to depose them. He had come a long way in a short time since he had made a *casus belli* out of the violation of the sacrosanctity of tribunes.

It was unfortunate that Caesar displayed contempt for the senators when they approached him to outline the latest honours voted to him. He was sitting down when the delegation came up to him, either in his new Temple of Venus, or on the Rostra, but he did not rise to greet the senators, a shocking mark of disrespect.[23] Afterwards he claimed that he had a problem with his bowels and could not risk standing up, but this seemed a feeble excuse. Since he suffered from epilepsy, he may have sensed a seizure coming on, but if so he may have considered his affliction a sign of weakness that he did not want to acknowledge. The incident may seem of little importance, but it caused considerable offence. Suetonius singles out this episode as the one that roused hatred against him, and contrasts it with Caesar's own anger when Pontius Aquila did not rise to greet him as his triumphal chariot passed him. Caesar was already far above everyone else, but he did not need to rub it in.

It was known by early February 44 that Caesar had accepted the Dictatorship for life.[24] The situation escalated at a festival celebrated on 15 February – the Lupercalia – a fertility rite of extreme antiquity. The consul Mark Antony took part in the ceremony, which entailed running round the streets of Rome with other young men, wearing only a loincloth. One of the main objects was to strike people – especially young women – with goat-skin thongs, which was supposed to make the women fertile and bear sons for Rome. Antony had another role to play for Caesar. He carried a diadem with him, which he offered to Caesar when he approached his chair, offering him in effect the title and rank of king. Caesar refused it. The audience roared approval that he had rejected it. Antony offered it again, with the same result.[25] Caesar pronounced that the diadem should be placed in the Temple of Jupiter, the only king in Rome. Antony ordered an official record to be made that Caesar had been offered the kingship and had refused it. Motives in this little scenario are obscure. Goldsworthy finds it hard to believe that the episode was not staged, and Gelzer finds it hard to believe that it was an idea of Antony's, carried out without the prior knowledge of Caesar, either to make him accept the kingship, or to give him an opportunity to reject it in front of the whole of Rome.[26] Alternatively Caesar may have put Antony up to it in order to test the waters of popular opinion, seeking the approval of the crowd, and if they gave it, then he could assume the kingship with impunity.[27] It may have been an attempt to kill off rumour altogether by a public demonstration that he definitely did not wish to be king. Meier makes the point that if Caesar had staged this event because he wanted to be made king with the support of the people, he could easily have orchestrated applause on a sufficient scale to make it seem that the people approved, therefore the fact that this did not happen suggests that Caesar genuinely did not want a crown or a kingship.[28] Whatever Caesar intended, the speculation did not cease, and all he had achieved was to compound the situation.

Caesar was preparing to go to war again, this time against the Dacians and then the Parthians.[29] The defeat of Crassus had still not been avenged, though it seems to have been forgotten that there had been no definite cause for the Roman attack on Parthia. Even before the civil wars the problem of a strong and potentially hostile Parthian regime had emerged, and troops had been assembled to deal with the problem. This is the occasion when Pompey had asked Caesar to contribute a legion from Gaul, and contributed one himself, but nominated the legion he had lent to Caesar. Then after the defeat of Pompey at Pharsalus, the Parthian problem surfaced again. When Caesar had settled accounts with Pharnaces in the East, he had installed a relative of his, Sextus Caesar, as governor of Syria, but the Pompeian Quintus Caecilius Bassus had emerged from hiding and taken over the province, intriguing to have Sextus Caesar murdered. At the time, Caesar could spare only two legions as reinforcements for the eastern troops, and he had appointed Quintus Cornificius and then Gaius Antistius Vetus to deal with Bassus. It remained a purely Roman matter until Pacorus, the son of the King of Parthia, entered the scene and tipped the balance, expressing too strong an interest in the Roman provinces of the East. A war with Parthia was being discussed while Caesar was still in Spain in 45 BC, but to Cicero's relief Caesar had resolved to settle affairs in Rome before he embarked upon the project.[30]

As soon as Caesar was free to turn his attention to it, he intended to conduct the Parthian war himself. His plans were more ambitious than simply attacking Parthia. He intended to wage war against the up and coming king Burebista in Dacia (roughly modern Romania) and then go on to the eastern provinces. According to Plutarch he was even planning to return to Rome via Germany, and Appian offers several possible reasons for all this strenuous activity: Caesar was hoping to cure his epilepsy which afflicted him during periods of inactivity, or he wanted to escape potential plots, or he may have decided to give up Rome to his enemies.[31] Caesar has been accused of deliberately abandoning Rome to its fate by finding another war to wage.[32] He could not find the ultimate solution for the tangled mess that Roman politics had sunk into. After Caesar's death, his friend Gaius Matius Calvena, a friend of both Caesar and Cicero, discussed the problems of state with Cicero, expressing the view that 'if Caesar with his genius could not find a solution, who will find it now?'[33] It seems that even with all his advantages as an autocrat with overwhelming powers, considerable charm and influence, and moreover lots of cash, Caesar could not create out of Rome the Empire that he desired.

As a preliminary to the war in Dacia, towards the end of 45 he had sent his great-nephew Gaius Octavius to gain military experience among the legions already stationed in Macedonia. It was rumoured that he intended to make Octavius his master of horse, *magister equitum*, in place of Marcus Aemilius Lepidus.[34] But there are doubts on the part of certain scholars that Caesar would have entrusted an adolescent, kinsman or not, with such a responsibility. It depends upon the extent to which Caesar intended to groom Octavius as his successor, a factor which cannot be known even with hindsight. The focus of attention would not be wholly upon Octavius at the time, since inflammatory stories had begun to circulate that the college of fifteen priests, the *Quindecemviri*, had discovered a prophecy in the Sibylline books to the effect that Parthia could be conquered only by a king.[35] Very soon it was said that the *Quindecemviri* were going to propose that Caesar should be made king, and that Lucius Cotta was to put this proposal before the Senate.[36] Cicero referred to it obliquely in a reply to a letter from Atticus, mentioning Cotta, but not mentioning the circumstances.[37]

The title of king was antithetical to the ideals of the Republic, but whatever he chose to call himself, Caesar was *de facto* king already. He held supreme power and he had no intention of giving it up. It was inevitable that one man with so much power would engender suspicion about his motives and his future plans. Not all the distinguished honours voted to him were well-intentioned. Some of them were probably proposed out of a desire to flatter and then perhaps be noticed and obtain appointments or money, but others seemed to be deliberately designed to foster ridicule or to discover the lengths to which Caesar would go in accepting them. Plutarch bluntly suggests that it was Caesar's enemies who proposed honours for him, to provide good grounds for attacking him, and Dio says that the design was to make him envied and disliked, so that he would probably perish sooner rather than later.[38] Caesar was elevated far above his peers, and whilst no one could accuse him of modesty or low self-esteem, it was perhaps only now that he began to take himself so seriously that he lost touch with reality. Perhaps he thought that honours and powers were no more than he deserved, or perhaps he trusted the senators who thus favoured him, and imagined that they would never harm him.[39]

It could be said that the fault lay not with Caesar but the political system that had evolved from the late sixth century BC to ensure that no one could ever be called king or accrue so much power ever again. In combatting the potential tyranny of one man, the Romans had instituted collegiality of political offices, and temporal restraints on post holders to prevent anyone from achieving too much power or retaining it. As a result, long term planning had become impossible, because legislation and social measures proposed at any time could be blocked, and anything that was put into effect in one year could be nullified in the next. A legally appointed Dictator could sort out the problems, as Sulla had done to his own satisfaction, but any success could be eroded if the Dictator stepped down, or died, leaving all his legislation vulnerable to attack from other politicians. Long-term supreme powers were necessary if anything positive was to be achieved, and even then there would be argument about what was positive for whom. Working under a long-established Imperial regime, Dio interpolates into his discussion of Caesar's achievements a little digression on the benefits of monarchy, the best form of government to live under, he asserts. If Brutus and Cassius had thought of this, he says, they would not have assassinated Caesar, and when they did so, they brought disorder onto the city at a time when it had a stable government.[40] He could well have added that from Caesar's point of view autocracy saved so much time. To his opponents that in itself was just about bearable, because there was still just a small chance that his autocracy might be temporary. Sulla had achieved what he set out to do and then retired. Caesar had said that Sulla 'did not know his letters', meaning that he was foolish to lay down his powers, but this need not be too depressing, since there was always hope that Caesar would rest contented when the state was running along the lines he laid down for it. He had been appointed Dictator for ten years in 46 BC, a disturbing concept but not irreversible, since in 36 BC it might all come to an end, and then normal life could be resumed bit by bit. Caesar's third, fourth and fifth consulships from 46 to 44 BC could be viewed in the same light, as a necessary evil, held conjointly with the Dictatorship. His censorial powers embodied in his office as *praefectus morum* could be tolerated, as could his appointment as sole censor, if they were to disappear along with the Dictatorship.

But then, in February 44 came the Dictatorship for life, *Dictator perpetuo*. There was no possibility that he would ever lay down his powers after he accepted this honour, no possibility that Rome would ever be restored to the governance of the Senate and the leading men, no paths to promotion except through Caesar and his agents, no offices that were not for the most part filled by Caesar's adherents, or those who pretended to be his adherents in order to rise. There was no debate, no discussion, not even any real share in government, no place for individuality or initiative, and certainly nothing to be gained from holding opinions that differed from Caesar's. And so Caesar was converted from Dictator and consul to tyrant.

There had already been murmurs of dissatisfaction while Caesar was in Spain. Mark Antony and Gaius Trebonius were travelling companions on the way to meet Caesar on his return from Spain after the Battle of Munda, and the possibility of removing Caesar had been delicately broached by Trebonius. While he was out of favour, Antony would seem the likely candidate for conversion to the cause, as a bitter casualty of Caesar's displeasure, but he was far from that. According to Plutarch, when the conspirators were forming their plans to assassinate Caesar, Trebonius told them that though Antony had disapproved of the scheme, he had not revealed anything to Caesar.[41] But it is equally possible that Antony did tell Caesar what he had heard, and then they both decided to pretend that he had said nothing. Dio says that Caesar refused to listen to information about plots and punished anyone who tried to give him news of this kind.[42] Absolutism runs the risk of assassination at all times, and Caesar knew it. If he had any inkling of dissension he did not show it. He was probably protected by his entourage from full knowledge of the discontent, and information would be filtered as a matter of course. Cicero vacillated about writing to Caesar while he was still in Spain, among other things offering advice. He liked to think of himself playing the part of Aristotle advising Alexander the Great, but when he showed the letter to Balbus and Oppius, as prompted by Atticus, they responded with frankness, suggesting so many alterations that in the end Cicero regretted writing the letter and since he was reluctant to write it all again, incorporating the amendments, he did not send it.[43] It cannot have been an isolated example, but letters from other people describing similar experiences have not been preserved. Only Cicero stands as a contemporary voice to describe what it was like to deal with Caesar. Almost a month after Caesar had been assassinated, Cicero was staying at the villa of Gaius Matius, and wrote to Atticus on 7 and 8 April explaining how he had visited Caesar at the behest of Statius, and was kept waiting. He reports that Caesar had said that he must be heartily detested when a man such as Cicero was kept waiting and could not visit when he wished to. The next day he toned down his tale, relaying that Matius informed him that Caesar had said that he could not be foolish enough to think that after sitting and waiting for him, Cicero should still be friendly towards him.[44] The filtration system had grown up around him, as it did around the Emperors. Doorkeepers could make a fortune out of facilitating and fast-tracking visits to the Imperial presence; it is said that the Emperor Vespasian demanded a share of his doorkeeper's profits.

Dictator, king, sole consul, tyrant, by whatever name Caesar was known, mere semantics could not disguise the fact that there was only one way to wrest Rome from his grasp. Appian deduced that the prospect of Caesar being made king was what triggered the conspiracy against Caesar, though he also considered that it would have made no difference to them, since 'dictator' is the same as 'king'.[45] The foremost among the conspirators was the praetor Marcus Junius Brutus, the son of Caesar's mistress Servilia, now called Quintus Caepio Brutus after his adoption by his uncle Quintus Servilius Caepio. According to Dio, people turned to him, calling on him and reminding him of the much earlier Brutus who had overthrown the Tarquins, the last kings of early Rome.[46] Brutus had always been opposed to Caesar, says Dio, even though he had accepted benefits from him. He was married to Cato's daughter Porcia, better known from Shakespeare as Portia, and educated in philosophy and oratory, absorbing the lofty ideals about the Republic from his father-in-law. Given his background and his loyalty to Cato, he probably recoiled at the suggestion that since his mother and Caesar had been lovers, he could have been Caesar's natural son. Gaius Cassius Longinus was the next most ardent anti-Caesarian. He had fought on the side of Pompey and been pardoned by Caesar, but never really settled down in the shadow of Caesar's clemency. Then there were Caesarians like

Decimus Brutus and Gaius Trebonius who had held commands under Caesar. Others may have joined the conspiracy because they thought that their careers were advancing too slowly. They could have been betrayed at any time, were it not for the fact that Caesar refused to listen to warnings of plots.[47]

The Liberators, as they called themselves, would have to act quickly. They could have chosen to wait until Caesar left for the east, and then tackled the problems of state in their own way, hoping to have remedied all the ills by the time he returned. There was always a chance that Caesar might die or be killed in Dacia or in Parthia, but the Liberators could not take the risk that he might also survive and be successful. If he won yet more victories, especially over a foreign enemy, Caesar's prestige and power would be considerably enhanced. Even while he was absent his influence would still be preponderant, exercised through his adherents. The Senate had authorised the appointment of officials for three years, the length of time that was thought necessary for the wars. All magistrates for the first year were appointed, but according to Dio only the tribunes and the consuls had been selected for the second year.

Once they had worked themselves up into a cold hatred and convinced themselves of the need to act, the Liberators could not afford to delay in case their resolve weakened. It was a heavy undertaking to kill someone, especially one so prominent, and more importantly, one to whom several of the conspirators owed their careers. There were sixty men in total who were party to the plot, according to Suetonius, far too many according to Dio, almost leading to the detection of the plot.[48]

Caesar was to leave for Parthia on 18 March. More significantly he had dismissed his bodyguard.[49] As Suetonius says, perhaps it was better to be exposed to plots than to be on guard at all times, and perhaps Caesar desired death because he was ill.[50] While dining at the house of Lepidus, Caesar was asked what sort of death he would prefer, and he had replied 'sudden and unexpected'.[51]

There was a meeting of the Senate planned for 15 March, in the meeting room in Pompey's theatre. The conspirators had formulated different plans for the assassination, including throwing Caesar off a bridge, but there would never be a better opportunity than the meeting on the Ides of March. They thought that Caesar would not expect to be attacked in the Senate, and decided upon that date and venue.[52] They swore oaths of loyalty to themselves and Rome, and braced themselves for the event.

On the morning of 15 March, Caesar felt ill and decided not to attend the Senate, especially as his wife Calpurnia had some premonition of disaster. The conspirators perhaps had not thought of this possibility. If Caesar did not turn up, it would mean that they would all have to sit through a meeting with their daggers hidden somewhere about them, and then go home and start again. And there were only three days left. Decimus Brutus was sent to persuade Caesar to attend the meeting.[53] So Caesar arrived at Pompey's theatre with a man he thought his friend. When Antony came up to meet Caesar he was drawn away for a conversation with Gaius Trebonius, another of Caesar's friends.[54] Plutarch gives this role of distracting Antony to Decimus Brutus.[55] The conspirators had decided spare Antony, mainly at the behest of Brutus.[56] Cicero lamented the fact that a golden opportunity to kill Antony was lost.

Before Caesar went into the meeting, Artemidorus of Cnidus presented him with a scroll, trying to warn him of the danger, but Caesar never read scrolls when they were presented to him; they were given to a member of his staff to be read later.[57] Spurinna the augur had warned Caesar of catastrophe of the Ides of March, but Caesar had scoffed; seeing him now he said, 'The Ides of March have come', meaning that nothing had come of the prophecy of doom. Spurinna, according to legend, replied, 'But not yet gone, Caesar.' Inside Pompey's theatre, the conspirators were waiting. They had decided that each one of them should strike a blow so that they should all share the responsibility for the murder. The story is told that when he saw Brutus, Caesar said 'And you, Brutus', or 'And you, my son?'[58] The phrase that has entered the mythology is '*et tu Brute*' in Latin, but according to Suetonius Caesar spoke in Greek.[59]

Caesar died from twenty-three stab wounds, pulling his cloak over his head as he fell at the foot of Pompey's statue. Suetonius says that he was justly killed, because he had accepted too many honours, and these, coupled with his powers, which he abused, were too great for a mortal man.[60]

The senators who were not aware of the plot were terrified and fled. It could not be known then that there were to be no massacres or rampaging through the city. The Liberators had made no plans to fill the gap left by Caesar, no plans to take over the state and form a government, no plans to remove all the adherents closest to Caesar, and no plans to take over the troops to support them in their new-found supremacy. After all, that would have been to act like Caesar himself, in a high handed and unorthodox manner. Brutus addressed the people, according to Dio just after Caesar had been killed, and before the conspirators went up to the Capitol, and according to Plutarch the day after the murder.[61] The people remained unmoved by Brutus, and the conspirators were surprised and disappointed that cries of joy that the tyrant was dead had not resounded through the streets of Rome.

Antony and Caesar's other supporters went home to barricade their houses, expecting loud kicks at the door at any moment, closely followed by men with swords. When nothing happened, gradually they would find out the state of affairs and begin to plan for the future themselves. Antony was the only official in high office, being consul. He took charge as soon as he could, first securing armed assistance from Lepidus, who brought troops to the Tiber Island.

The conspirators had gone to the Capitol and prepared for a siege. They had not worked out that the only people whose liberty had been seriously curtailed by Caesar the tyrant were themselves and men like them, who wished to rule the mob in Rome, and the provincials, in the time-honoured exploitative manner. The vast majority in Rome mourned Caesar. Cicero went to the Capitol to talk with the Liberators on that first day, and recommended that the praetors should convene the Senate on the Capitol. But this did not happen, and Cicero lamented later to Atticus 'what might we have accomplished then?'[62] It is to Antony's credit that he kept his head and prevented a blood bath in Rome and another civil war from breaking out there and then. Antony came to a precarious understanding with the conspirators. He sent his infant son to them on the Capitol as hostage, to indicate that there was no intention of storming the hill, and Lepidus did the same. Later Antony and Lepidus entertained the so-called Liberators to dinner, during which Antony asked Cassius if he had a dagger concealed on his person, and Cassius replied he had a large one in case Antony should make himself tyrant.[63]

In the two days since Caesar's murder, Antony had been very busy. It is not known how he stood with Balbus and Oppius, but they would be the first men whom he approached, or who may have approached him. Caesar's *clientelae* would be a useful source of support, so he cultivated them, as well as Caesar's secretaries and assistants. Only the secretary Faberius is known by name, and he co-operated with Antony, after Calpurnia, now Caesar's widow, gave up all the Dictator's papers.[64]

Antony convened the Senate on 17 March in the Temple of Tellus which was close to his house.[65] He did not call out the troops to line the streets, having learned the hard way when he suppressed the disturbances caused by Dolabella and his cronies over their chronic debts. But no doubt Lepidus' soldiers were close by. In the Senate Antony let everyone have their say, so the meeting was a riotous one, but the outcome was as good as it was going to get in the circumstances. The restoration of law and order was of prime importance. Dio produces a long speech for Cicero, mostly appealing for calm and unity, and citing historical examples of dissensions that had affected Rome and Greece.[66] The main proposal led by Cicero was for a general amnesty, and everyone breathed a sigh of relief when the motion was adopted. Common sense had won the day, but Cicero privately despaired; his verdict on the assassination was that the conspirators had planned with the courage of men but the understanding of boys. Perhaps he had not thought of asking them what they were going to do after Caesar was dead, assuming that it went without saying that they had formulated plans for the government of the Empire. A month after Caesar's death, Cicero summed up what had been achieved: 'The tyrant is dead, but the tyranny still lives.'[67]

There was a major dilemma that Antony had to solve, and he skilfully steered a middle course. Caesar had been murdered, so the murderers ought to be punished. That would divide Rome into two factions once again and cause civil war. But if the assassins were not punished, it was equivalent to declaring that they had been justified in killing the man they called tyrant, and if Caesar had been justly killed, then strictly speaking all his acts should be annulled. That would mean that most of the magistrates and provincial governors would have to be replaced, so the annulment of Caesar's acts was not to be recommended. There was a suspenseful neutrality, while Antony carried on the government of Rome along Caesarian lines. He took Dolabella as his consular colleague, according to Dio because he feared that Dolabella would stage a revolt.[68] Antony also abolished the Dictatorship. He used the notes that Caesar had left to put forward all the measures which had been planned but not implemented, perhaps selecting those he thought more useful than others, or even inventing projects. Cicero complained that Rome was being governed by Caesar's acts, notes, words, promises and projects, which were more valid now he was dead than when he was alive, and he accused Antony of forging some of the notes and memos.[69] Antony also mixed up his financial accounts with Caesar's, and managed to pay off all his debts, so men began to feel suspicious that he had defrauded the state, but in view of the alternative of civil war, perhaps it did not matter too much.

At the behest of Piso, Caesar's father-in-law, Caesar's will was read, in Antony's house according to Suetonius.[70] Antony and the Senate ratified the terms on 18 March. There was a sum of money for every Roman citizen in the city, and Caesar's gardens were to be opened to the public. There were legacies to most of the conspirators, and some for Antony, though he was not in the first rank of the legatees.[71] Caesar had left a quarter of his fortune to his kinsmen Pedius and Pinarius, but the main beneficiary was Gaius Octavius, Caesar's great-nephew, currently at Apollonia in Macedonia with the legions destined for the Parthian campaign. In a codicil to his will, Caesar had adopted Octavius as his son. Initially this may not have seemed significant. The youth was only nineteen years old; he had fought no battles and had no political experience; he was of a delicate disposition, and could withstand neither heat nor cold; he never went out in summer without a hat and in winter he wore layers of clothes to keep warm. And anyway, he was always ill. Antony and the Senate had more to think about than the ailing teenage heir of Caesar.

There was the funeral to arrange, where emotions would run high. Cicero's friend Atticus had foretold that a public funeral for Caesar would sound the death knell for the Liberators, and Cicero reminded him of what he had said, in two letters written in April.[72] On 20 March Antony opened the funeral ceremony. Caesar's body was brought to the Forum, where Antony had prepared well, having arranged to display on the Rostra a gilded shrine based on the model of the Temple of Venus Genetrix, an ivory couch with purple and gold coverlets, and Caesar's bloodied robe displayed on a pillar.[73] Nobody knows what Antony included in his funeral oration. Suetonius is probably closest to the truth when he says that Antony had a herald read out the decree of the Senate voting Caesar divine and human honours, and the text of the oath that the people had sworn to preserve Caesar's safety. Then Antony added a few words of his own. Suetonius' version sounds plausible. Antony was trained as an orator and was used to public speaking, but in the circumstances he could not have been heard except by the crowd nearest to him, and if the mob was restless there would have been no point in prolonging the agony. Antony's theatrical props on the Rostra would speak louder than words. Another reason why Suetonius' version may be more accurate is that he was closer to the era than the later authors, and he had access to the state archives when he was writing his first biographies. When he fell out with the Emperor Hadrian it is thought that he was denied access to this valuable resource and had to resort to hearsay and anecdotes when he wrote his later biographies. The main point is that he may have seen official records of what happened at Caesar's funeral, which were perhaps no longer extant when other writers wrote Caesar's biography. Dio invents a truly monumental speech for Antony, describing Caesar's family, his descent from Venus, his career and achievements, and underlining what benefits the people had received from him.[74] Appian's version is similar, but with Antony gesticulating and gesturing to Caesar's corpse, emphasising Caesar's clemency to all who found refuge with him, and reminding the people that an oath had been taken to protect him, just as Suetonius says.[75] Both these later authors use the speeches to present their view of Caesar and his achievements. A funeral pyre had been prepared in the Campus Martius, near to the tomb of Julia, but after Antony's showmanship, the people made another pyre in the Forum. After the funeral was over, a column was set up on the site where Caesar had been burned, inscribed with the words *Pater Patriae*, father of his country, a title awarded to Caesar in his lifetime. The role of Amatius in setting up a shrine, and his execution without trial by Mark Antony has been described in chapter one, but it is worth adding that the cult of *Divus Julius* served Octavian-Augustus well, especially as a viable alternative to Caesar the Dictator.

Then there was the question of who should govern which provinces. It was essential to remove Brutus and Cassius from

Rome, so they were given the task of administering the corn supply in Asia and Sicily. Antony chose Cisalpine Gaul, where he would be closer to Italy, exchanging his designated province of Macedonia, which had been part of Caesar's plans for the campaign first into Dacia and then into Parthia. For this exchange to work, Antony had to have a law passed to remove the governor that Caesar had chosen for Cisalpine Gaul, the conspirator Decimus Brutus, who had already gone to take up his post. Antony also commandeered the legions from Macedonia, since there would now be no need for them in a Parthian campaign.

In the midst of all these arrangements, the young Gaius Octavius returned to Rome. He had changed his name after his adoption to Gaius Julius Caesar, to which he ought to have added Octavianus, indicating that he had been adopted into the Julii Caesares from the Octavii. But he never used this name by which historians identify him. He had to make strenuous efforts to have his adoption ratified by law, possibly because testamentary adoption was not strictly legal, but more importantly he had to establish a firm basis for his use of Caesar's name. He devoted considerable efforts to gathering political support; he took over as many of Caesar's clients as he could, and secured the services of Cornelius Balbus, a valuable ally. Ultimately he acquired an army with which to shore up his position. Reticent and cautious, Octavian was never shy and retiring, and he utilised to good effect Caesar's divinity. If not actually a living god, Caesar had been destined for deification after his death, a fact that Octavian did not allow the Roman populace to forget. He called himself *divi Juli filius*, son of the divine Julius, or simply *divi filius*, eventually issuing coins bearing this proud legend.

Octavian had accepted his position as Caesar's heir, and clung to it tenaciously through the next fifty years, reshaping the Empire slowly and patiently, perhaps along the lines that Caesar had in mind, though with much less haste. Caesar was a man in a hurry, and in his frenetic desire for rapid results he abandoned tradition and rode roughshod over those who clung to it. Octavian was more fortunate in that he could allow so much more time for achieving what he wanted, and in 27 BC a grateful Senate renamed him Augustus. He became in time Rome's first Emperor, using the personal name Imperator that had been awarded to Caesar, and with more power in his hands than any king.

Notes

Abbreviations

Appian *BC The Civil wars*
Caesar *BC The Civil War*
Caesar *BG The Gallic War*
Cic. *Ad Att.* Cicero *Letters to Atticus*
Cic. *Ad Fam.* Cicero *Letters to his Friends*
Cic. *Ad QFr.* Cicero *Letters to his brother Quintus*
ILS Inscriptiones Latinae Selectae
Sall. *Cat.* Sallust *The War with Catiline*
Sall. *Jug.* Sallust *The War with Jugurtha*
Suet. *DJ* Suetonius *Divine Julius* in *Lives of the Caesars*.
Vell. Velleius Paterculus *Compendium of Roman History*.

1 Caesar: An Extraordinary Life

1. Canfora 2007, ix.
2. Suet. *Caesar* 1.1.
3. Plut. *Caesar* 2; Suet. *Caesar* 4.2.
4. Plut. *Caesar* 1; Suet. *Caesar* 1.3.
5. Suet. *Caesar* 9.1–2.
6. Plut. *Caesar* 4; Waterfield 502 comments on Caesar's ability to seem less dangerous than he really was.
7. Honours: Gelzer 1968, 278; Meier 1995, 432–434; power: Goldsworthy 2006, 600.
8. Dio 43.14; Suet. *Caesar* 76.1; Cic. *Ad Fam.* 9.15.5; Gelzer 278 n. 1.
9. Goldsworthy 2006, 602, 'it makes it hard to argue against the view that Caesar was declared at least semi-divine during his lifetime, and was perhaps said to be a god'.
10. Cic. *Ad Fam.* 10.21.4, Plancus to Cicero, 15 May 43 BC, re: the Canidii and the Rufreni; see also *ILS* 73 and 73a.
11. Canfora 2007, 342; Appian BC 3.2–3; 36.
12. Cic. *Philippics* 2. 43.1 on Antony as *flamen*.
13. Suet. *Caesar* 88.
14. Suet. *Caesar* 56.7.
15. Taylor 1949, 186 n.3 referring to Carcopino *Les Secrets de la Correspondence de Ciceron*. 1947.
16 Suet. *Caesar* 88; Taylor 1949, 178–9; Goldsworthy 2006, 7.
17 Grant 1972, 239 for corrective to pro-Augustan tradition; 240–241 for Appian's reliance upon Pollio, for example in his unfavourable references to Plancus.

18. Taylor 1949, 179; 240 n.70 quoting Seneca *NQ* 5.18.4, frg. 48 ed. Weissenborn.
19. Vell. 2. 41.1.
20. Canfora 2007, xv.
21. Dio 72.36.4.

2 The Last Years of the Roman Republic

1. Suet. *DJ* 77.
2. Gelzer 1968, 27; Gruen 1974, 174.
3. Taylor 1949, 3.
4. Cooley 2009, 58.
5. Goldsworthy 2006, 19–20.
6. Gruen 1974, 160–161; 209; 442–444 for summary of disruptive electoral proceedings.
7. Gruen 1974, 457; the only source is Cicero *de Provinciis Consularibus*.
8. Suet. *DJ* 19.
9. Suet. *DJ* 18; Appian BC 2.28–30; Dio 37.54.1.
10. Sallust *Cat.* 38.
11. Plut. *Marius* 9; Gelzer 1968, 9.
12. Dio 36.71.4.
13. Dio 36.23–24; Appian *Mithridatic War* 94.
14. Rich 1983.

3 Caesar's Family and Early Life, 100–83 BC

1. Gelzer 1968, 19.
2. Goldsworthy 2006, 40–41.
3. *ILS* 7272.
4. Plut. *Marius* 6.
5. Plut. *Marius* 4.
6. Plut. *Marius* 5.
7. Sallust *Jug.* 95.3; 96.
8. Plut. *Marius* 9.
9. Plut. *Sulla* 12.
10. Suet. *DJ* 46.
11. Suet. *DJ* 46.
12. Goldsworthy 2006, 42.
13. Plut. *Caesar* 9–10.

14. Suet. *Grammaticis et Rhetoribus* 7.
15. Suet. *DJ.* 55.
16. Plut. *Caesar* 3–4.
17. Suet. *DJ* 48.
18. Suet. *DJ* 64.
19. Goldsworthy 2006, 48.
20. Plut. *Caesar* 17.
21. Plut. *Marius* 35; *Sulla* 7–8; Appian BC 1.55.
22. Appian BC 1.57–59.
23. Appian BC 1.57.
24. Appian BC 1.71.
25. Appian BC 1.65; 1.74.
26. Appian BC 1.71–75.
27. Seager, 1992, 165–207 esp. 179.
28. Plut. *Marius* 46.
29. Goldsworthy 2006, 59–60; Gellius *Attic Nights* 10.15.
30. Plut. *Caesar* 1.
31. Meier 1995, 86.
32. Tacitus *Annals* 3.58.2; Dio 54.36.1.
33. Gelzer 1968, 21.
34. Suet. *DJ* 59
35. Appian BC 1.76.
36. Gelzer 1968, 19 n.1.
37. Plut. *Caesar* 5.

4 Early Career, 83–69 BC

1. Suet. *DJ* 45; Plut. *Caesar* 17.
2. Suet. *DJ* 45.
3. Plut. *Sulla* 22.
4. Appian BC 1.80.
5. Appian BC 1.80; Plut. *Pompey* 6.
6. Appian BC 1.87–88; 1.92.
7. Appian BC 1.93; Plut. *Sulla* 29.
8. Plut. *Sulla* 30.
9. Plut. *Pompey* 10–11.
10. Plut. *Pompey* 14.
11. Plut. *Sulla* 31.
12. Suet. *DJ* 1.
13. Plut. *Caesar* 1.
14. Plut. *Pompey* 9.
15. Suet. *DJ* 1.3.
16. Plut. *Caesar* 1.
17. Goldsworthy 2006, 78.
18. Cic. *Philippics* 44–45.

19. Suet. *DJ* 49.
20. Suet. *DJ* 1; Plutarch does not mention the award.
21. Suet. *DJ* 2.
22. Appian BC 1.98.
23. Appian BC 1.99.
24. Appian BC 1.101.
25. Appian BC 1.104.
26. Plut. *Sulla* 36.
27. Suet. *DJ* 3.
28. Meier 1995, 105.
29. Suet. *DJ* 4.
30. Goldsworthy 2006, 86.
31. Plut. *Caesar* 4.
32. Suet. *DJ* 4.1; Meier 1995, 108.
33. Plut. *Caesar* 4.
34. Plut. *Caesar* 1.
35. Suet. *DJ* 4.1–2.
36. Plut. *Caesar* 2.
37. Suet *DJ* 74.
38. Meier 1995, 109.
39. Vell. 2.42.2–3.
40. Meier 1995, 109.
41. Suet. *DJ* 4.2.
42. Appian 1.111.
43. Goldsworthy 2006, 95; 650 n. 25 referring to Vell. 2.93.2 and Gruen 1974, 528.
44. Suet. *DJ* 5; Plut. *Caesar* 5.
45. Meier 1995, 131.
46. Appian BC 1.14.121.
47. Plut. *Pompey* 23.
48. Suet. *DJ* 5.
49. Gruen 1974, 27.

5 Senator, 69–63 BC

1. Plut. *Caesar* 5
2. Plut. *Caesar* 5.
3. Gelzer 1968, 32
4. Suet. *DJ* 7; Dio 37.52.2.
5. Plut. *Caesar* 11.
6. Suet. *DJ* 7.
7. Suet. *DJ* 7.
8. Suet. *DJ* 8.
9. Gelzer 1968, 32; Meier 1995, 142–143.
10. Suet. *DJ* 9.

11. Plut. *Caesar* 11.
12. Plut. *Caesar* 5; Meier 1995,145.
13. Plut. *Pompey* 25.
14. Dio 36.36a.
15. Plut. *Pompey* 25.
16. Gelzer 1968, 33; Meier 1995, 145.
17. Goldsworthy 2006, 125.
18. Gelzer 1968, 41.
19. Dio 36.14.4; 36.16.3.
20. Gelzer 1968, 34; Meier 1995, 146.
21. Gelzer 1968, 20.
22. Meier 1995, 158.
23. Gruen 1974.
24. Dio 36.43.2–3.
25. Dio 37.8.1–2.
26. Suet. *DJ* 10; Plut. *Caesar* 5.
27. Plut. *Caesar* 6.
28. Plut. *Caesar* 6.
29. Appian BC 2.1.1.
30. Meier 1995, 148.
31. Gelzer 1968, 39.
32. Suet. *DJ* 11; Gelzer 1968, 40 points out that Suetonius includes events that do not belong to 65 but also to 59 and 57.
33. Gelzer 1968, 42.
34. Appian BC 2.1.1.
35. Wiseman 1992a, 349.
36. Gruen 1974, 389.
37. Gruen 1974, 389–396.
38. Gruen 1974, 389.
39. Wiseman 1992a, 349.
40. Gruen 1974, 392.
41. Suet. *DJ* 71.
42. Suet. *DJ* 12; Dio 37.26.1.
43. Dio 37.27.2.
44. Suet. *DJ* 12.
45. Dio 37.38.4.
46. Suet. *DJ* 13.
47. Gruen 1974, 282; Dio 37.37.1–2.
48. Goldsworthy 2006, 151.
49. Dio 37.37.1–3.
50. Gelzer 1968, 47.
51. Plut. *Caesar* 7.
52. Suet. *DJ* 13; Plut, *Caesar* 7.
53. Gruen 1974, 80–81.
54. Sallust *Cat.* 51–52.

55. Gruen 1974, 416–417.
56. Goldsworthy 2006, 157–158.
57. Dio 37.29.1.
58. Dio 37.34.1.
59. Dio 37.30.4.
60. Sallust *Cat.* 49.
61. Appian BC 2.1.6.
62. Goldsworthy 2006, 160.
63. Gelzer 1968 54; Cic. *Ad Att.* 2.1.3; 6; 9.
64. Cic. *Ad Att.* 12.21; see also Suet. *DJ* 14; Plut. *Caesar* 7; Appian BC 2.6; Dio 37.36.
65. Sallust *Cat.* 51.1–3.
66. Suet. *DJ* 14.
67. Dio 37.36.1–2.
68. Appian BC 2.6.
69. Sallust *Cat.* 51.
70. Suet. *DJ* 14.
71. Plut. *Caesar* 8; Appian BC 2.6.
72. Suet. *DJ* 15.

6 Praetor and Proprietor, 62–60 BC

1. Plut. *Caesar* 8.
2. Suet. *DJ* 15; Dio 37.44.1–3.
3. Dio 37.43.1–3.
4. Dio 37.44.3.
5. Suet. *DJ* 55.3.
6. Suet. *DJ* 16.
7. Dio 37.41.2–3.
8. Suet. *DJ* 17.
9. Suet. *DJ* 6; Dio 37.45.
10. Gruen 1974, 248; Cic. *Ad Att.* 1.14.1; 1.14.5.
11. Stadter 1999, 503, note to Plut. *Caesar* 5.
12. Appian BC 2.8.1; Plut. *Caesar* 11.
13. Suet. *DJ* 18.
14. Cic. *Ad Att.* 1.13; 1.14.
15. Suet. *DJ* 18.
16. Plut. *Caesar* 12.
17. Dio 37.52–53.
18. Plut. *Caesar* 11.
19. Suet. *DJ* 54.
20. Appian BC 2.8.

21. Suet. *DJ* 84.
22. Plut. *Pompey* 43.
23. Cic. *Ad Att.* 1.16.
24. Cic. *Ad Att.* 1.16.
25. Cic. *Ad Att.* 1.16.
26. Plut. *Pompey* 46; *Lucullus* 42; *Cato* 31; Dio 37.50.1.
27. Cic. *Ad Att.* 1.19.
28. Dio 37.47.1.
29. Cic. *Ad Att.* 1.19.
30. Cic. *Ad Att.* 1.18.
31. Cic. *Ad Att.* 2.1.
32. Cic. *Ad Att.* 1.18.
33. Cic. *Ad Att.* 2.1.
34. Cic. *Cat.* 4.9–10.
35. Dio 37.54.1–5.
36. Goldsworthy 2006, 193–140.
37. Gruen 1974, 457.
38. Suet. *DJ* 19.

7 Consul, 59 BC

1. Appian BC 2.2.9.
2. Suet. *DJ* 19.
3. Dio 37.57.1–3.
4. Goldsworthy 2006, 201.
5. Suet *DJ* 19.
6. Appian BC 2.2.9.
7. Plut. *Caesar* 13; *Pompey* 47.
8. Vell. 2.44.2.
9. Gruen 1974, 88.
10. Cic. *Ad Att.* 2.3.
11. Gruen 1917, 88.
12. Dio 37.56–57.
13. Goldsworthy 2006, 201; Dio 37.58.1
14. Canfora 2007, 64.
15. Cic. *Ad Att.* 2.1.
16. Suet. *DJ* 20.
17. Suet. *DJ* 20.
18. Goldsworthy 2006, 198–9.
19. Cic. *Ad Att.* 2.3.
20. Gelzer 1968, 72.
21. Gruen 1974, 398.
22. Gelzer 1968, 72.
23. Plut. *Caesar* 14.
24. Gruen 1974, 404.

25. Dio 38.5.1–2; Gruen 1974, 399; 403.
26. Gelzer 1968, 72.
27. Meier 1995, 207.
28. Cic. *Ad Att.* 1.17.
29. Dio 38.2.2–3.
30. Meier 1995, 207.
31. Dio 38.3.2.
32. Plut. *Caesar* 14.
33. Suet. *DJ* 20.4
34. Meier 1995, 208–9.
35. Dio 38.4.3.
36. Goldsworthy 2006, 206.
37. Appian BC 2.10–11.
38. Suet. *DJ* 20.
39. Appian BC 2.10; Dio 38.4.
40. Plut. *Pompey* 47.
41. Meier 1995, 210.
42. Plut. *Caesar* 14.
43. Gruen 1974, 397.
44. Appian BC 2.2.11.
45. Appian BC 2.2.12; Dio 38.7.1.
46. Vell. 44.2.5.; Appian BC 2.2.11.
47. Plut. *Caesar* 14.
48. Suet. *DJ* 20.1.
49. Cic. *Ad Att.* 2.16.
50. Suet. *DJ* 20.1; Appian BC 2.12.
51. Cic. *Ad Att.* 2.15.
52. Dio 33.8.2.
53. Gelzer 1968, 69.
54. Appian 2.2.13.
55. Vell. 2.44.4; Suet. *DJ* 20.3; Appian BC 2.10; Dio 38.7.3.
56. Cic. *Ad Att.* 2.6.1.
57. Cic. *Ad Att.* 2.15.
58. Cic. *Ad Att.* 2.16.
59. Gruen 1974, 400–403.
60. Suet. *DJ* 20.4.
61. Appian BC 2.2.13.
62. Dio 38.7.4–6.
63. Appian BC 2.2.13.
64. Gruen 1974, 239–240.
65. Appian BC 2.14; Plut. *Caesar* 14.
66. Appian BC 2.12.
67. Dio 37.41.2–4.
68. Appian BC 2.12.
69. Dio 38.9.2.
70. Cic. *Ad Att.* 2.24.
71. Appian BC 2.12.
72. Suet. *DJ* 20; Plutarch *Lucullus* 47.2.
73. Cic. *Ad Att.* 2.18; 2.19.
74. Suet. *DJ* 22.
75. Dio 37.47.1.
76. Cic. *Ad Att.* 1.19.
77. Suet. *DJ* 22.1
78. Suet. *DJ* 22.1
79. Suet. *DJ* 22.2
80. Suet. *DJ* 23.
81. Suet. *DJ* 27; Cic. *Ad Att.* 2.18.
82. Cic. *Ad Att.* 2.18; 2.19; Plut. *Cicero* 39.3–5; Dio 38.17.1–2.
83. Appian BC 2.2.14.
84. Suet. *DJ* 20.4.
85. Plut. *Caesar* 14.

8 Caesar, the Gauls and the Roman Army, 58–50 BC

1. Suet. *DJ* 56.1.
2. Suet. *DJ* 56.4.
3. Suet. *DJ* 25.
4. Suet. *DJ* 54.
5. Suet. *DJ* 28.
6. Suet. *DJ* 24.
7. Plut. *Caesar* 15.
8. Vell 2.46–47.
9. Caesar BG 2.14.
10. Caesar BG 6.12.
11. Caesar BG 1. 2–4.
12. Caesar BG 1.41.
13. Caesar BG 5.25.
14. Caesar BG 7.32–33.
15. Caesar BG 7.40.
16. Caesar BG 6.15.
17. Caesar BG 1.16–18.
18. Caesar BG 6.11.
19. Caesar BG 5.42.
20. Caesar BG 1.47.
21. Caesar BG 1.29.
22. Caesar BG 6.14.
23. Caesar BG 5.48.
24. Suet. *DJ* 56
25. Caesar BG 6.11–28.

26. Caesar *BG* 1.10.
27. Caesar *BG* 2.2.
28. Caesar *BG* 5.25.
29. Caesar *BG* 6.1.
30. Suet. *DJ* 24.
31. Caesar *BG* 5.36–37.
32. Caesar *BG* 3.2.
33. Caesar *BG* 8.4.
34. Gruen 1974, 374.
35. Caesar *BG* 1.24.
36. Caesar *BG* 1.51.
37. Caesar *BG* 4.14.
38. Caesar *BG* 2.25.
39. Caesar *BG* 6.40.
40. Caesar *BG* 7.60.
41. Caesar *BG* 5.48–49.
42. Caesar *BG* 5.44.
43. Caesar *BG* 6.40.
44. Caesar *BG* 7.51.
45. Caesar *BG* 2.25.
46. Caesar *BG* 4.22.
47. Caesar *BG* 5.24–25; 6.6
    (Crassus); 8.2; 8.24 (Antony).
48. Caesar *BG* 5.24.
49. Caesar *BG* 1.21
50. Caesar *BG* 1.8–10.
51. Caesar *BG* 5.8.
52. Caesar *BG* 5.11.
53. Caesar *BG* 3.11.
54. Caesar *BG* 5.24.
55. Caesar *BG* 6.5–8.
56. Caesar *BG* 8. 23–25; 45.
57. Caesar *BG* 7.57–62; Dio 40.31.
58. Caesar *BG* 7.86–87.
59. Caesar *BG* 8.52.
60. Caesar *BG* 5.11.
61. Caesar *BG* 1.42.
62. Caesar *BG* 3.24–25.
63. Caesar *BG* 8.10.
64. Caesar *BG* 2.7,10,19, 24; 4.25;
    8.40.
65. Caesar *BG* 2.24.
66. Caesar *BG* 36–40.
67. Caesar *BG* 5.24.
68. Caesar *BG* 5.49–51.
69. Caesar *BG* 8.9.
70. Caesar *BG* 7.72–73.

71. Suet. *DJ* 58.
72. Caesar *BG* 1.21; 2.11.
73. Caesar *BG* 7.66–67.
74. Caesar *BG* 1.19; 47; 53.

9 Gaul and Britain, 58–50 BC

1. Caesar *BG* 1 2–29; Dio
   38.31conflates the influence of
   Orgetorix in getting the tribe
   to move their homes with the
   actual migration, by which time
   Orgetorix was already dead.
2. Cic. *Ad Att.* 2.18; 2.19; Plut.
   Cicero 39.3–5; Dio 38.17.1–2.
3. The war is described in Caesar
   BG 1.30–53.
4. Dio 38.34.3.
5. Caesar *BG* 1.31.
6. Caesar *BG* 1.40.
7. Dio 38.36–46.
8. Dio 38.45.1.
9. Dio 38.50.4.
10. Caesar *BG* 2.1.
11. Caesar *BG* 2.3–5.
12. Caesar *BG* 2.16–28.
13. Caesar *BG* 2. 35; Dio 39.5.
14. Dio 39.6.
15. Gruen 1974, 100.
16. Gelzer 1968, 124; Cic. *Ad Fam.*
    1.7.10; Dio 39.25.1.
17. Caesar *BG* 3.7–16; Dio 39.40–43.
18. Caesar *BG* 4.1–15.
19. Caesar *BG* 4.16–17.
20. Caesar *BG* 4.20–21; Suet. *DJ* 58.
21. Caesar *BG* 4.25.
22. Caesar *BG* 4.33.
23. Caesar *BG* 4.37–38.
24. Dio 39.53.
25. Dio 40.1–3.
26. Caesar *BG* 5.6–7.
27. Caesar *BG* 5.8.
28. Caesar *BG* 5.10.
29. Caesar *BG* 5 18–23.
30. Cicero *QF* 3.1.17 places the
    death in September; see also Dio
    39.64.1.

31. Dio 39.64.
32. Dio 39.64.
33. Plut. *Pompey* 53; *Caesar* 23; Suet. *DJ* 26.1.
34. Suet. *DJ* 27.
35. Dio 40.44.
36. Gruen 1974, 450–1 says that the two men co-operated until 50.
37. Caesar *BG* 5.26–37.
38. Dio 40.9.
39. Caesar *BG* 5.39–52.
40. Caesar *BG* 5.53–58.
41. Caesar *BG* 6.1–4.
42. Caesar *BG* 6.34.
43. Caesar *BG* 6.38.
44. Caesar *BG* 6.36–42.
45. Caesar *BG* 6.43.
46. Dio 40.45.1.
47. Dio 40.46–50.
48. Dio 40.33–41.
49. Caesar *BG* 7.10.
50. Caesar *BG* 6.10–13.
51. Caesar *BG* 7.15.
52. Caesar *BG* 7.16–25.
53. Caesar *BG* 7.27–34.
54. Dio 40.35.
55. Caesar *BG* 7.35–36.
56. Caesar *BG* 7.39–40; Dio 40.37.
57. Caesar *BG* 7.44–52; Dio 40.36.
58. Caesar *BG* 7.55–63.
59. Caesar *BG* 7.64–65.
60. Caesar *BG* 7.66–67.
61. Caesar *BG* 7.69–74.
62. Caesar *BG* 7.75–88.
63. Caesar *BG* 7.89. Dio 40.41.
64. Caesar *BG* 7.90.
65. Caesar *BG* 8.2.
66. Caesar *BG* 8.3.
67. Dio 40.42 says that the Romans broke through the fire screen and killed many of the Gauls.
68. Caesar *BG* 8.4–23.
69. Caesar *BG* 8.24.
70. Caesar *BG* 8.30–38.
71. Caesar *BG* 8.44.
72. Caesar *BG* 8.48.
73. Caesar *BG* 8.49.

10 The Road to War, 58–50 BC

1. Plut. *Caesar* 13.
2. Suet. *DJ* 23.
3. Vell. 2.45.1; Plut. *Cicero* 30.4; Appian BC 2.15.
4. Plut. *Cato* 34; *Pompey* 48; *Caesar* 21; Vell. 2.45; Dio 38.30.5.
5. Plut. *Pompey* 48; Dio 38.30.1–2; Cic. *Ad Att.* 3.8.
6. Dio 38.30.3.
7. The date is provided by Cicero *Pro Sestio* 69.
8. Dio 38.12–14.
9. Cicero *Pro Sestio* 55.
10. Cic. *Ad Att.* 4.1; Plut. *Pompey* 45.
11. Plut. *Pompey* 49.
12. Cic. *Ad Att.* 4.1.
13. Suet. *DJ* 41; see also Rickman 1980, 169–175.
14. Cic. *Ad Q.Fr* 2.3; *Ad Att.* 4.3.
15. Gruen 1974, 100–1; 106–9.
16. Cic. *Ad Fam.* 1.9; see also Plut. *Pompey* 51.3; *Caesar* 21.2.
17. Appian BC 2.17; See also Plut. *Caesar* 21.5; *Pompey* 51.
18. Gelzer1968, 121; Gruen 1974, 72; 101.
19. Suet. *DJ* 24.
20. Gelzer 1968, 122; Cic. *Ad Q.Fr* 2.6; *Ad Fam.* 1.9.9–10.
21. Appian BC 2.17.
22. Meier 1995, 273.
23. Gelzer 1968, 122.
24. Plut. *Pompey* 51; *Crassus* 15; Dio 39.27–3.
25. Plut. *Pompey* 52; *Crassus* 15; Dio 39.31–32.
26. Appian BC 2.18.
27. Cic. *Ad Att.* 4.9.1; 4.10.2.
28. Vell. 2.46.2; 2.48.1; Plut. *Pompey* 53; *Crassus* 15; *Caesar* 28; Dio 38.33.2.
29. Dio 39.39 (Pompey); 39.60 (Crassus).
30. Cicero *Ad Att.* 8.3.3; Vell. 2.46.2.
31. Dio 39.33.3; 44.43.2

32. Syme 1939, 32.
33. Dio 39.37.1.
34. Dio 39.29.1.
35. Plut. *Pompey* 52; Pliny *NH* 7.34–36; Tacitus *Ann.* 14.20; Dio 39.38.2.
36. Gruen 1974, 331.
37. Gruen 1974, 148–151; 451.
38. Appian BC 2.18.
39. Appian BC 2.18; Dio 39.39.4.
40. Appian BC 2. 23.
42. Plut *Pompey* 53.3–4; *Caesar* 23; Suet. *DJ* 26.1; Dio 39.32.2.
43. Dio 41.6; Vell. 2.47.1.
45. Suet. *DJ* 83.1.
46. Gruen 1974, 450–1.
47. Suet. *DJ* 27; Gruen 1974, 453 places it in 53 perhaps just after the death of Crassus, but others argue that it was in 52.
48. Cic. *Ad Fam.* 5.8.1; Dio 39.60.3.
49. Gruen 1974, 330.
50. Cic. *Ad Q.Fr.* 2.15.3; 3.9.5; *Ad Att.* 4.15.9; 11.5.4; 11.9.2; *Ad Fam.* 5.9; Plut. *Cicero* 26. 51. Cic. *Ad Att.* 4.18; 4.19.
52. Dio 39.55.6; 39.62–63.
53. Appian BC 2.3.19; Dio 40.45.
54. Gruen 1974, 149 n.20 and Seager 1979, 134–6 both disagree with this theory.
55. Plut. *Crassus* 17–33; *Pompey* 53; *Caesar* 28; Appian BC 2.28; Dio 40.27; Vell. 2.46.4. 56. Gruen 1974, 453–4 detects no evidence of the slightest rift, nor did Syme1939, 38.
57. Dio 40.46.3.
58. Dio 40.48–49; Appian BC 2.21.
59. Cic. *pro Milone* 13; 61; 67; 70; Dio 40.49.
60. Caesar *BG* 7.1.1.
61. Appian BC 2. 23; Dio 40.50.4–5; see also Suet. *DJ* 26.1; Plut. *Pompey* 54; *Caesar* 28; *Cato* 47; Vell. 2.47.3.
62. Suet. *DJ* 26.1.
63. Appian BC 2.3.20; Vell. 2.47.3; Dio 40.50.
64. Gruen 1974, 475–6.
65. Appian BC 2.23.
66. Plut. *Pompey* 55; Dio 40.52.1; 40.55.2.
67. Tacitus *Annals* 3.28.
68. Appian BC 2.22.
69. Cic. *Ad Fam.*3.10.
70. Dio 40.54.4.
71. Dio 40.51.
72. Suet. *DJ* 28.
73. Meier 1995, 327–8.
74. Gelzer 1968, 153; Meier 1995, 327.
75. Gelzer 1968, 152; Dio 40.46.2; 40.56.1.
76. Dio 40.56.
77. Gelzer 1968, 153; Meier 1995, 372–8.
78. Caesar BC 1.85.
79. Caesar *BG* 8.53.1.
80. Gruen 1974, 492–3.
81. Suet. *DJ* 28–29; Caesar *BG* 8.53; Gruen 1974, 463.
82. Dio 40.59.2.
83. Suet. *DJ* 28; Dio 40.59.
84. Cic. *Ad Fam.* 8.3.3; 8.9.
85. Cic. *Ad Att.* 5.2.3; 5.11.2 ; Suet. *DJ* 28.3; Plut. *Caesar* 29; Appian BC 2.26.
86. Caelius to Cicero *Ad Fam.* 8.10.2.
87. For Curio's hostility to Caesar see Cic. *Ad Att.* 2.18; 2.19; Suet. *DJ* 50.
88. Caelius to Cicero *Ad Fam.* 8.8.9; 8.9.5.

11 Escalation: The Outbreak of the Civil War, 48–47 BC

1. Caelius to Cicero *Ad Fam.* 8.6; 8.10; Dio 40.61–62; Appian BC 2.27.
2. Gruen 1974, 480–485.
3. Caelius to Cicero *Ad Fam.* 8.11; Dio 40.40.2; 62.1; Plut. *Pompey* 58.1; *Caesar* 29.2–3; Appian BC 2.26.

4. Cic. *Ad Att.* 5.20.7; Appian BC 2.27; Suetonius *DJ* 29; Plut. *Pompey* 58; *Caesar* 30; Dio 40.62.3; Vell. 2.48.2.
5. Appian BC 2.27.
6. Appian BC 2.26.
7. Caelius to Cicero *Ad Fam.* 8.11.3.
8. Gelzer 1968, 181.
9. Gruen 1974, 476.
10. Goldsworthy 2006, 445.
11. Gelzer 1968, 181.
12. Vell. 2.48.2.
13. Cicero *Ad Att.* 6.3; 8.16. Dio 41.6.3; Appian BC 2.28; Vell. 2.48.2.
14. Plut. *Pompey* 57.
15. Appian BC 2.28.
16. Appian BC 2.28.
17. Caelius to Cicero *Ad Fam.* 8.13; 8.14.
18. Caesar *BG* 8.54; Appian BC 2.29; Plut. *Pompey* 56.3; 57.4; *Caesar* 29.
19. Appian BC 2.29.
20. Caesar *BG* 8.52–55; Caesar BC 1.9.
21. Appian BC 2.30; Dio 41.2, places the vote in January 49, when Caesar sent a letter to the Senate.
22. Appian BC 2.30.
23. Plut. *Pompey* 59; Appian BC 2.31; Dio 40.64.4; 40.66.1.
24. Appian BC 2.31.
25. Appian BC 2.33.
26. Cic. *Philippics* 2.4.
27. Appian BC 2.32.
28. Cic. *Ad Att.* 7.6.
29. Cic. *Ad Att.* 7.7.
30. Cic. *Ad Att.* 7.8.5.
31. Cic. *Ad Att.* 7.7.
32. Cic. *Ad Att.* 7.8.
33. Caesar BC 1.1; Plut. *Pompey* 59; *Caesar* 30; Appian BC 2.32; Dio 41.1.
34. Caesar BC 1.2.
35. Caesar BC 1.3.
36. Caesar BC 1.2–6.
37. Caesar BC 1.5.
38. Appian BC 2.33; Dio 41.3.2.
39. Caesar BC 1.5.
40. Caesar BC 1.7–9.
41. Appian BC 2.33.
42. Plut. *Caesar* 31.
43. Suet. *DJ* 33.
44. Suet. *DJ* 31–32; Plut. *Caesar* 32.
45. Appian BC 2.32.
46. Dio 41.4.
47. Suet. *DJ* 31–2. 48. Plut. *Pompey* 60; *Caesar* 32.
49. Caesar BC 1.1–4.
50. Caesar BC 1.7.
51. Caesar BC 1.22.
52. Caesar BC 1.32.
53. Appian BC 2.37.
54. Caesar BC 1.6; Dio 41.3.3; Appian BC 2.34.
55. Cic. *Ad Fam.* 2.16; *Ad Att.* 6.8; 7.8; 7.13; 7.14; 7.21; 8.11; 9.7; 9.10; Plut. *Pompey* 59; Appian BC 2.36.
56. Caesar BC 1.14; Plut. *Pompey* 60; *Caesar* 33; Dio 41.6.1; Appian BC 2.37; Suet. *DJ* 75.1. 57. Cic. *Ad Att.* 9.10.
58. Dio 41.4.
59. Cic. *Ad Att.* 7.12; 7.13.
60. Plut. *Caesar* 34.
61. Caesar BC 1.9.
62. Caesar BC 1.10–11.
63. Cic. *Ad Att.* 7.14.
64. Caesar BC 1.11–16.
65. For Pompey's correspondence see Cic. *Ad Att.* 8.11a; 8.12b; 8.12c; 8.12d.
66. Cic. *Ad Att.* 7.20.
67. Caesar BC 1.15–23.
68. Caesar BC 1.24–5.
69. Caesar BC 1.26; Cic. *Ad Att.* 9.13.
70. Cic. *Ad Att.* 9.7c.
71. Caesar BC 1.26.
72. Dio 41.5.1; 6.1.
73. Dio 41.10.3.
74. Caesar BC 1.27.
75. Caesar BC 1.25.
76. Cic. *Ad Fam.* 15.15.
77. Caesar BC 1.25–26.
78. Caesar BC 1.28.

12 *The Civil War 48–47*, BC

1. Appian BC 2.36. Cic. *Ad Att.* 8.11; 9.7; 9.10.
2. Caesar BC 1.29–30; Appian BC 2.41.
3. Plut. *Caesar* 35; Dio 41.18; Cic. *Ad Att.* 9.2a.
4. Caesar BC 2.33–44; Appian BC 2.40; 44–46; Dio 41.41.
5. Dio 41.17; Plut. *Caesar* 35.
6. Appian BC 2.41.
7. Caesar BC 3.10.
8. Suet. *DJ* 34.
9. Caesar BC 1.33–37
10. Caesar BC 1.37–87; Appian BC 2.42–43; Dio 41.18–24; Plutarch *Caesar* 36; Gelzer 1968, 212–219.
11. Appian BC 2.47; Dio 41.35.
12. Caesar BC 3.4–5.
13. Plut. *Pompey* 64.
14. Appian BC 2.50; 2.65; Plut. *Pompey* 66; Vell. 2.52.1.
15. Caesar BC 3.1–2; Plut. *Caesar* 37; on the debt problem: Cic. *Ad Att.* 7.18; 9.9; 10.11; Dio 41.38.
16. Appian BC 2.48; 2.54.
17. Dio 41.43.
18. Caesar BC 3.2; Dio 41.44; Plut. *Caesar* 37; Suet. *DJ* 58; Appian BC 2.54; Vell. 2.51.
19. Appian BC 2. 52.
20. Caesar BC 3.11–13.
21. Caesar BC 3.13.
22. Plut. *Caesar* 38; Appian BC 2.56–57; Dio 41.46.
23. Dio 41.47.
24. Caesar BC 3.15–17.
25. Caesar BC 3.18.
26. Caesar BC 3.19.
27. Dio 41.48.
28. Appian BC 2.59.
29. Dio 41. 48; 41.49.
30. Caesar BC 29–30.
31. Caesar BC 3.45–7.
32. Gelzer 1968, 230–231.
33. Caesar BC 3.48.
34. Plut. *Caesar* 39; Suet. *DJ* 68.

35. Plut. *Pompey* 67.
36. Cic. *Ad Fam.* 9.9; Appian BC 2.67.
37. Caesar BC 3.82–83.
38. Caesar BC 3.49
39. Caesar BC 3.52–3; Appian BC 2.60; Dio 41.50.
40. Caesar BC 3.59–71; Dio 41.51; Appian BC 2.61.
41. Plut. *Caesar* 39; Appian BC 2.62.
42. Appian BC 2.63.
43. Dio 41.51.
44. Cic. *Ad Fam.* 4.9; Plut. *Pompey* 66–7; *Caesar* 40; Appian BC 2.65–6; Dio 41.52; Vell. 2.52. 48. BC 3.85. Plutarch *Pompey* 67.
45. Caesar BC 3.80–81; Plut. *Caesar* 41; Dio 41.51.4.
46. Caesar BC 3.81.
47. Caesar BC 3.84.
48. Caesar BC 3.85. Plutarch *Pompey* 67.
49. Caesar BC 3.82; Plut. *Caesar* 41.
50. Appian BC 2.67.
51. Caesar BC 3.86.
52. Caesar BC 3.88; Plut. *Caesar* 42.
53. Caesar BC 3.89.
54. Plut. *Pompey* 69; *Caesar* 45; Appian BC 2.78 echoes this, but he says that it was Caesar's reserve line who aimed at the faces of the Pompeian cavalry.
55. Caesar BC 3.88–97; Plut. *Pompey* 69; *Caesar* 44; Appian BC 2.75–82.
56. Dio 41.58–63.
57. Dio 41.55; 41.63.
58. Caesar BC 3.97–98.
59. Caesar BC 3.99.
60. Suet. *DJ* 30.
61. Plut. *Caesar* 46.
62. Caesar BC 3.100–101.
63. Plut. *Pompey* 76; Appian BC 2.83.
64. Dio 41.55.3; 42.2.
65. Caesar BC 3.102.
66. Plut. *Pompey* 77.
67. Plut. *Pompey* 73–80; Appian 2.86; Dio 41.3–4.
68. Caesar BC 3.106; Dio 42.7.

69. Plut. *Pompey* 80; *Caesar* 48; Dio 42.8; Caesar BC 3.103.
70. Dio 42.8.
71. Appian BC 2.90.
72. Caesar BC 3.107.
73. Dio 42.38.1
74. Caesar BC 3.112.
75. Caesar *Alex. War* 14–17.
76. Caesar BC 3.103.
77. Plut. *Caesar* 48–49.
78. Plut. *Caesar* 49.
79. Dio 42.34–35.
80. Caesar *Alex. War* 1–2.
81. Caesar BC 3.112; Dio 42.39; Appian BC 2.90 says that Caesar killed them both, though Achillas was killed by Arsinoe and Ganymede.
82. Caesar *Alex. War* 4–9.
83. Caesar *Alex. War* 9–12.
84. Caesar *Alex. War* 14–2.
85. Plut. *Caesar* 49; Suet. *DJ* 64; Dio 42.40.
86. Caesar *Alex. War* 23–25.
87. Caesar *Alex. War* 20–31.
88. Caesar *Alex. War* 33.
89. Appian BC 2.90.
90. Suet. *DJ* 52; Plut. *Antony* 54; 81.
91. Caesar *Alex. War* 34.
92. Caesar *Alex. War* 42–47 (Illyricum); 48–64 (Spain).
93. Caesar *Alex. War* 35–41; Plut. *Caesar* 50.
94. Caesar *Alex. War* 65.
95. Caesar *Alex. War* 67–76.
96. Plut. *Caesar* 50.
97. Dio 42.49.

13 Africa and Spain, 47–45 BC

1. Caesar *Alex. War* 65.
2. Dio 42.21.
3. Dio 42.27–28.
4. Plut. *Antony* 9.2.
5. Dio 42.32–33.
6. Plut. *Antony* 10.1.
7. Plut. *Caesar* 51; Dio 42.52–54.
8. Plut. *Caesar* 51.
9. Appian BC 2.93.
10. Plut. *Caesar* 52–54.
11. Dio 42.56–58; 43.1–14.
12. Caesar *African War* 1–2.
13. Caesar *African War* 3.
14. Dio 42.58.
15. Caesar *African War* 6–7.
16. Caesar *African War* 11.
17. Appian BC 2.95.
18. Caesar *African War* 17.
19. Caesar *African War* 13–18.
20. Dio 43.2.4.
21. Plut. *Caesar* 52; Appian BC 2.95.
22. Caesar *African War* 19.
23. Caesar *African War* 24.
24. Caesar *African War* 25.
25. Dio 43.3.
26. Caesar *African War* 30–32.
27. Caesar *African War* 34.
28. Dio 43.5.
29. Caesar *African War* 37.
30. Caesar *African War* 39–40.
31. Caesar *African War* 41–42.
32. Caesar *African War* 47.
33. Caesar *African War* 48.
34. Caesar *African War* 50.
35. Caesar *African War* 51.
36. Caesar *African War* 56.
37. Caesar *African War* 51–52.
38. Caesar *African War* 32; 55.
39. Caesar *African War* 53.
40. Caesar *African War* 62–63.
41. Caesar *African War* 68–69.
42. Caesar *African War* 71.
43. Caesar *African War* 75–76.
44. Caesar *African War* 79–80; Dio 43.7.
45. Caesar *African War* 80.
46. Caesar *African War* 82.
47. Caesar *African War* 87.
48. Caesar *African War* 88; Dio 43.10–11.
49. Dio 43.12.
50. Caesar *African War* 94.

51. Dio 43.9.
52. Caesar *African War* 90.
53. Dio 43.14.1.
54. Dio 43.14.4–7.
55. Dio 43.14.6; 43.21.2.
56. Gelzer 1968, 278 n.1.
57. Dio 43.14.4; Gelzer 1968, 288; Meier 1995, 432.
58. Dio 43.47.3.
59. Dio 43.15.1.
60. Plut. *Caesar* 55.
61. Dio 43.19.
62. Suet. *DJ* 41.3; Plut. *Caesar* 55.
63. Dio 43.22.4.
64. Dio 43.21.3.
65. Dio 43.24.4.
66. Cic. *Ad Fam.* 9.15.5.
67. Dio 43.25.2.
68. Dio 43.25.3.
69. Dio 43.27.1
70. Dio 43.27.2.
71. Cic. *Ad Fam.* 9.15.4.
72. Suet. *DJ* 40; Dio 43.26.
73. Suet. *DJ* 40; Dio 43.26.
74. Dio 43.29.
75. Dio 43.30.5.
76. Dio 43.28.1.
77. Dio 43. 31.4.
78. Caesar *Spanish War* 3–5; Dio 43.32.3–6.
79. Dio 43.33.2.
80. Caesar *Spanish War* 6.
81. Caesar *Spanish War* 16.
82. Caesar *Spanish War* 19
83. Caesar *Spanish War* 22.
84. Caesar *Spanish War* 22.
85. Caesar *Spanish War* 24.
86. Caesar *Spanish War* 27–28.
87. Caesar *Spanish War* 29.
88. Caesar *Spanish War* 29–31.
89. Plut. *Caesar* 56.
90. Caesar *Spanish War* 31.
91. Caesar *Spanish War* 36–39.
92. Caesar *Spanish War* 32.
93. Caesar *Spanish War* 41.
94. Caesar *Spanish War* 33–34.
95. Caesar *Spanish War* 35; Dio 43.39.1–2.
96. Caesar *Spanish War* 36.
97. Caesar *Spanish War* 42.
98. Dio 43.39.5.

14 Finale 45–44, BC

1. Suet. *DJ* 83.
2. Dio 43.44.2–5.
3. Dio 43.43.1.
4. Dio 43.44.
5. Dio 44.4.
6. Dio 44.6.3.
7. Appian BC 3.28.
8. Dio 44.6.4.
9. Suet. *DJ* 88.
10. Dio 43.45.2.
11. Dio 44.6.2.
12. Plut. *Caesar* 58.
13. Plut. *Caesar* 58.
14. Dio 43.47.1; 43.51.3.
15. Dio 43.22.2.
16. Dio 43.49.3.
17. Plut. *Caesar* 58; Dio 44.5.1.
18. Dio 43.50.3–5.
19. Cic. *Ad Att.* 13.52.
20. Suet. *DJ* 79.
21. Dio 44.9.3.
22. Dio 44.10.2.
23. Suet. *DJ* 78; Plut. *Caesar* 60; Dio 44.8.2–3; Appian BC 2.107.
24. Plut. *Caesar* 57; Dio 44.8.4.
25. Appian BC 2.109.
26. Goldsworthy 2006, 607; Gelzer 1968, 321.
27. Plut. *Caesar* 61; Dio 44.11.
28. Meier 1995, 476–477.
29. Dio 43.51.1; 44.1.1.
30. Cic. *Ad Att.* 13.31, written 28 May 45.
31. Plut. *Caesar* 58, Appian BC 110.
32. Meier 1995, 456–458.
33. Cic. *Ad Att.* 14.1.
34. Dio 43.51.7–8.
35. Plut. *Caesar* 60.

36. Suet. *DJ* 79; Dio 44.15.3.
37. Cic. *Ad Att.* 13.44.
38. Plut. *Caesar* 57; Dio 44.7.1–3.
39. Dio 44.3.2; 44.7.4.
40. Dio 44.1.2–5.
41. Plut. *Antony* 13.
42. Dio 44.15.1.
43. Cic. *Ad Att.* 13.27; 13.28.
44. Cic. *Ad Att.* 14.1; 14.2.
45. Appian BC 2.111.
46. Dio 44.11–12.
47. Dio 44.15.1.
48. Suet. *DJ* 80; Dio 44.15; Appian BC 2.113 provides twelve names besides Brutus and Cassius.
49. Appian BC 2.107.
50. Suet. *DJ* 86.
51. Suet. *DJ* 87; Plut. *Caesar* 63; Appian BC 2.115.
52. Suet. *DJ* 80; Dio 44.16.
53. Appian BC 2.115; Dio 44.18.1.
54. Appian BC 2.117; Dio 44.19.1.
55. Plut. *Caesar* 66.
56. Appian BC 2.114.
57. Plut. *Caesar* 65; Dio 44.18.3 does not name Artemidorus.
58. Dio 44 19.4.
59. Suet. *DJ* 82.
60. Suet. *DJ* 76.
61. Dio 44.21; Plut. *Caesar* 67.
62. Cic. *Ad Att.* 14.10.1.
63. Dio 44.34.6–7.
64. Appian BC 3.5.
65. Dio 44.22.3.
66. Dio 44.23–33.
67. Cic. *Ad Att.* 14.9; 14.14.1.
68. Dio 44.53.1.
69. Cic. *Ad Att.* 14.10; 14.13; 14.14.
70. Suet. *DJ* 83.
71. Dio 44.35.2–3.
72. Cic. *Ad Att.* 14.14.2.
73. Suet. *DJ* 84.
74. Dio 44.36–49.
75. Appian BC 2.144–147.

Bibliography

ANCIENT SOURCES
Latin and Greek sources available in translation:

Appian, *Roman History*. Loeb Classical Library. 4 vols.
Caesar, *The Alexandrian, African and Spanish Wars*. Loeb Classical Library.
Caesar, *The Civil Wars*. Loeb Classical Library.
Caesar, *The Gallic Wars*. Loeb Classical Library.
Cicero, *In Catilinam*. Loeb Classical Library.
Cicero, *Letters to Atticus*. Loeb Classical Library. 4 vols.
Cicero, *Letters to his Friends*. Loeb Classical Library. 3 vols.
Cicero, *Letters to his Brother Quintus*. Loeb Classical Library.
Cicero, *Philippics*. Loeb Classical Library.
Cicero, *Pro Sestio*. Loeb Classical Library.
Dio, *Roman History*. Loeb Classical Library. 9 vols.
Gellius, *Attic Nights*. Loeb Classical Library. 3 vols.
Plutarch, *Roman Lives*. (Trans.) R. Waterfield. Oxford University Press, 1999.
Sallust, *The War with Catiline*. Loeb Classical Library.
Sallust, *The War with Jugurtha*. Loeb Classical Library.
Suetonius, *The Lives of the Caesars*. Loeb Classical Library. 2 vols.
Suetonius, *Grammaticis et Rhetoribus*, in vol. 2 of *The Lives of the Caesars*.
    Loeb Classical Library.
Tacitus, *Annals*. Loeb Classical Library. 3 vols.
Velleius Paterculus, *Compendium of Roman History*. Loeb Classical Library.

MODERN WORKS
Beard, M. and Crawford, M., *Rome in the Late Republic: Problems and Interpretations*. Duckworth, 1985.
Brunt, P. A., *Social Conflicts in the Roman Republic*. New York: W. W. Norton & Co., 1971.
Canfora, L. *Julius Caesar: The People's Dictator*. Edinburgh University Press, 2007.
Cooley, A., *Res Gestae Divi Augusti*. Cambridge University Press, 2008.

Crook, J. A. et al. (eds), *The Last Age of the Roman Republic146–43* BC. Cambridge Ancient History Volume IX. 2nd ed. Cambridge University Press, 1992

Everitt, A., *Cicero: A Turbulent Life*. John Murray, 2001.

Fields, N., *Warlords of Republican Rome: Caesar versus Pompey*. Pen & Sword, 2008.

Fuller, Major-General J. F. C., *Julius Caesar: Man, Soldier and Tyrant*. London: Eyre & Spottiswoode, 1965.

Gelzer, M., *Caesar: Politician and Statesman*. Harvard University Press, 1968.

Goldsworthy, A., *Caesar*. Phoenix, 2006.

Goodman, R. and Sony, J., *Rome's Last Citizen: The Life and Legacy of Cato, Mortal Enemy of Caesar*. Thomas Dunne Books, 2012.

Grant, M., *Cleopatra*. Weidenfeld & Nicolson, 1972.

Grant, M., *Caesar*. Weidenfeld & Nicolson, 1974.

Greenhalgh, P., *Pompey: The Roman Alexander*. Weidenfeld & Nicolson, 1980.

Greenhalgh, P., *Pompey: The Republican Prince*. Weidenfeld & Nicolson, 1981.

Gruen, E. S., *The Last Generation of the Roman Republic*. University of California Press, 1974.

Meier, C., *Caesar*. London: Harper Collins, 1995.

Rawson, E., 'Caesar: civil war and dictatorship', in Crook et al. 1992, pp. 424–67.

Rich, J. W., 'The supposed manpower shortage of the late second century BC', Historia 32, pp. 287–331, 1983.

Rickman, G., *The Corn Supply of Ancient Rome*. Clarendon Press, 1980.

Sabben-Clare, J. (ed.), *Caesar and Roman Politics 60–50 BC: source material in translation*. Oxford University Press, 1971

Seager, R., *Pompey: A Political Biography*. Blackwell, 1979.

Seager, R., 'Sulla' in Crook et al. 1992, pp.165–207, esp. p. 179.

Shotter, D., *The Fall of the Roman Republic*. London: Routledge, 1994.

Smith, R. E., *The Failure of the Roman Republic*. New York; Russell and Russell, 1955.

Stadter, P. A., Introduction and Notes to *Roman Lives*. (Trans.) Waterfield, R., Oxford University Press, 1999.

Syme, R., *The Roman Revolution*. Oxford University Press, 1939.

Taylor, L. R., *Party Politics in the Age of Caesar*. University of California Press, 1949.

Tempest, K., *Cicero: Politics and Persuasion in Ancient Rome*. Bloomsbury, 2014.

Waterfield, R., *Plutarch: Roman Lives*. Oxford University Press, 1999.

Wiseman, T. P., 'The Senate and the *populares*, 69–60 BC', in Crook et al., 1992, pp. 327–367.

Wiseman, T. P., 'Caesar, Pompey and Rome, 59–50 BC', in Crook et al., 1992, pp. 368–423.

Index